FOR ORGANS, PIANOS & ELECTRONIC KEYBOARDS

E-Z PLAY® TODAY

347

Anthology of COUNTRY SONGS

MW00668015

COUNTRY

ISBN 978-1-4234-9660-1

HAL•LEONARD® CORPORATION

7777 W. BLUEMOUND RD. P.O. BOX 13819 MILWAUKEE, WI 53213

Visit Hal Leonard Online at
www.halleonard.com

Always on My Mind

Registration 10
Rhythm: Ballad or Slow Rock

Words and Music by Wayne Thompson,
Mark James and Johnny Christopher

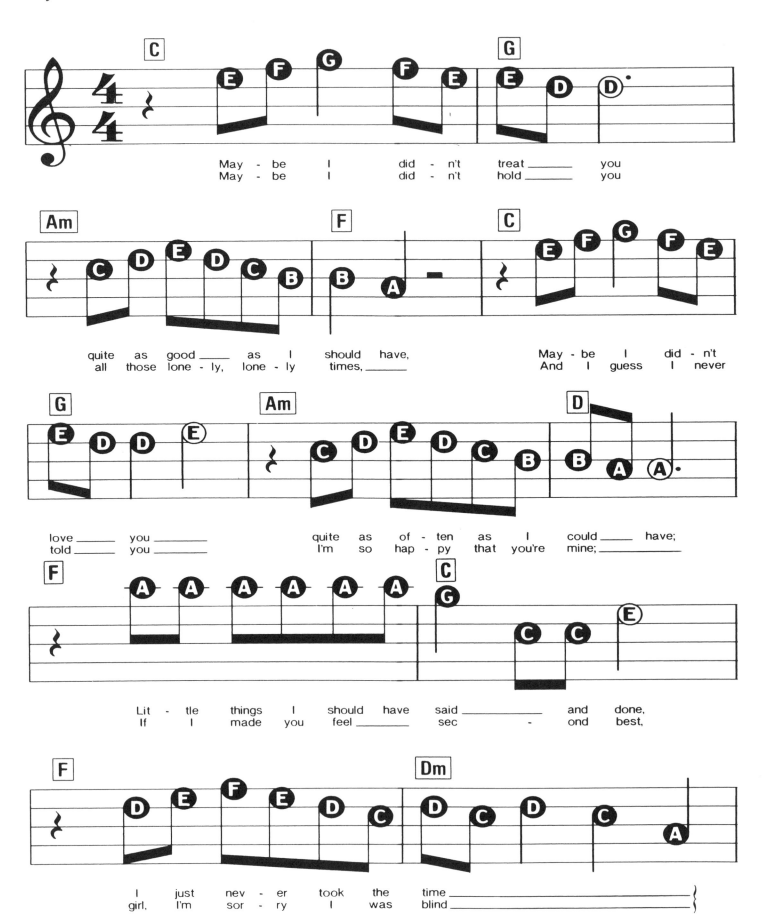

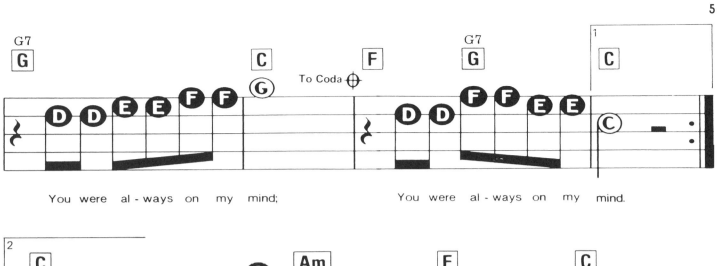

You were al - ways on my mind; You were al - ways on my mind.

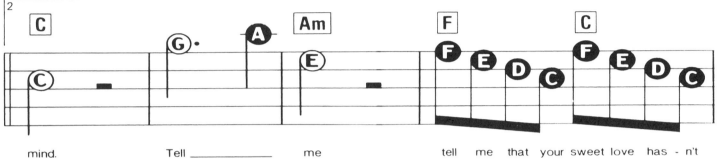

mind. Tell _____ me tell me that your sweet love has - n't

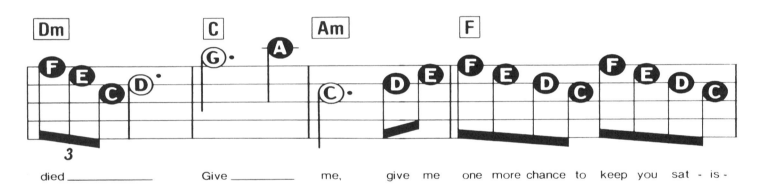

died _____ Give _____ me, give me one more chance to keep you sat - is -

D.C. al Coda (Lyric 1)
(Return to beginning
Play to ⊕ and skip to Coda)

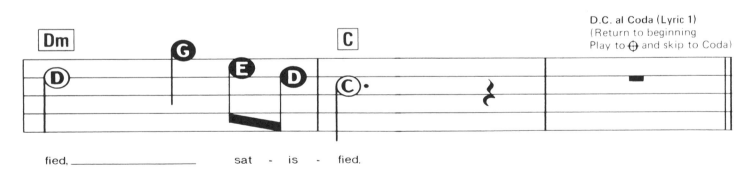

fied, _____ sat - is - fied.

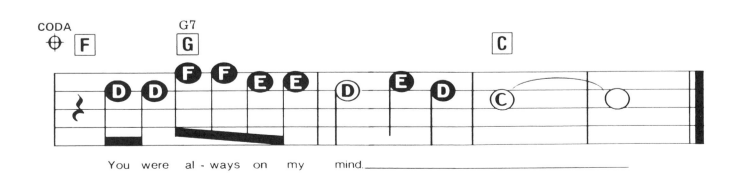

You were al - ways on my mind._____

Amanda

Registration 10
Rhythm: Waltz

Words and Music by
Bob McDill

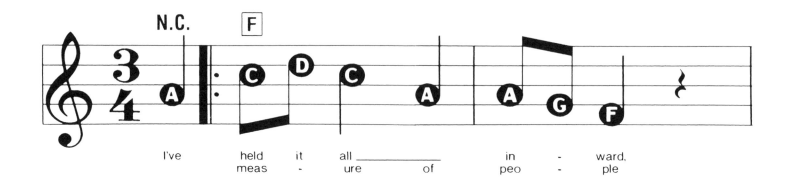

I've held it all _____ in - ward,
meas - ure of peo - ple

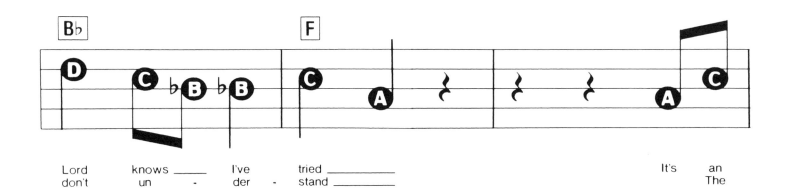

Lord knows _____ I've tried _____ It's an
don't un - der - stand _____ The

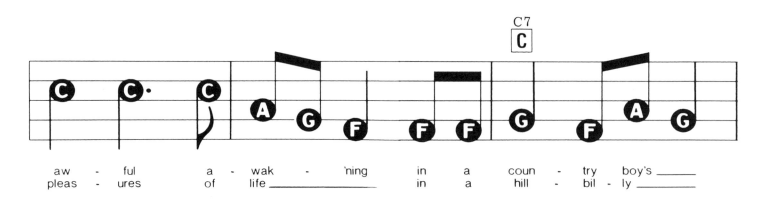

aw - ful a - wak - 'ning in a coun - try boy's _____
pleas - ures of life _____ in a hill - bil - ly

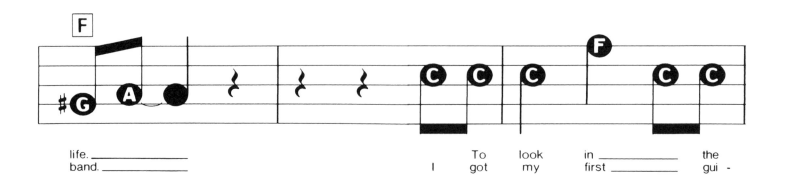

life. _____ To look in _____ the
band. _____ I got my first _____ gui -

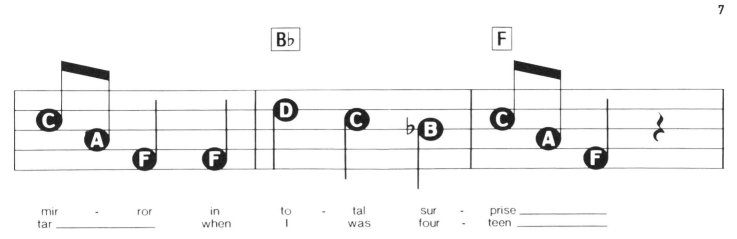

mir - ror   in   to - tal   sur - prise _____
tar _____   when   I   was   four - teen _____

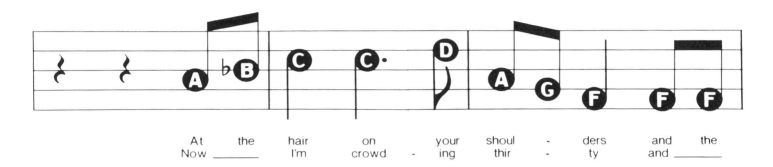

At   the   hair   on   your   shoul - ders   and   the
Now _____   I'm   crowd - ing   thir - ty   and _____

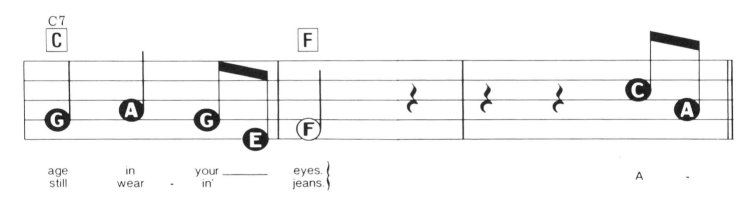

age   in   your _____   eyes. }
still   wear - in'   jeans. }   A -

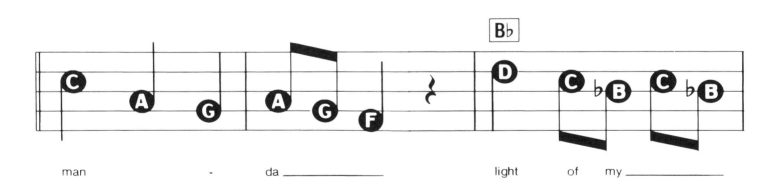

man _____ - da _____   light   of   my _____

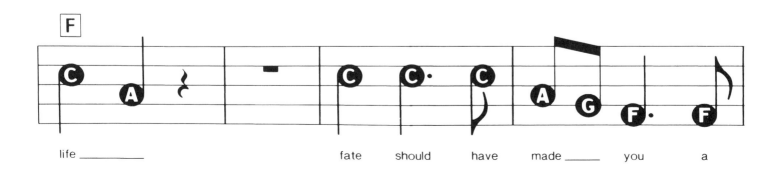

life _____   fate   should   have   made _____   you   a

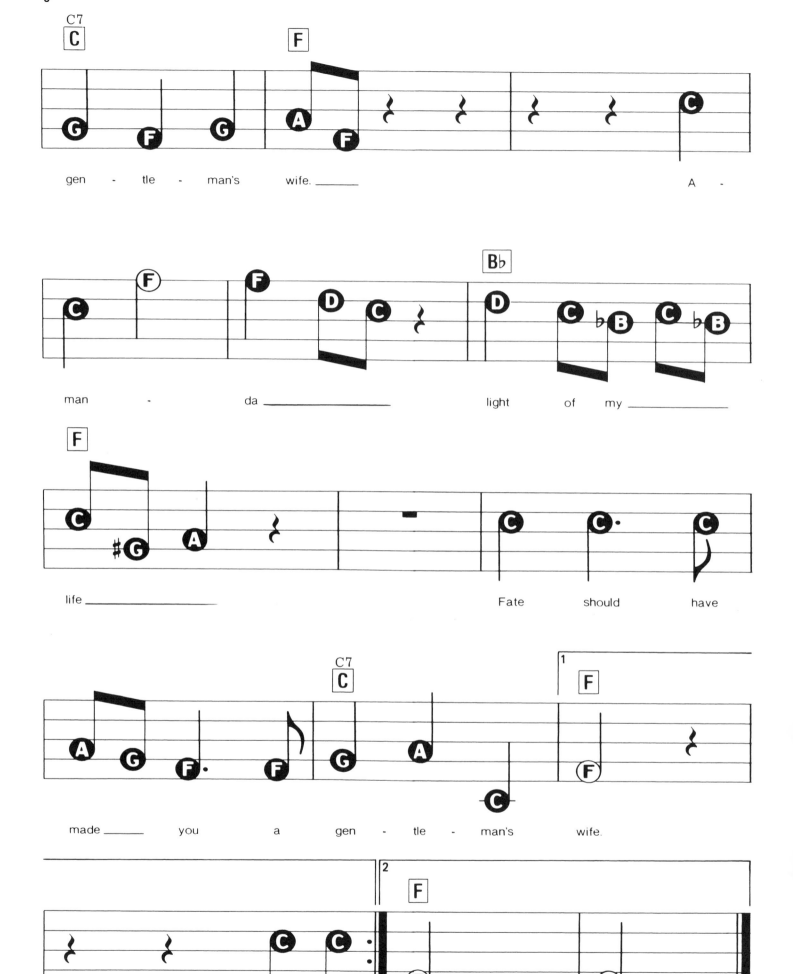

Angel Flying Too Close to the Ground

Registration 3
Rhythm: Country or Fox Trot

Words and Music by
Willie Nelson

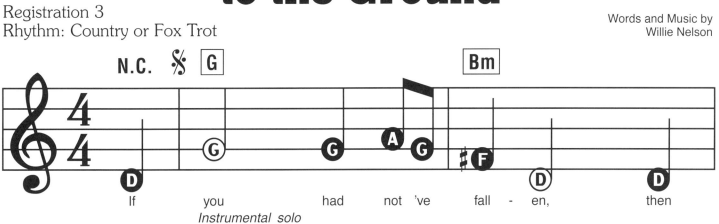

If you had not 've fall - en, then
Instrumental solo

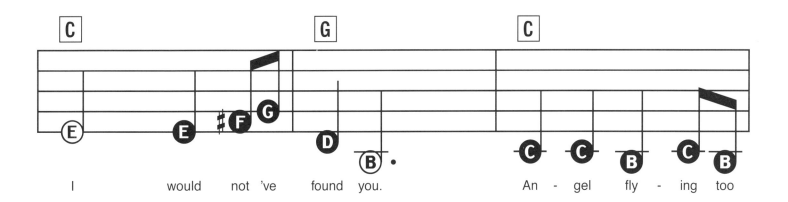

I would not 've found you. An - gel fly - ing too

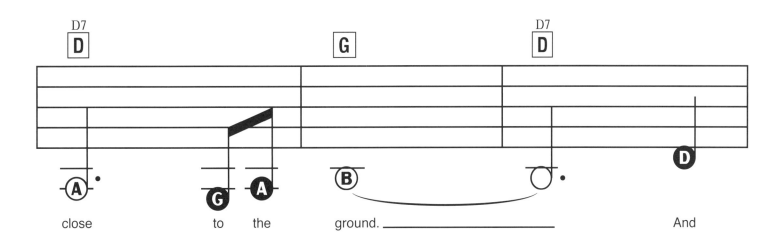

close to the ground. _____ And

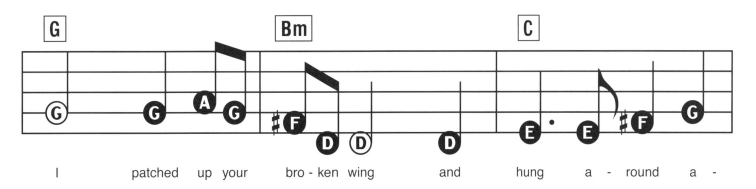

I patched up your bro - ken wing and hung a - round a -

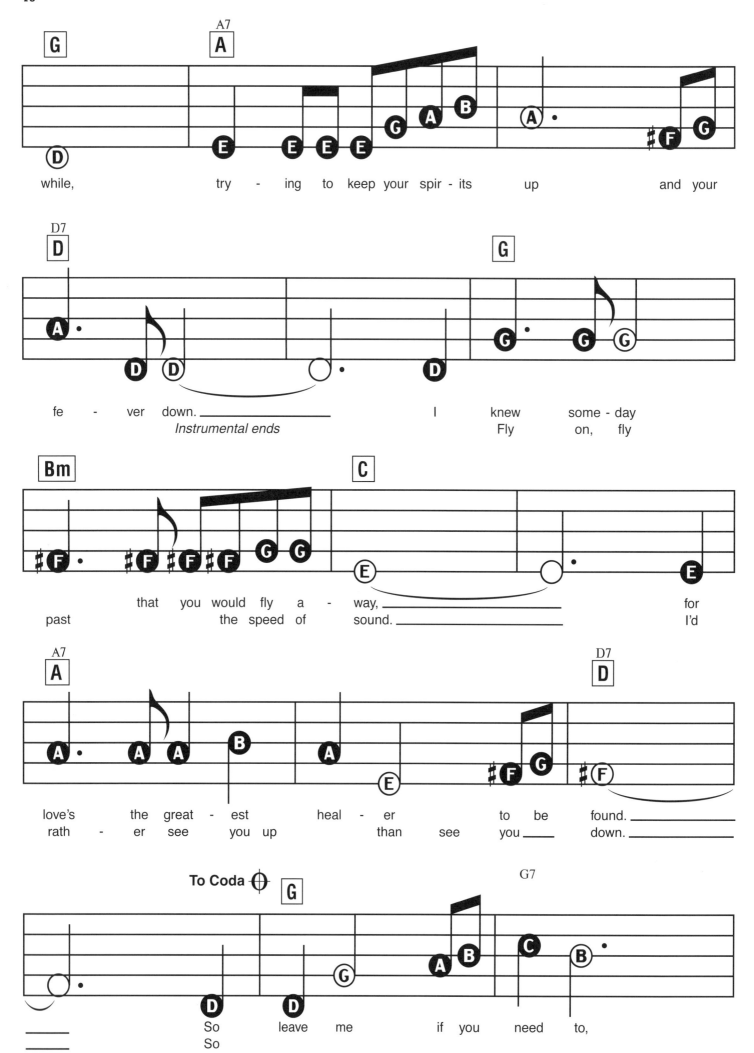

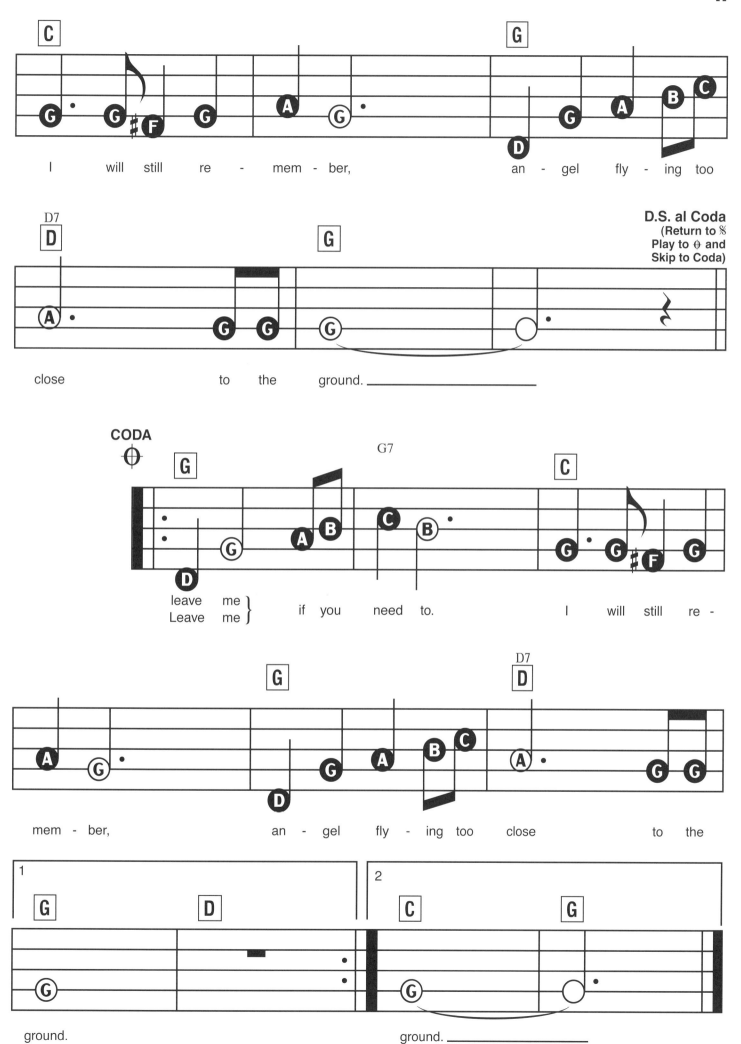

Angel of the Morning

Registration 1
Rhythm: Rock

Words and Music by
Chip Taylor

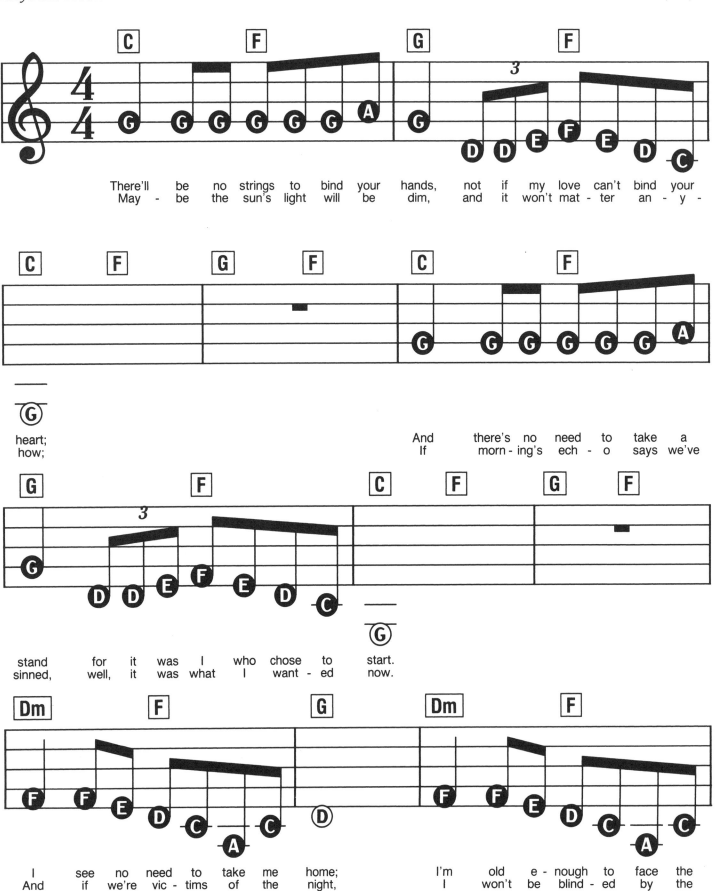

There'll be no strings to bind your hands, not if my love can't bind your
May - be the sun's light will be dim, and it won't mat - ter an - y -

heart;
how;

And there's no need to take a
If morn - ing's ech - o says we've

stand, for it was I who chose to start.
sinned, well, it was what I want - ed now.

I see no need to take me home;
And if we're vic - tims of the night,

I'm old e - nough to face the
I won't be blind - ed by the

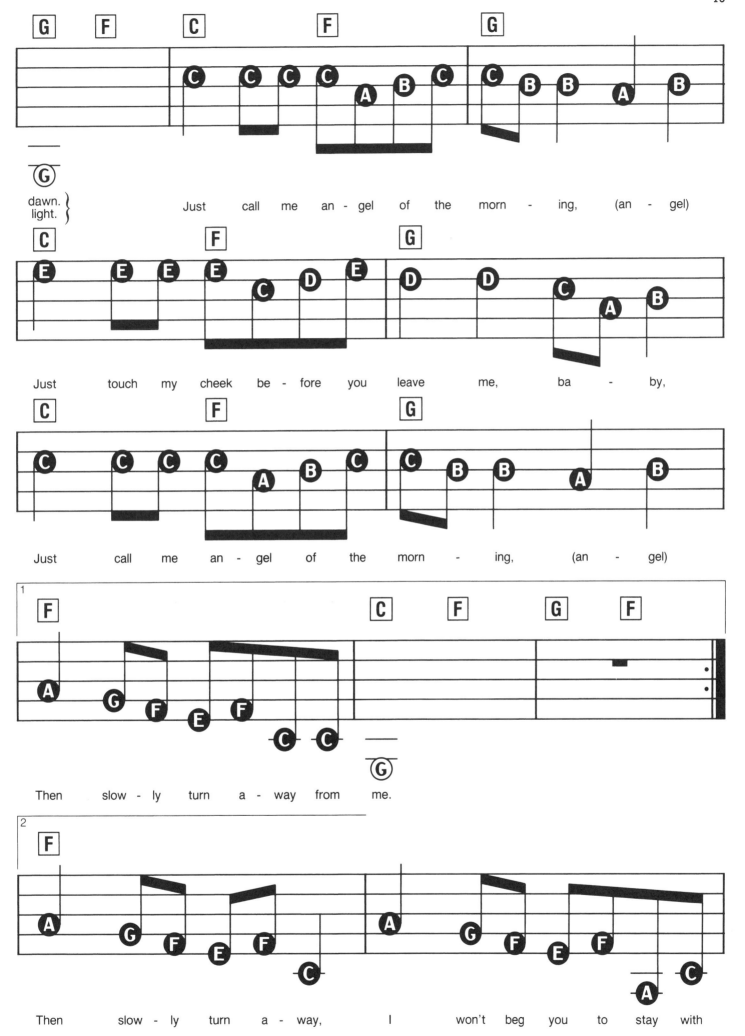

14

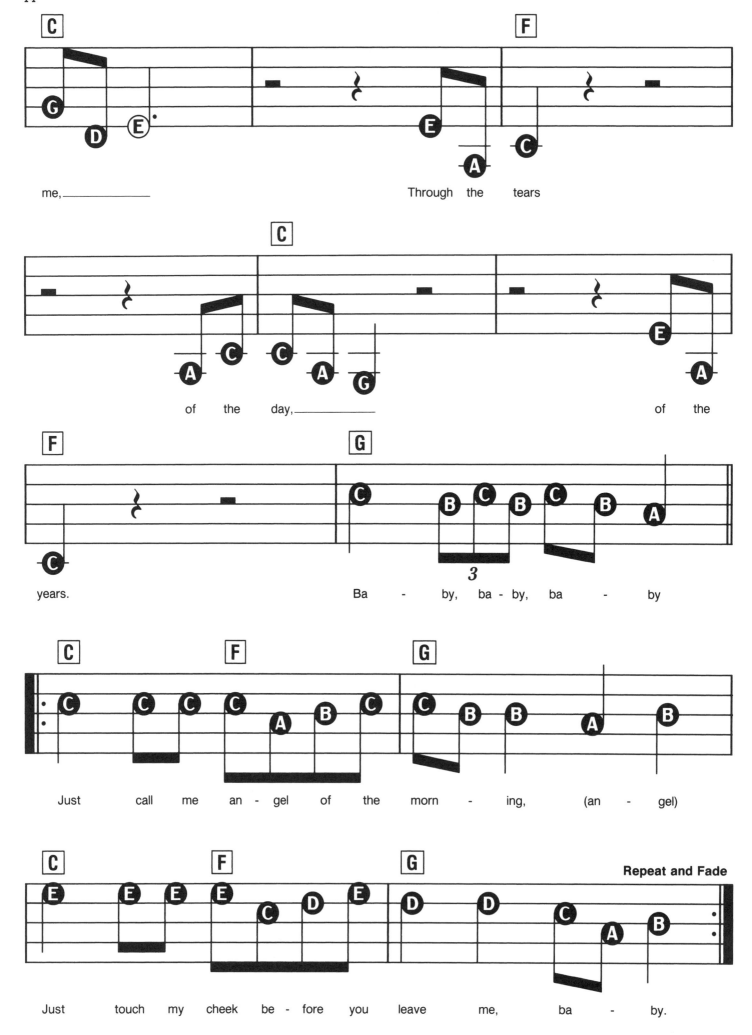

Blue Bayou

Registration 2
Rhythm: Rock or 8-Beat

Words and Music by Roy Orbison
and Joe Melson

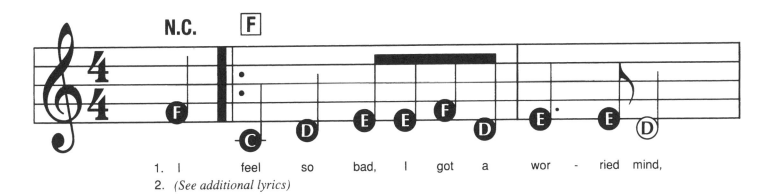

1. I feel so bad, I got a wor - ried mind,
2. *(See additional lyrics)*

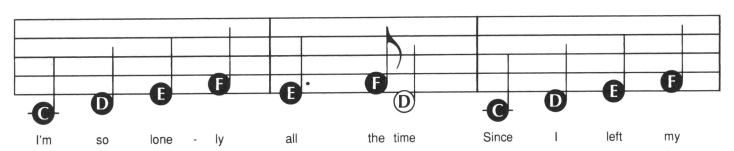

I'm so lone - ly all the time Since I left my

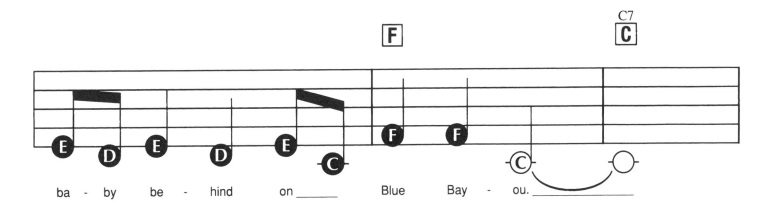

ba - by be - hind on _____ Blue Bay - ou. _____

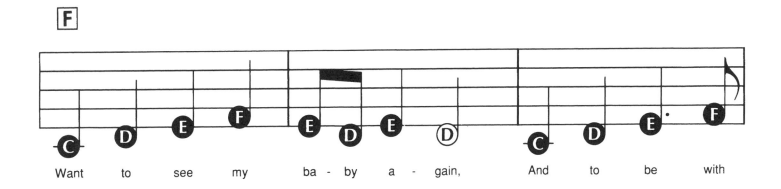

Want to see my ba - by a - gain, And to be with

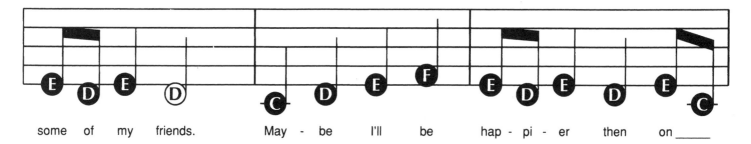

some of my friends. May - be I'll be hap - pi - er then on _____

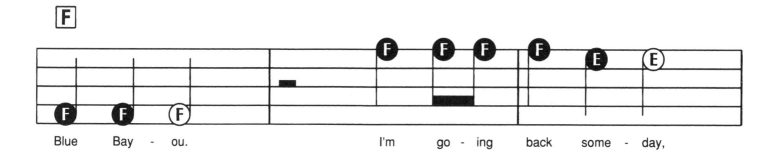

Blue Bay - ou. I'm go - ing back some - day,

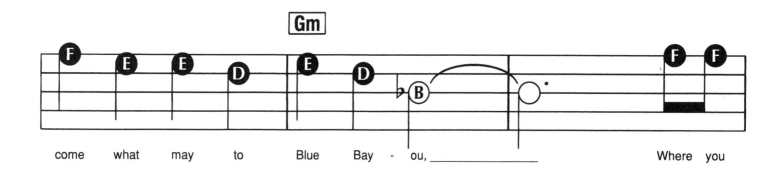

come what may to Blue Bay - ou, _____ Where you

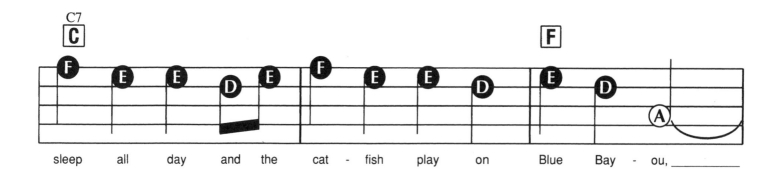

sleep all day and the cat - fish play on Blue Bay - ou, _____

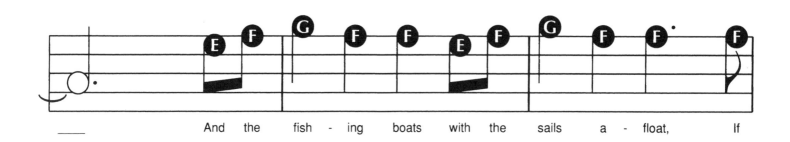

_____ And the fish - ing boats with the sails a - float, If

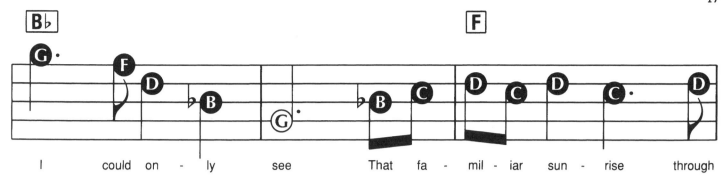

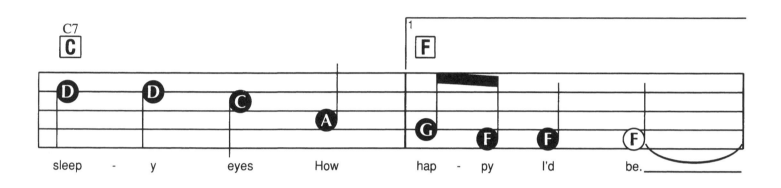

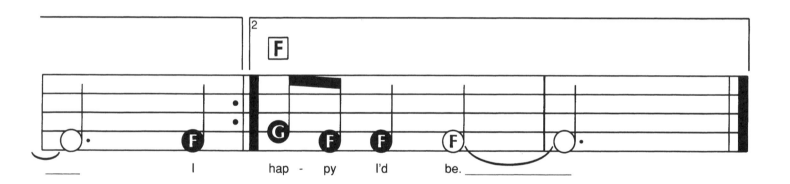

Additional Lyrics

2nd Verse:

I feel so bad, I got a worried mind, I'm so lonely all the time
Since I left my baby behind on Blue Bayou
Saving nickles, saving dimes, working till the sun don't shine
Looking forward to happier times on Blue Bayou.

2nd Chorus

I'm going back someday, gonna stay on Blue Bayou
Where my folks I'll find, all the time on Blue Bayou
With that girl of mine by my side till the moon in the evening dies
Oh, some sweet day, gonna take away this hurtin' inside.

Bonaparte's Retreat

Registration 4
Rhythm: Country Swing or Fox Trot

Words and Music by Redd Stewart
and Pee Wee King

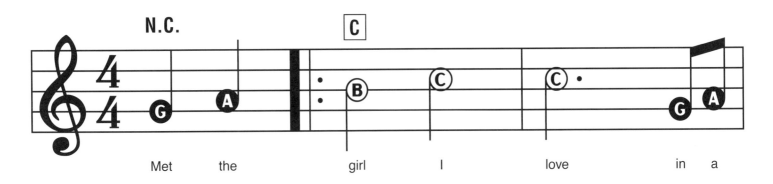

Met the girl I love in a

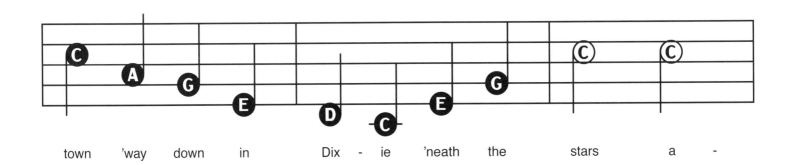

town 'way down in Dix - ie 'neath the stars a -

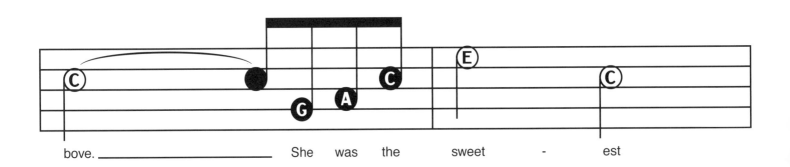

bove. _____ She was the sweet - est

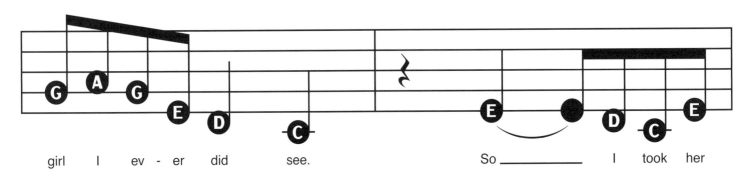

girl I ev - er did see. So _____ I took her

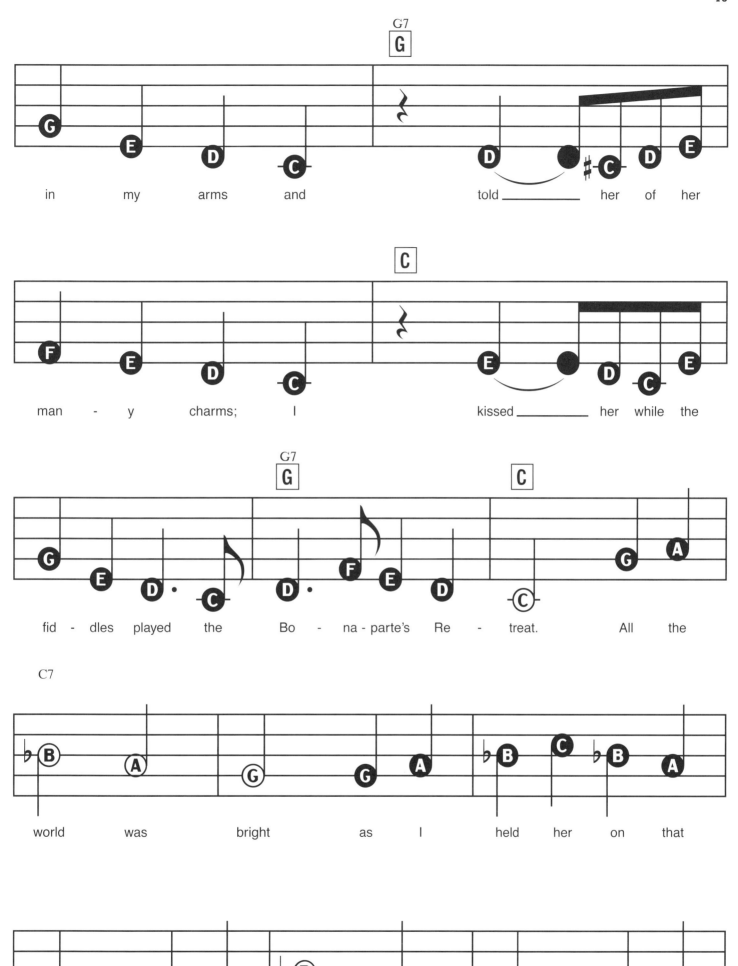

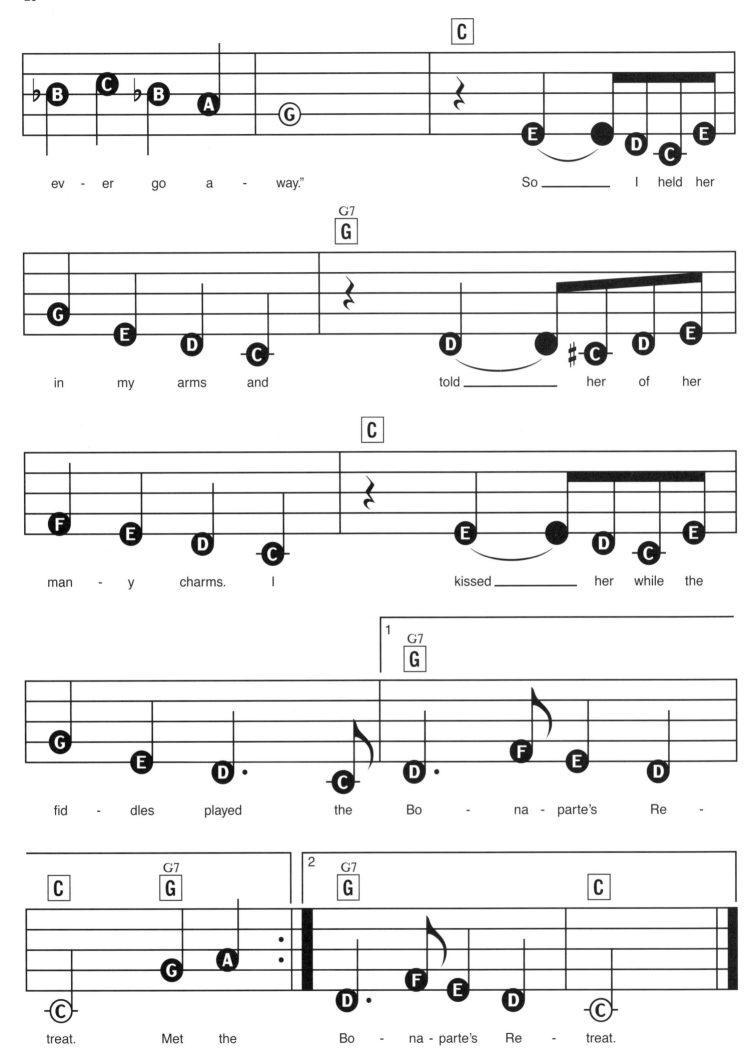

A Broken Wing

Registration 4
Rhythm: Country Pop or Fox Trot

Words and Music by Sam Hogin,
Phil Barnhart and James House

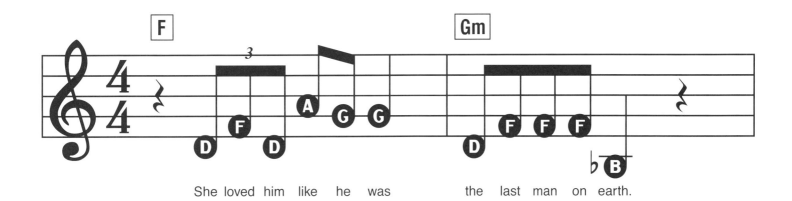

She loved him like he was   the last man on earth.

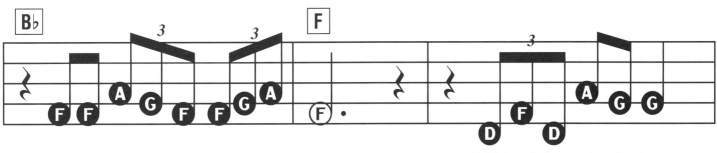

Gave him ev -'ry-thing she ev - er had.   He'd break her spir - it down,

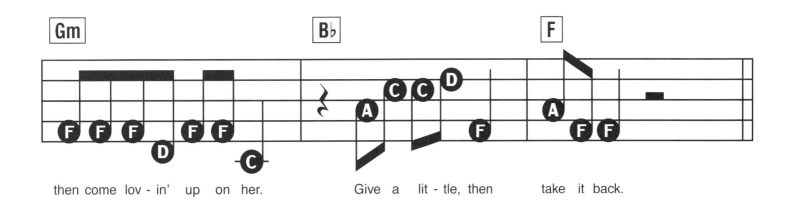

then come lov - in' up on her.   Give a lit - tle, then   take it back.

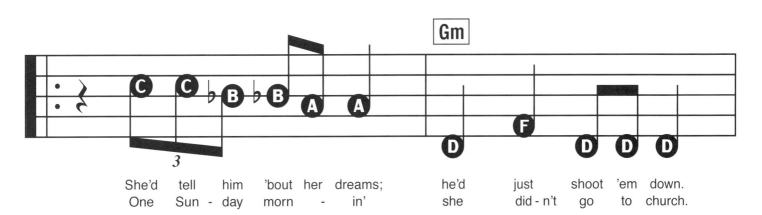

She'd tell him 'bout her dreams;   he'd   just   shoot 'em down.
One Sun - day morn - in'   she   did - n't   go   to church.

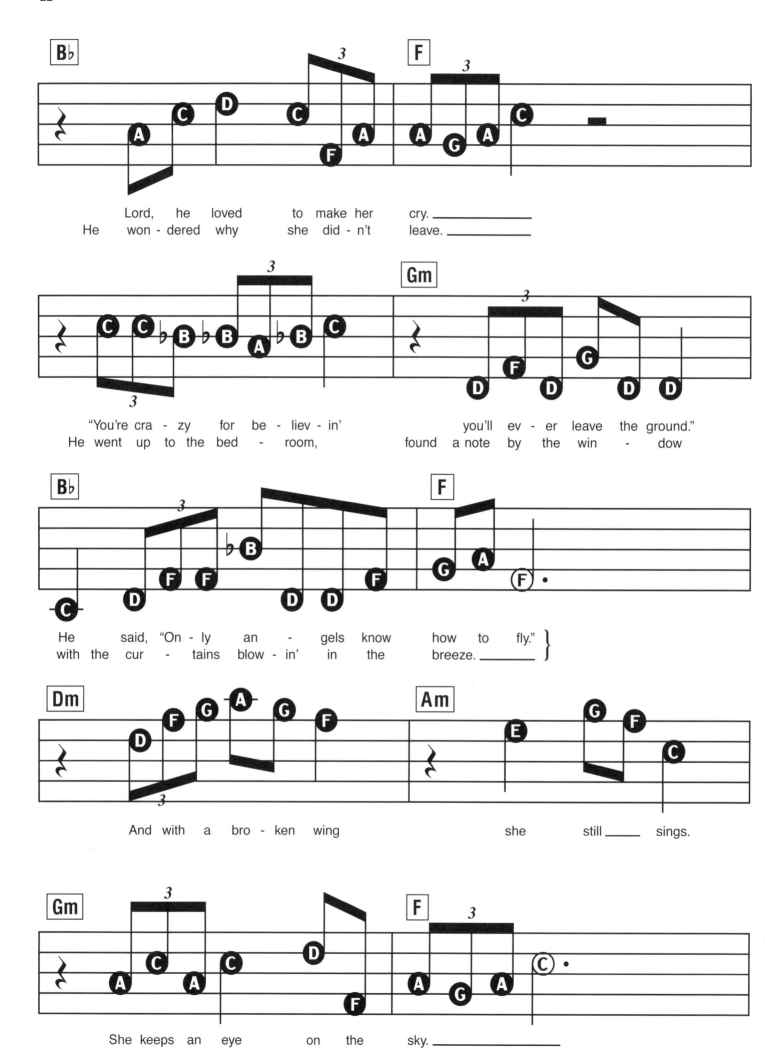

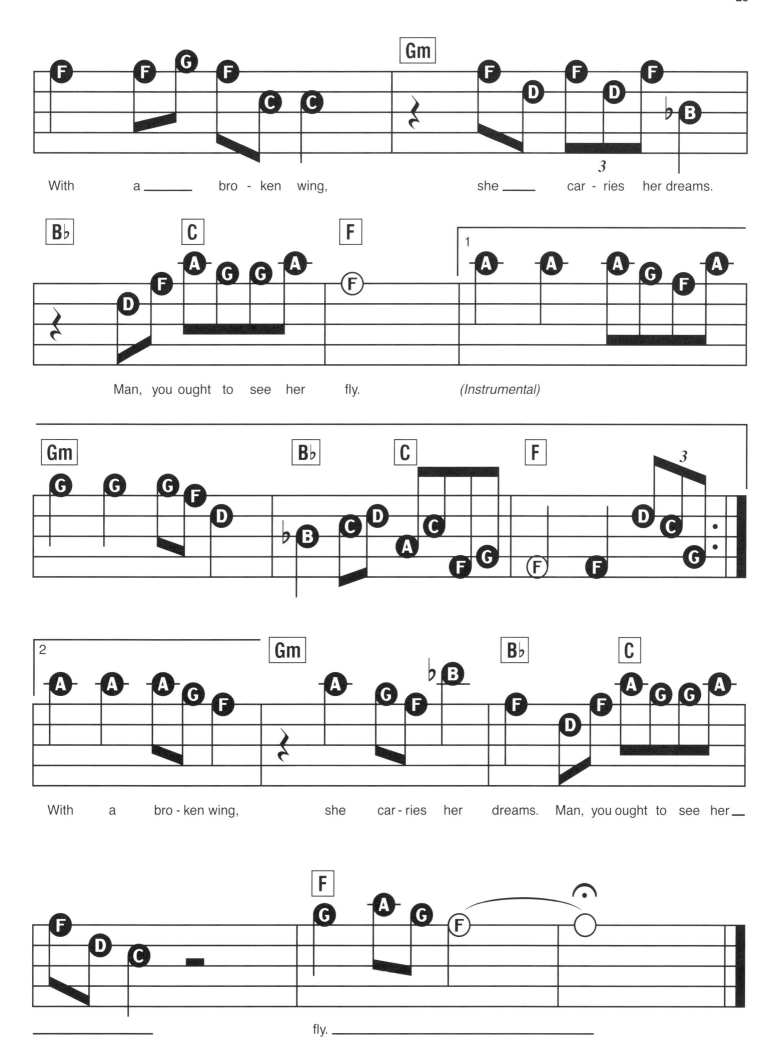

With a _____ bro - ken wing, she _____ car - ries her dreams.

Man, you ought to see her fly. *(Instrumental)*

With a bro - ken wing, she car - ries her dreams. Man, you ought to see her __

fly. _____

Born to Lose

Registration 1
Rhythm: Country Swing or Fox Trot

Words and Music by
Ted Daffan

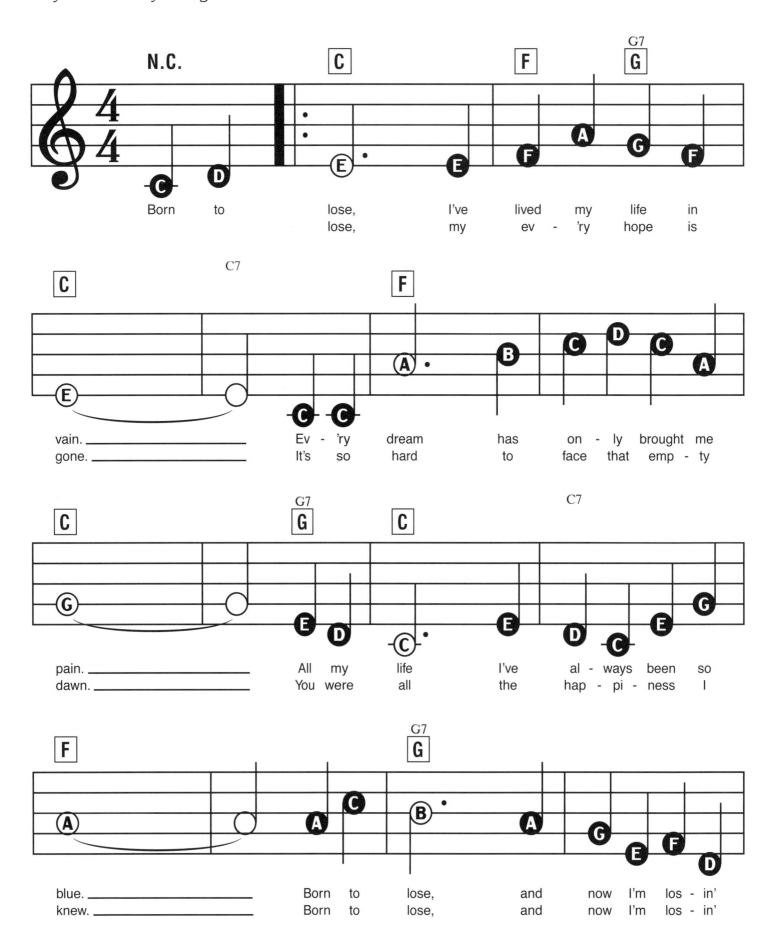

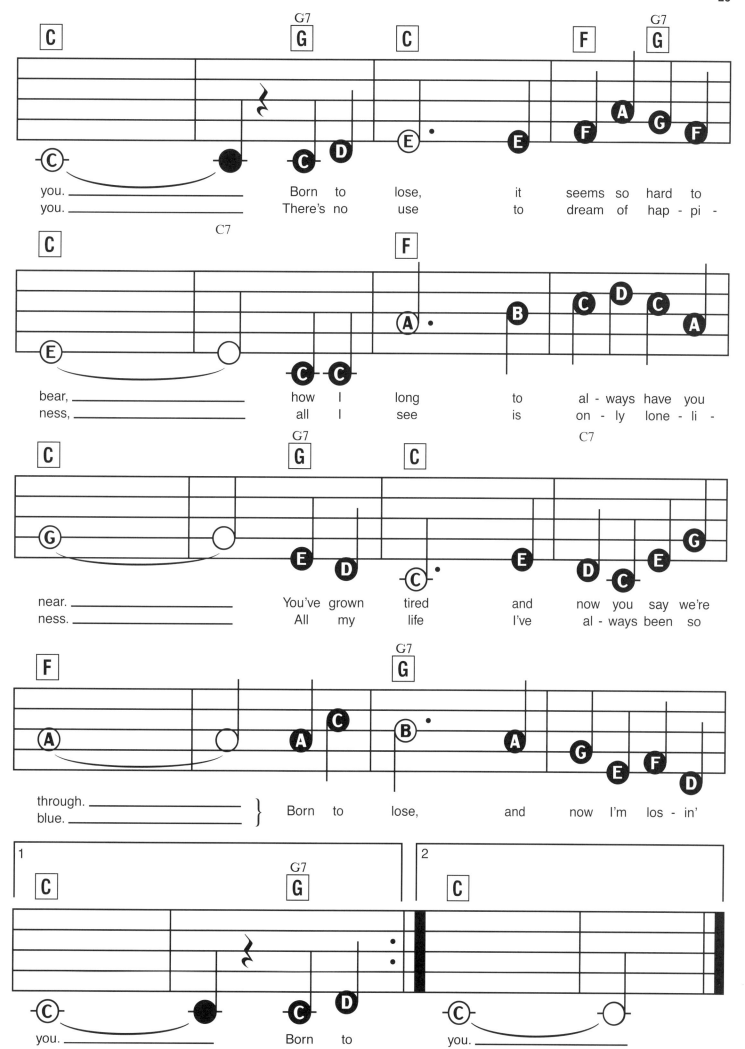

Busted

Registration 4
Rhythm: Country

Words and Music by
Harlan Howard

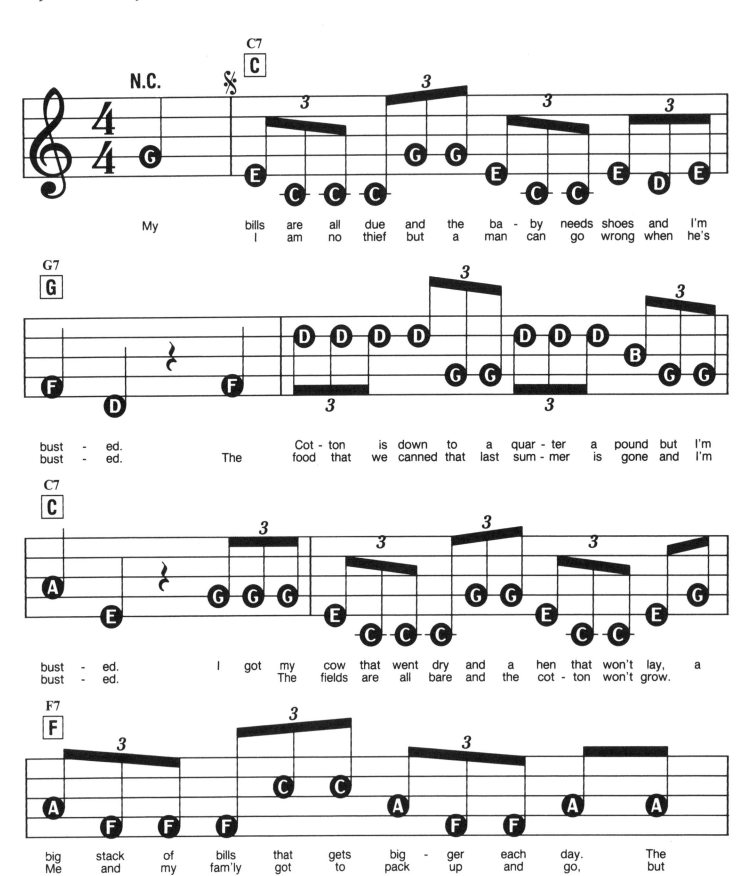

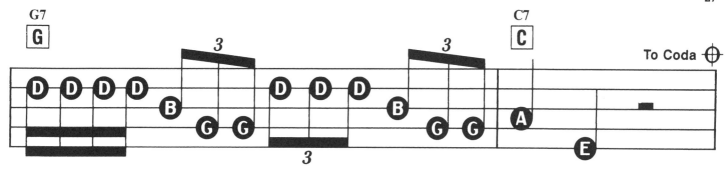

To Coda

coun - ty's gon - na haul my be - long - ings a - way 'cause I'm bust - ed.
I'll make a liv - ing just where I don't know 'cause I'm bust - ed.

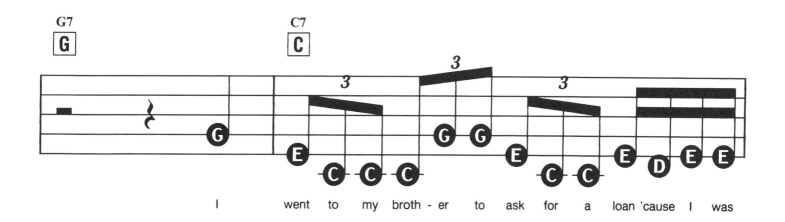

I went to my broth - er to ask for a loan 'cause I was

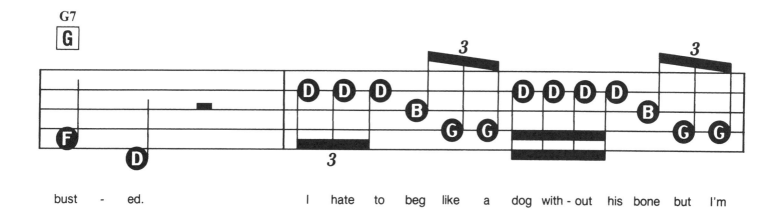

bust - ed. I hate to beg like a dog with - out his bone but I'm

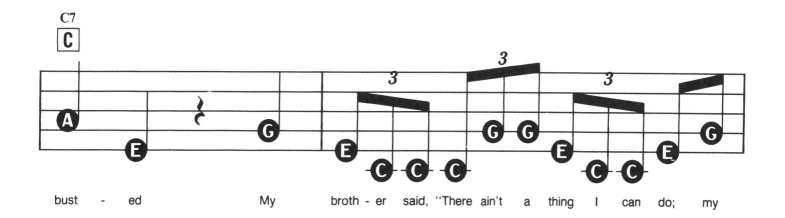

bust - ed My broth - er said, "There ain't a thing I can do; my

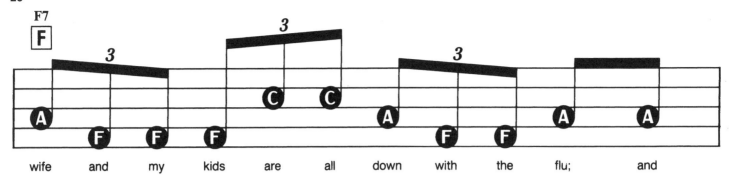

wife   and   my   kids   are   all   down   with   the   flu;   and

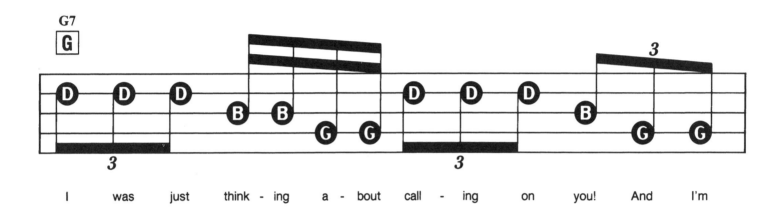

I   was   just   think - ing   a - bout   call - ing   on   you!   And   I'm

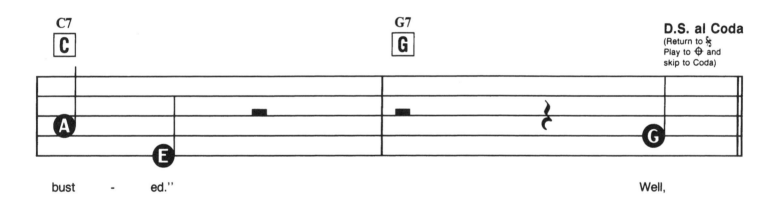

bust - ed."   Well,

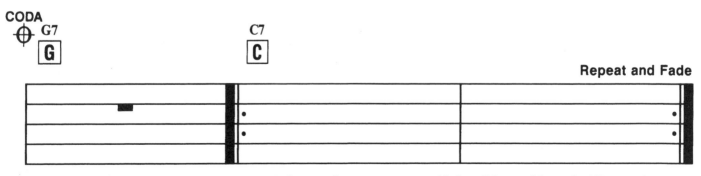

(Spoken:) I'm broke!   *No bread! I mean like nothin' Forget it!*

Butterfly Kisses

Registration 8
Rhythm: Ballad

Words and Music by Bob Carlisle
and Randy Thomas

30

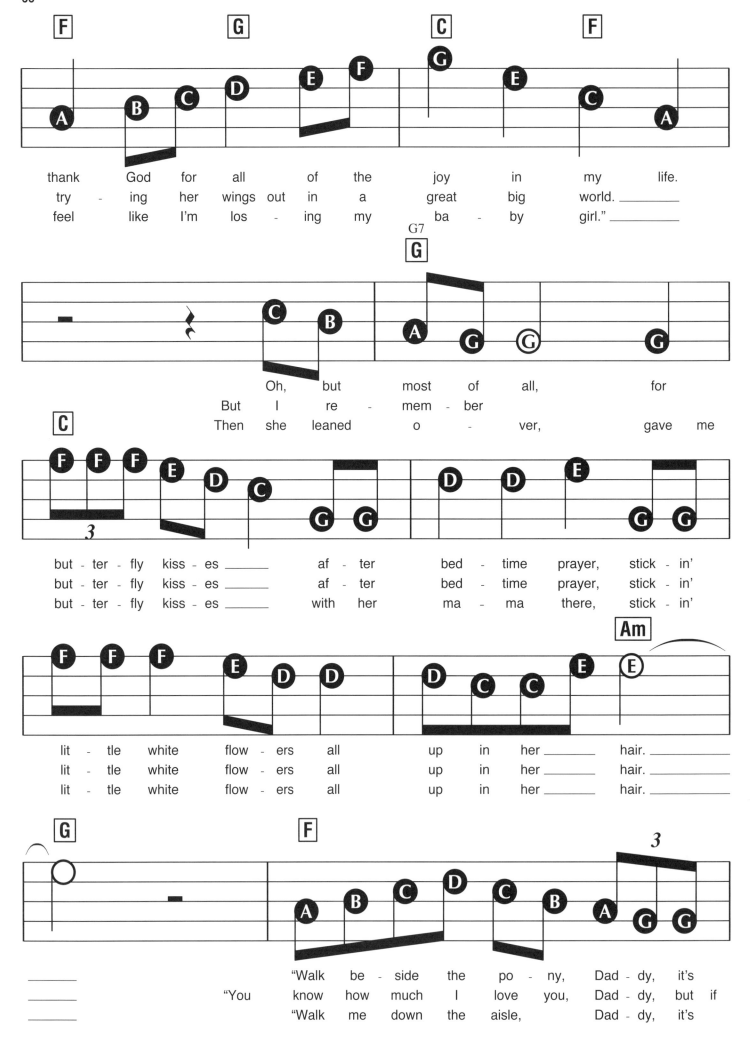

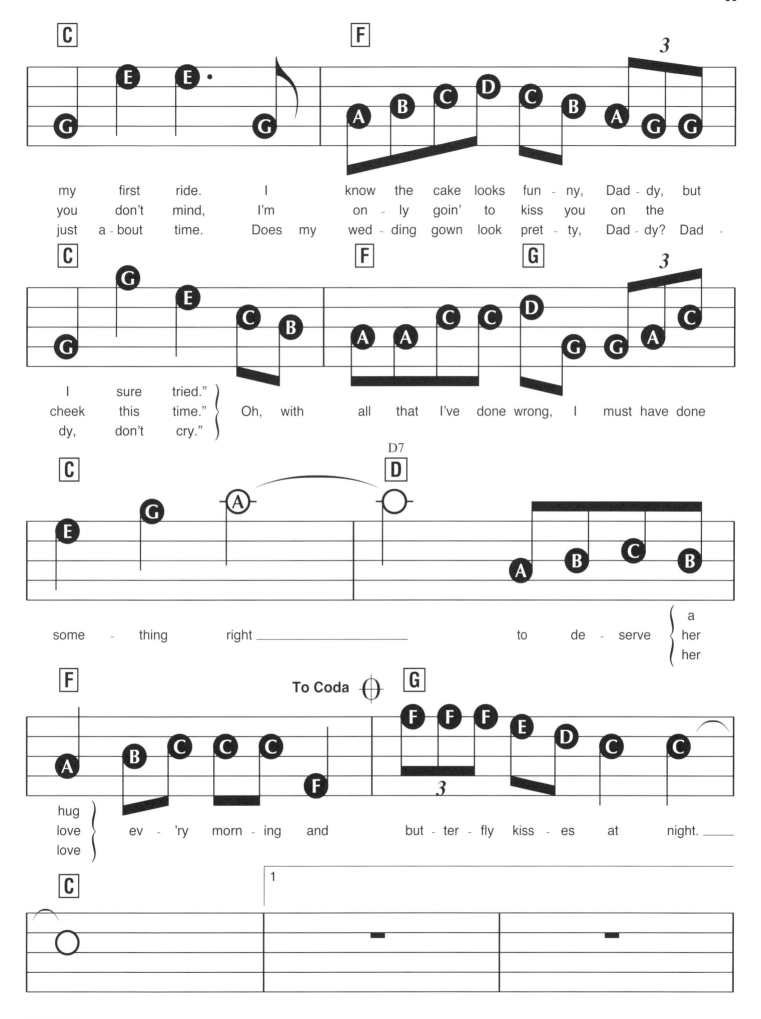

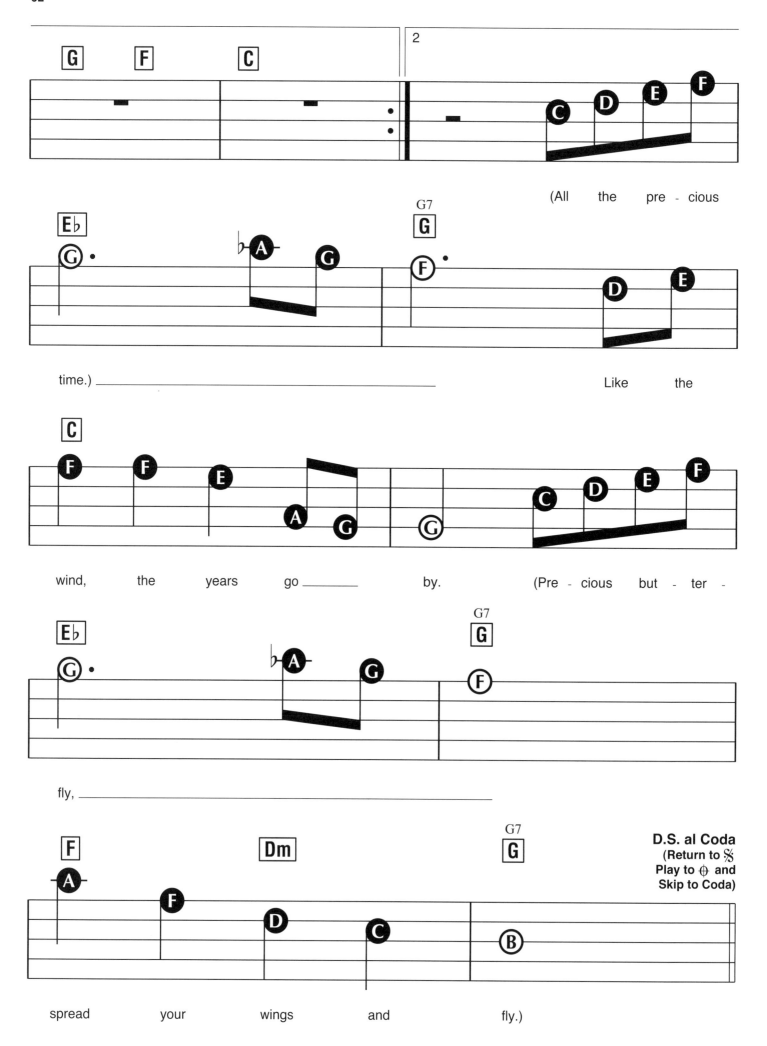

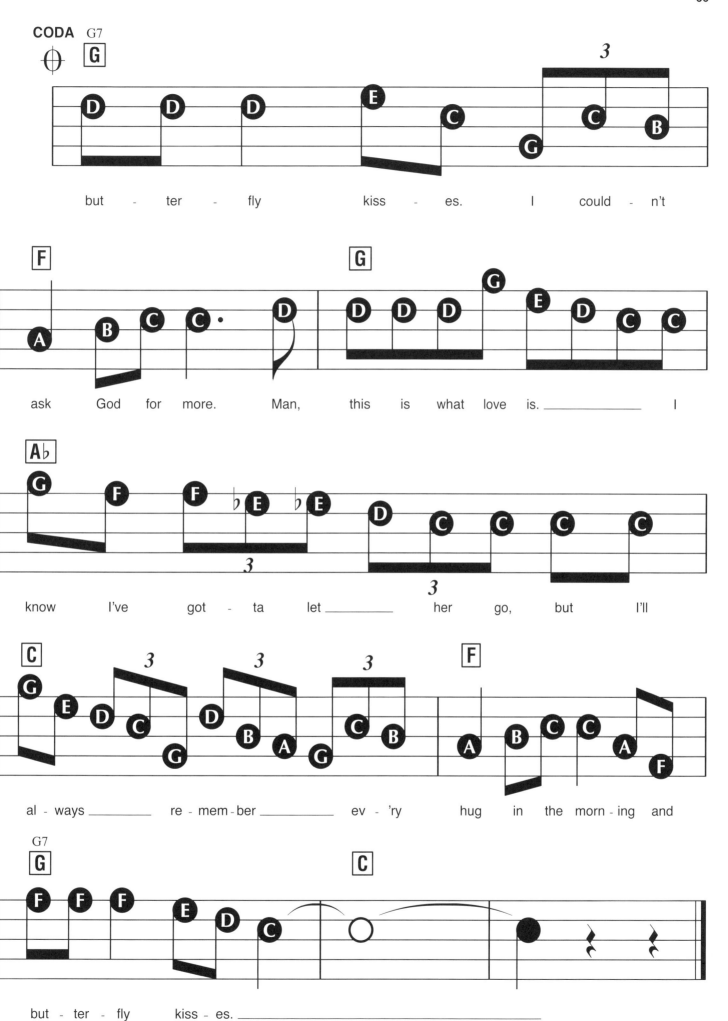

Can't Help Falling in Love

from the Paramount Picture BLUE HAWAII

Registration 3
Rhythm: Ballad or Swing

Words and Music by George David Weiss,
Hugo Peretti and Luigi Creatore

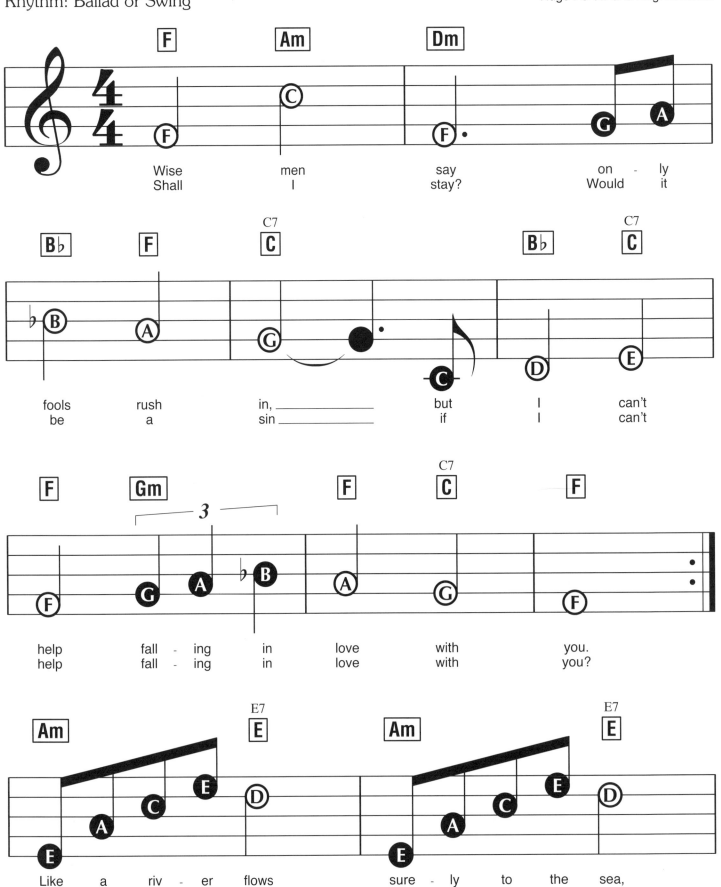

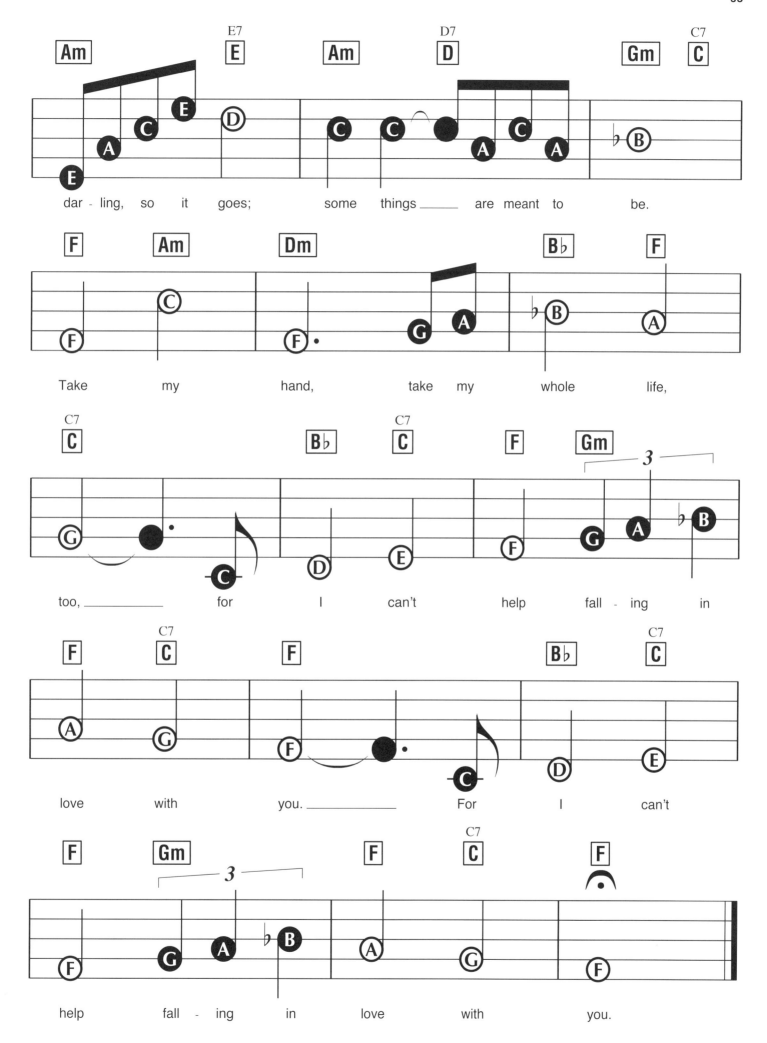

The Closer You Get

Registration 4
Rhythm: Country or Shuffle

Words and Music by James Pennington
and Mark Gray

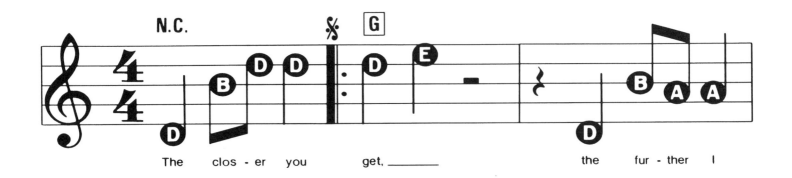

The clos - er you get, _____ the fur - ther I

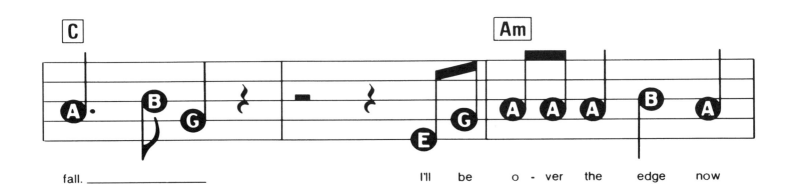

fall. _____ I'll be o - ver the edge now

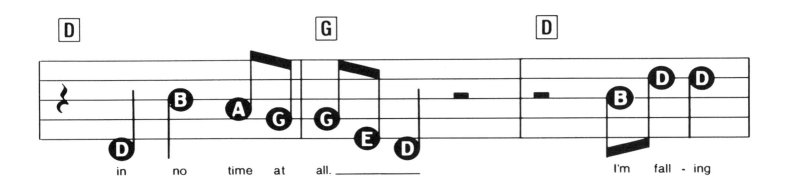

in no time at all. _____ I'm fall - ing

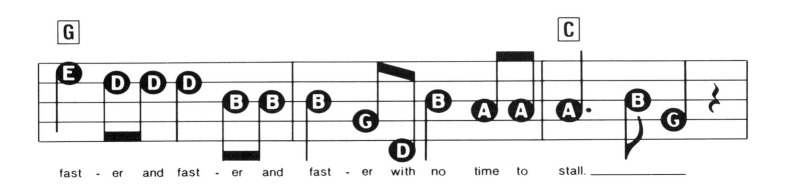

fast - er and fast - er and fast - er with no time to stall. _____

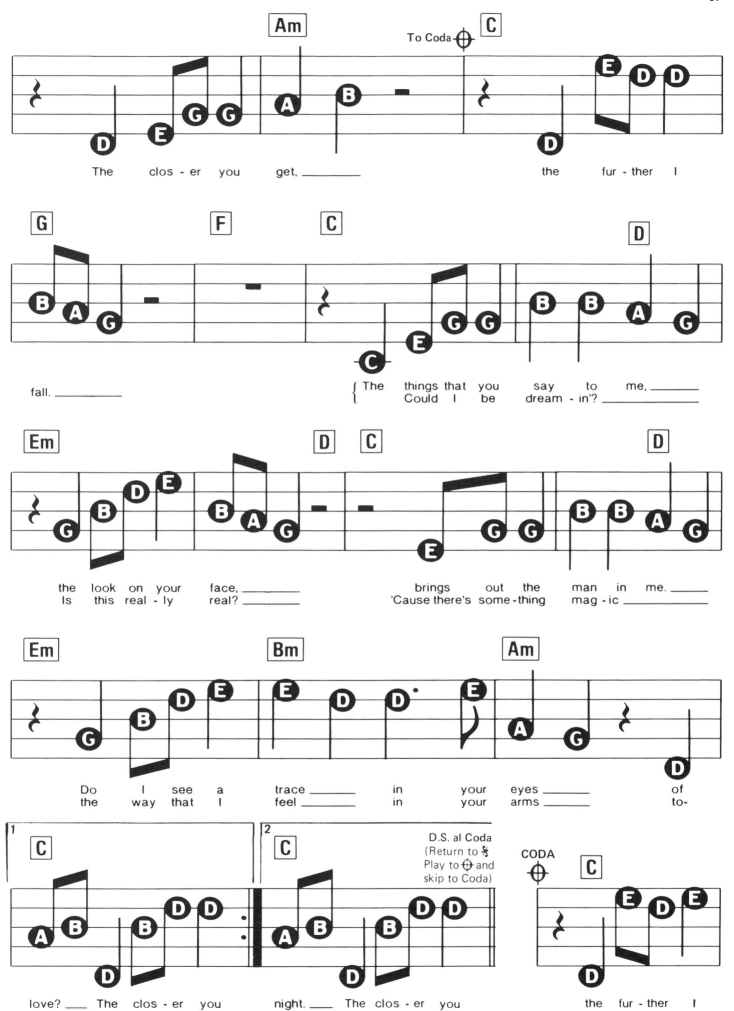

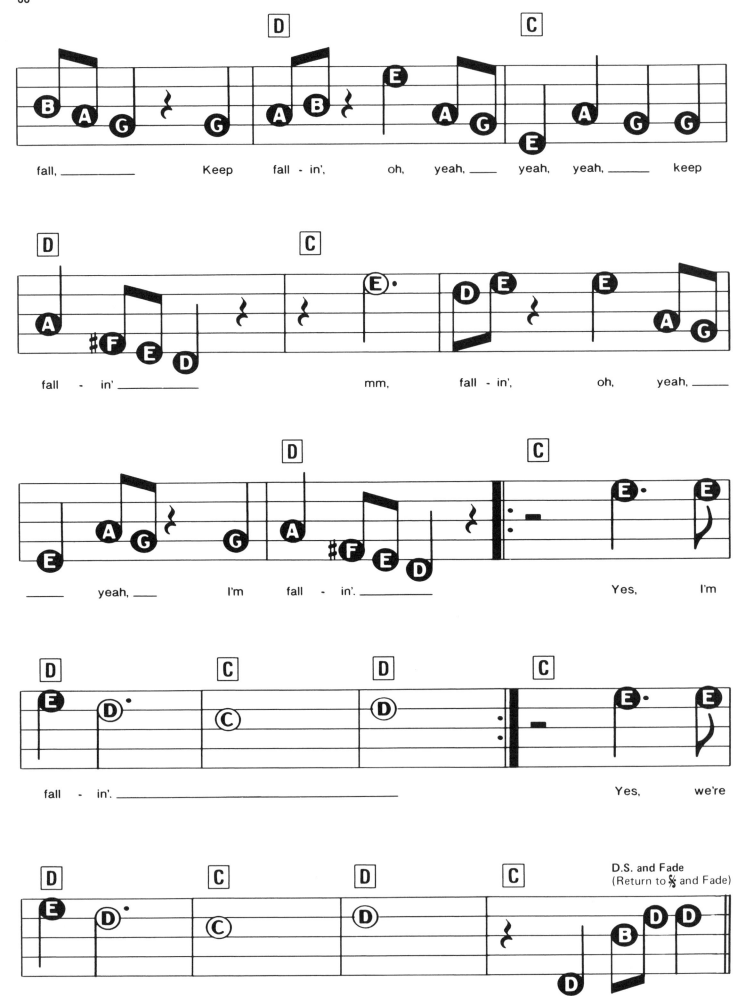

Coal Miner's Daughter

Registration 8
Rhythm: Country or Fox Trot

Words and Music by
Loretta Lynn

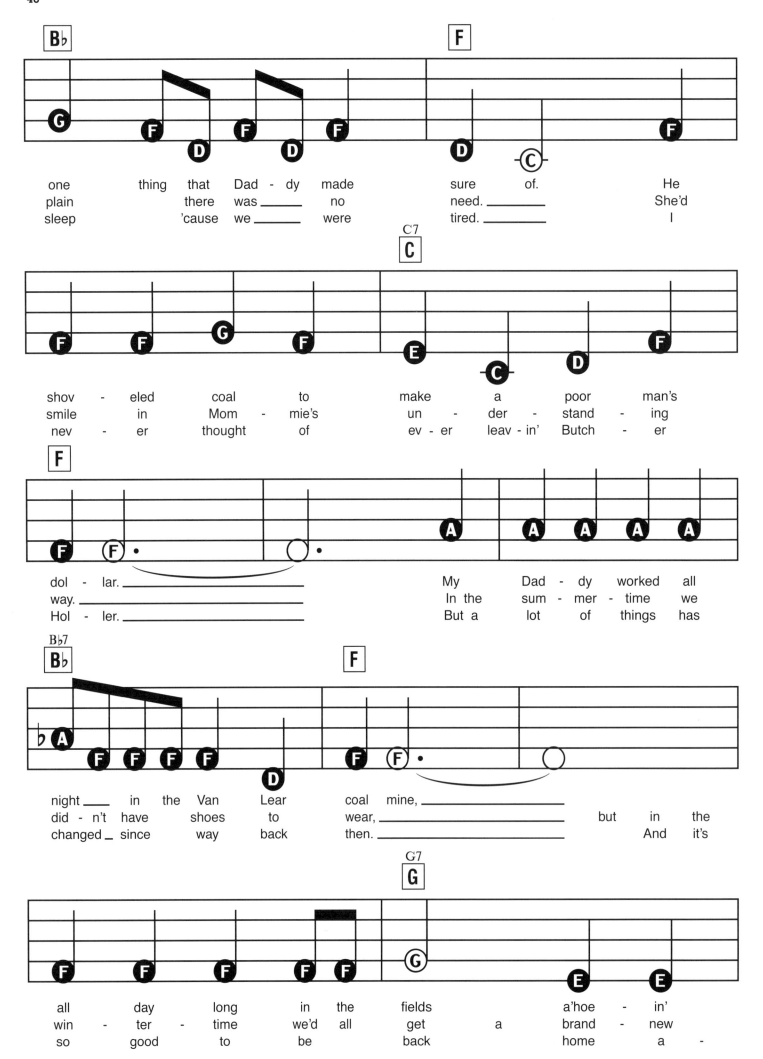

Cold, Cold Heart

Registration 4
Rhythm: Country or Fox Trot

Words and Music by
Hank Williams

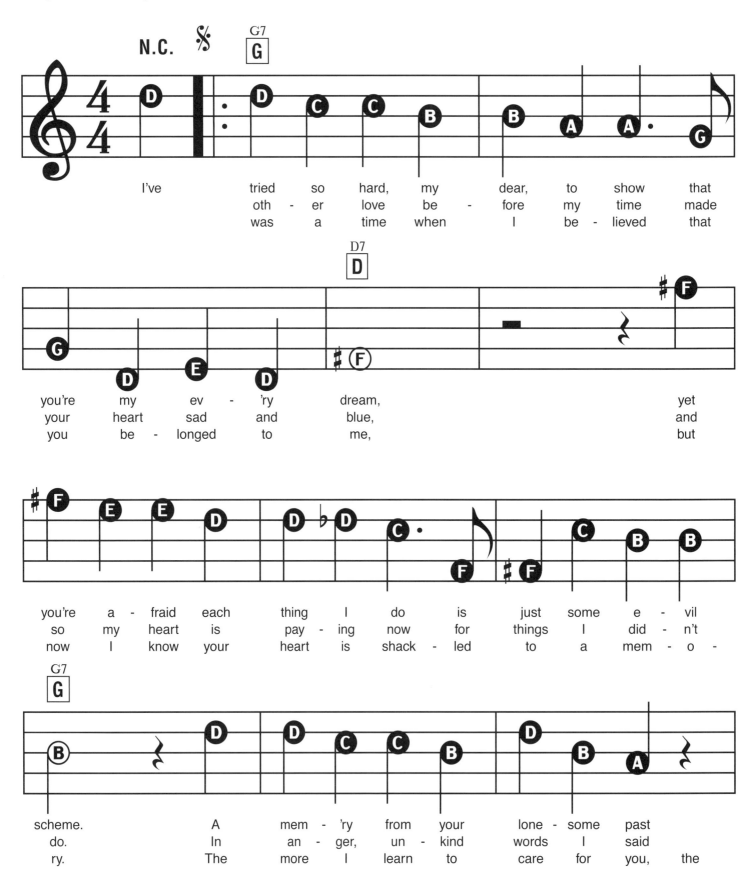

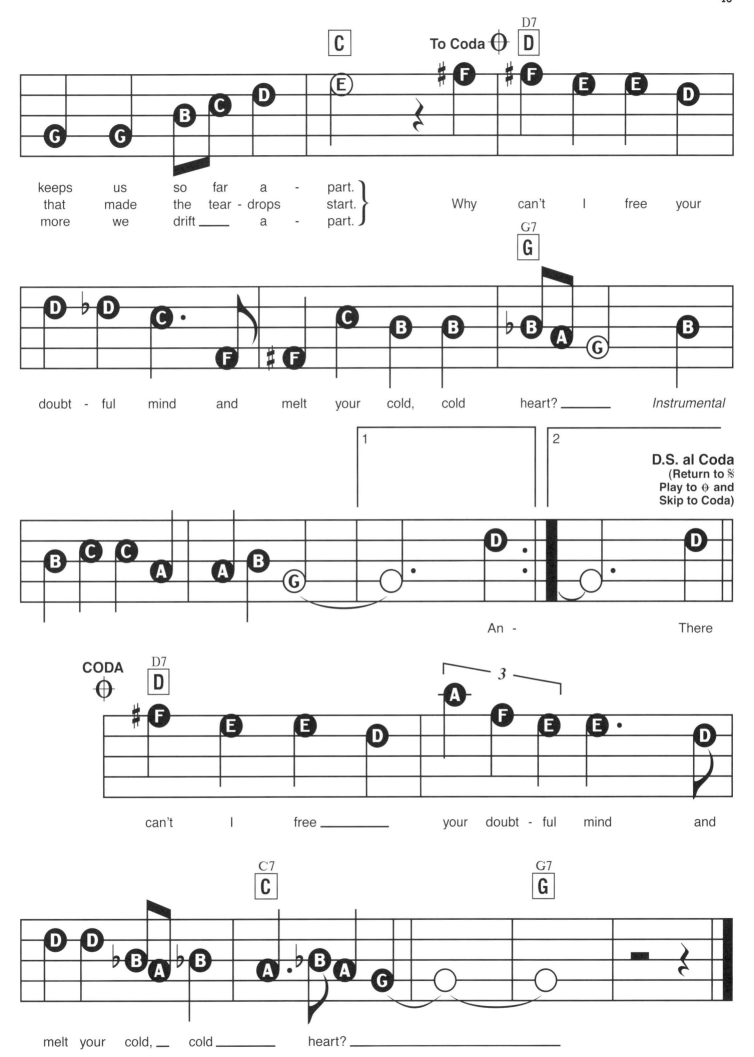

Country Sunshine

Registration 1
Rhythm: Country

Words and Music by Dottie West,
Bill Davis and Dianne Whiles

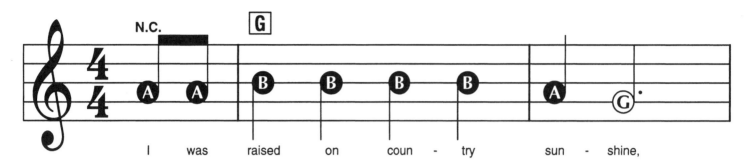

I was raised on coun - try sun - shine,

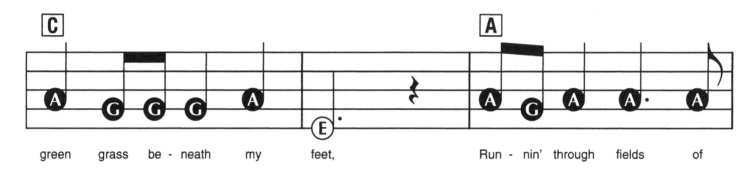

green grass be - neath my feet, Run - nin' through fields of

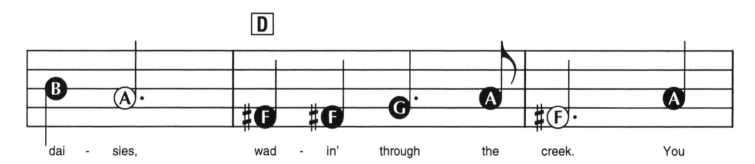

dai - sies, wad - in' through the creek. You

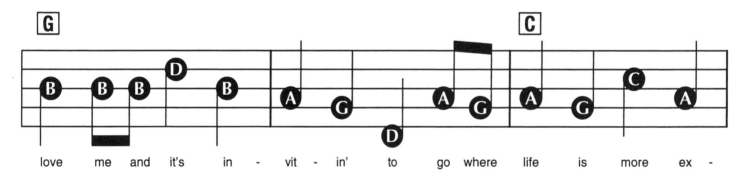

love me and it's in - vit - in' to go where life is more ex -

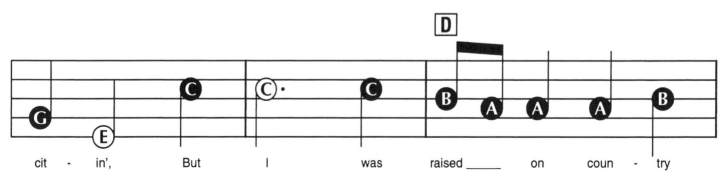

cit - in', But I was raised _____ on coun - try

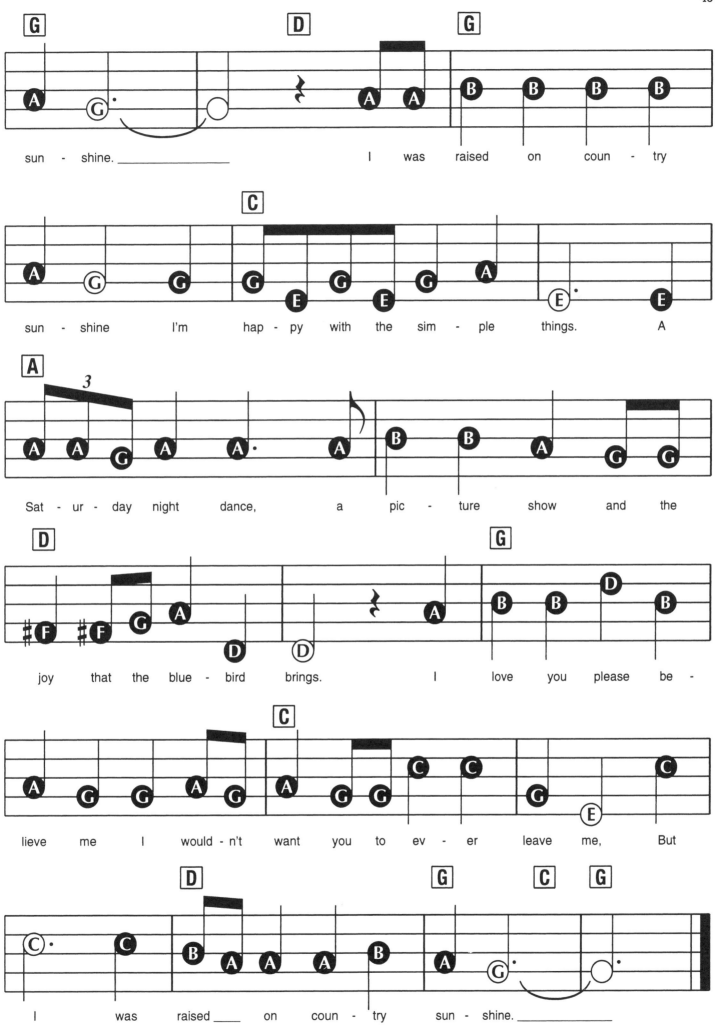

Cryin' Time

Registration 3
Rhythm: Country

Words and Music by
Buck Owens

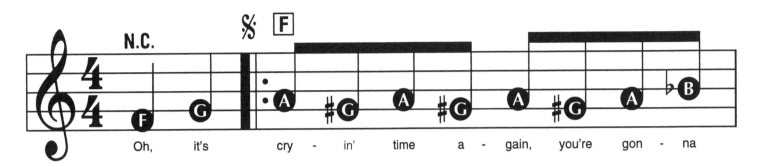

Oh, it's cry - in' time a - gain, you're gon - na

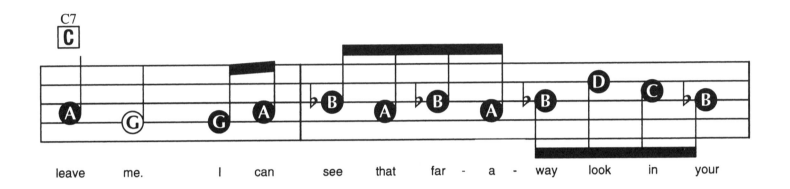

leave me. I can see that far - a - way look in your

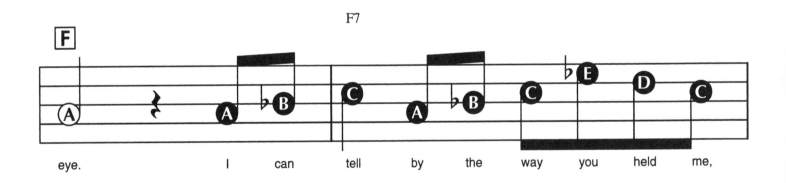

eye. I can tell by the way you held me,

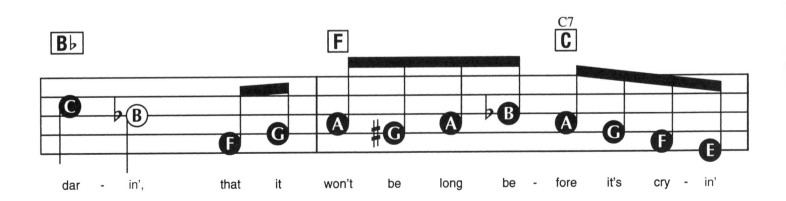

dar - in', that it won't be long be - fore it's cry - in'

Crying

Registration 4
Rhythm: Ballad or Slow Rock

Words and Music by Roy Orbison
and Joe Melson

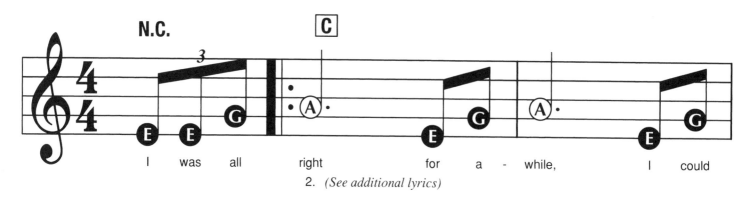

I was all right for a - while, I could

2. *(See additional lyrics)*

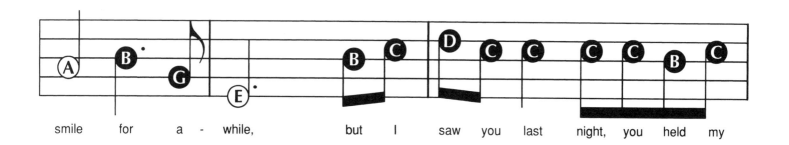

smile for a - while, but I saw you last night, you held my

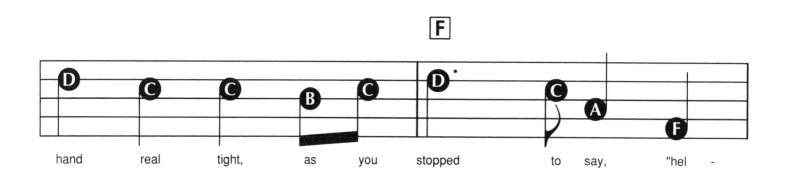

hand real tight, as you stopped to say, "hel -

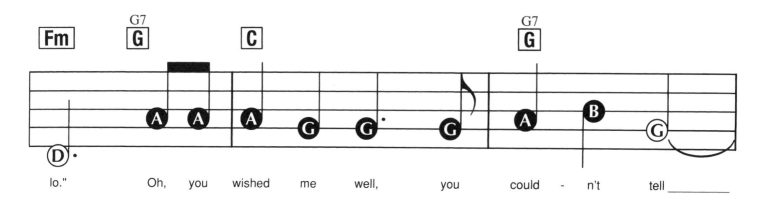

lo." Oh, you wished me well, you could - n't tell _____

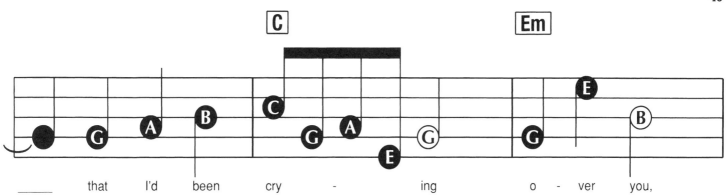

that I'd been cry - ing o - ver you,

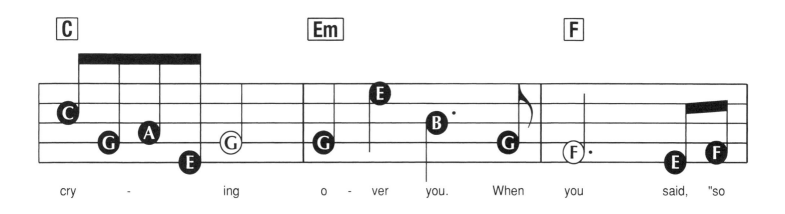

cry - ing o - ver you. When you said, "so

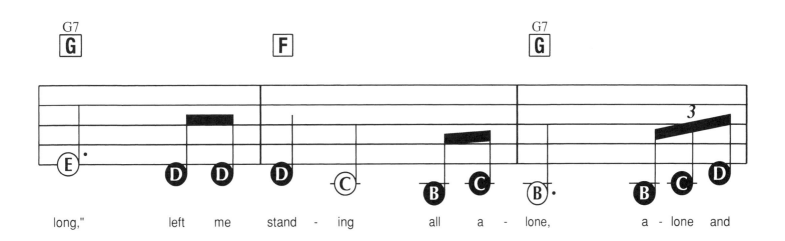

long," left me stand - ing all a - lone, a - lone and

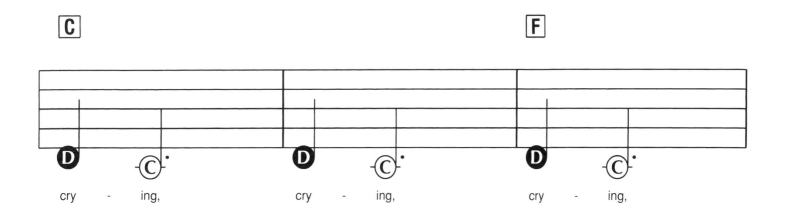

cry - ing, cry - ing, cry - ing,

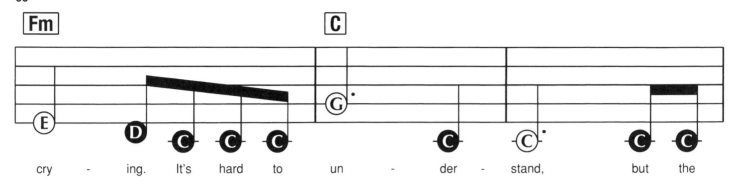

cry - ing. It's hard to un - der - stand, but the

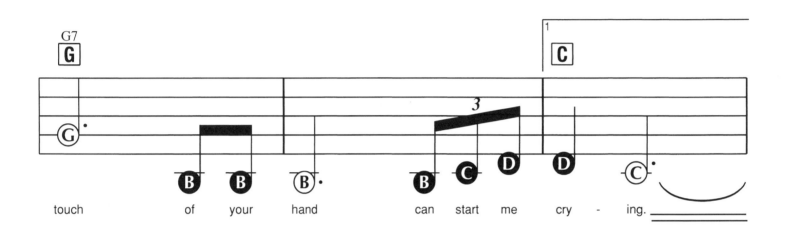

touch of your hand can start me cry - ing.

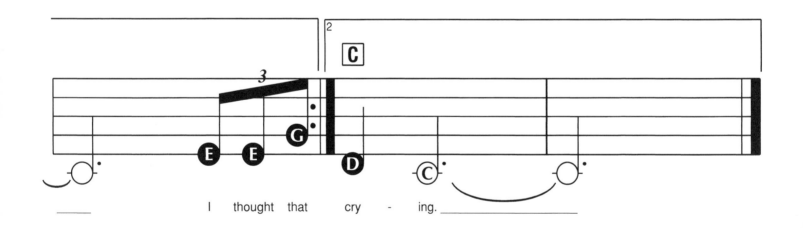

I thought that cry - ing.

Additional Lyrics

2   I thought that I was over you,
    But it's true, so true:
    I love you even more than I did before.
    But darling, what can I do?
    For you don't love me and I'll always be
    Crying over you, crying over you.
    Yes, now you're gone and from this moment on
    I'll be crying, crying, crying, crying,
    Yeah, crying, crying over you.

Eighteen Wheels and a Dozen Roses

Registration 8
Rhythm: Country Rock or Country Pop

Words and Music by Gene Nelson
and Paul Nelson

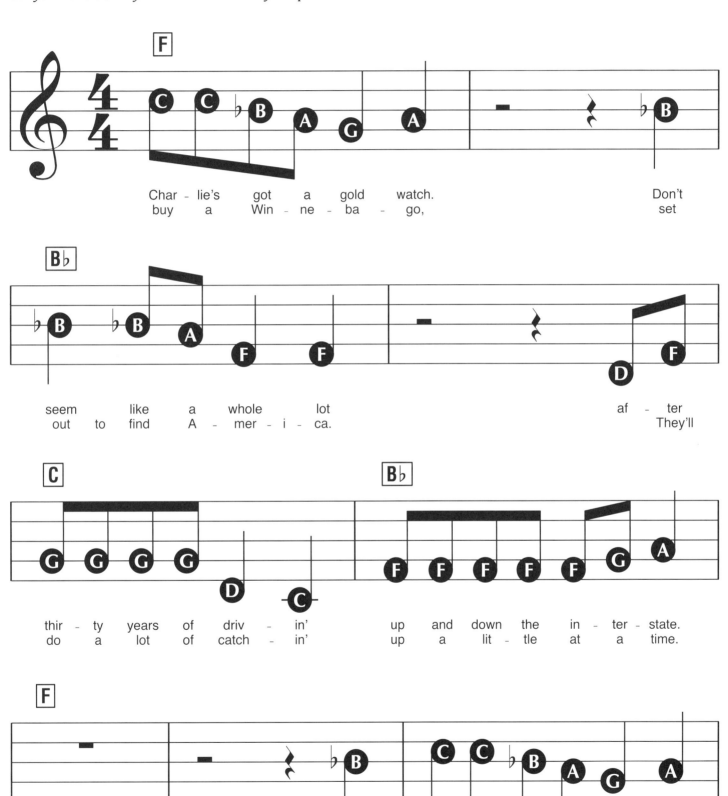

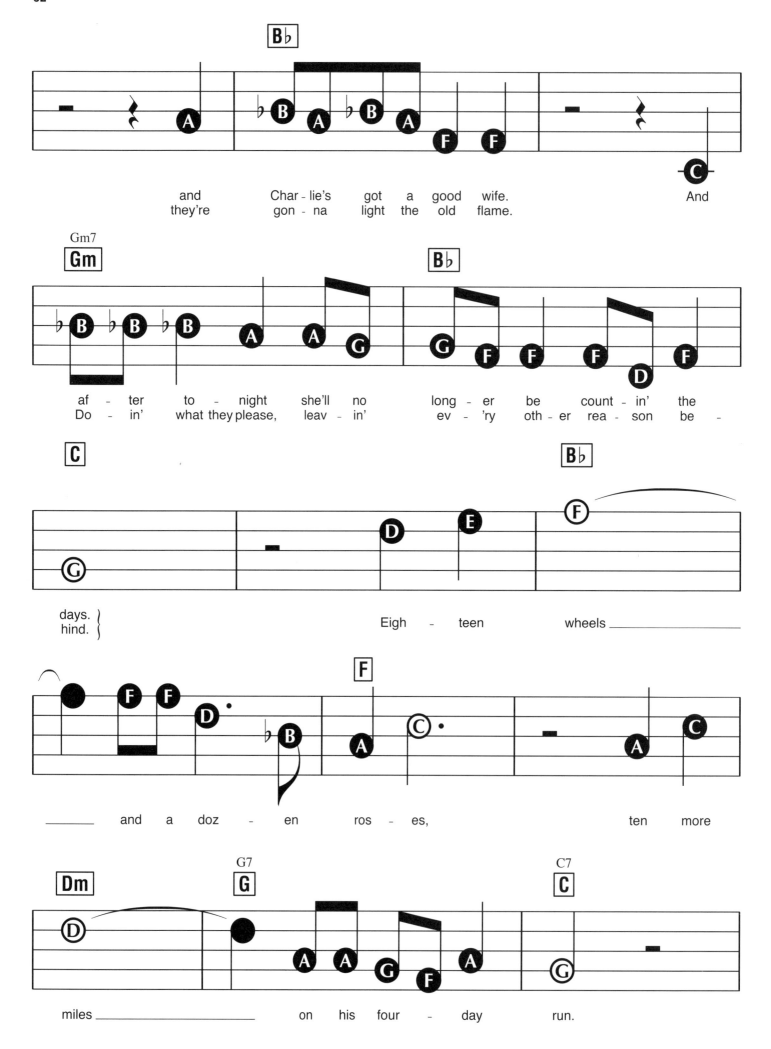

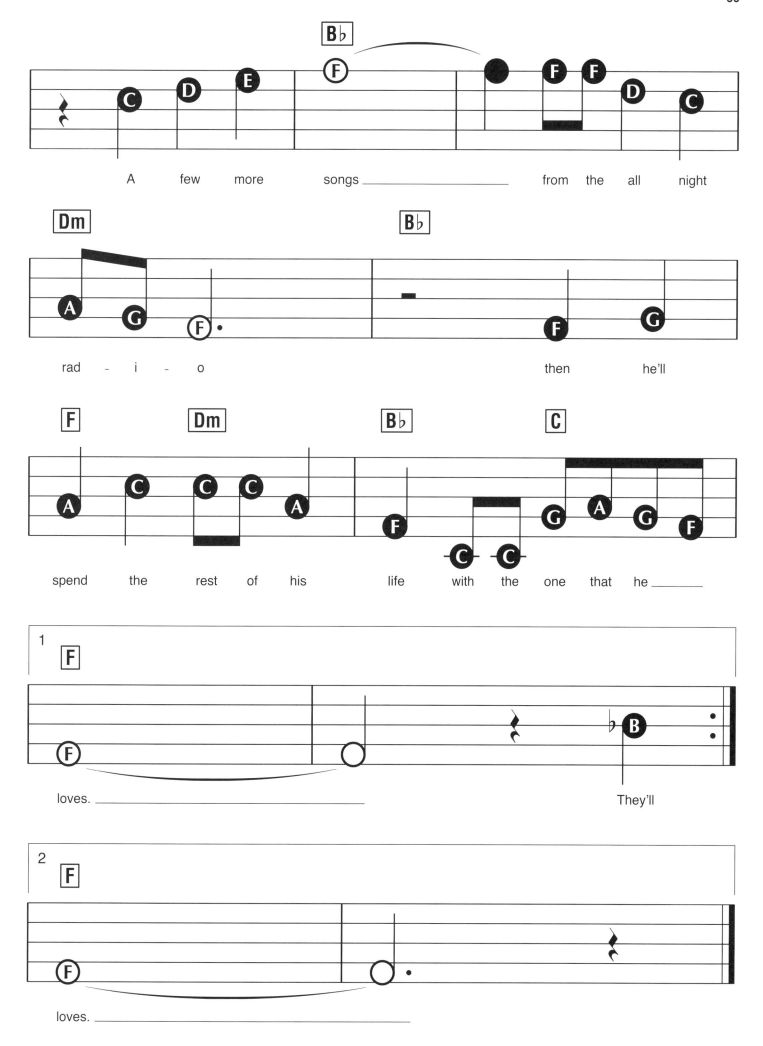

Don't Rock the Jukebox

Registration 9
Rhythm: Shuffle or Swing

Words and Music by Roger Murrah,
Alan Jackson and Keith Stegall

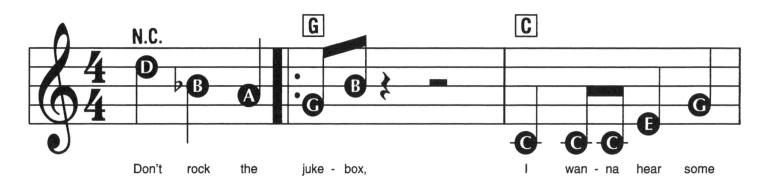

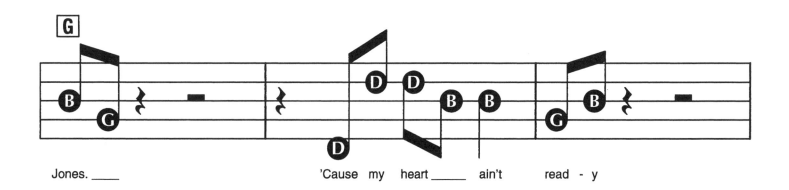

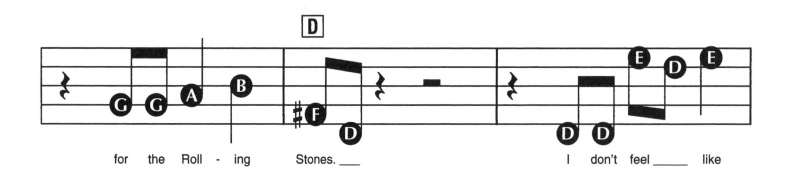

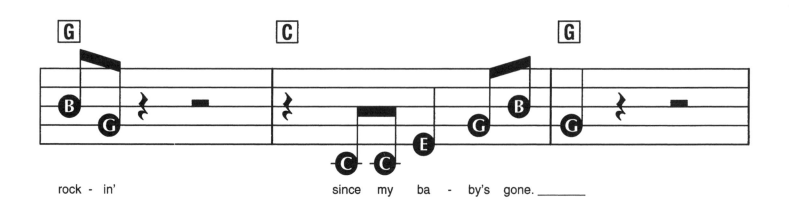

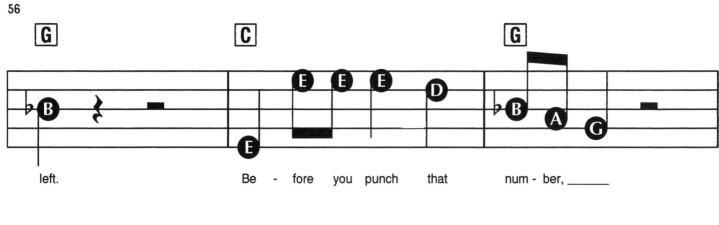

left. Be - fore you punch that num - ber, _____

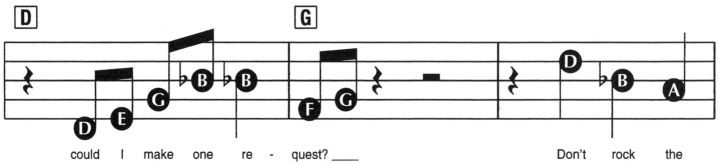

could I make one re - quest? ____ Don't rock the

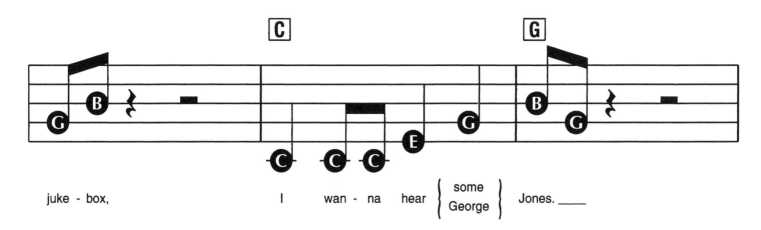

juke - box, I wan - na hear { some / George } Jones. ____

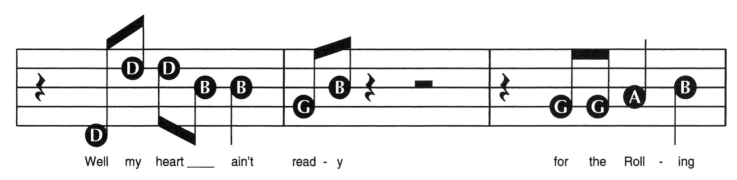

Well my heart ____ ain't read - y for the Roll - ing

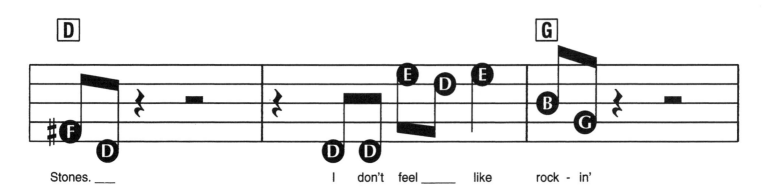

Stones. ___ I don't feel ____ like rock - in'

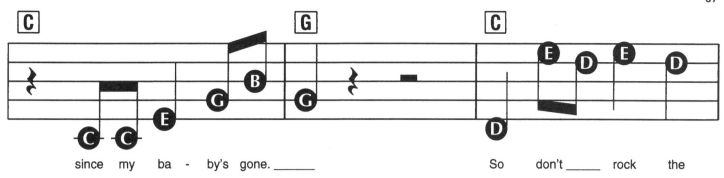

since my ba - by's gone. _____ So don't _____ rock the

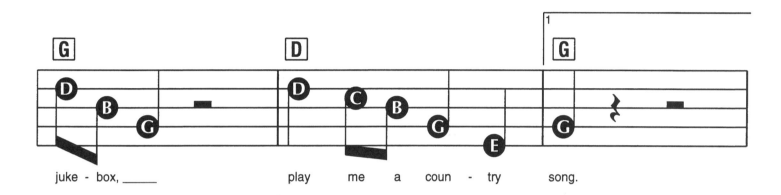

juke - box, _____ play me a coun - try song.

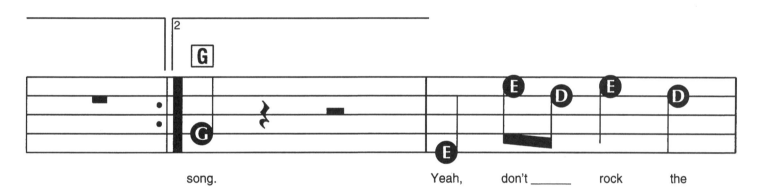

song. Yeah, don't _____ rock the

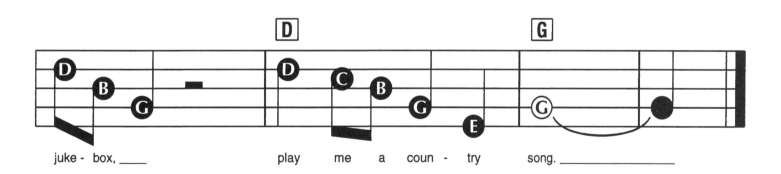

juke - box, _____ play me a coun - try song. _____

Additional Lyrics

I ain't got nothin' against rock & roll,
But when your heart's been broken,
You need a song that's slow.
Ain't nothin' like a steel guitar
To drown a memory.
Before you spend your money, baby.
Play a song for me.

Chorus

Down at the Twist and Shout

Registration 1
Rhythm: Country or Polka

Words and Music by
Mary Chapin Carpenter

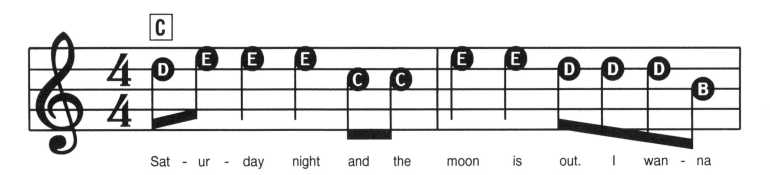

Sat - ur - day night and the moon is out. I wan - na

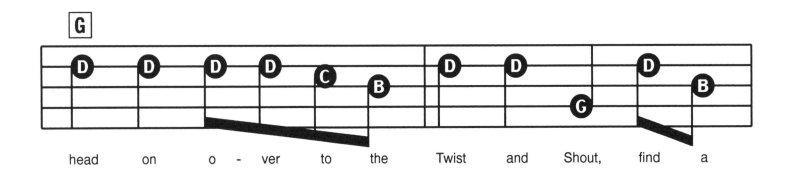

head on o - ver to the Twist and Shout, find a

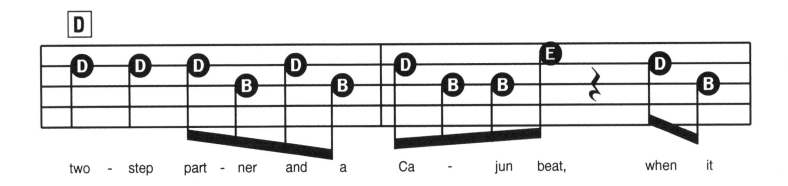

two - step part - ner and a Ca - jun beat, when it

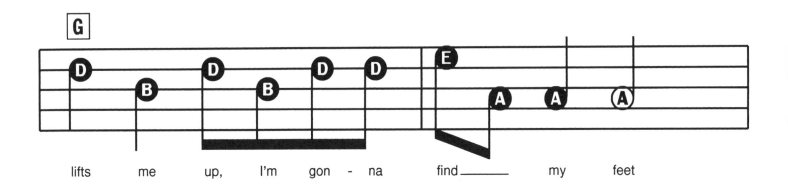

lifts me up, I'm gon - na find_____ my feet

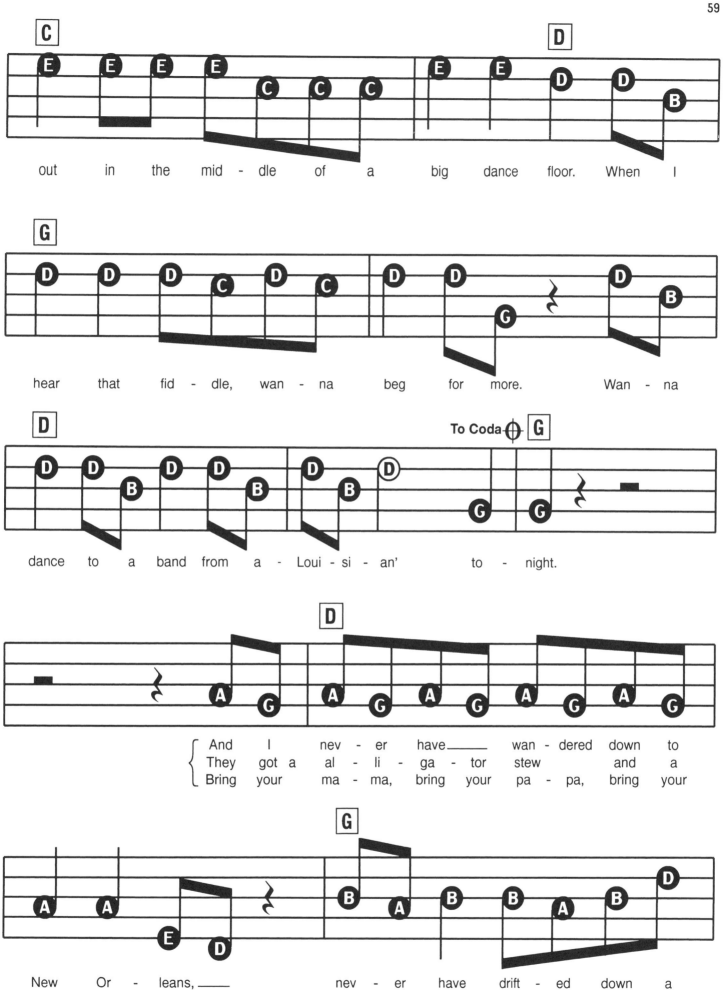

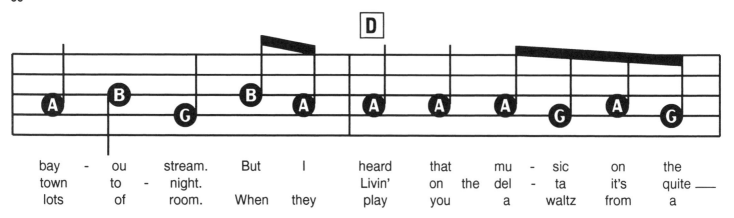

bay	-	ou	stream.	But	I	heard	that	mu	-	sic	on	the
town		to	- night.	When	they	Livin'	on	the	del	- ta	it's	quite ___
lots		of	room.			play	you	a	waltz	from		a

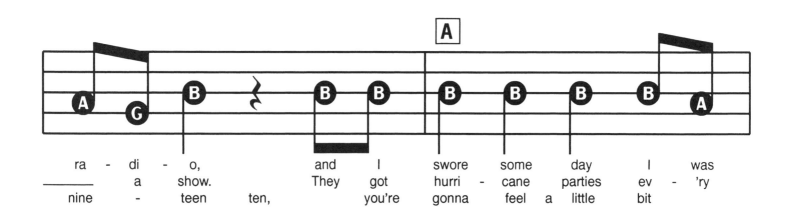

ra	-	di	- o,		and	I	swore	some	day	I	was
___		a	show.		They	got	hurri	- cane	parties	ev	- 'ry
nine		- teen	ten,		you're	gonna	feel	a	little		bit

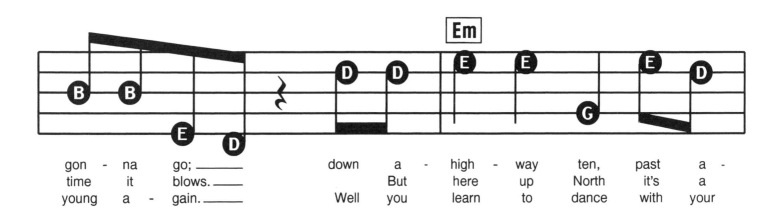

gon	- na	go; ___		down	a	- high	- way	ten,	past	a -
time	it	blows. ___		But	here	up	North	it's		a
young	a -	gain. ___	Well	you	learn	to	dance	with	your

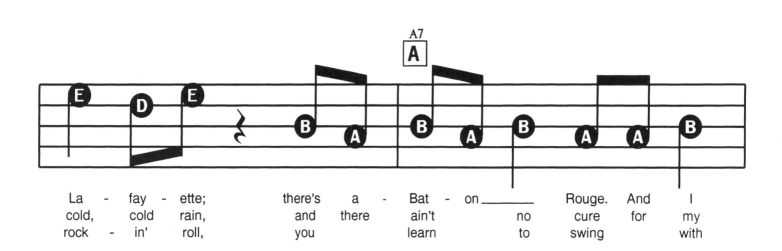

La	- fay	- ette;		there's	a	- Bat	- on ___	Rouge.	And	I
cold,	cold	rain,		and	there	ain't	no	cure	for	my
rock	- in'	roll,	you		learn	to	swing	with

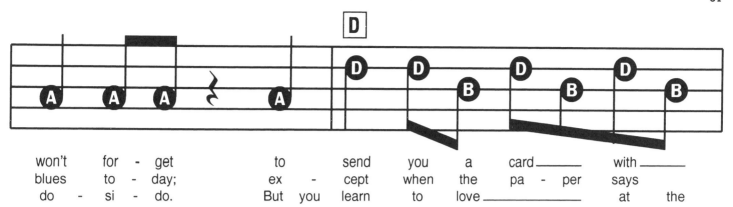

won't for - get to send you a card_____ with _____
blues to - day; ex - cept when the pa - per says
do - si - do. But you learn to love _____ at the

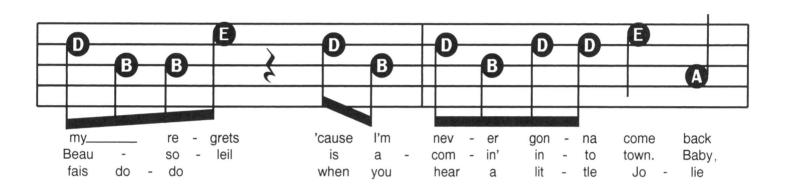

my_____ re - grets 'cause I'm nev - er gon - na come back
Beau - so - leil is a - com - in' in - to town. Baby,
fais do - do when you hear a lit - tle Jo - lie

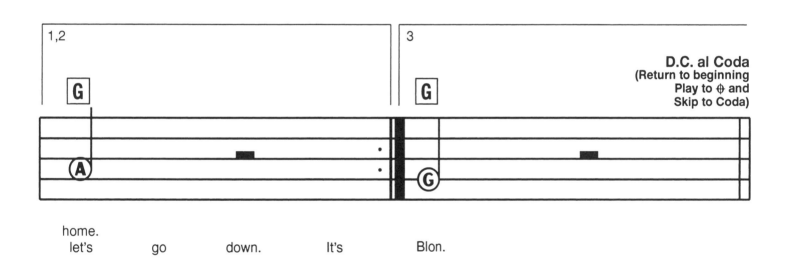

D.C. al Coda
(Return to beginning
Play to ⊕ and
Skip to Coda)

home.
let's go down. It's Blon.

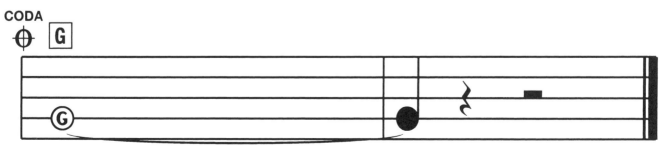

night._____

Dream Baby
(How Long Must I Dream)

Registration 7
Rhythm: Ballad or Fox Trot

Words and Music by
Cindy Walker

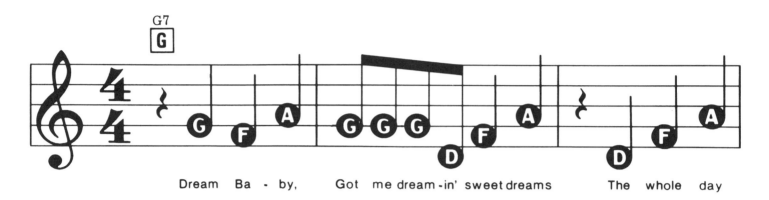

Dream Ba - by, Got me dream-in' sweet dreams The whole day

through. Dream Ba - by, Got me dream - in' sweet dreams Night time,

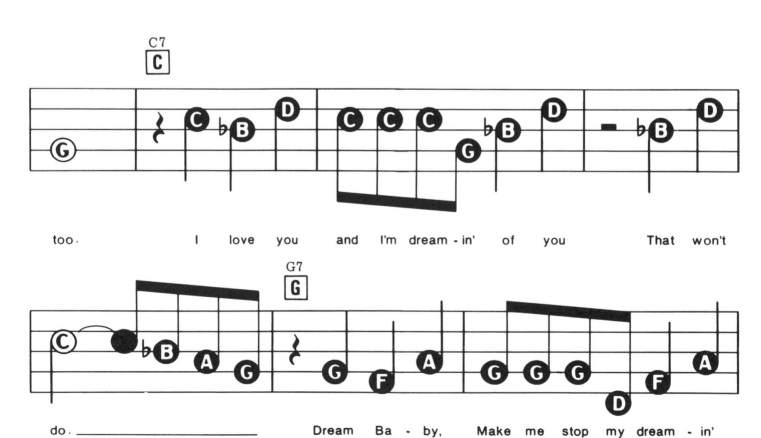

too. I love you and I'm dream-in' of you That won't

do. _____ Dream Ba - by, Make me stop my dream - in'

East Bound and Down
from the Universal Film SMOKEY AND THE BANDIT

Registration 4
Rhythm: Bluegrass or Fox Trot

Words and Music by Jerry Reed
and Dick Feller

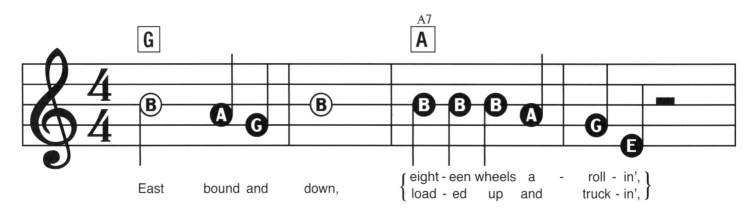

East bound and down, { eight - een wheels a - roll - in', load - ed up and truck - in', }

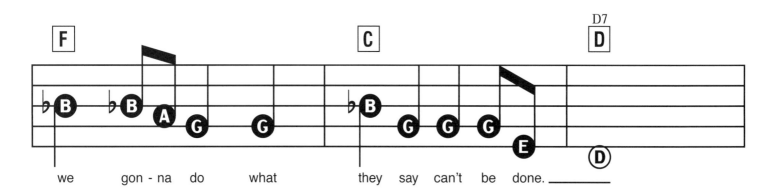

we gon - na do what they say can't be done. _____

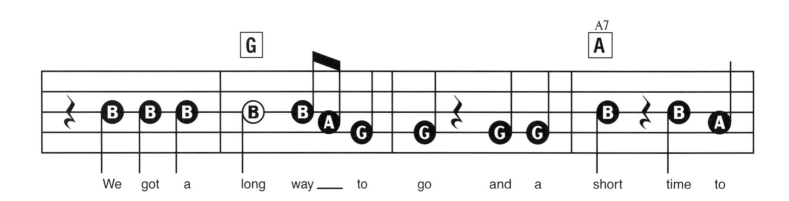

We got a long way ___ to go and a short time to

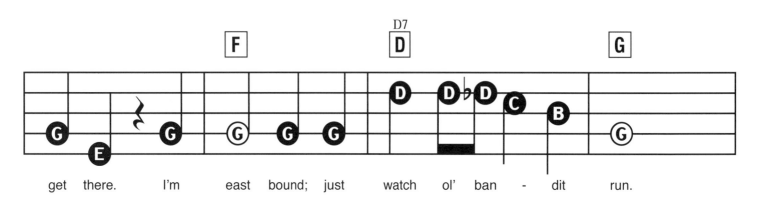

get there. I'm east bound; just watch ol' ban - dit run.

65

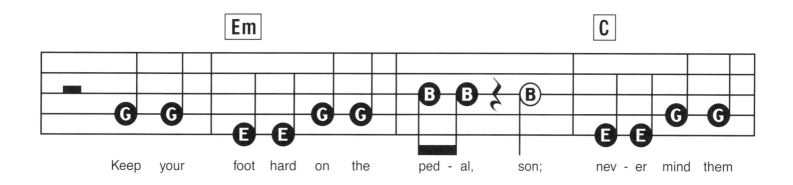

Keep your foot hard on the ped - al, son; nev - er mind them

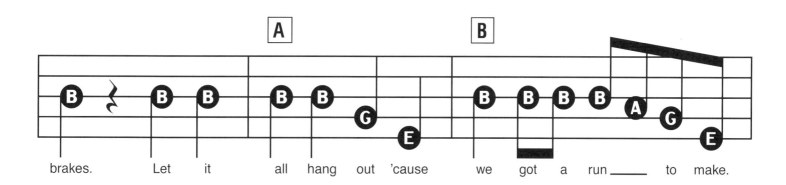

brakes. Let it all hang out 'cause we got a run ___ to make.

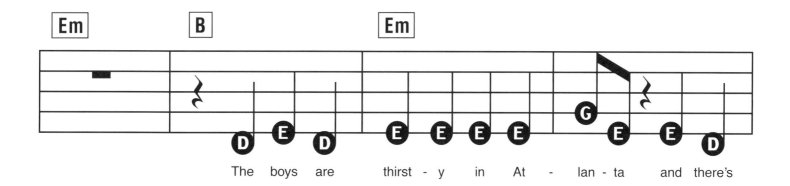

The boys are thirst - y in At - lan - ta and there's

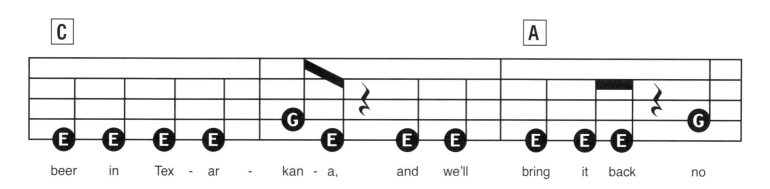

beer in Tex - ar - kan - a, and we'll bring it back no

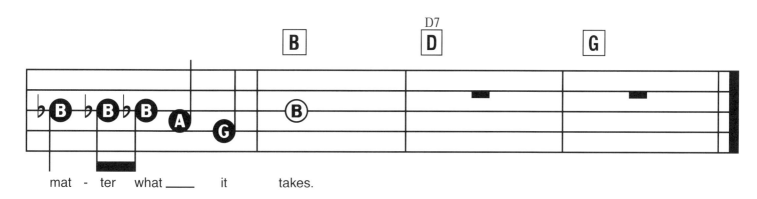

mat - ter what ___ it takes.

England Swings

Registration 8
Rhythm: Polka or Fox Trot

Words and Music by
Roger Miller

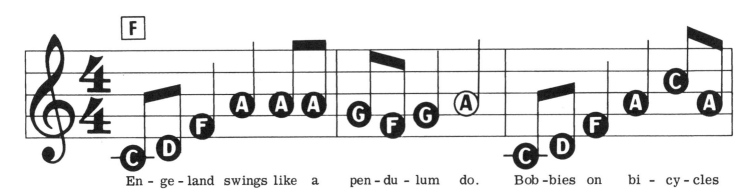

En - ge - land swings like a pen - du - lum do. Bob - bies on bi - cy - cles

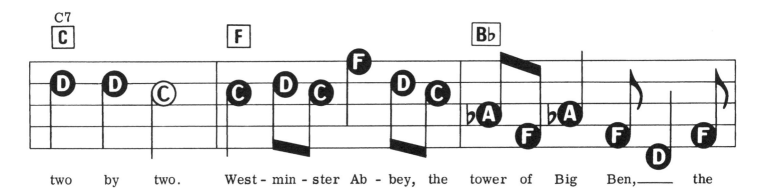

two by two. West - min - ster Ab - bey, the tower of Big Ben,____ the

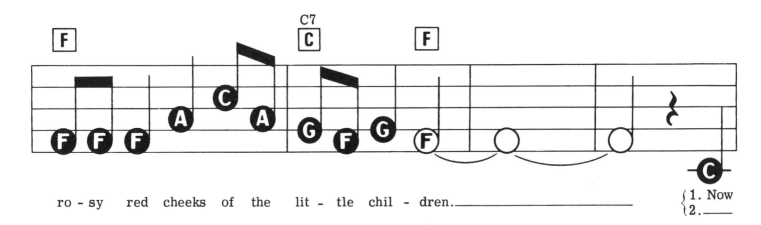

ro - sy red cheeks of the lit - tle chil - dren.____ {1. Now
2.____

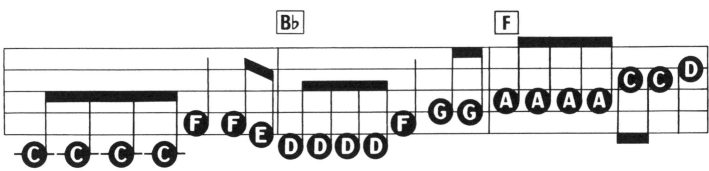

if you huff and puff, and you fin -'lly save e - nough mon - ey up to take your fam - i - ly
Ma - ma's old pa - jamas and your pa - pa's mus - tache,____ fall - in' out the win - dow sill,

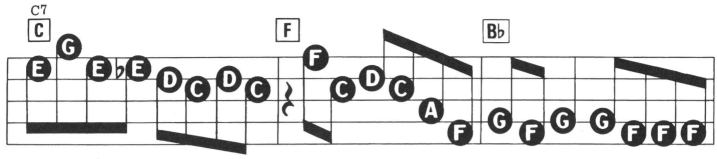

on a trip a-cross the sea,___ take a tip be-fore you take your trip, let me tell you
fro-lic in the grass.___ Try'n to mock the way they talk but with all in vain;___

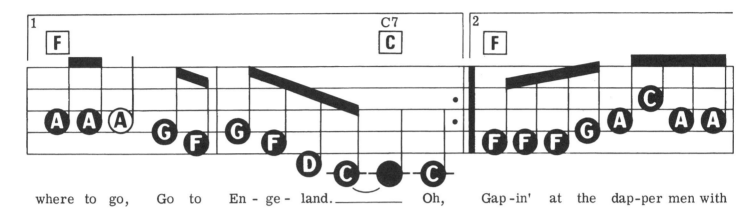

where to go, Go to En - ge - land.___ Oh, Gap-in' at the dap-per men with

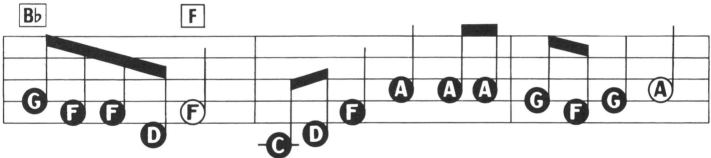

der - by hats and canes. En - ge - land swings like a pen - du - lum do.

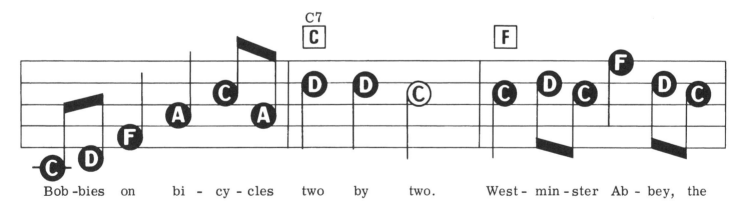

Bob-bies on bi - cy - cles two by two. West - min - ster Ab - bey, the

tower of Big Ben,___ the ro - sy red cheeks of the lit - tle chil - dren.

Every Which Way But Loose
from EVERY WHICH WAY BUT LOOSE

Registration 7
Rhythm: Shuffle

Words and Music by Steve Dorff,
Milton Brown and Thomas Garrett

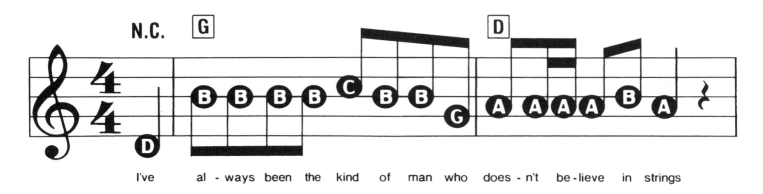

I've al-ways been the kind of man who does-n't be-lieve in strings

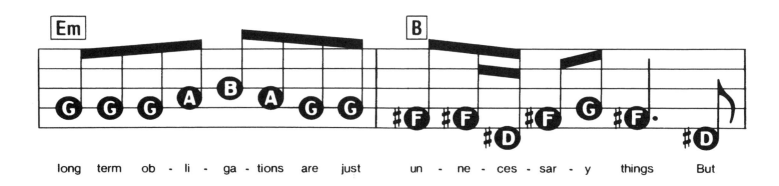

long term ob-li-ga-tions are just un-ne-ces-sar-y things But

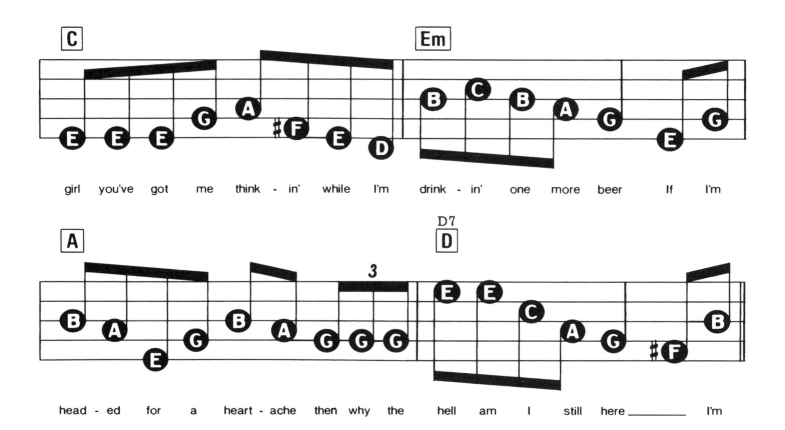

girl you've got me think-in' while I'm drink-in' one more beer If I'm

head-ed for a heart-ache then why the hell am I still here _____ I'm

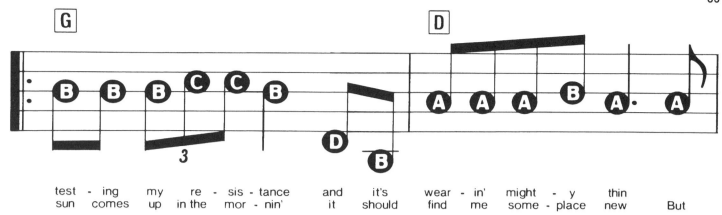

test - ing my re - sis - tance and it's wear - in' might - y thin
sun comes up in the mor - nin' it should find me some - place new But

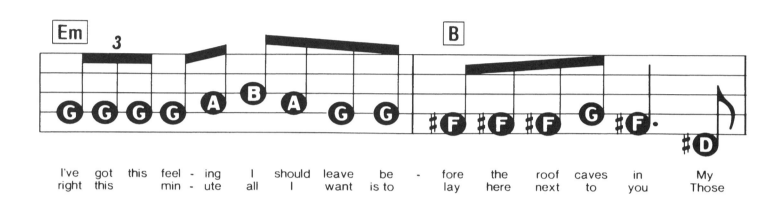

I've got this feel - ing I should leave be - fore the roof caves in My
right this min - ute all I want is to lay here next to you Those

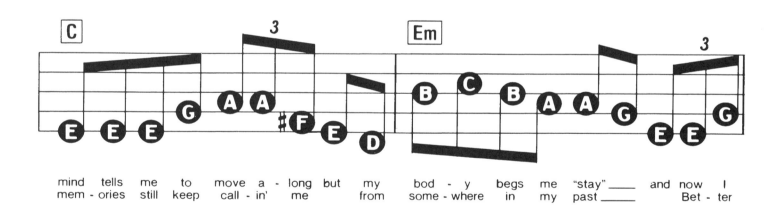

mind tells me to move a - long but my bod - y begs me "stay" ___ and now I
mem - ories still keep call - in' me from some - where in my past ___ Bet - ter

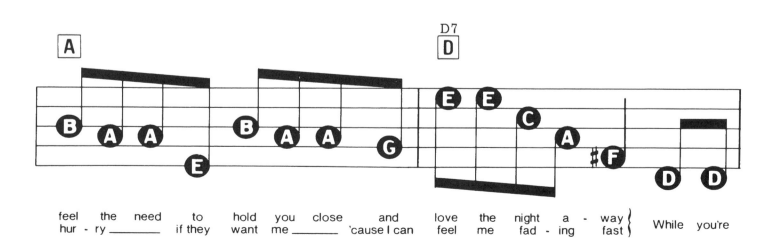

feel the need to hold you close and love the night a - way } While you're
hur - ry ___ if they want me ___ 'cause I can feel me fad - ing fast }

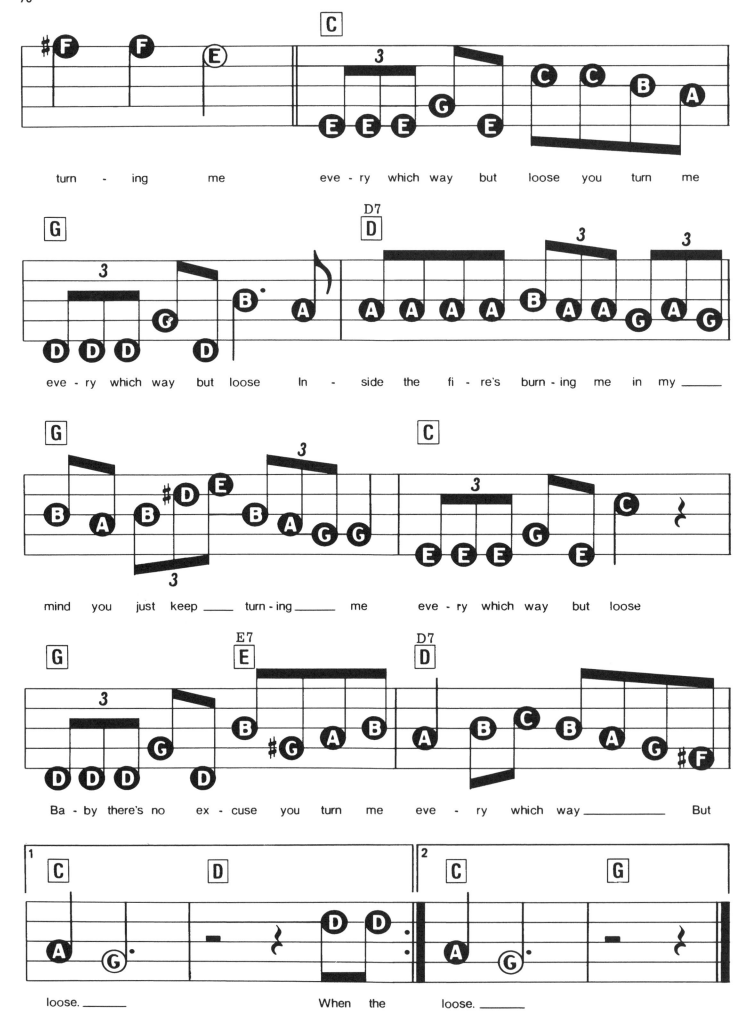

Games People Play

Registration 4
Rhythm: Country

Words and Music by
Joe South

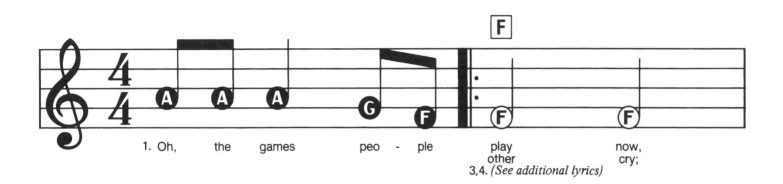

1. Oh, the games peo - ple play now,
other cry;
3,4. *(See additional lyrics)*

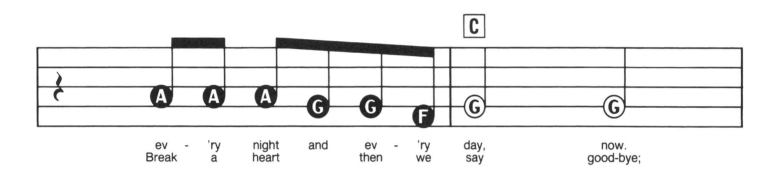

ev - 'ry night and ev - 'ry day, now.
Break a heart then we say good-bye;

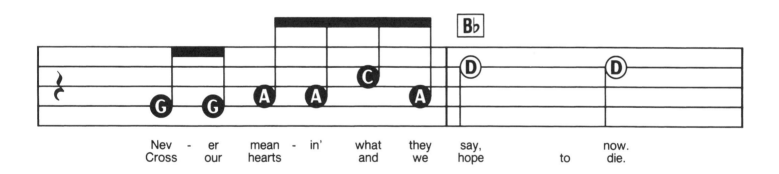

Nev - er mean - in' what they say, now.
Cross our hearts and we hope to die.

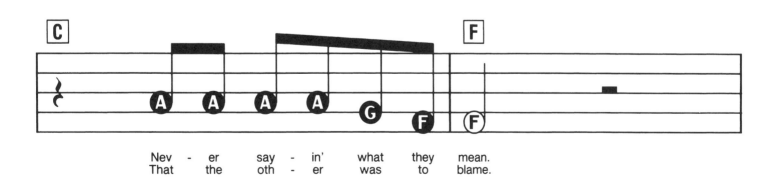

Nev - er say - in' what they mean.
That the oth - er was to blame.

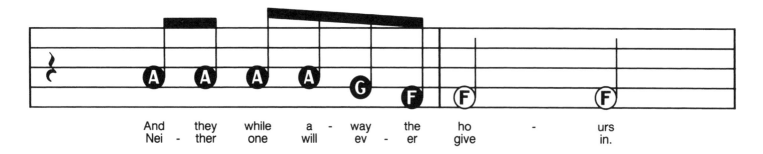

And they while a - way the ho - urs
Nei - ther one will ev - er give in.

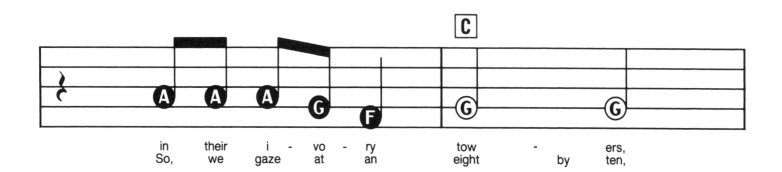

in their i - vo - ry tow - ers,
So, we gaze at an eight by ten,

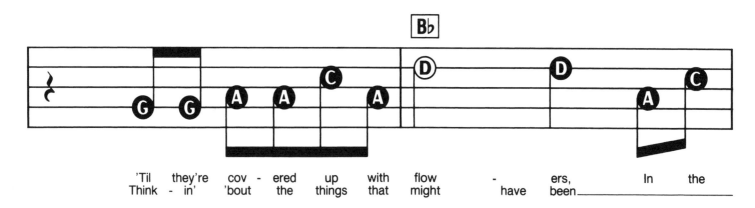

'Til they're cov - ered up with flow - ers, In the
Think - in' 'bout the things that might have been____

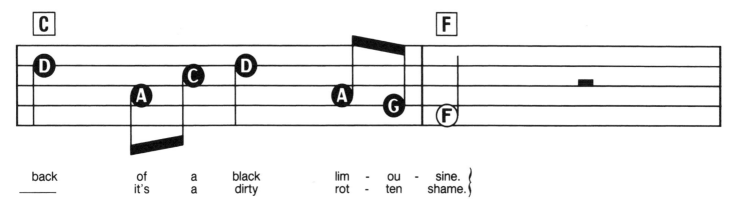

back of a black lim - ou - sine.
____ it's a dirty rot - ten shame.

Chorus

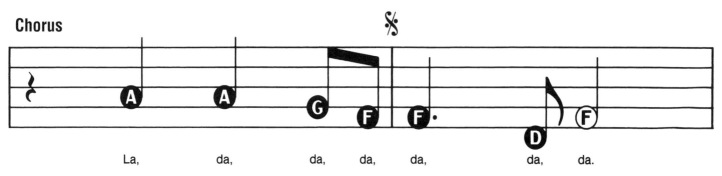

La, da, da, da, da, da, da.

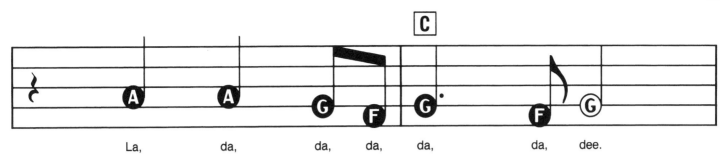

La, da, da, da, da, da, dee.

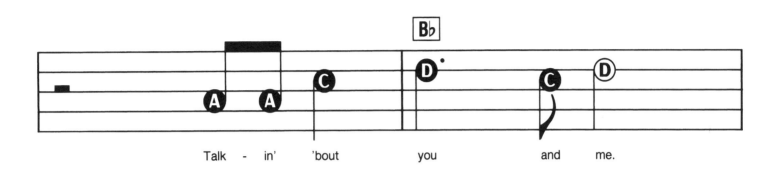

Talk - in' 'bout you and me.

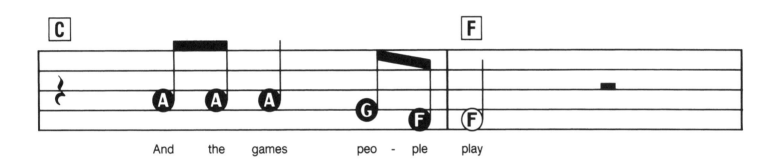

And the games peo - ple play

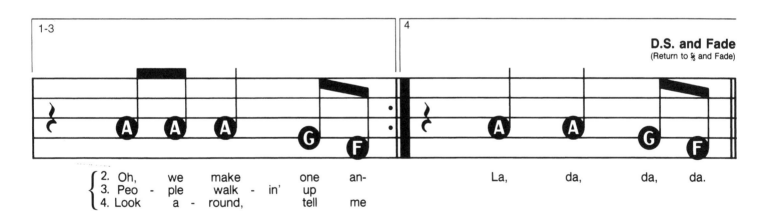

1-3

2. Oh, we make one an-
3. Peo - ple walk - in' up
4. Look a - round, tell me

4

D.S. and Fade
(Return to 𝄋 and Fade)

La, da, da, da.

Additional lyrics

3. People walkin up to you
Singin' "Glory Hallelujah!"
And they're tryin' to sock it to ya
In the name of the Lord.
They gonna teach you how to meditate,
Read your horoscope and cheat your fate,
And furthermore to hell with hate.
Come on get on board.
Chorus

4. Look around, tell me what you see.
What's happenin' to you and me?
God grant me the serenity
To remember who I am.
'Cause you're givin' up your sanity
For your pride and your vanity.
Turn your back on humanity,
And don't give a da da da da da.
Chorus

Folsom Prison Blues

Registration 3
Rhythm: Rock or Fox Trot

Words and Music by
John R. Cash

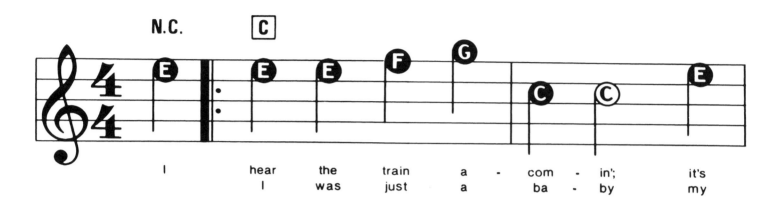

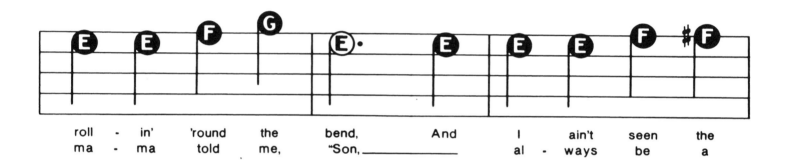

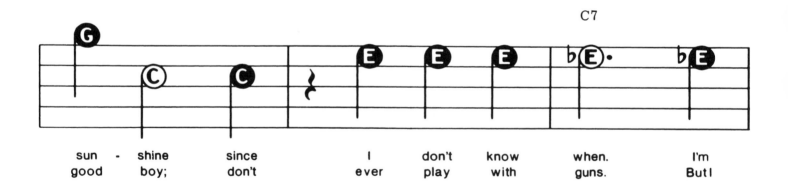

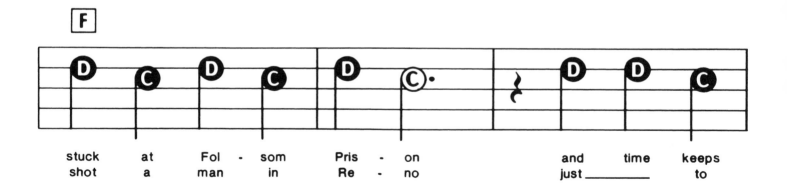

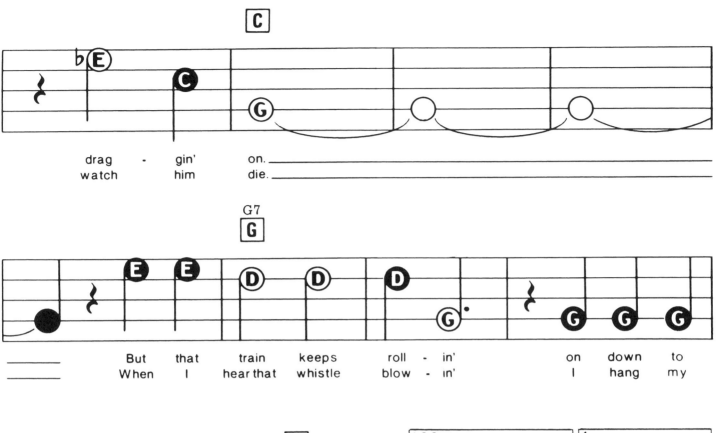

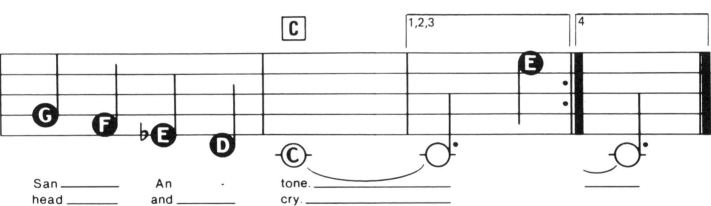

San_____	An -
head_____	and_____

3. I bet there's rich folks eatin' in a fancy dining car.
   They're prob'ly drinkin' coffee and smokin' big cigars,
   But I know I had it comin', I know I can't be free,
   But those people keep a-movin', and that's what tortures me.

4. Well, if they freed me from this prison, if that railroad train was mine,
   I bet I'd move over a little farther down the line,
   Far from Folsom Prison, that's where I want to stay.
   And I'd let that lonesome whistle blow my blues away.

Four Walls

Registration 8
Rhythm: Waltz

Words and Music by Marvin J. Moore
and George H. Campbell, Jr.

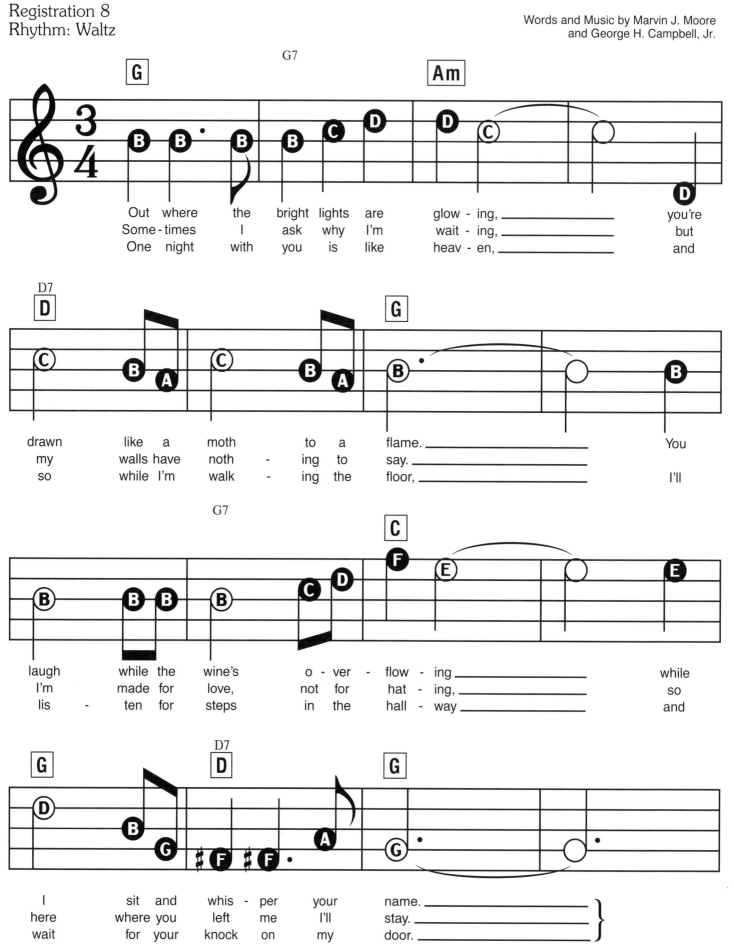

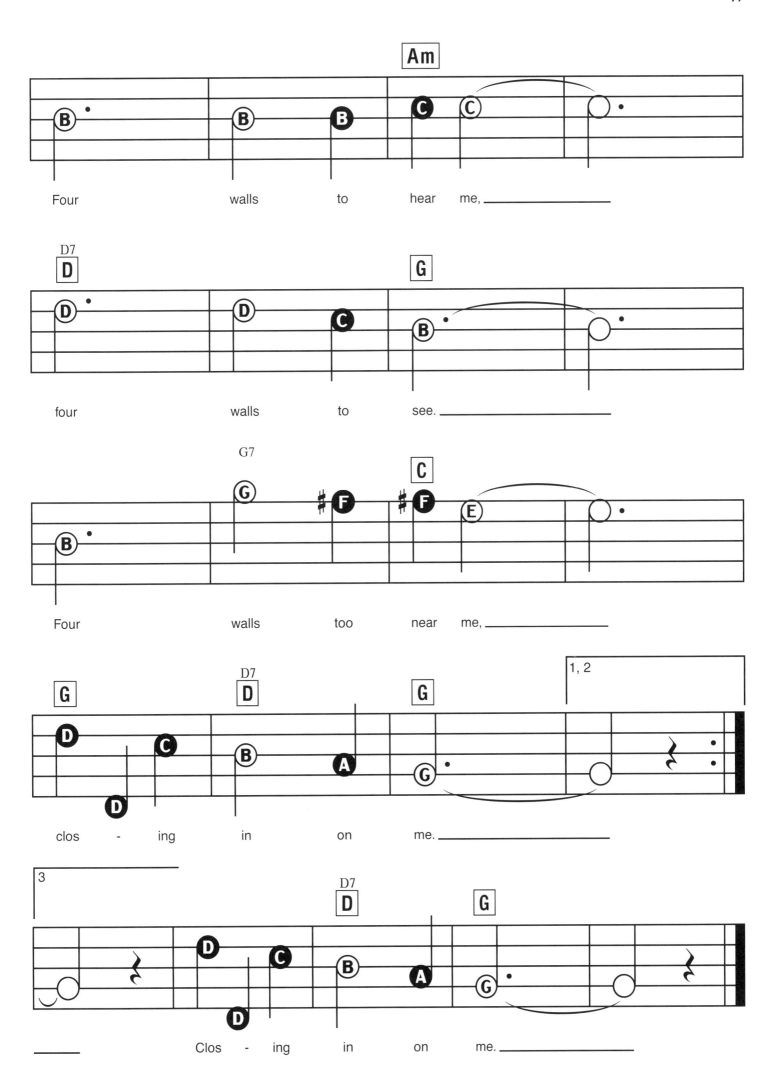

Gentle on My Mind

Registration 10
Rhythm: Fox Trot or Pops

Words and Music by
John Hartford

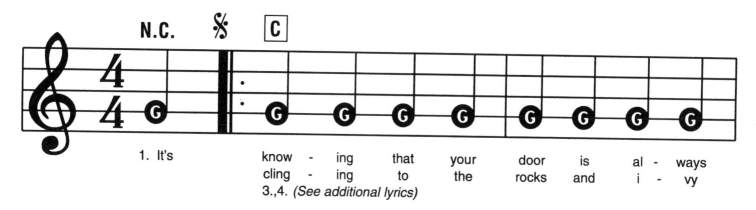

1. It's know - ing that your door is al - ways
cling - ing to the rocks and i - vy
3.,4. *(See additional lyrics)*

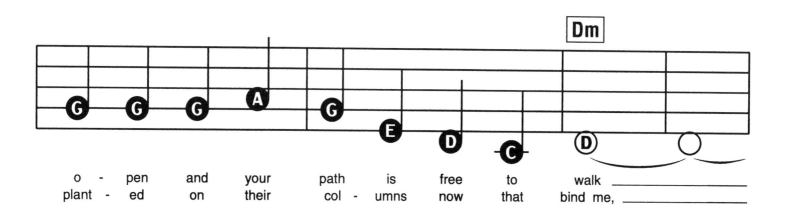

o - pen and your path is free to walk _____
plant - ed on their col - umns now that bind me, _____

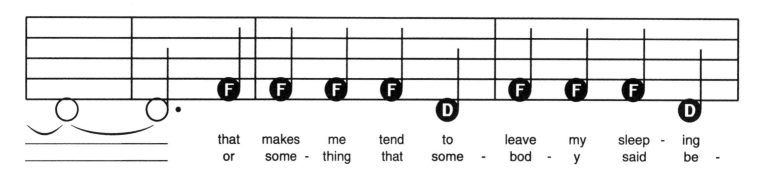

that makes me tend to leave my sleep - ing
or some - thing that some - bod - y said be -

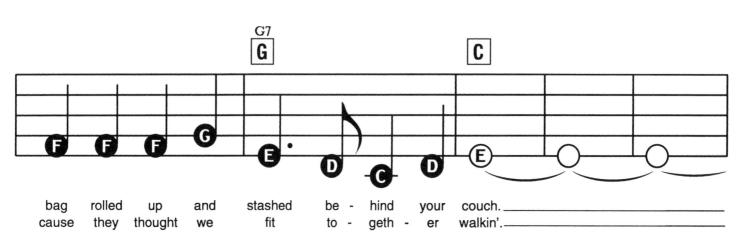

bag rolled up and stashed be - hind your couch. _____
cause they thought we fit to - geth - er walkin'. _____

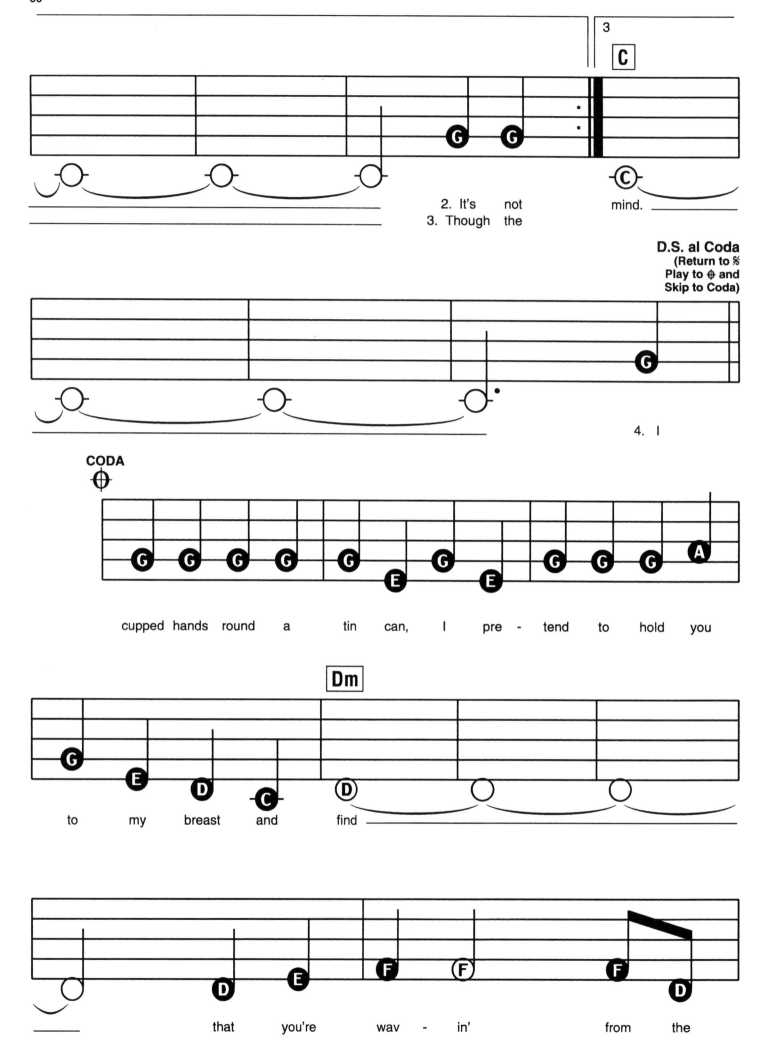

3

C

2. It's   not   mind.
3. Though   the

D.S. al Coda
(Return to ℅
Play to ⊕ and
Skip to Coda)

4. I

CODA
⊕

cupped   hands   round   a   tin   can,   I   pre - tend   to   hold   you

Dm

to   my   breast   and   find

that   you're   wav - in'   from   the

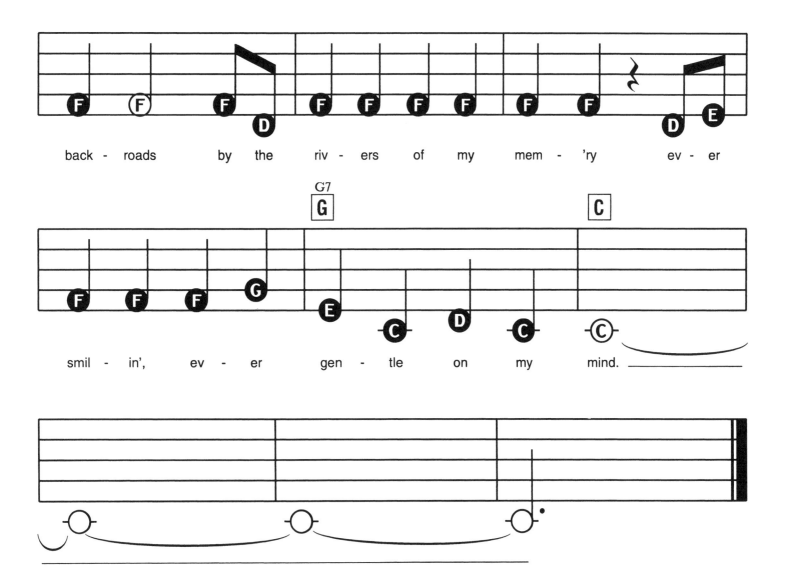

back - roads   by   the   riv - ers   of   my   mem - 'ry   ev - er

smil - in',   ev - er   gen - tle   on   my   mind. _____

Additional Lyrics

3. Though the wheat fields and the clotheslines
    and the junkyards and the highways come between us,
    and some other woman cryin' to her mother
    'cause she turned and I was gone.
    I still might run in silence,
    tears of joy might stain my face,
    and the summer sun might burn me till I'm blind,
    but not to where I cannot see you
    walkin' on the backroads
    by the rivers flowing gentle on my mind.

4. I dip my cup of soup back from some gurglin',
    cracklin' cauldron in some train yard,
    my beard a rough'ning coal pile and
    a dirty hat pulled low across my face.
    Through cupped hands round a tin can,
    I pretend to hold you to my breast and find
    that you're wavin' from the backroads
    by the rivers of my mem'ry,
    ever smilin', ever gentle on my mind.

Gone Country

Registration 8
Rhythm: Pop or Rock

Words and Music by
Bob McDill

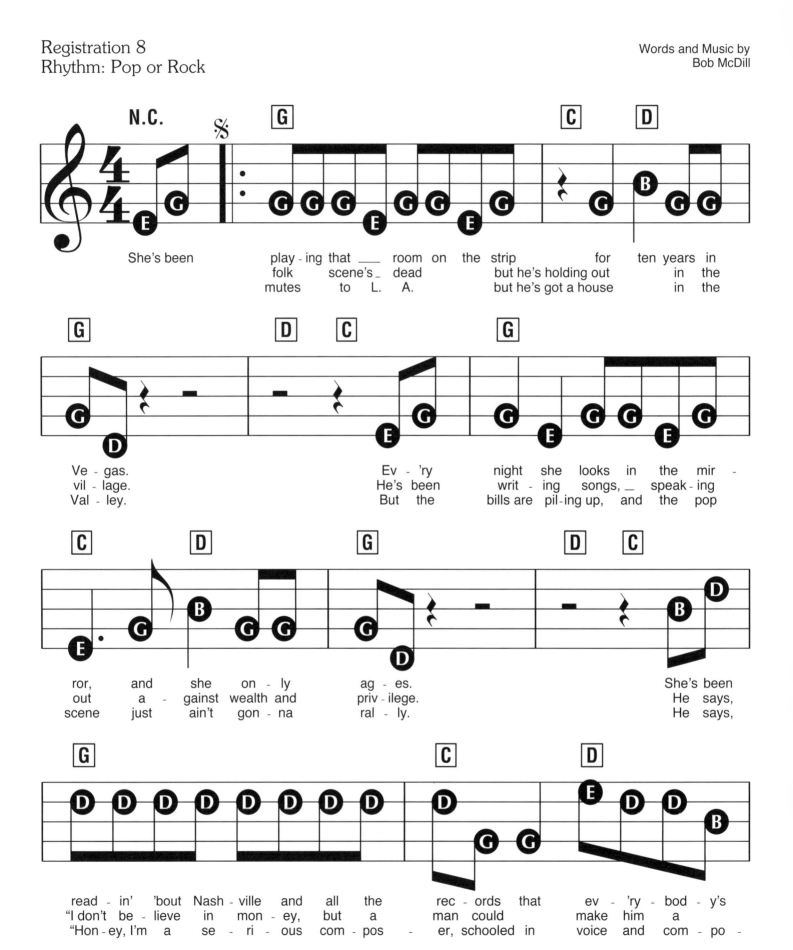

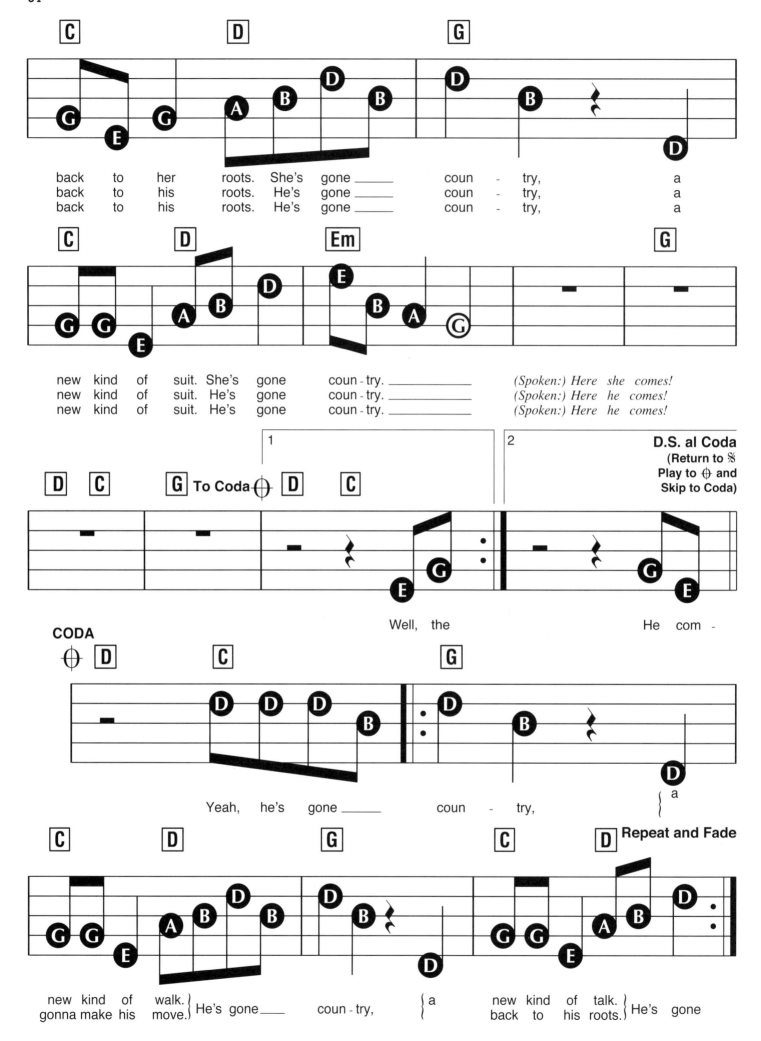

Happy Trails

from the Television Series THE ROY ROGERS SHOW

Registration 5
Rhythm: Swing or Pops

Words and Music by
Dale Evans

Hap - py trails to you un - til we meet a -

gain. Hap - py trails to you, keep smil - in' un - til

then. Who cares a - bout the clouds when we're to - geth - er? Just

sing a song and bring the sun - ny weath - er. Hap - py

trails to you till we meet a - gain. Hap - py gain.

Half as Much

Registration 2
Rhythm: Fox Trot

Words and Music by
Curley Williams

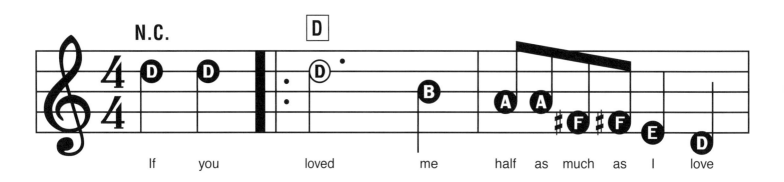

If you loved me half as much as I love

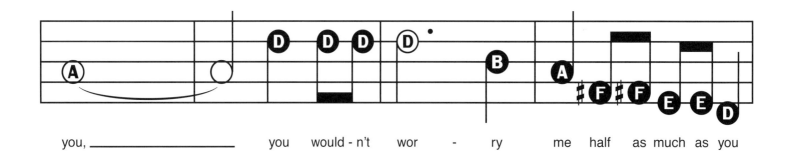

you, _____ you would-n't wor - ry me half as much as you

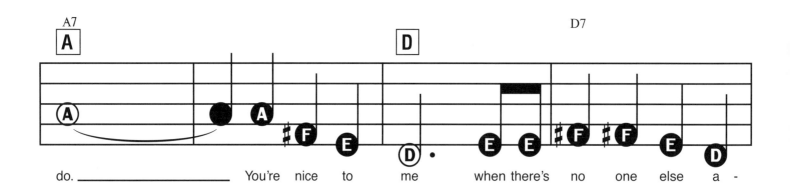

do. _____ You're nice to me when there's no one else a -

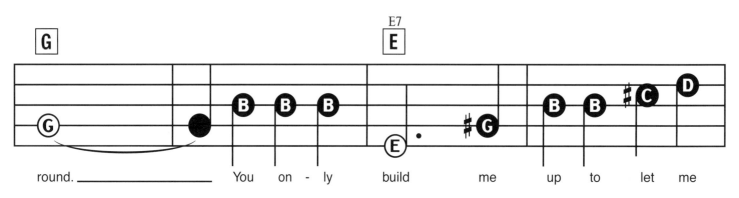

round. _____ You on - ly build me up to let me

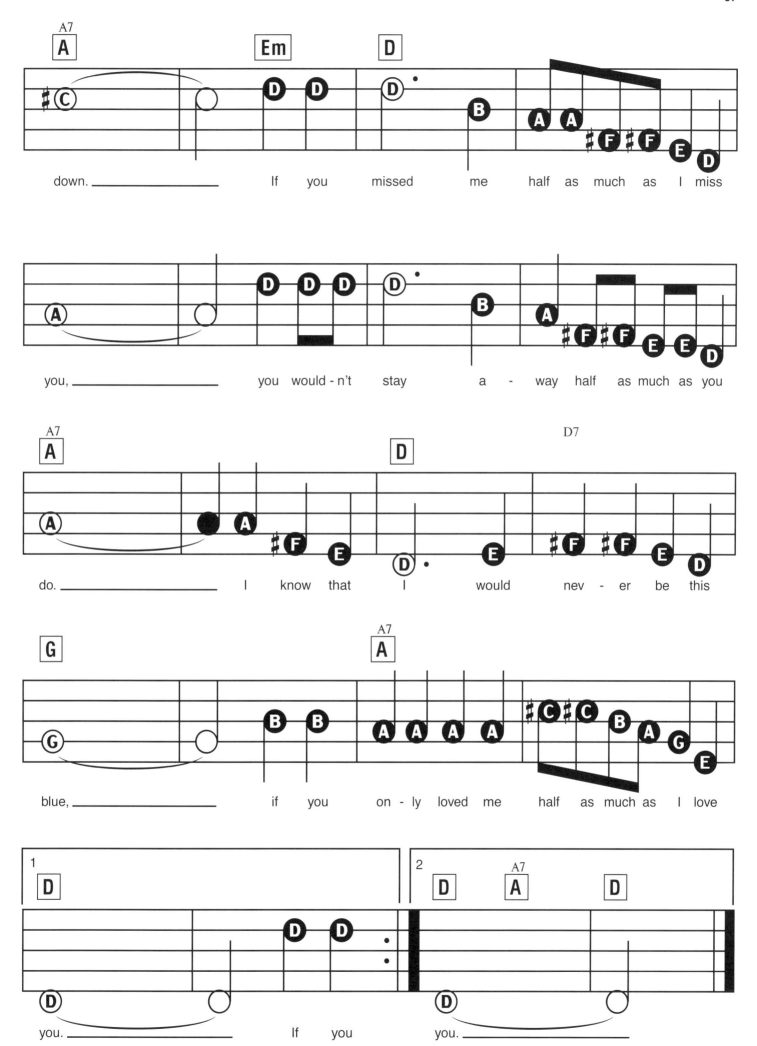

Heartaches

Registration 4
Rhythm: Fox Trot or Swing

Words by John Klenner
Music by Al Hoffman

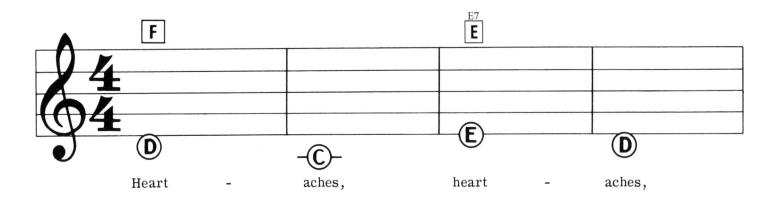

Heart - aches, heart - aches,

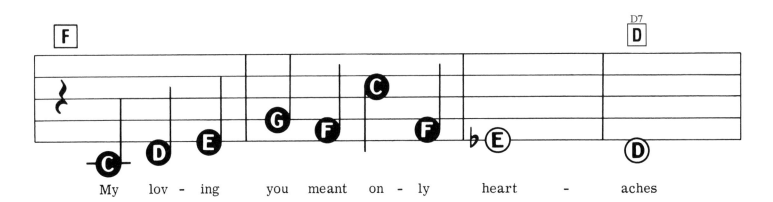

My lov - ing you meant on - ly heart - aches

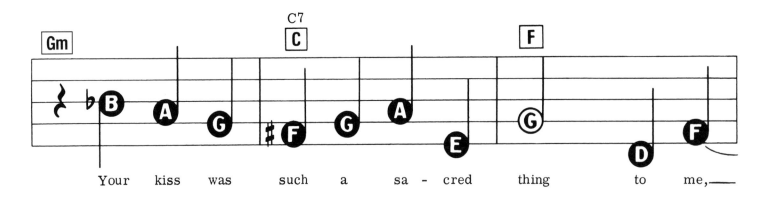

Your kiss was such a sa - cred thing to me,

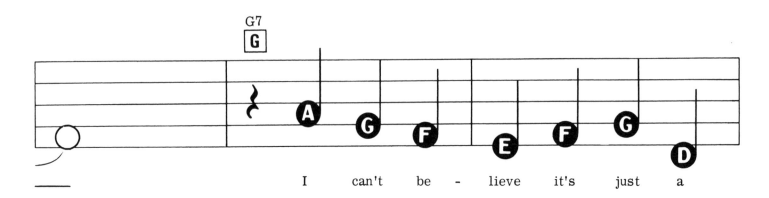

I can't be - lieve it's just a

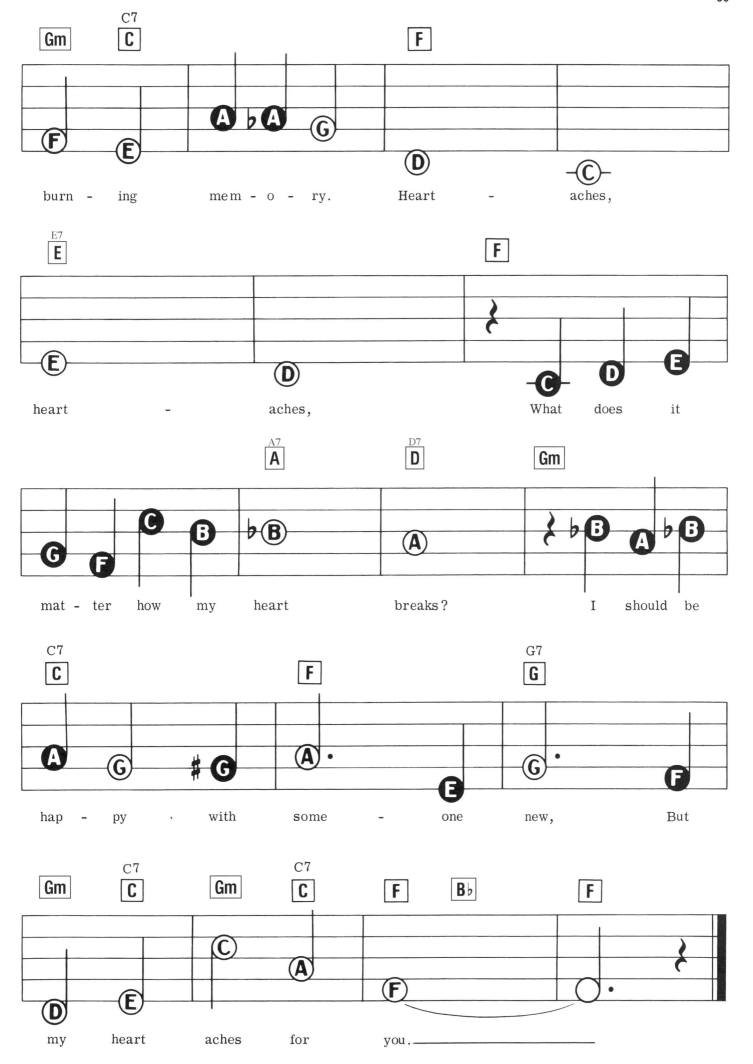

Gm C7 C F
burn - ing mem - o - ry. Heart - aches,
E7 E F
heart - aches, What does it
A7 A D7 D Gm
mat - ter how my heart breaks? I should be
C7 C F G7 G
hap - py with some - one new, But
Gm C7 C Gm C7 C F B♭ F
my heart aches for you.

Heartaches by the Number

Registration 4
Rhythm: Country

Words and Music by
Harlan Howard

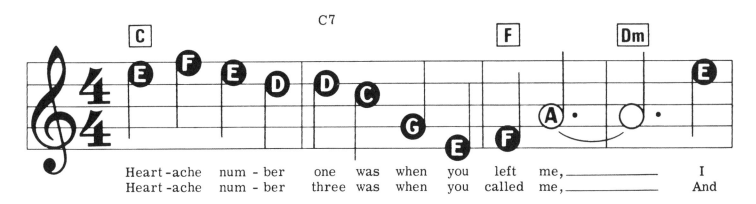

Heart-ache num-ber one was when you left me, _____ I
Heart-ache num-ber three was when you called me, _____ And

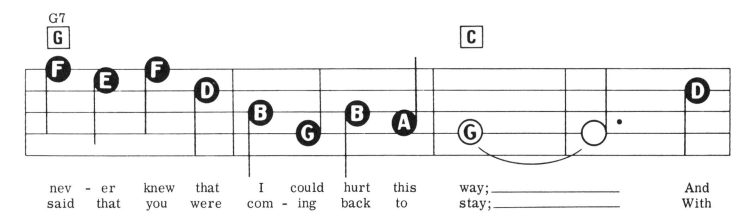

nev - er knew that I could hurt this way; _____ And
said that you were com - ing back to stay; _____ With

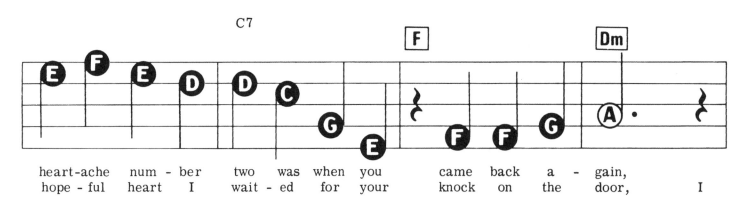

heart-ache num - ber two was when you came back a - gain, I
hope - ful heart I wait - ed for your knock on the door, I

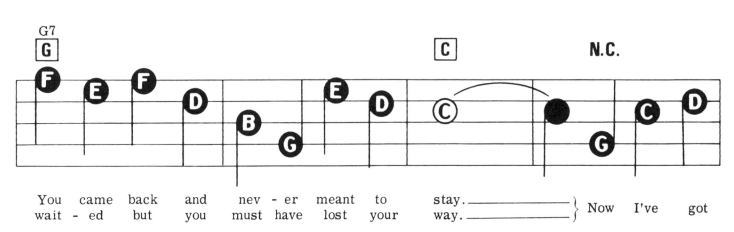

You came back and nev - er meant to stay. _____ } Now I've got
wait - ed but you must have lost your way. _____ }

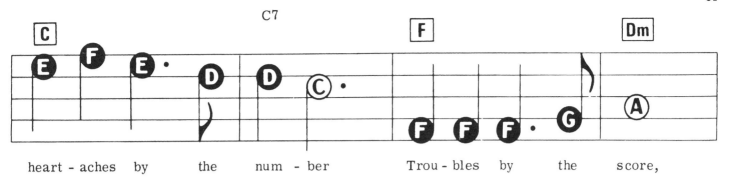

heart - aches by the num - ber Trou - bles by the score,

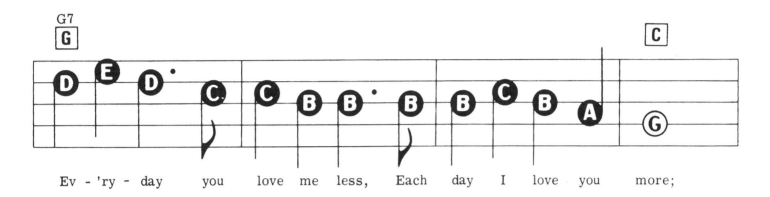

Ev - 'ry - day you love me less, Each day I love you more;

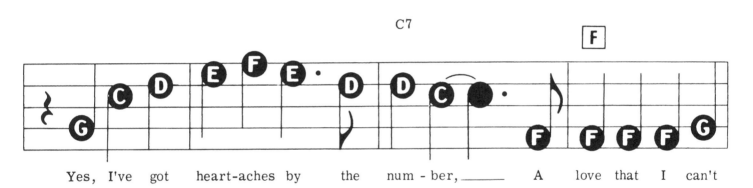

Yes, I've got heart-aches by the num - ber,_____ A love that I can't

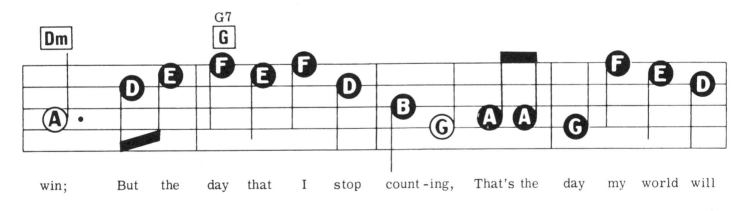

win; But the day that I stop count -ing, That's the day my world will

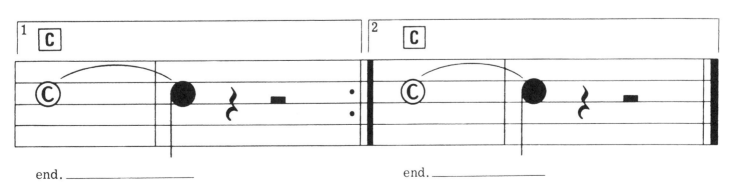

end._____ end._____

The Highwayman

Registration 3
Rhythm: Country Shuffle or Fox Trot

Words and Music by
Jimmy Webb

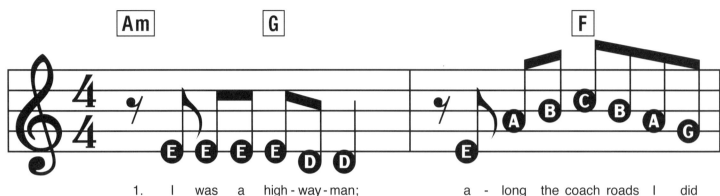

1. I was a high - way - man;   a - long the coach roads I did
2. - 4. (*See additional lyrics*)

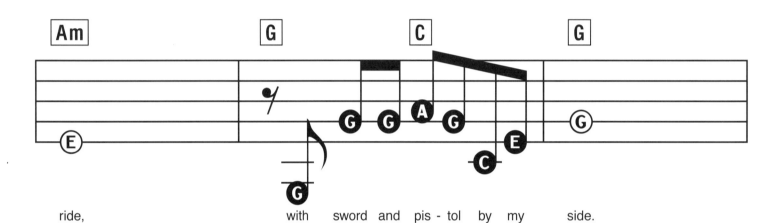

ride,   with sword and pis - tol by my side.

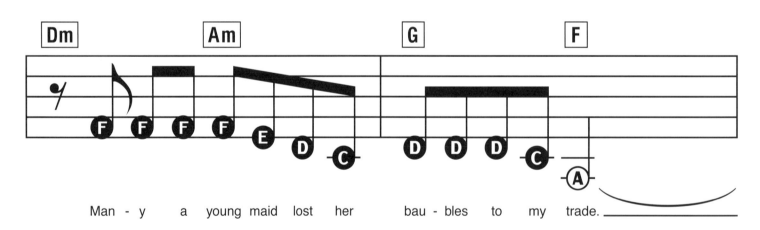

Man - y a young maid lost her bau - bles to my trade. ___

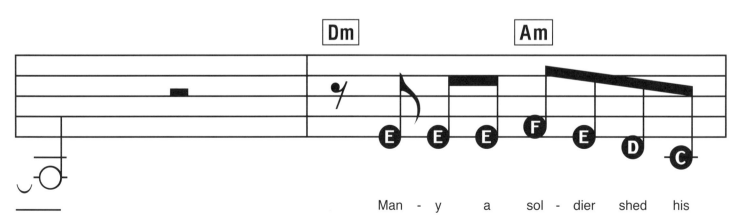

Man - y a sol - dier shed his

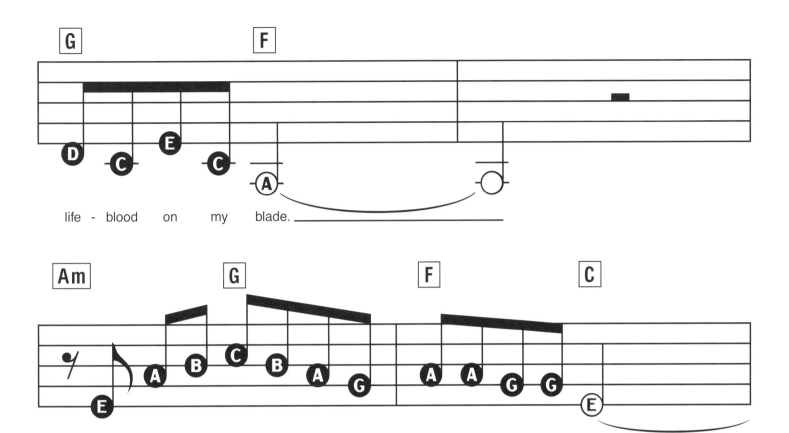

life - blood on my blade. _____

The bas - tards hung me in the spring of twen - ty - five. _____

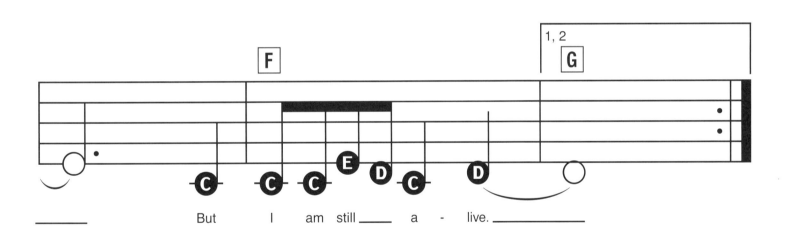

But I am still ___ a - live. _____

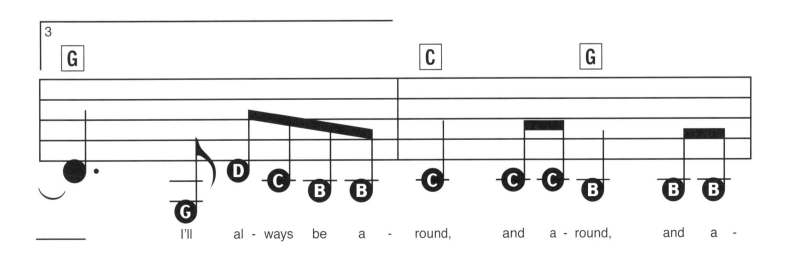

___ I'll al - ways be a - round, and a - round, and a -

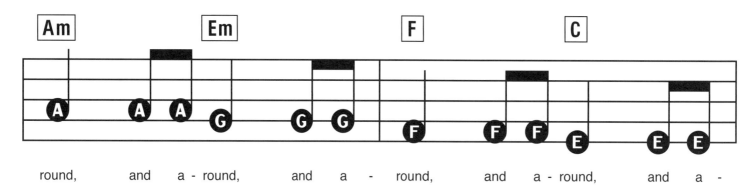

round,   and   a - round,   and   a -   round,   and   a - round,   and   a -

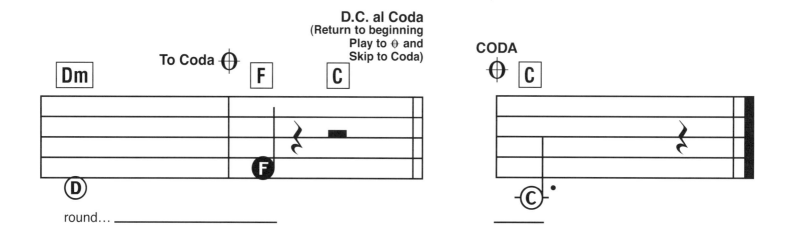

round… _____

Additional Lyrics

2. I was a sailor,
   And I was born upon the tide,
   And with the sea I did abide.
   I sailed a schooner 'round the Horn to Mexico;
   I went aloft to furl the mainsail in a blow.
   And when the yards broke off, they say that I got killed.
   But I am living still…

3. I was a dam builder
   Across the river deep and wide,
   Where steel and water did collide,
   A place called Boulder on the wild Colorado.
   I slipped and fell into the wet concrete below.
   They buried me in that great tomb that knows no sound,
   But I am still around.
   I'll always be around, and around, and around,
   And around, and around, and around, and around…

4. I'll fly a starship
   Across the universe divide.
   And when I reach the other side,
   I'll find a place to rest my spirit if I can.
   Perhaps I may become a highwayman again,
   Or I may simply be a single drop of rain.
   But I will remain.
   And I'll be back again, and again, and again,
   And again, and again, and again, and again…

Husbands and Wives

Registration 1
Rhythm: Waltz

Words and Music by
Roger Miller

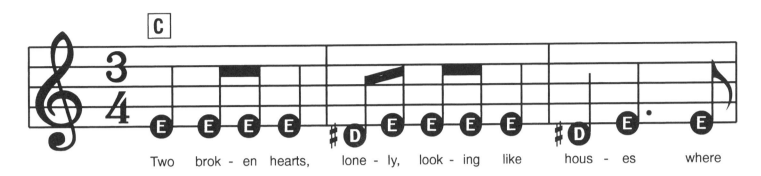

Two brok - en hearts, lone - ly, look - ing like hous - es where

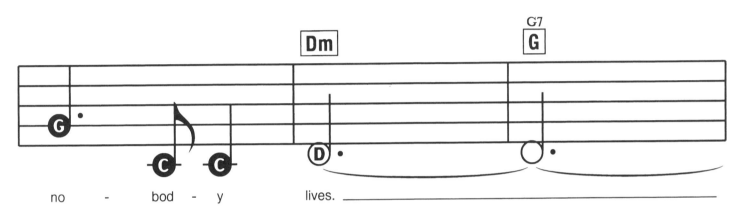

no - bod - y lives. _____

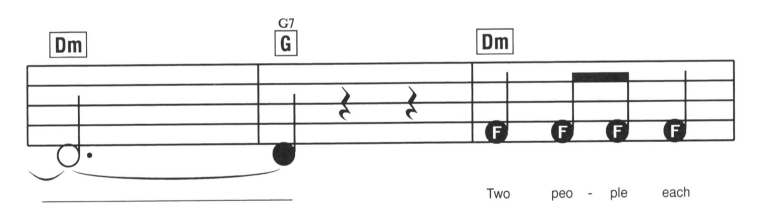

_____ Two peo - ple each

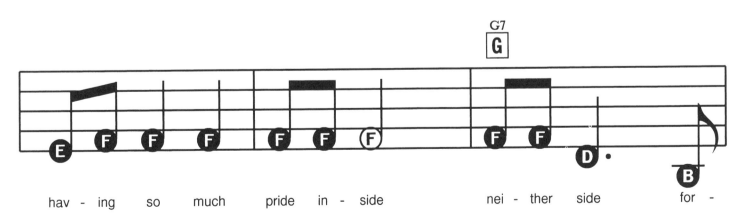

hav - ing so much pride in - side nei - ther side for -

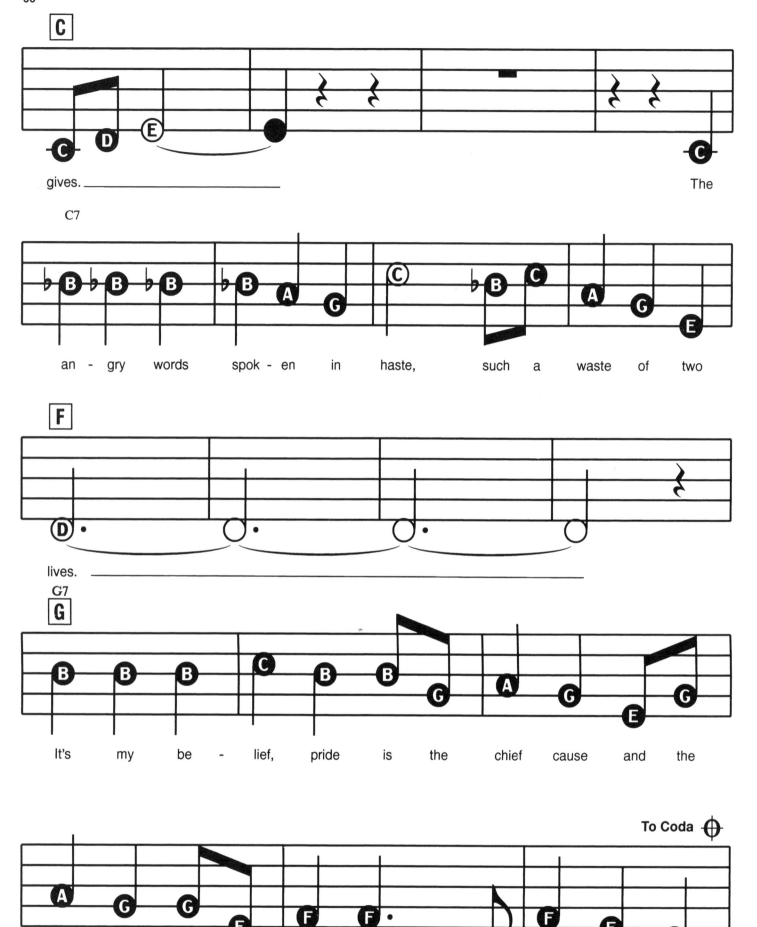

gives. _____ The

an - gry words spok - en in haste, such a waste of two

lives. _____

It's my be - lief, pride is the chief cause and the

To Coda

de - cline in the num - ber of hus - bands and

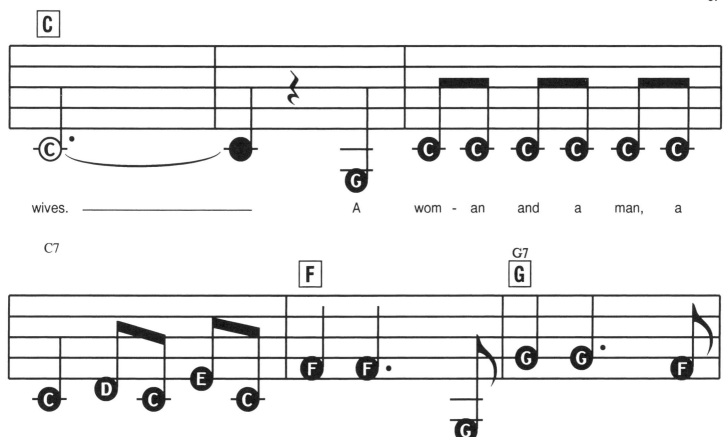

wives. _____ A wom - an and a man, a

man and a wom - an, some can and some can't and

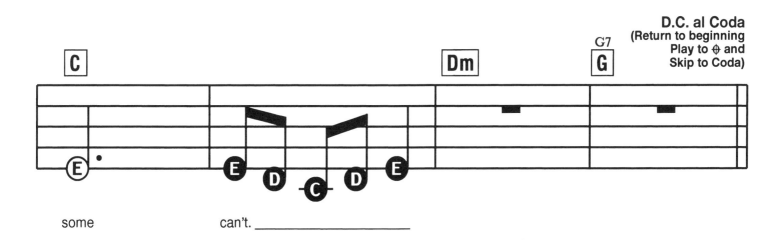

some can't. _____

D.C. al Coda
(Return to beginning
Play to ⊕ and
Skip to Coda)

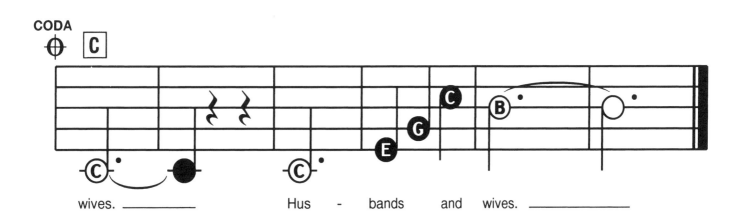

CODA

wives. _____ Hus - bands and wives. _____

I Can't Help It
(If I'm Still in Love with You)

Registration 3
Rhythm: Fox Trot or Ballad

Words and Music by
Hank Williams

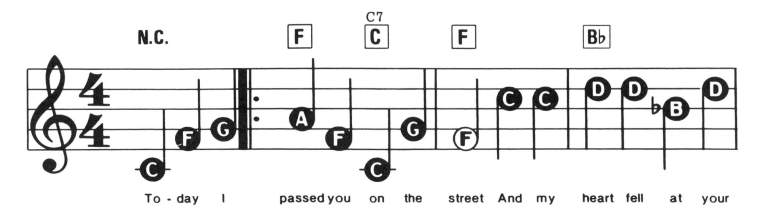

To - day I passed you on the street And my heart fell at your

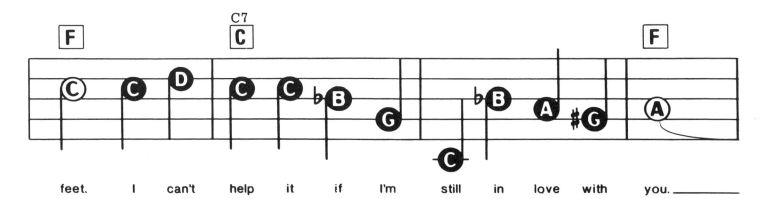

feet. I can't help it if I'm still in love with you. _____

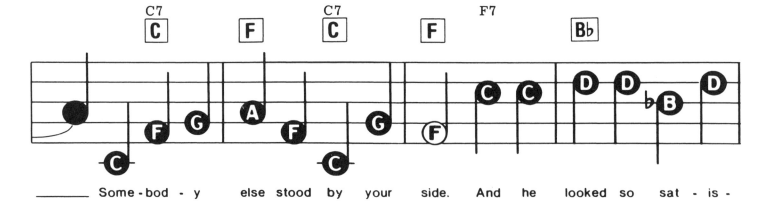

_____ Some - bod - y else stood by your side. And he looked so sat - is -

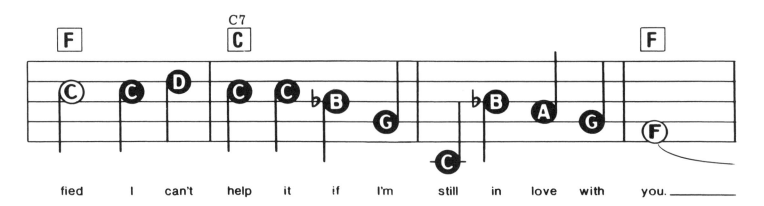

fied I can't help it if I'm still in love with you. _____

99

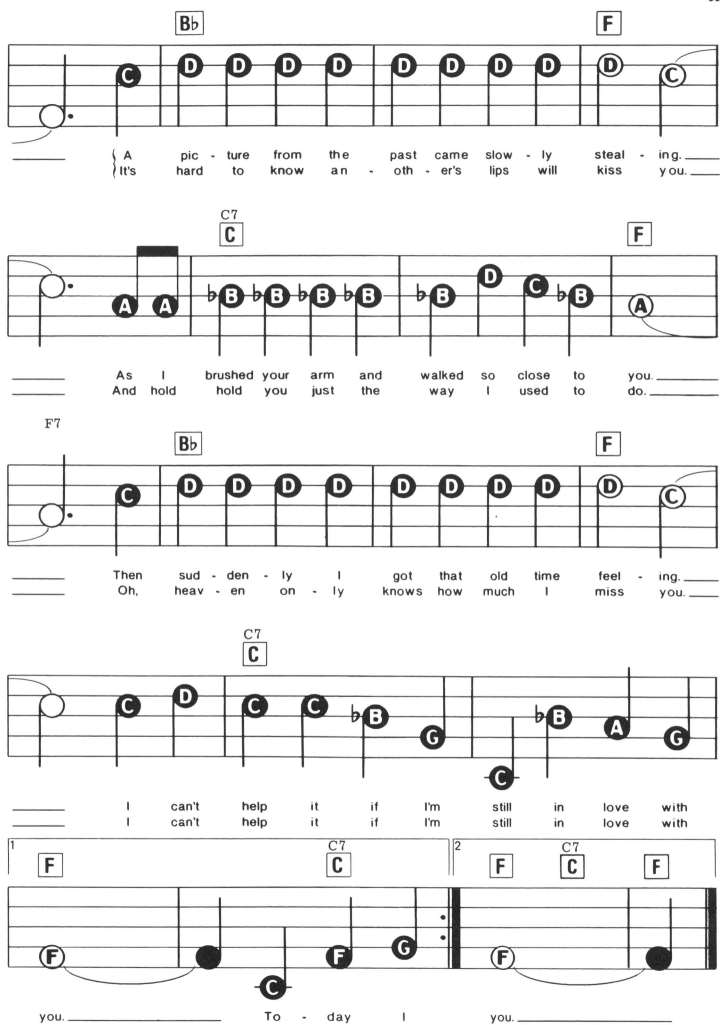

I Can't Stop Loving You

Registration 8
Rhythm: Swing or Fox Trot

Words and Music by
Don Gibson

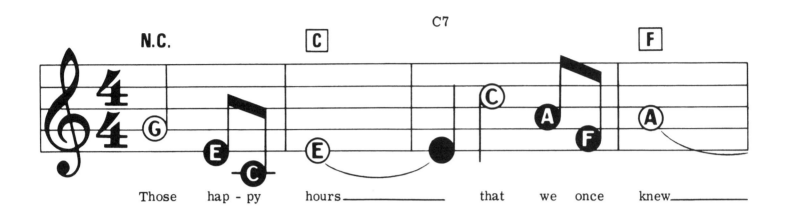

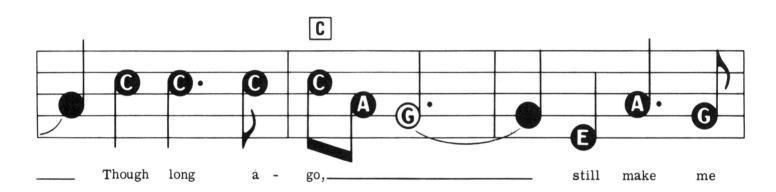

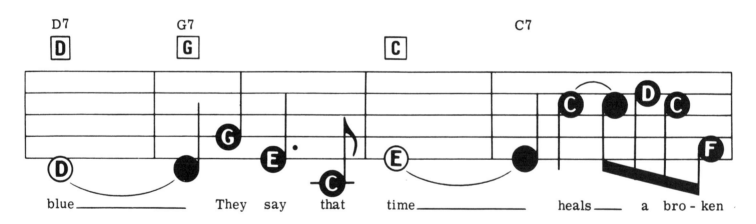

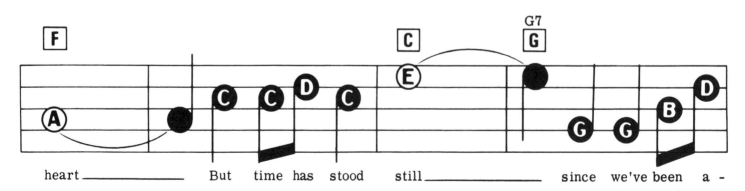

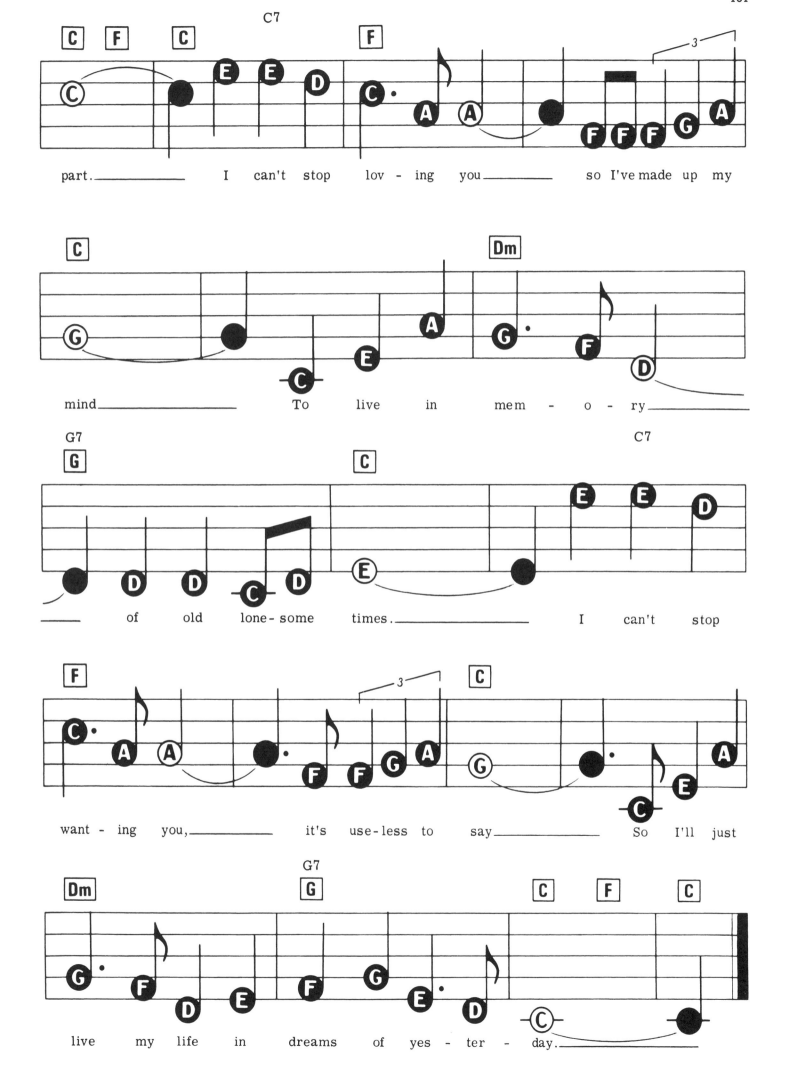

I Swear

Registration 7
Rhythm: Pops or 8-Beat

Words and Music by Frank Myers
and Gary Baker

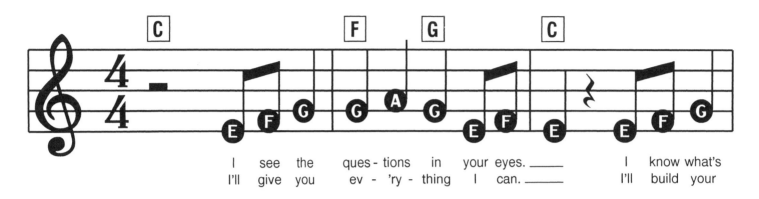

I see the ques - tions in your eyes. _____ I know what's
I'll give you ev - 'ry - thing I can. _____ I'll build your

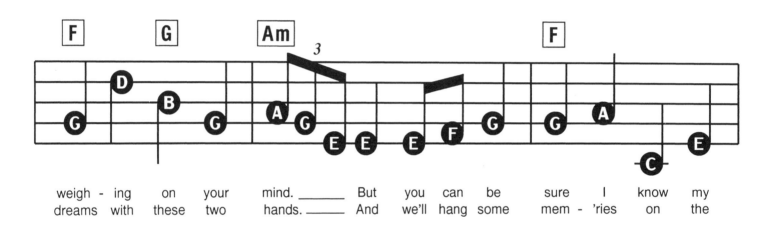

weigh - ing on your mind. _____ But you can be sure I know my
dreams with these two hands. _____ And we'll hang some mem - 'ries on the

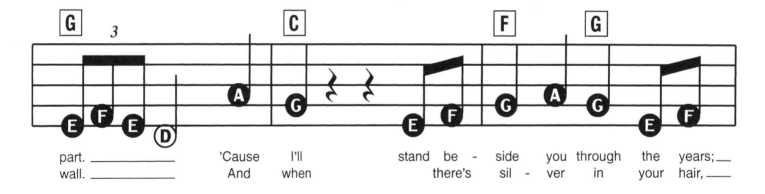

part. _____ 'Cause I'll stand be - side you through the years; _____
wall. _____ And when there's sil - ver in your hair, _____

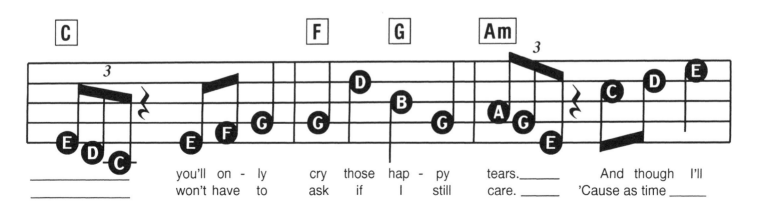

_____ you'll on - ly cry those hap - py tears. _____ And though I'll
_____ won't have to ask if I still care. _____ 'Cause as time _____

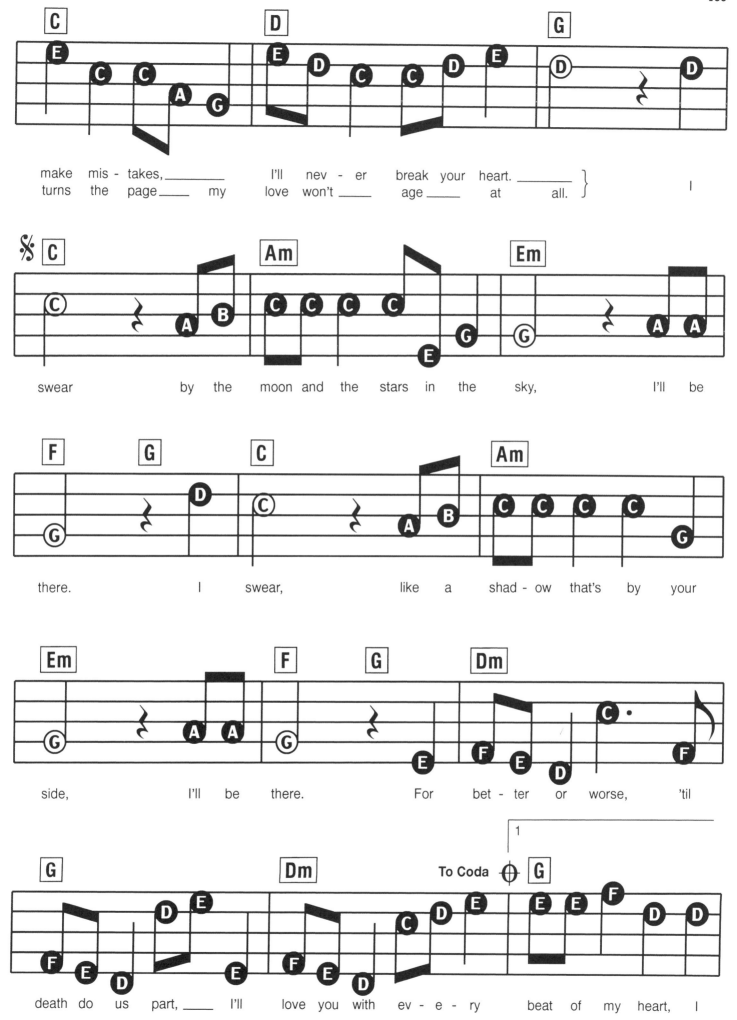

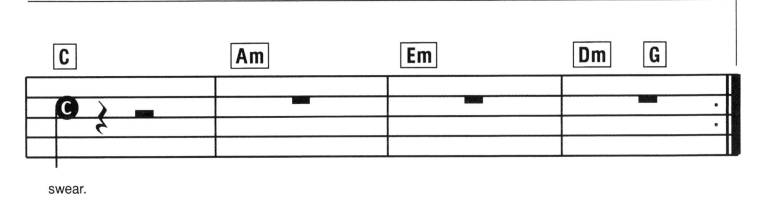

swear.

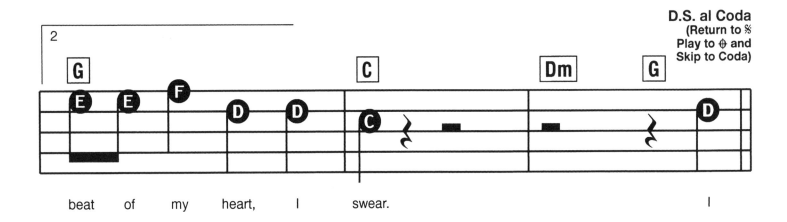

beat of my heart, I swear. I

CODA

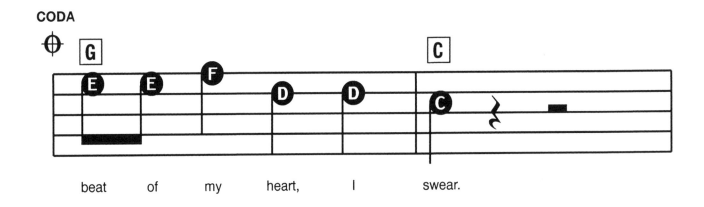

beat of my heart, I swear.

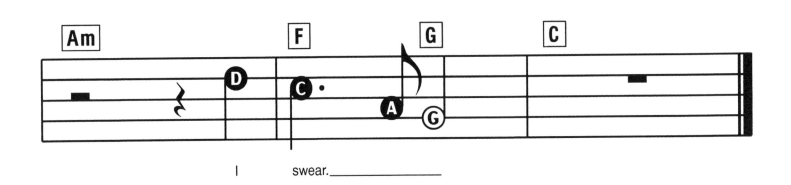

I swear._____

I'm Not Lisa

Registration 2
Rhythm: Country

Words and Music by
Jessi Colter

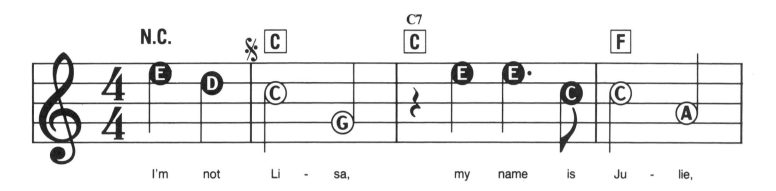

I'm not Li - sa, my name is Ju - lie,

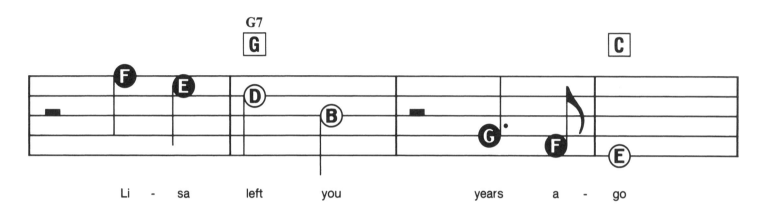

Li - sa left you years a - go

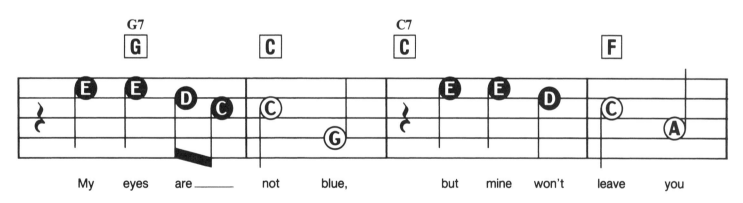

My eyes are _____ not blue, but mine won't leave you

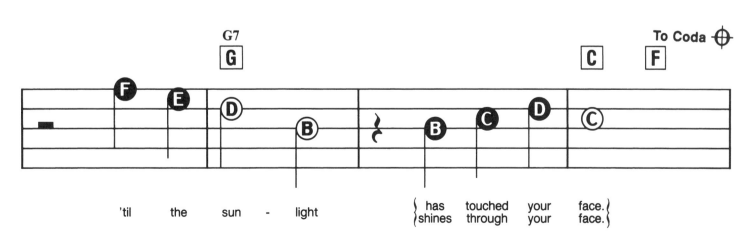

'til the sun - light { has touched your face. } { shines through your face. }

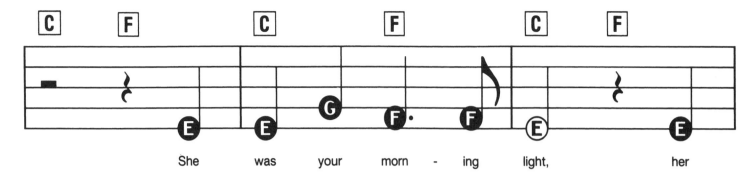

She was your morn - ing light, her

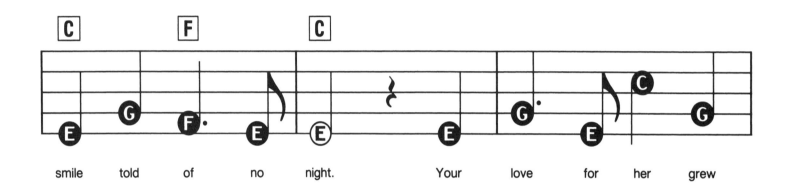

smile told of no night. Your love for her grew

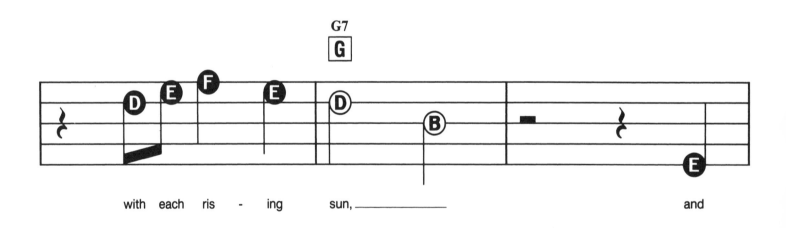

with each ris - ing sun, _____ and

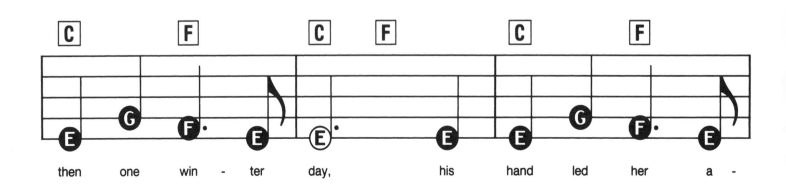

then one win - ter day, his hand led her a -

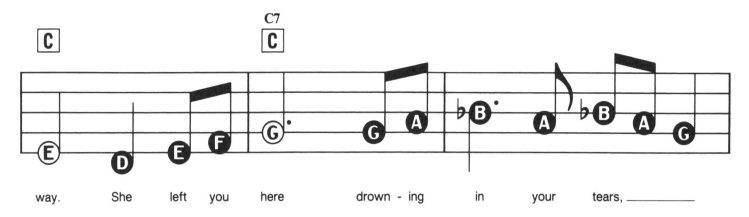

way. She left you here drown - ing in your tears, _____

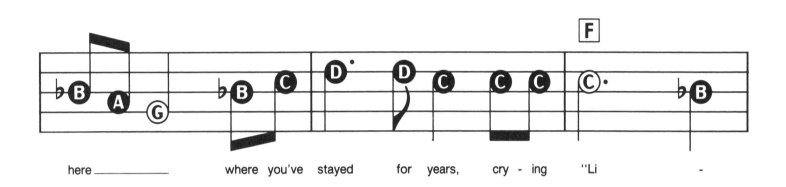

here _____ where you've stayed for years, cry - ing "Li -

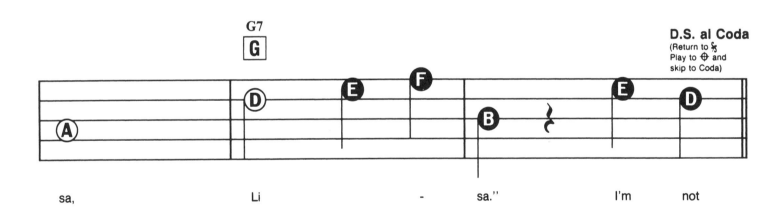

sa, Li - sa." I'm not

D.S. al Coda
(Return to 𝄋
Play to ⊕ and
skip to Coda)

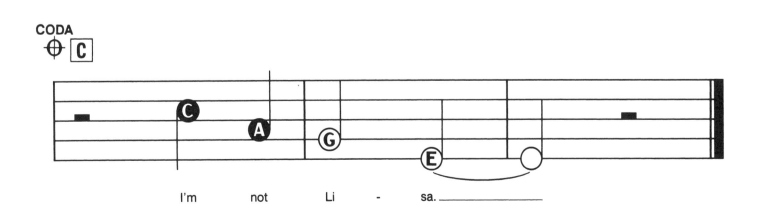

I'm not Li - sa. _____

I Will Always Love You

Registration 3
Rhythm: Pops or 8-Beat

Words and Music by
Dolly Parton

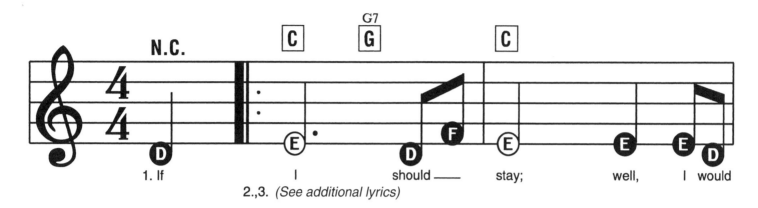

1. If I should —— stay; well, I would

2.,3. *(See additional lyrics)*

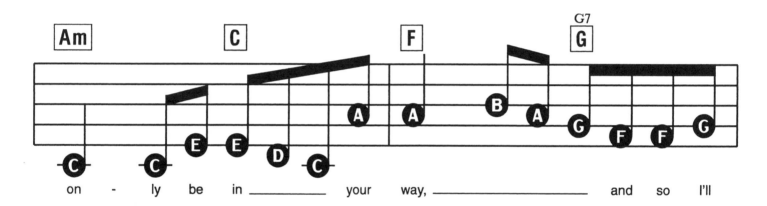

on - ly be in _____ your way, _____ and so I'll

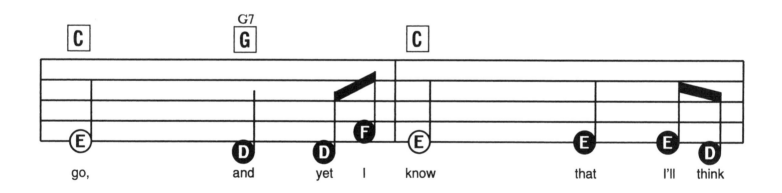

go, and yet I know that I'll think

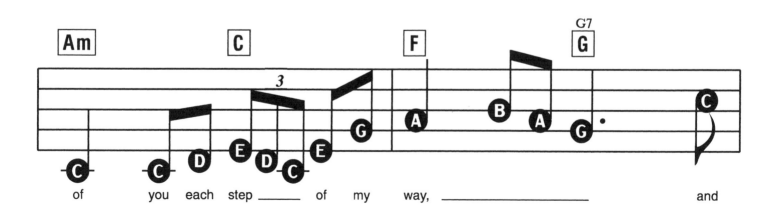

of you each step _____ of my way, _____ and

Chorus

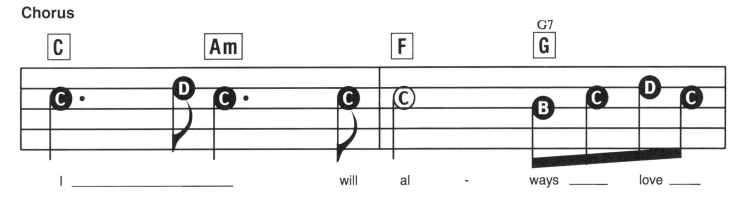

I _____ will al - ways _____ love _____

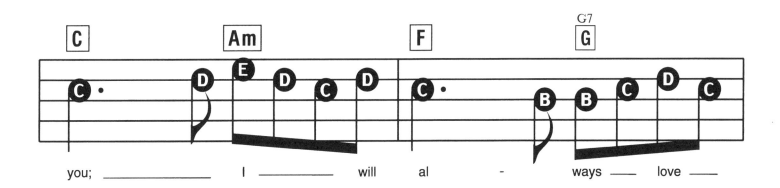

you; _____ I _____ will al - ways _____ love _____

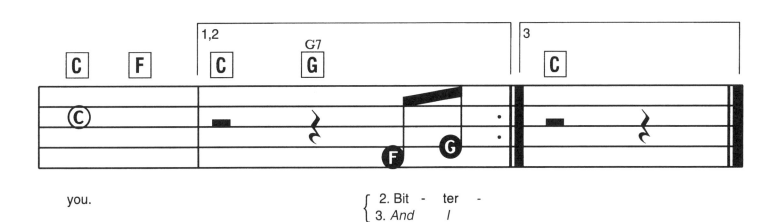

you.

{ 2. Bit - ter -
{ 3. *And* *I*

Additional Lyrics

2. Bittersweet memories, that's all I have and all I'm taking with me.
   Good-bye, oh please don't cry, 'cause we both know that I'm not what you need. But…
   Chorus

(Spoken:)
3. *And I hope life will treat you kind, and I hope that you have all that you ever dreamed of.*
   Oh, I do wish you joy, and I wish you happiness, but above all this, I wish you love. And…
   Chorus

I'm So Lonesome I Could Cry

Registration 2
Rhythm: Waltz

Words and Music by
Hank Williams

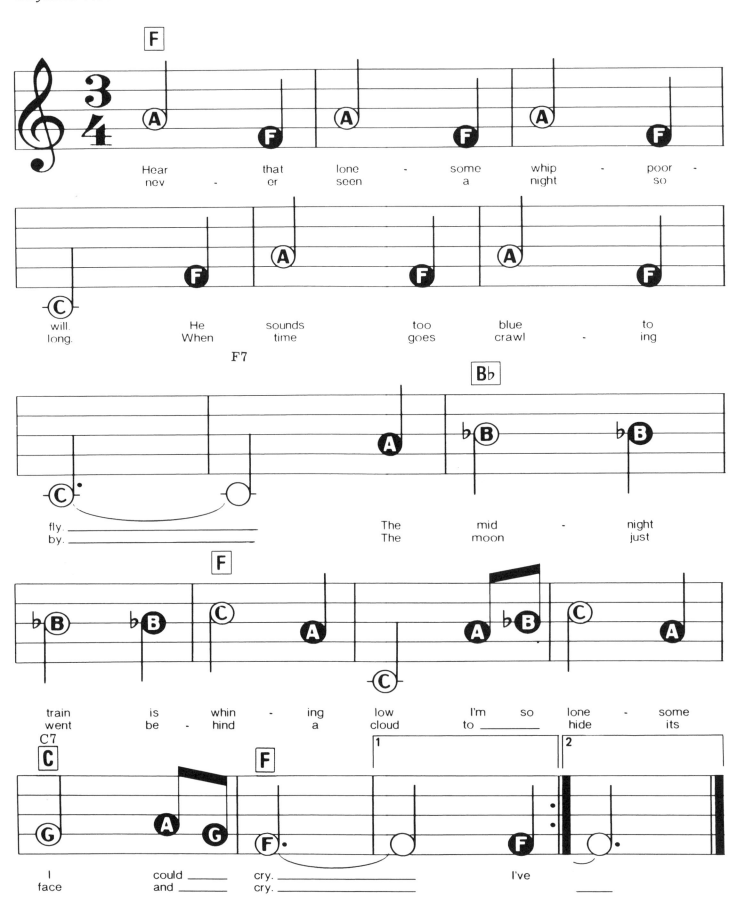

If I Said You Have a Beautiful Body Would You Hold It Against Me

Registration 8
Rhythm: Country Pop or 8-Beat

Words and Music by
David Bellamy

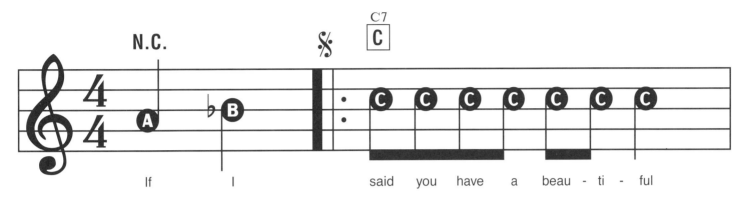

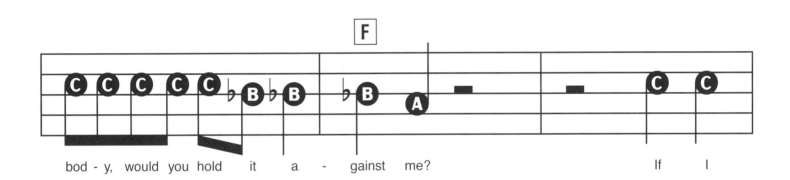

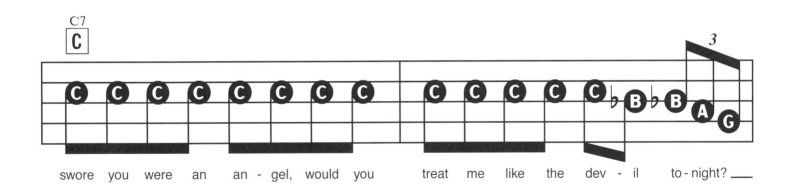

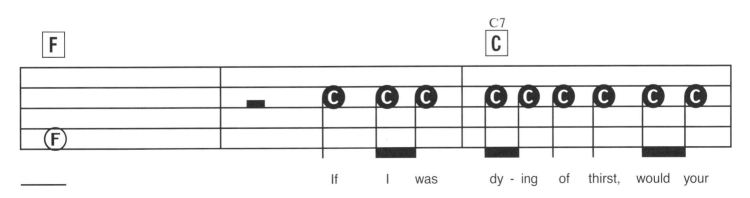

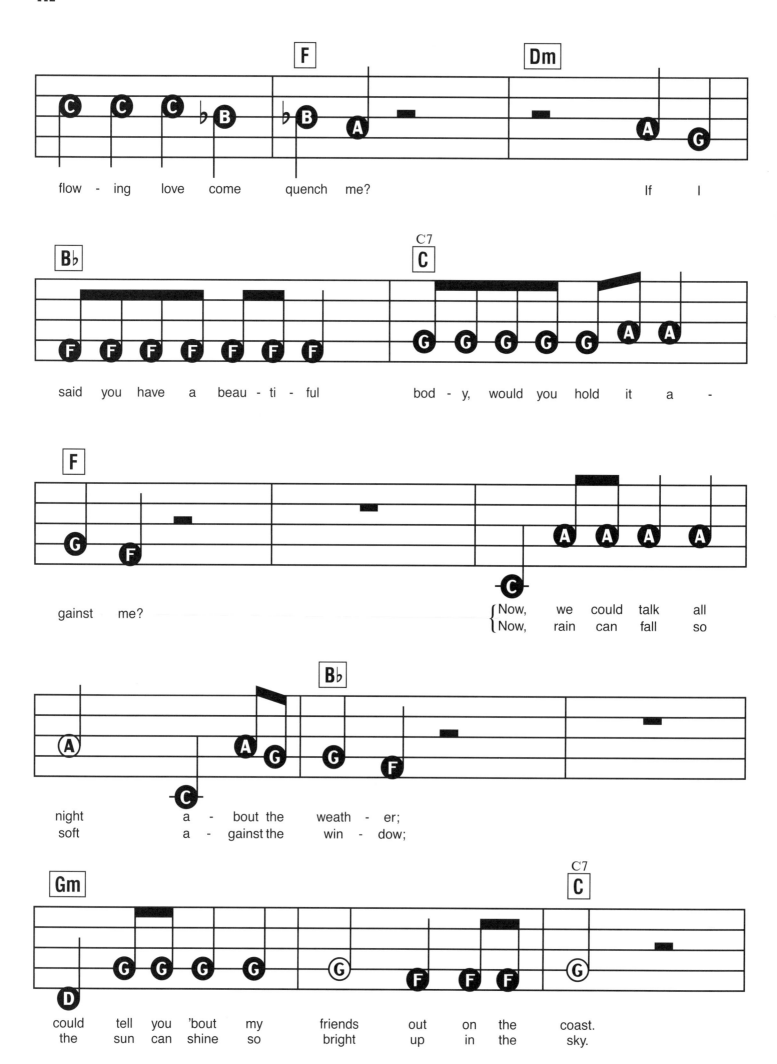

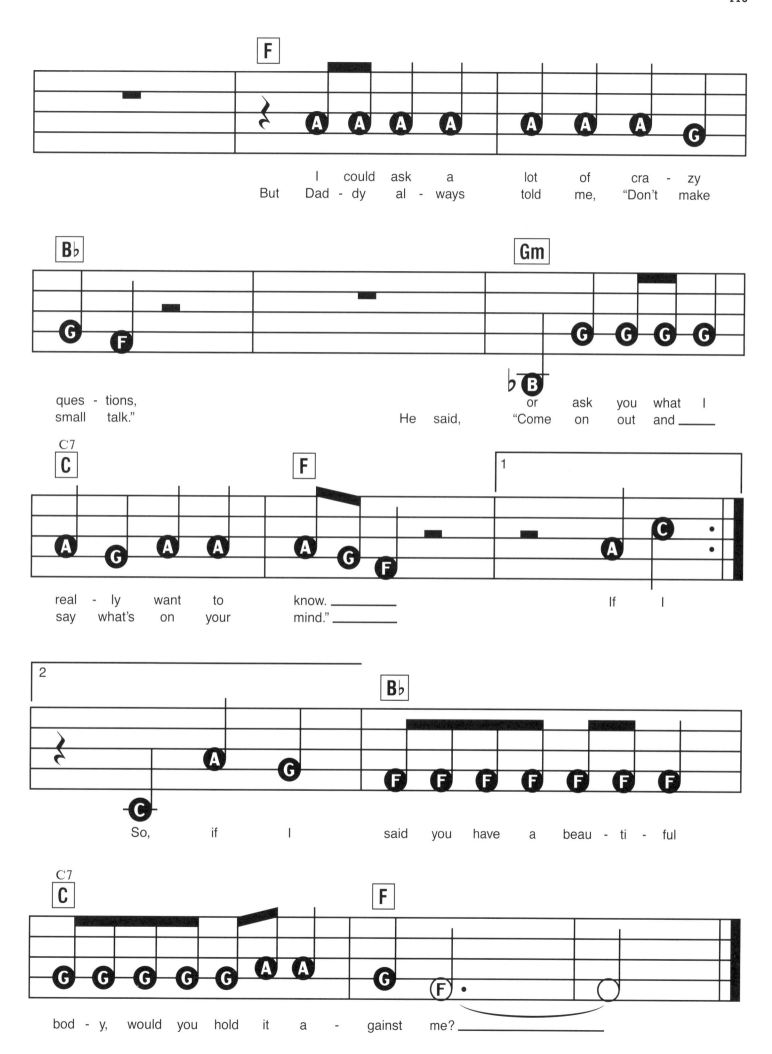

If We Make It Through December

Registration 4
Rhythm: Country or Shuffle

Words and Music by
Merle Haggard

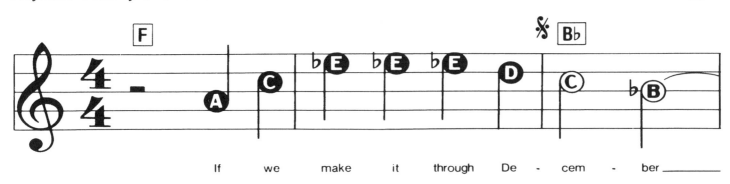

If we make it through De - cem - ber _____

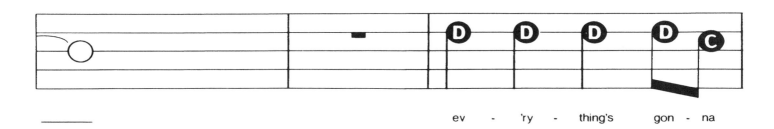

_____ ev - 'ry - thing's gon - na

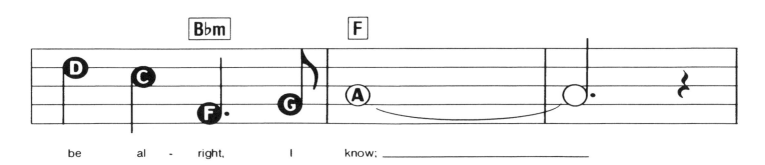

be al - right, I know; _____

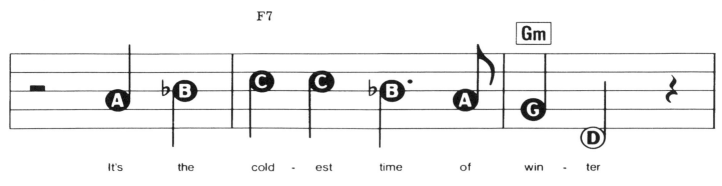

It's the cold - est time of win - ter

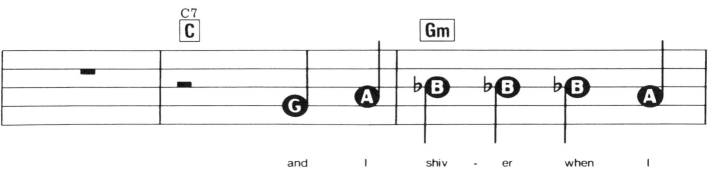

and I shiv - er when I

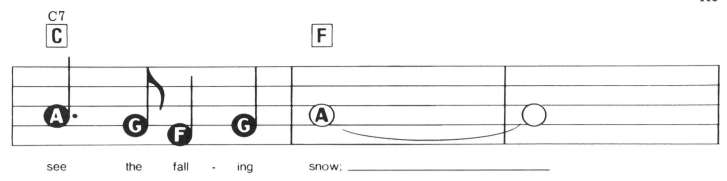

see the fall - ing snow; _____

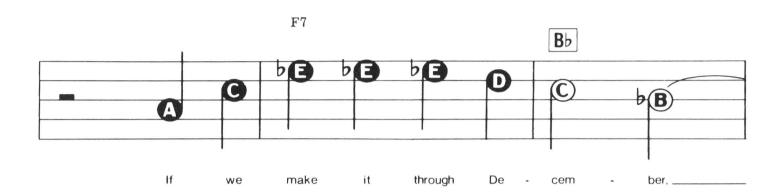

If we make it through De - cem - ber, _____

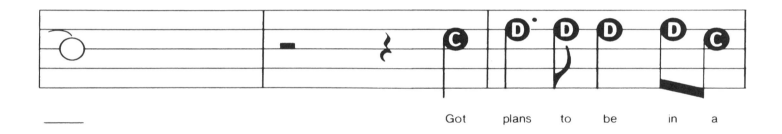

_____ Got plans to be in a

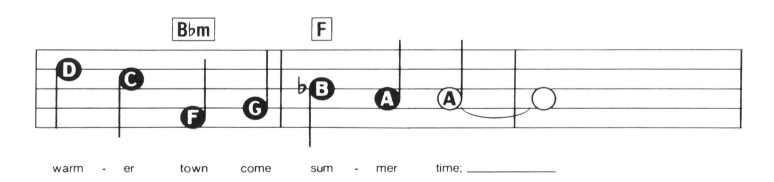

warm - er town come sum - mer time; _____

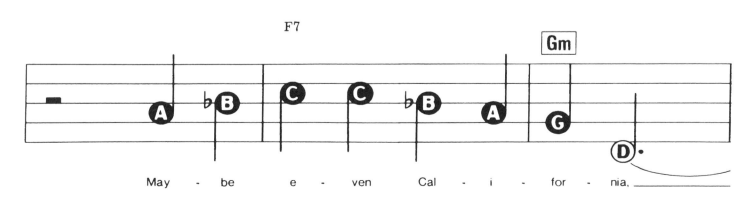

May - be e - ven Cal - i - for - nia, _____

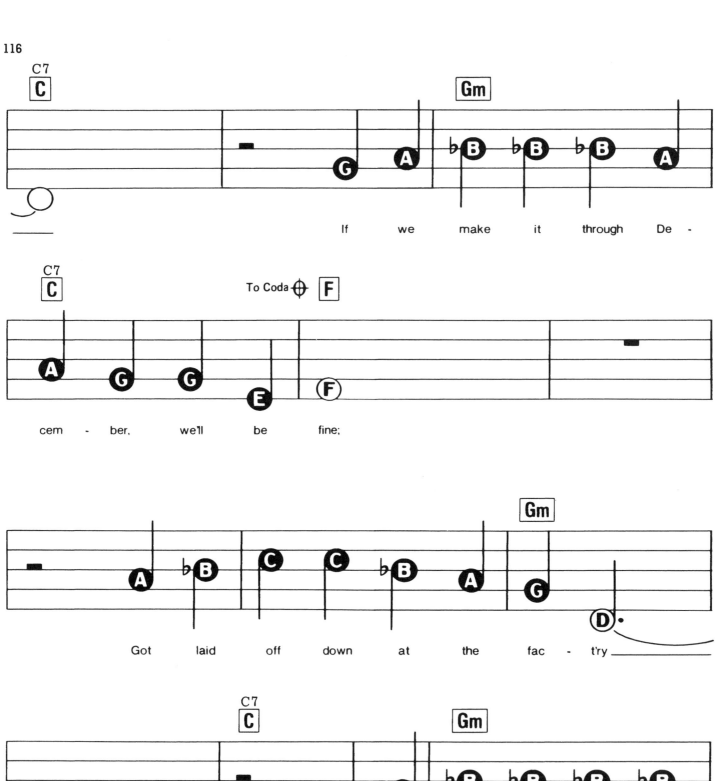

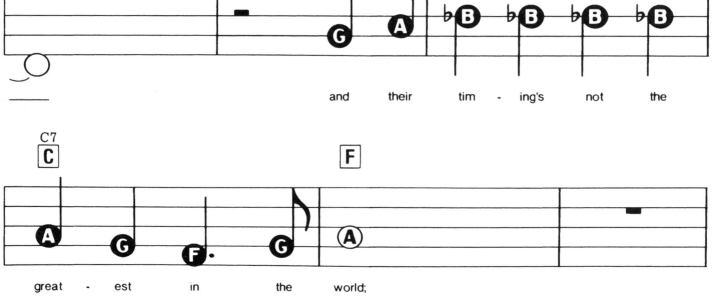

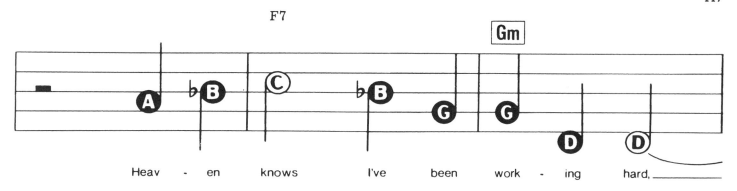

Heav - en knows I've been work - ing hard, ____

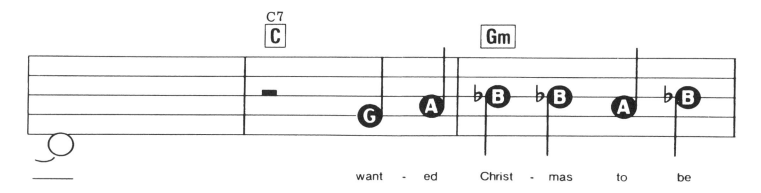

____ want - ed Christ - mas to be

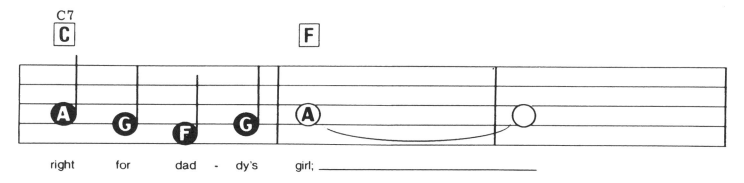

right for dad - dy's girl; ____

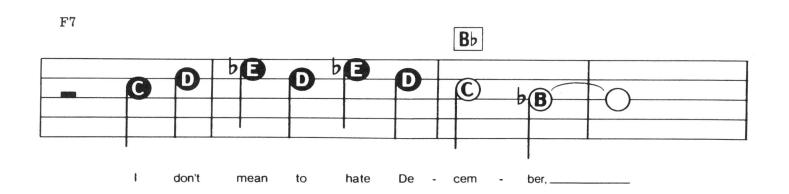

I don't mean to hate De - cem - ber, ____

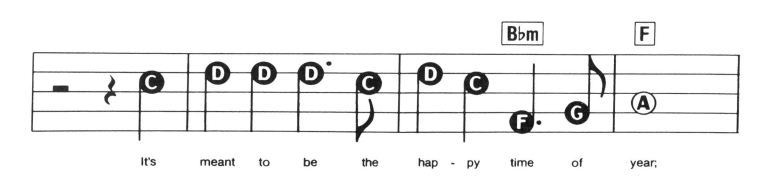

It's meant to be the hap - py time of year;

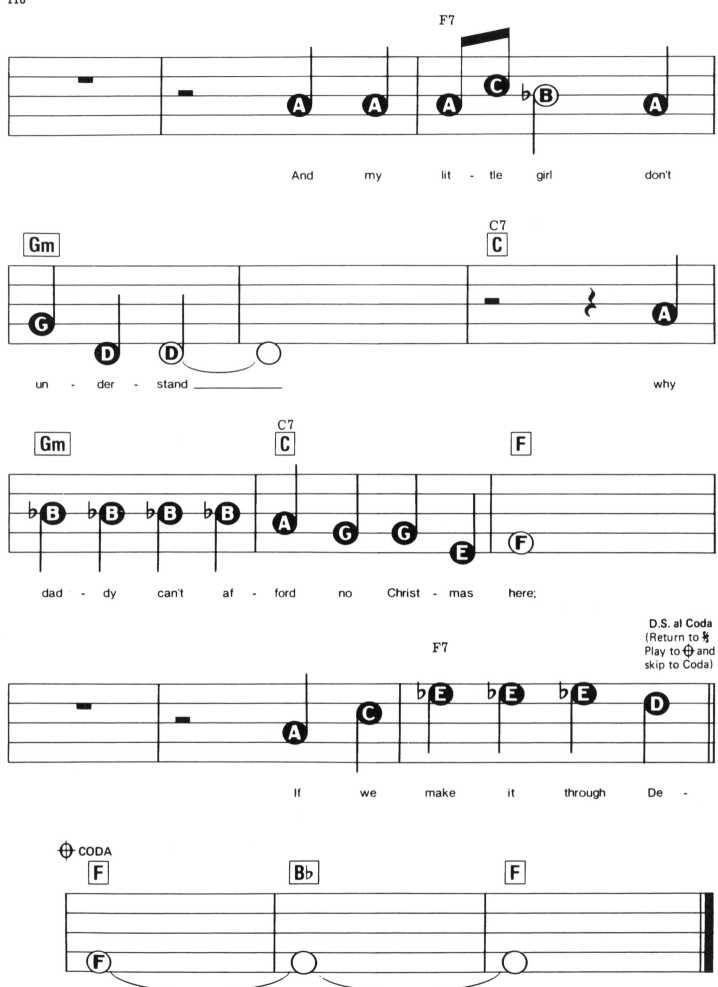

Jealous Heart

Registration 7
Rhythm: Country or Fox Trot

Words and Music by
Jenny Lou Carson

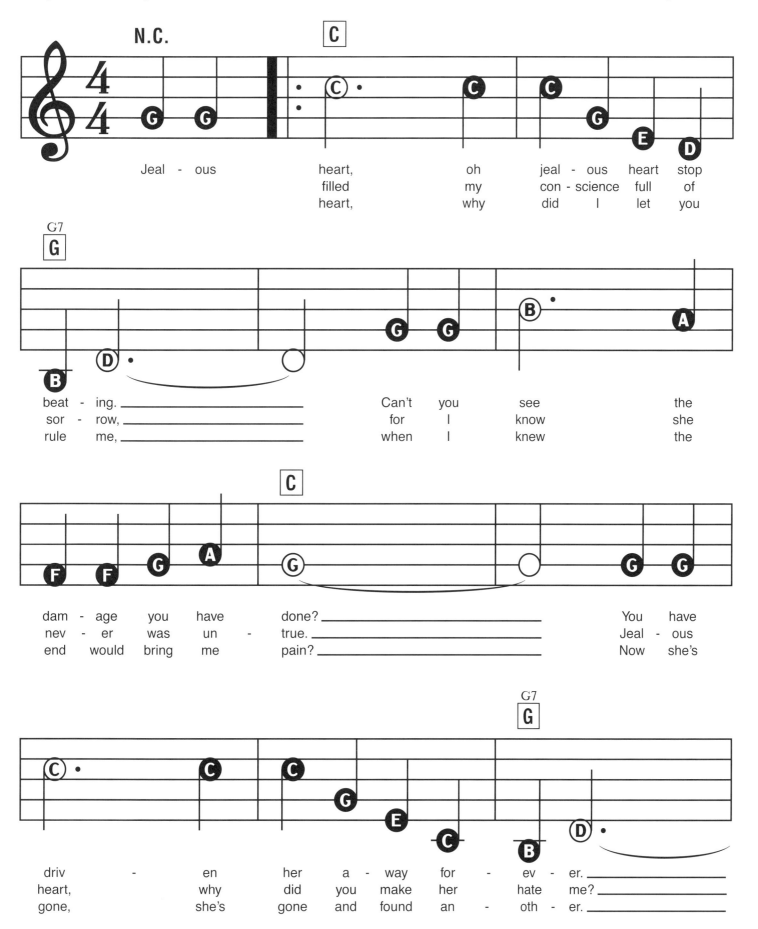

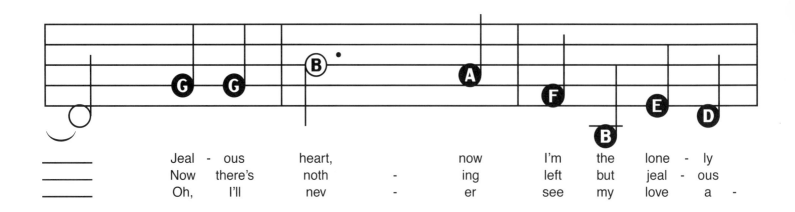

Jeal - ous   heart,   now   I'm   the   lone - ly
Now   there's   noth   -   ing   left   but   jeal - ous
Oh,   I'll   nev   -   er   see   my   love   a   -

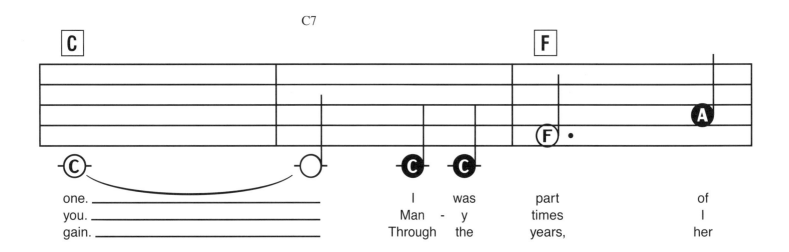

one. _____   I   was   part   of
you. _____   Man - y   times   I
gain. _____   Through the years,   her

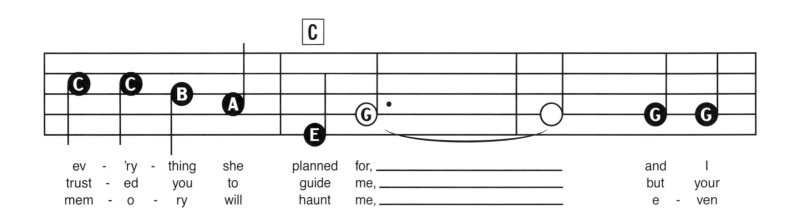

ev - 'ry - thing   she   planned   for, _____   and   I
trust - ed   you   to   guide   me, _____   but   your
mem - o - ry   will   haunt   me, _____   e - ven

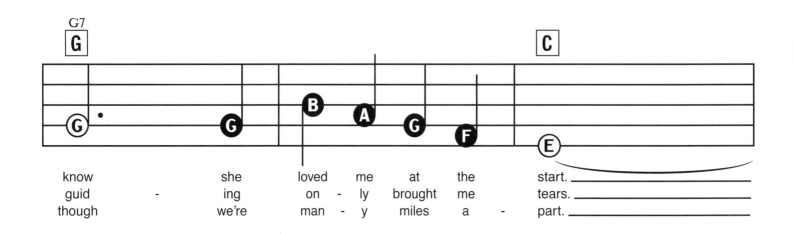

know   she   loved   me   at   the   start. _____
guid - ing   on - ly   brought   me   tears. _____
though   we're   man - y   miles   a - part. _____

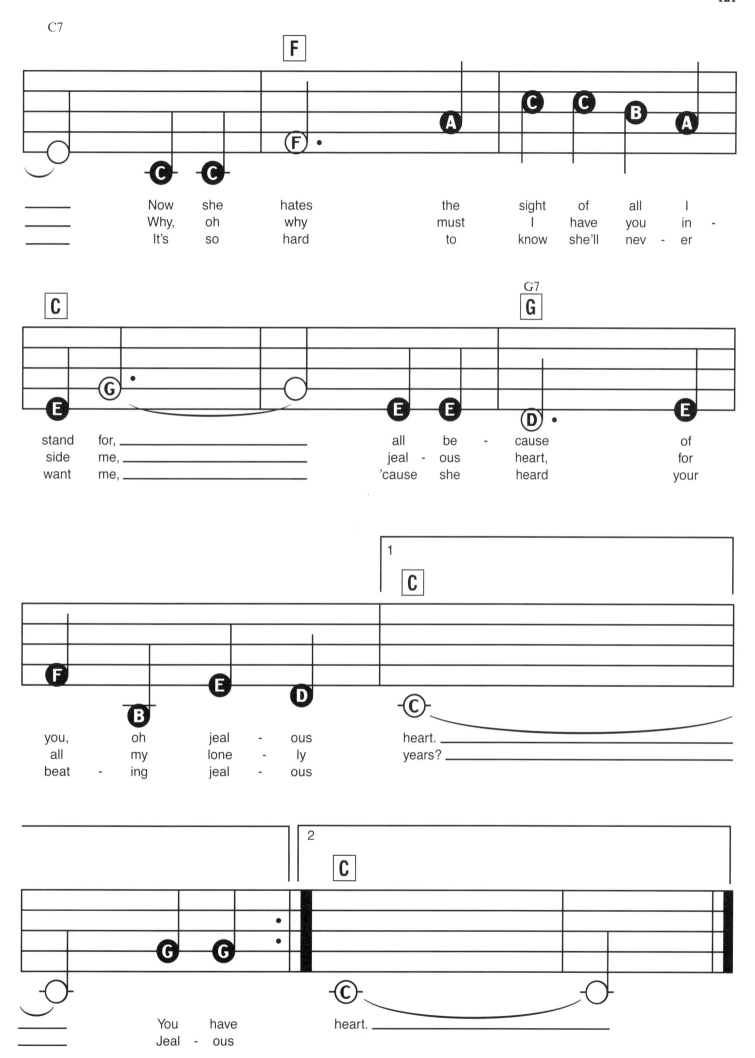

I.O.U.

Registration 10
Rhythm: Ballad

Words and Music by Kerry Chater
and Austin Roberts

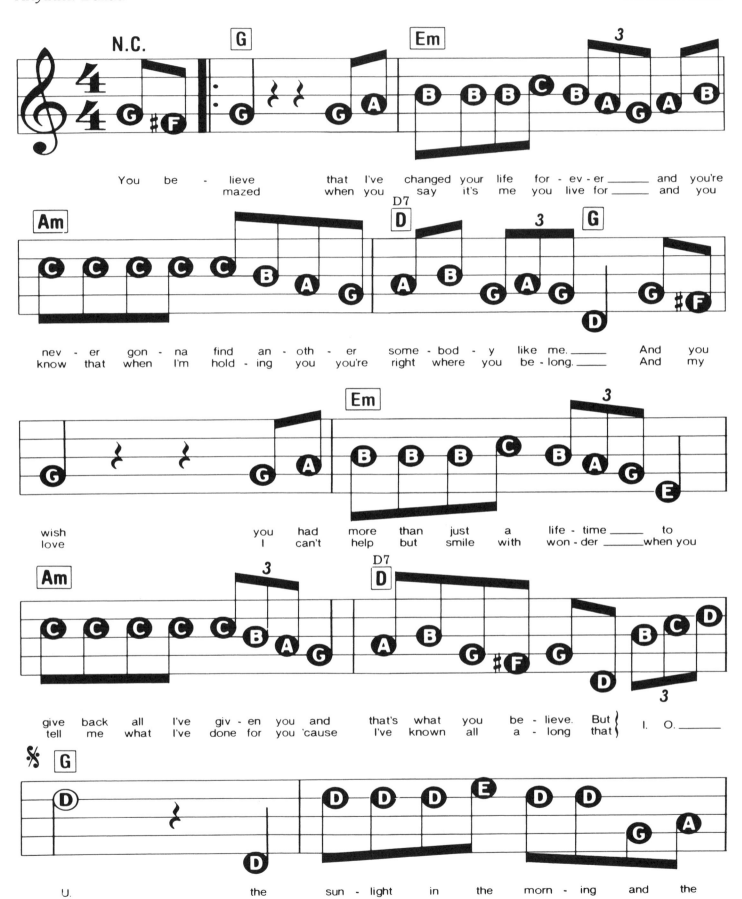

123

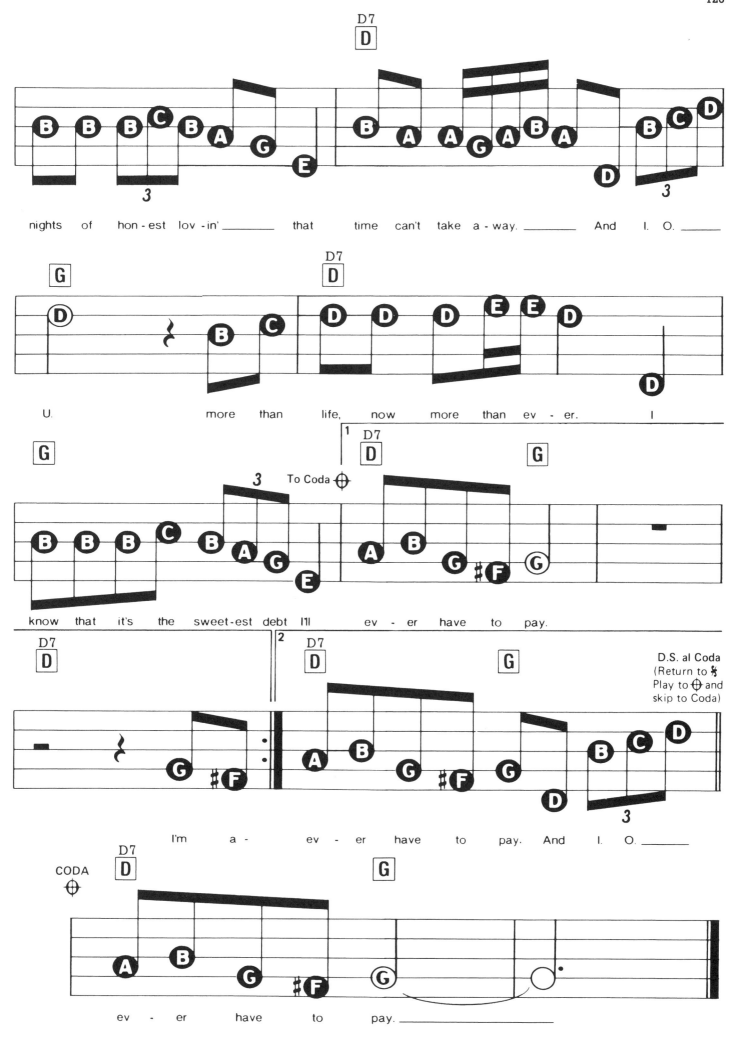

It's Now or Never

Registration 10
Rhythm: Fox Trot or Swing

Words and Music by Aaron Schroeder
and Wally Gold

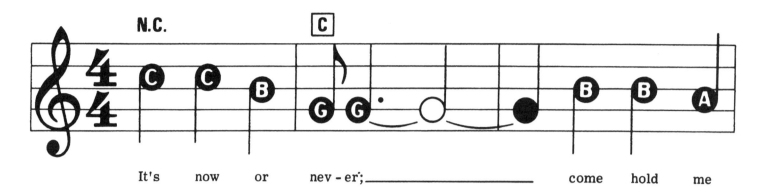

It's now or nev-er;_____ come hold me

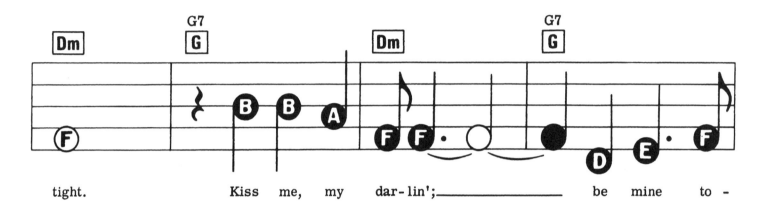

tight. Kiss me, my dar-lin';_____ be mine to-

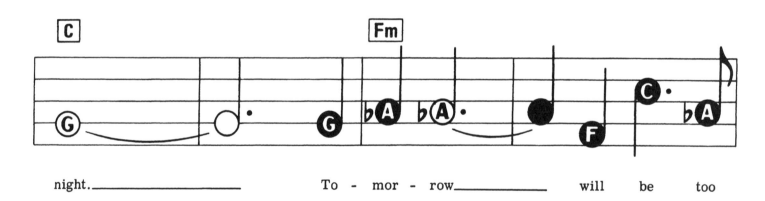

night._____ To - mor - row_____ will be too

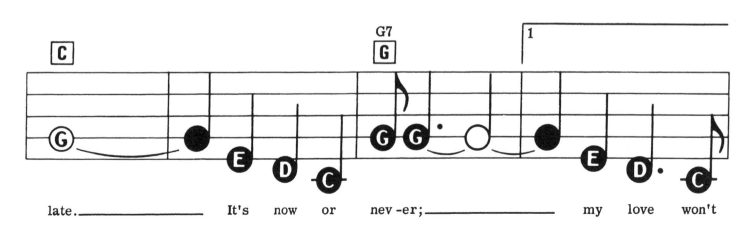

late._____ It's now or nev -er;_____ my love won't

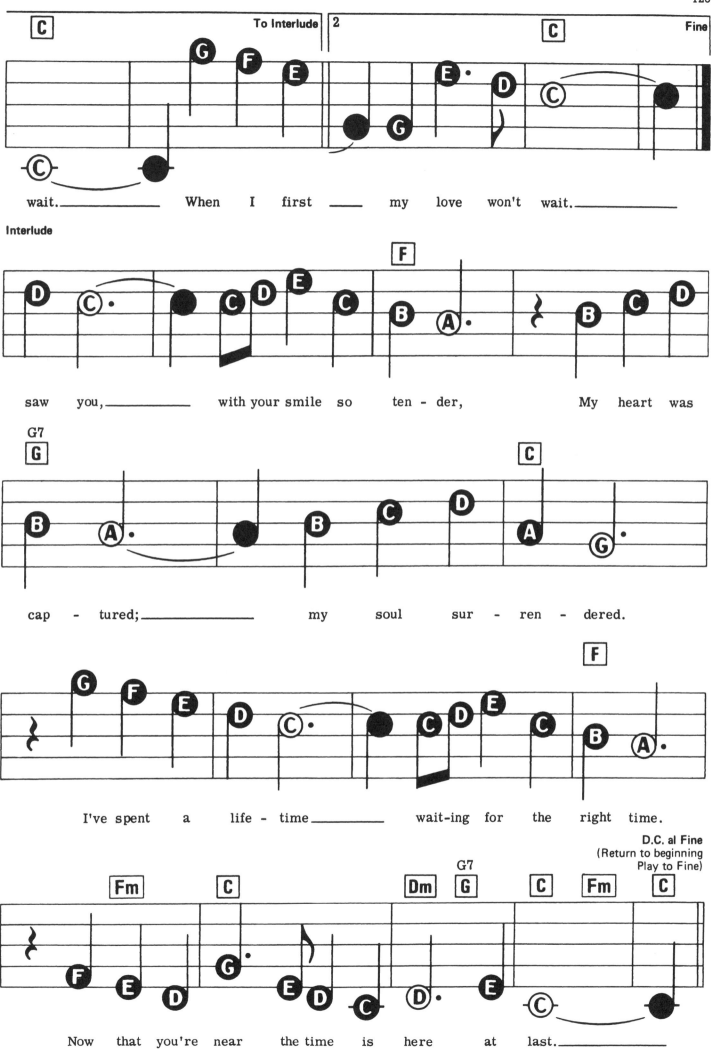

It's Such a Pretty World Today

Registration 4
Rhythm: Country or Shuffle

Words and Music by
Dale Noe

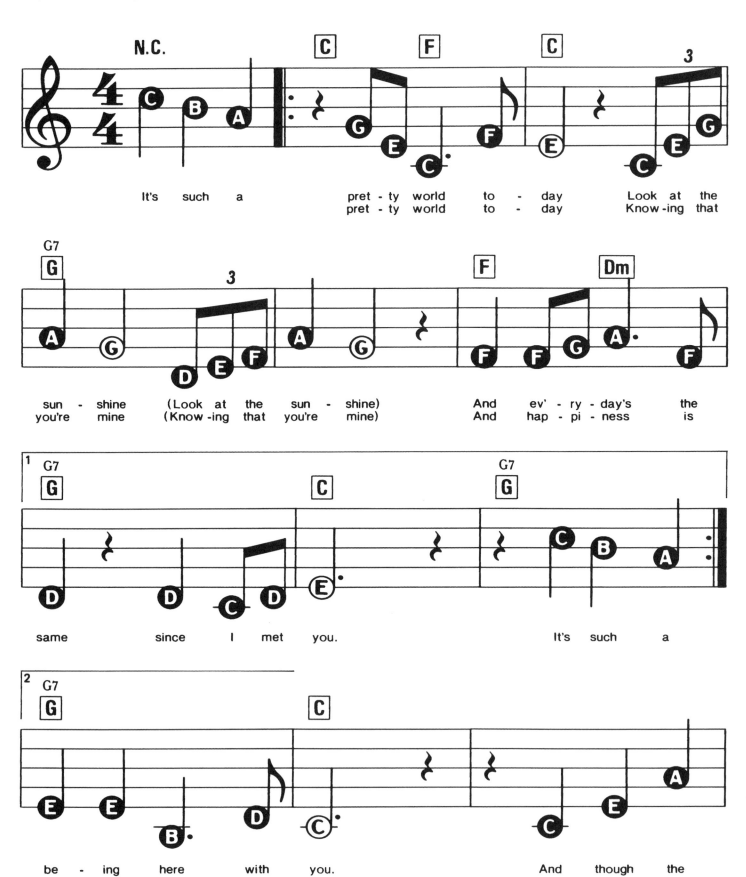

Jackson

Registration 10
Rhythm: Country or Bluegrass

Words and Music by Billy Edd Wheeler
and Jerry Leiber

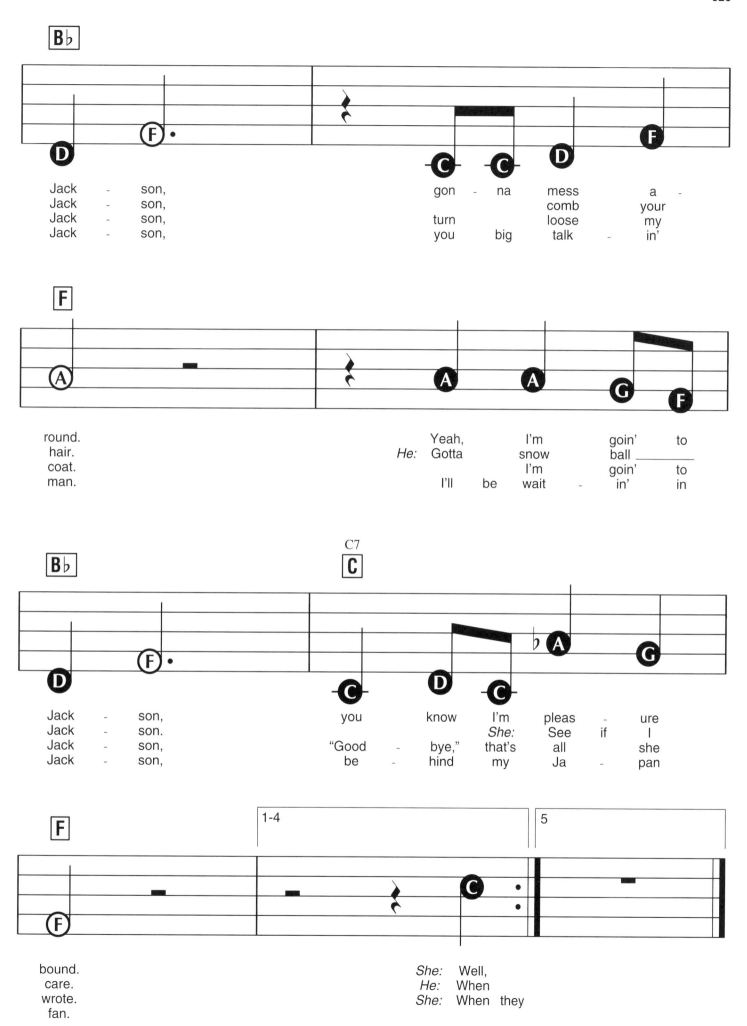

Jolene

Registration 7
Rhythm: Country Pop or 8-Beat

Words and Music by
Dolly Parton

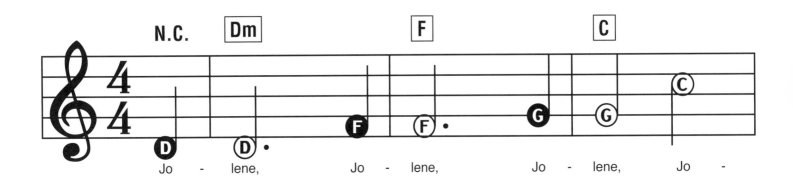

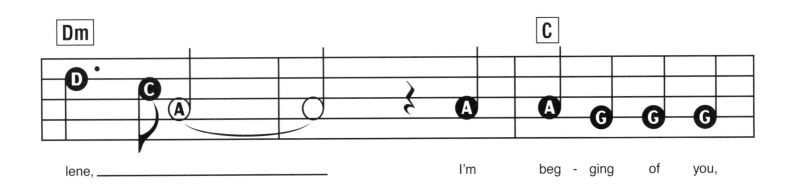

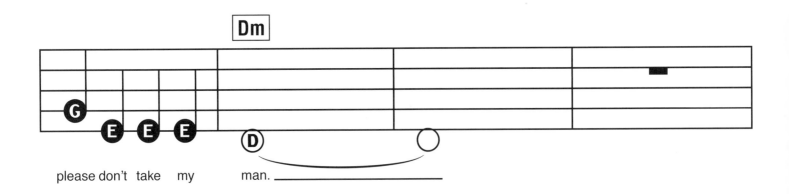

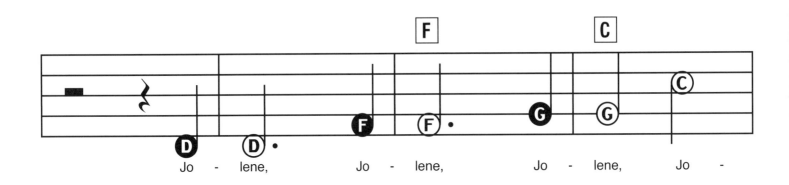

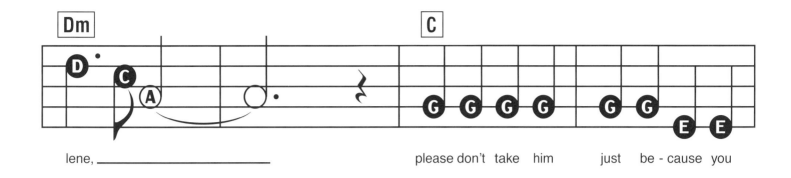

lene, _____ please don't take him just be - cause you

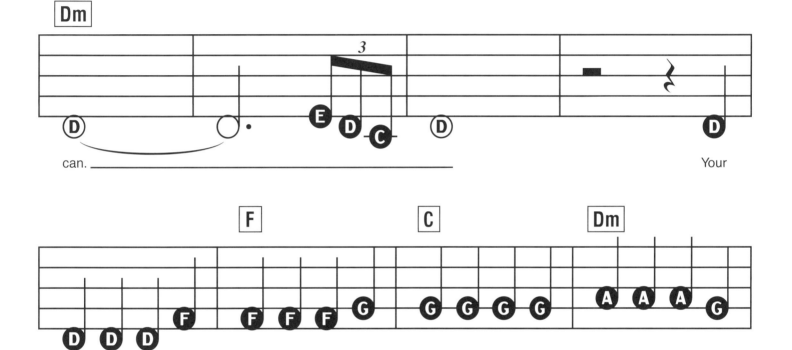

can. _____ Your

beau - ty is be - yond com - pare, with flam - ing locks of au - burn hair, with

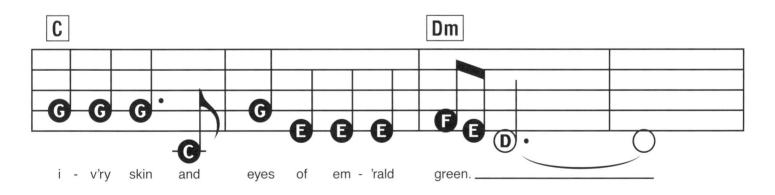

i - v'ry skin and eyes of em - 'rald green. _____

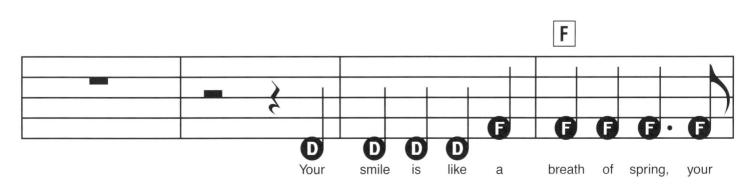

Your smile is like a breath of spring, your

132

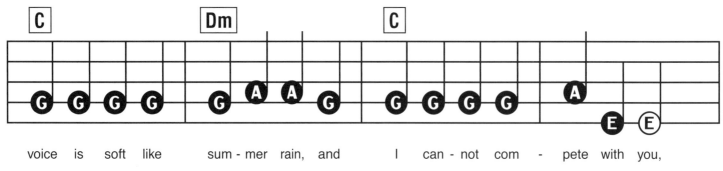

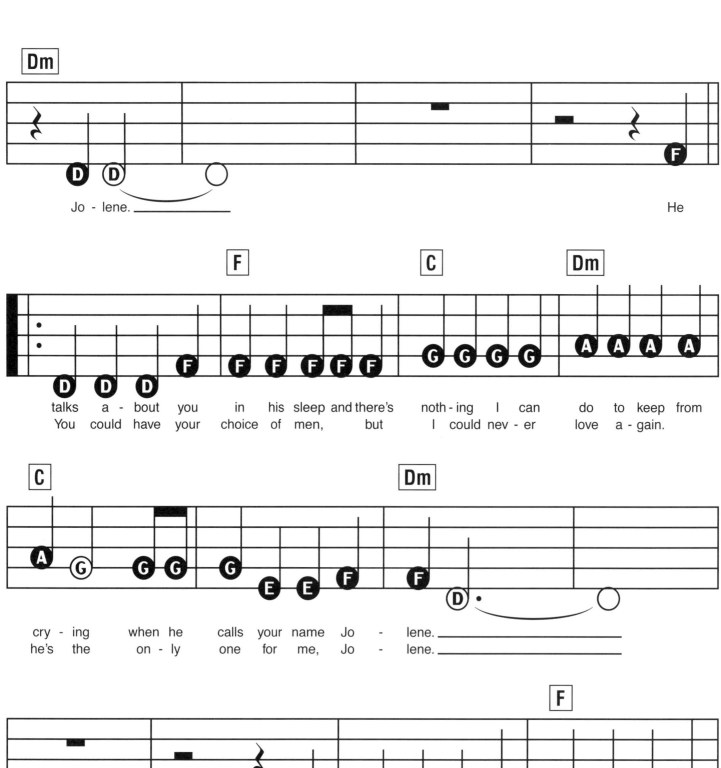

133

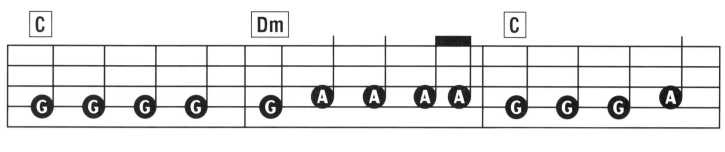

you could eas - 'ly take my man, but you don't know what he
hap - pi - ness de - pends on you and what - ev - er you de -

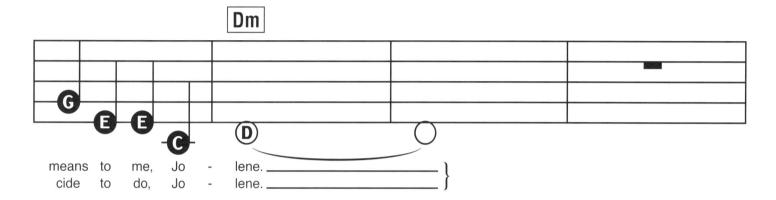

means to me, Jo - lene. _____
cide to do, Jo - lene. _____ }

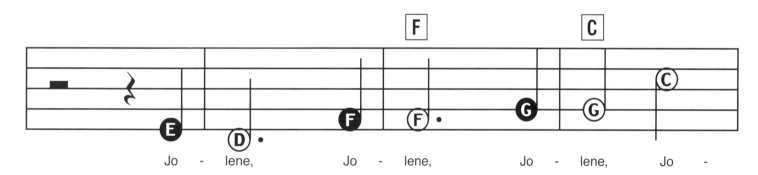

Jo - lene, Jo - lene, Jo - lene, Jo -

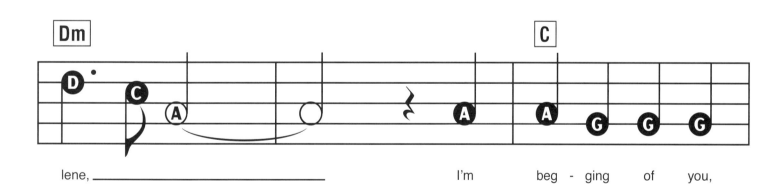

lene, _____ I'm beg - ging of you,

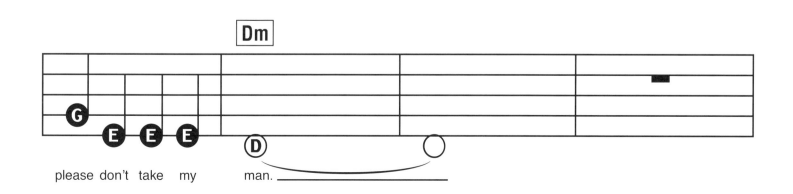

please don't take my man. _____

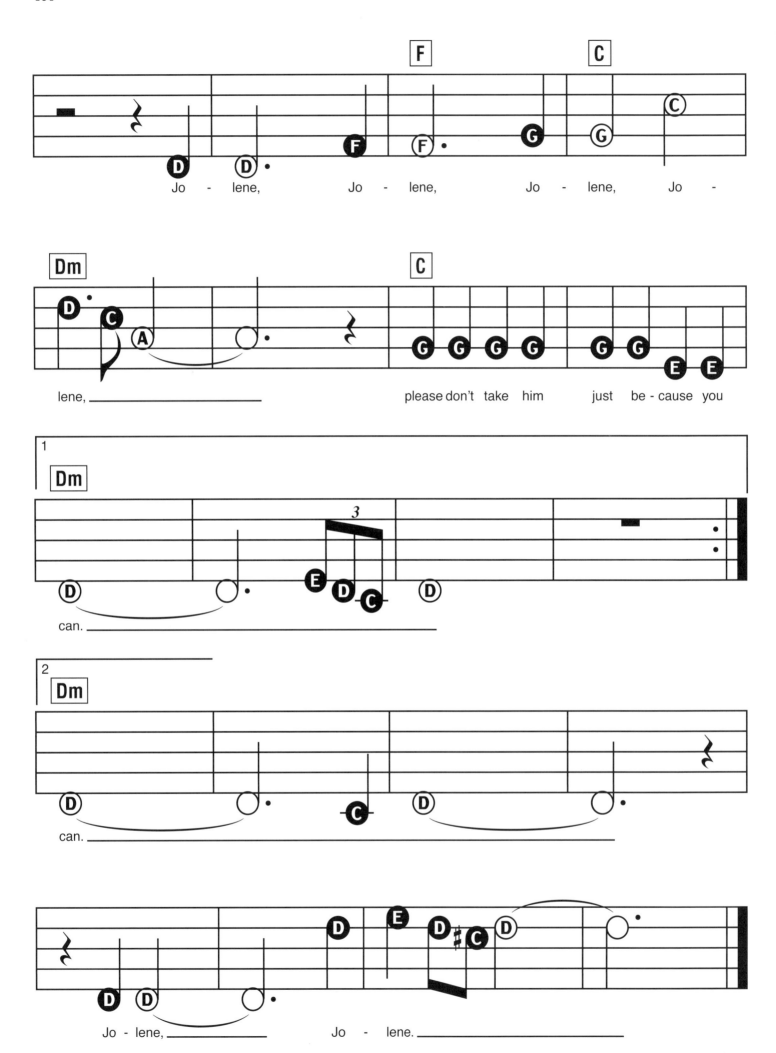

Kaw-Liga

Registration 4
Rhythm: Fox Trot or Ballad

Words by Fred Rose
Music by Hank Williams

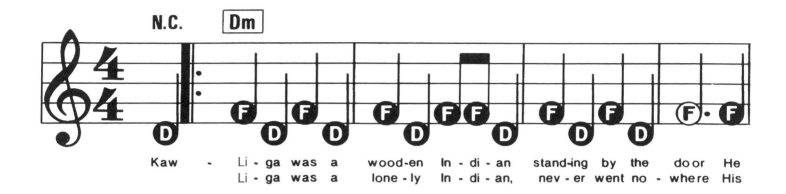

Kaw - Li - ga was a wood-en In - di - an stand-ing by the door He
Li - ga was a lone - ly In - di - an, nev - er went no - where His

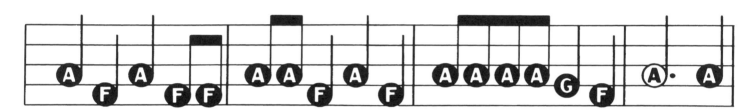

fell in love with an In - di - an maid - en o - ver in the an - tique store. Kaw-
heart was set on the In - di - an maid - en with ____ the ____ coal black hair. Kaw-

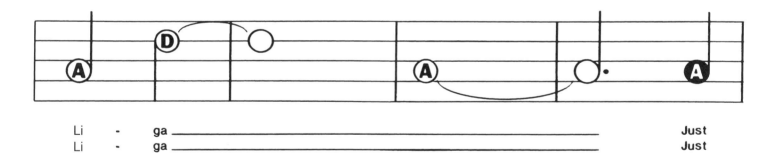

Li - ga ____ Just
Li - ga ____ Just

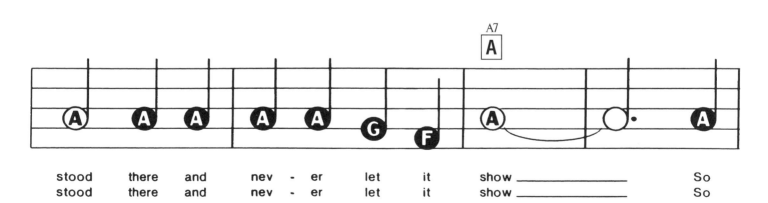

stood there and nev - er let it show ____ So
stood there and nev - er let it show ____ So

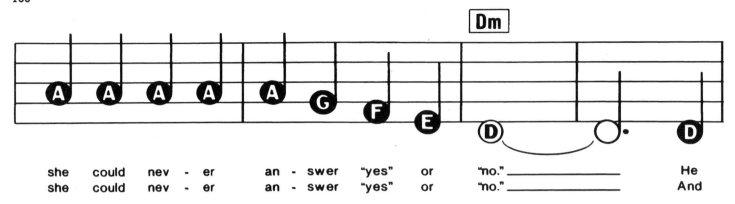

she could nev - er an - swer "yes" or "no." _____ He
she could nev - er an - swer "yes" or "no." _____ And

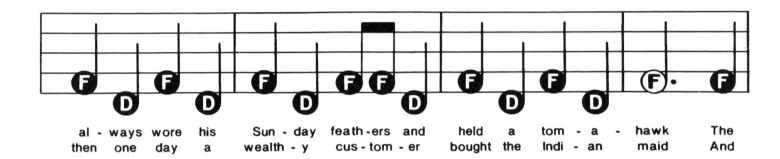

al - ways wore his Sun - day feath -ers and held a tom - a - hawk The
then one day a wealth - y cus - tom - er bought the Indi - an maid And

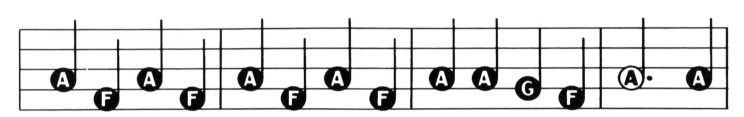

maid - en wore her beads and braids and hoped some - day he'd talk. Kaw-
took her, oh, so far a - way but ol' Kaw - Li - ga stayed. Kaw-

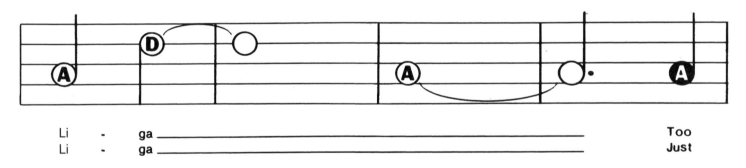

Li - ga _____ Too
Li - ga _____ Just

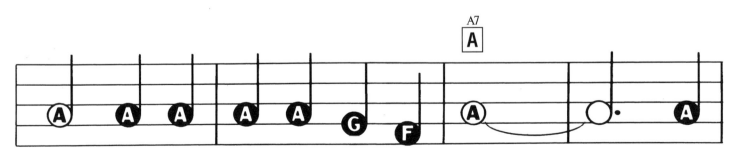

stub - born to ev - er show a sign _____ Be -
stands there as lone - ly as can be _____ And

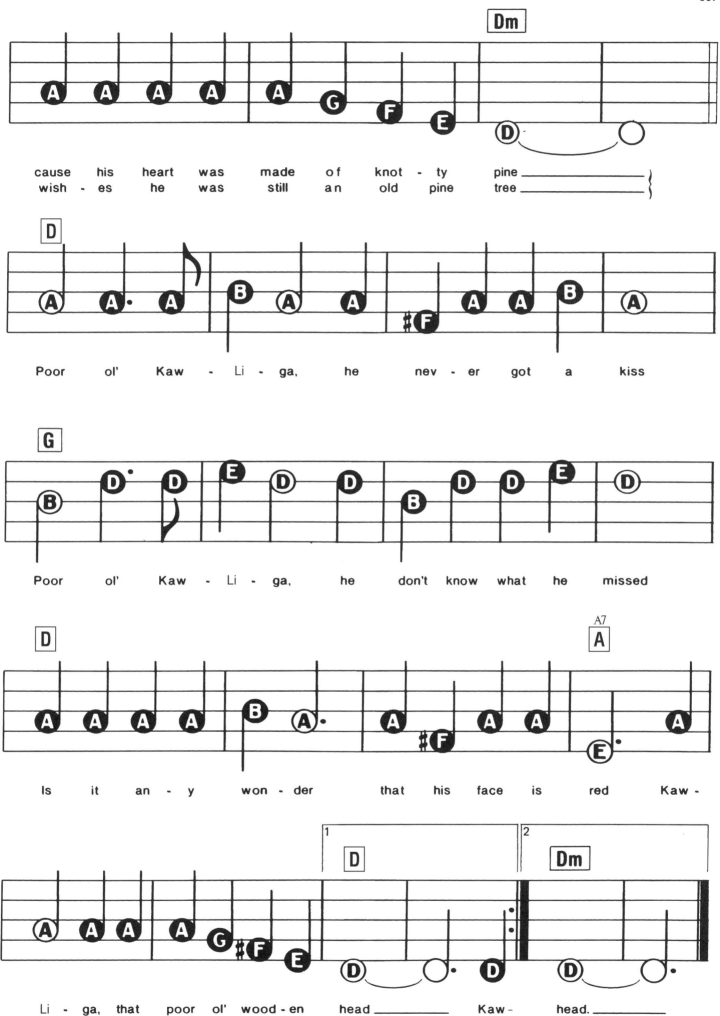

Kentucky Rain

Registration 8
Rhythm: Rock

Words and Music by Eddie Rabbitt
and Dick Heard

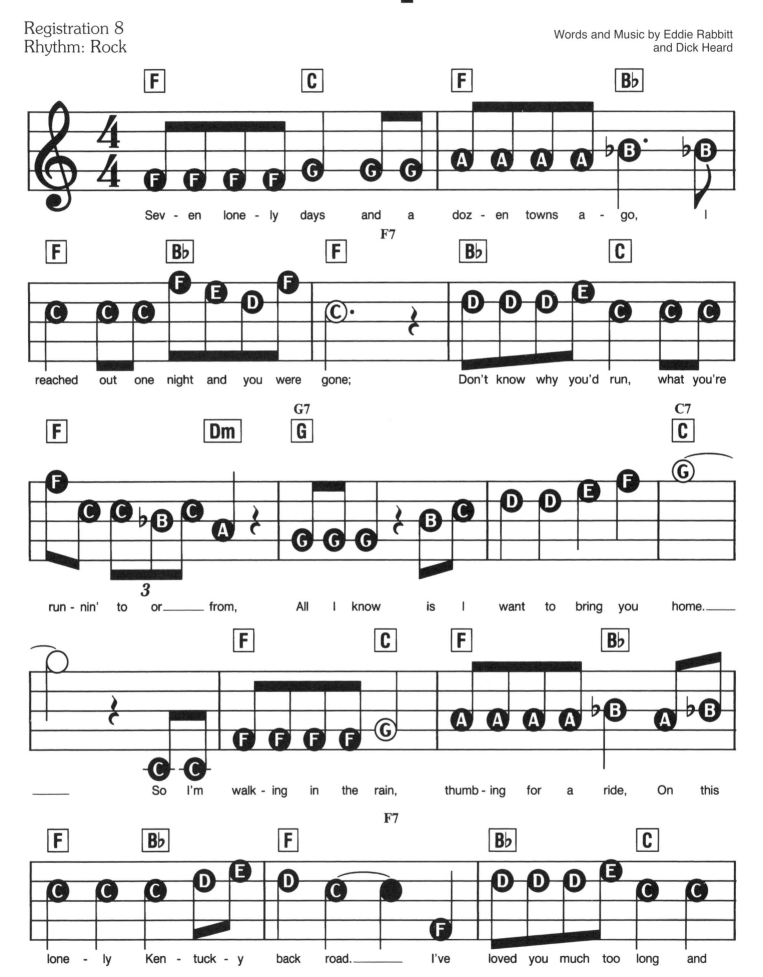

139

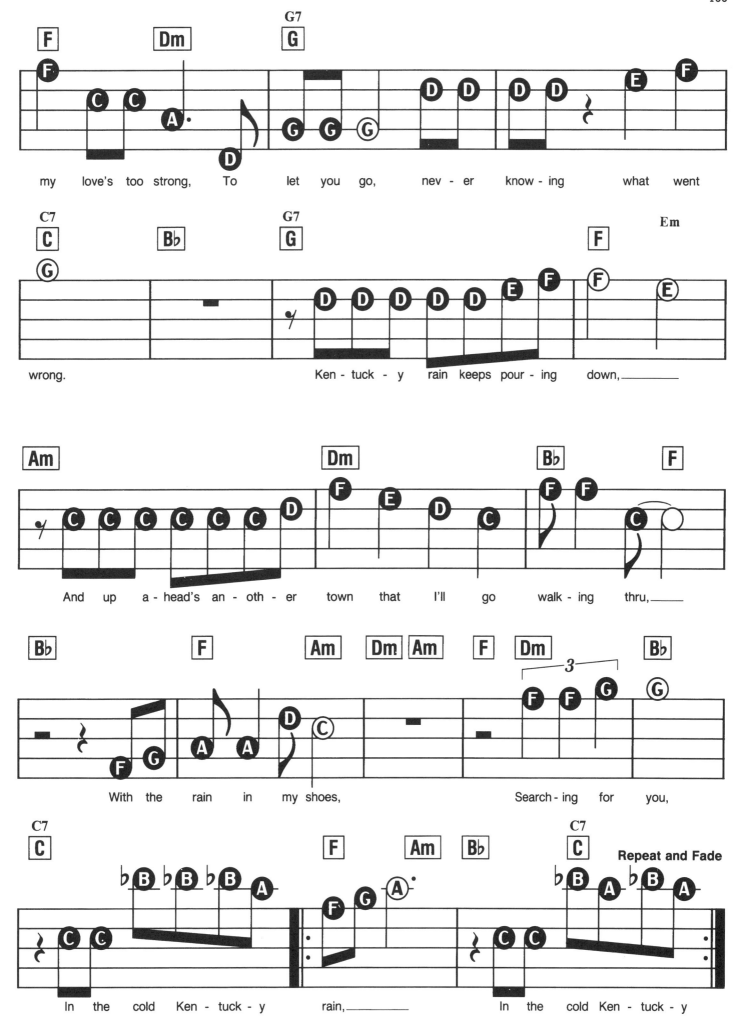

Kiss an Angel Good Mornin'

Registration 10
Rhythm: Swing or Fox Trot

Words and Music by
Ben Peters

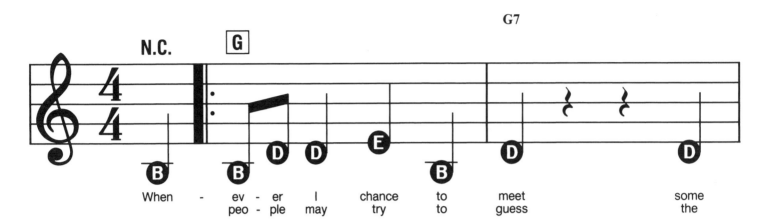

When - ev - er I chance to meet some
peo - ple may try to guess the

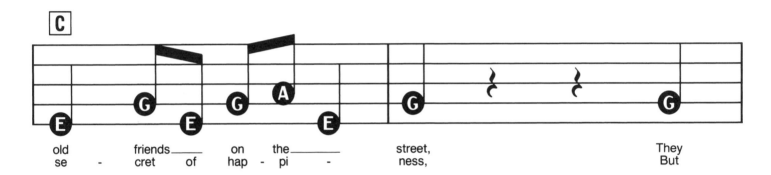

old friends___ on the___ street, They
se - cret of hap - pi - ness, But

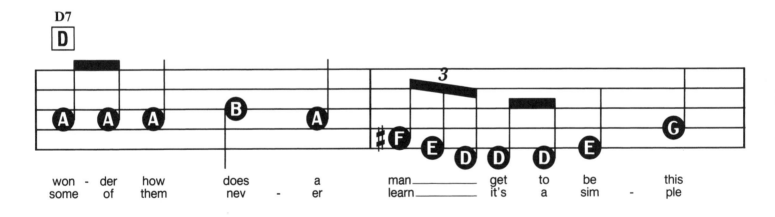

won - der how does a man___ get to be this
some of them nev - er learn___ it's a sim - ple

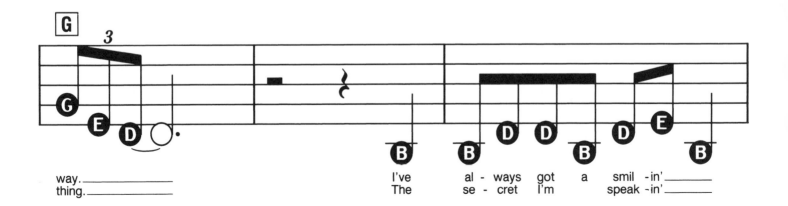

way.___
thing.___

I've al - ways got a smil - in'___
The se - cret I'm speak - in'___

141

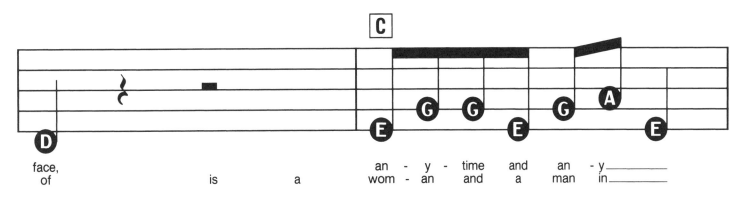

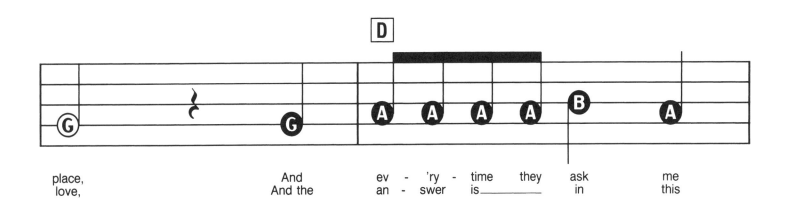

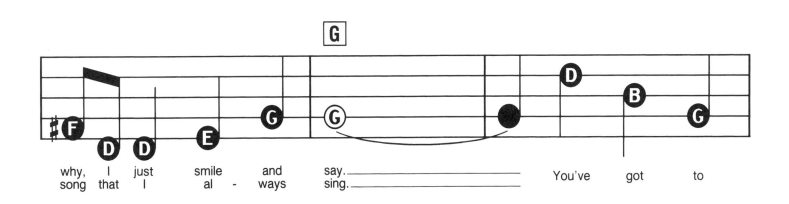

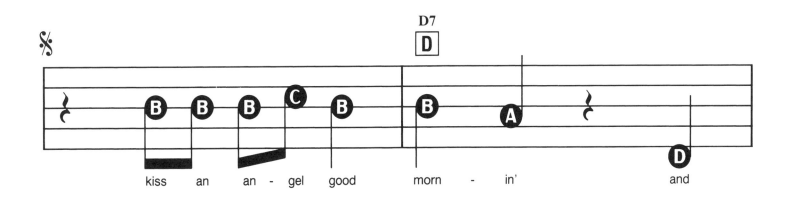

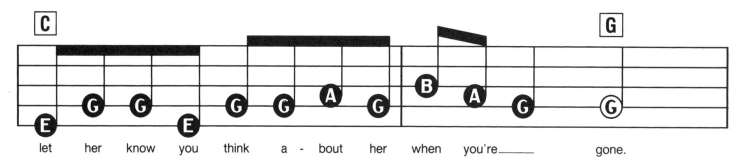

let her know you think a - bout her when you're_____ gone.

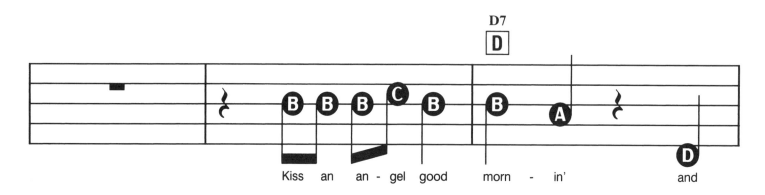

Kiss an an - gel good morn - in' and

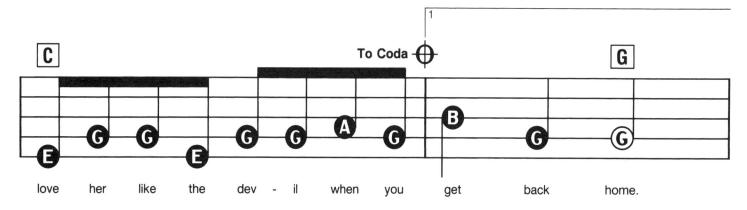

love her like the dev - il when you get back home.

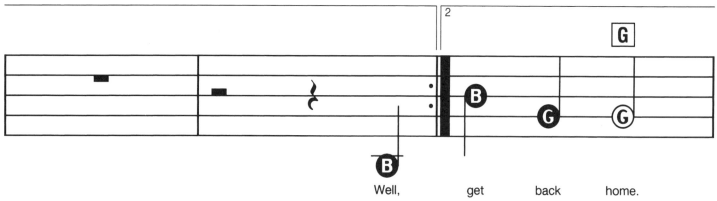

Well, get back home.

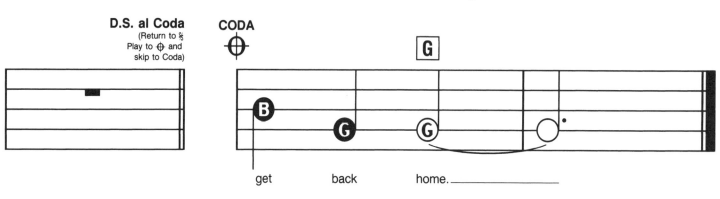

get back home._____

Little Green Apples

Registration 3
Rhythm: Country

Words and Music by
Bobby Russell

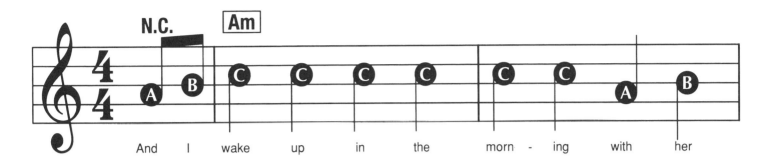

And I wake up in the morn - ing with her

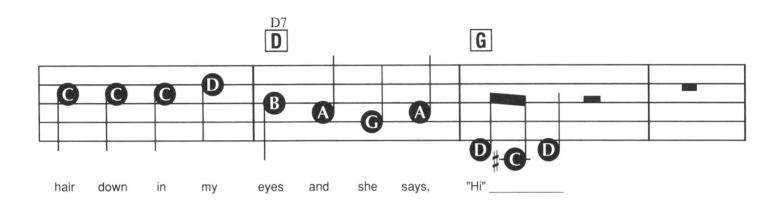

hair down in my eyes and she says, "Hi" _____

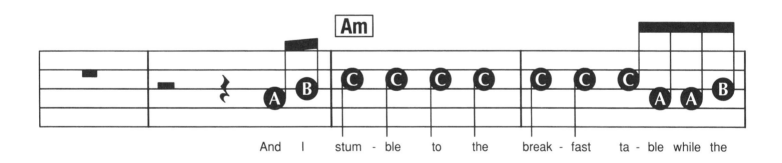

And I stum - ble to the break - fast ta - ble while the

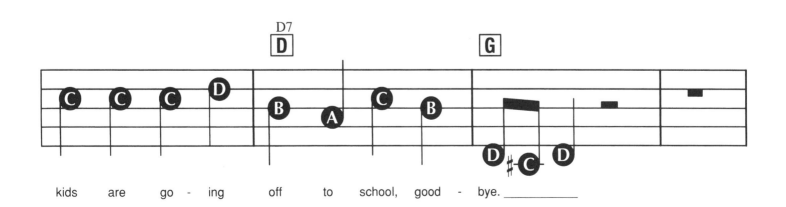

kids are go - ing off to school, good - bye. _____

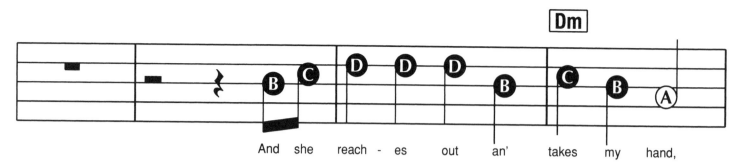

And she reach - es out an' takes my hand,

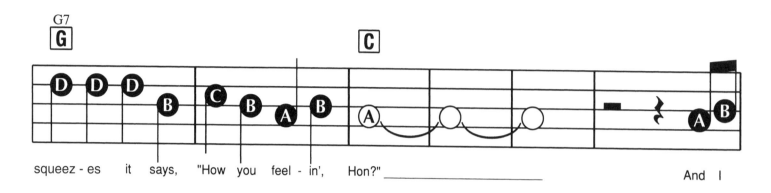

squeez - es it says, "How you feel - in', Hon?" And I

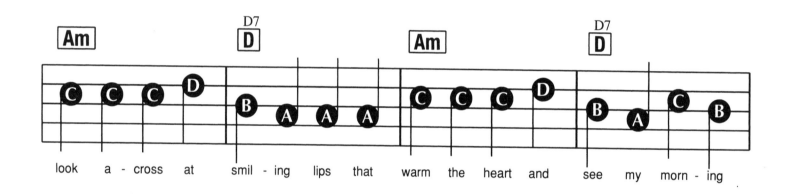

look a - cross at smil - ing lips that warm the heart and see my morn - ing

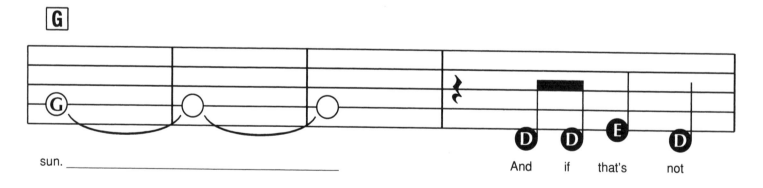

sun. And if that's not

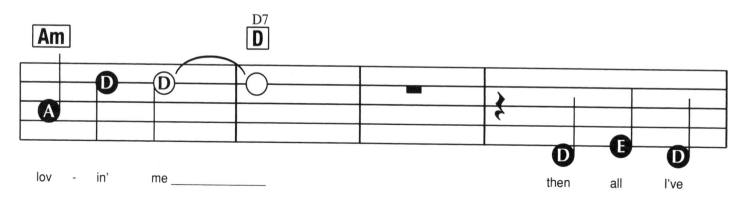

lov - in' me then all I've

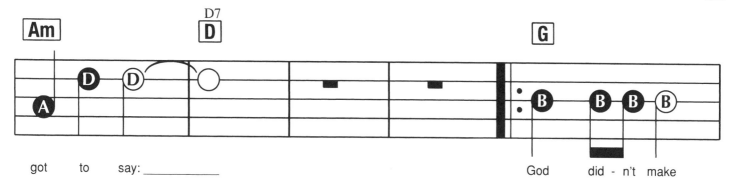

got to say: ____

God did - n't make

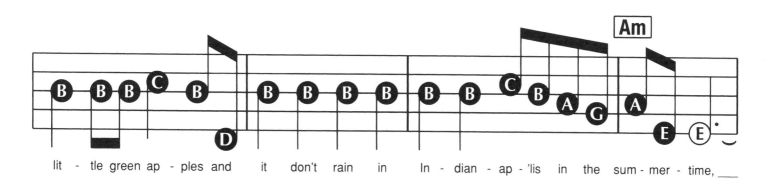

lit - tle green ap - ples and it don't rain in In - dian - ap - 'lis in the sum - mer - time, ___

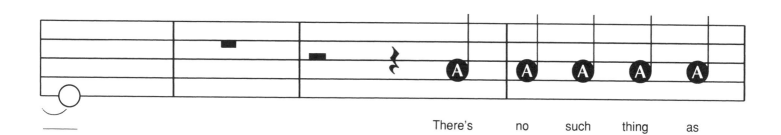

____ There's no such thing as

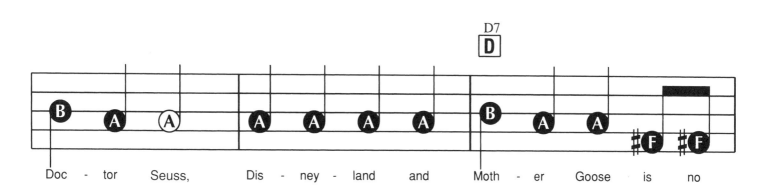

Doc - tor Seuss, Dis - ney - land and Moth - er Goose is no

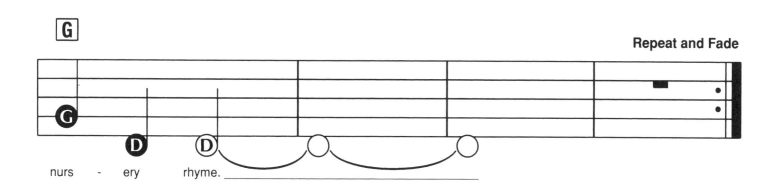

nurs - ery rhyme. _____

The Last Word in Lonesome Is Me

Registration 8
Rhythm: Waltz

Words and Music by
Roger Miller

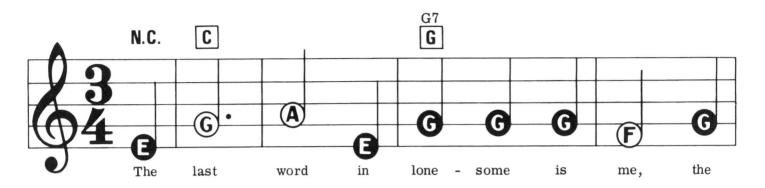

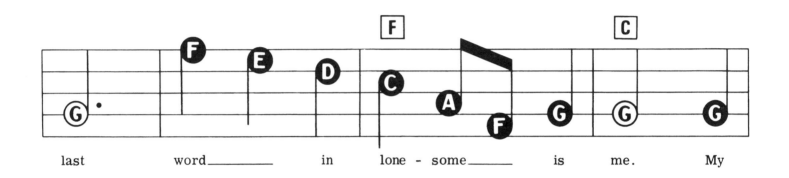

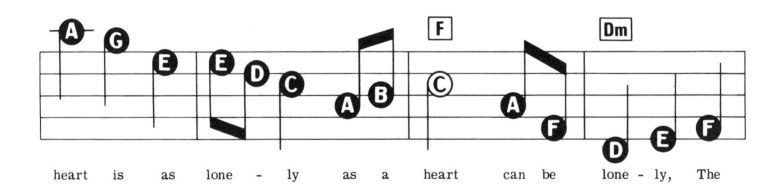

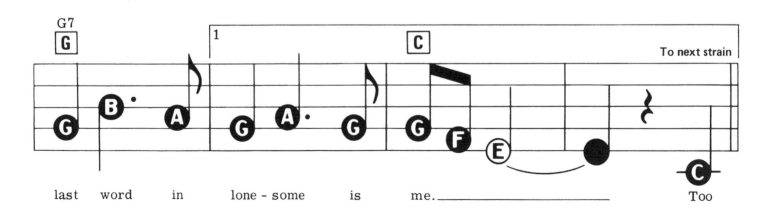

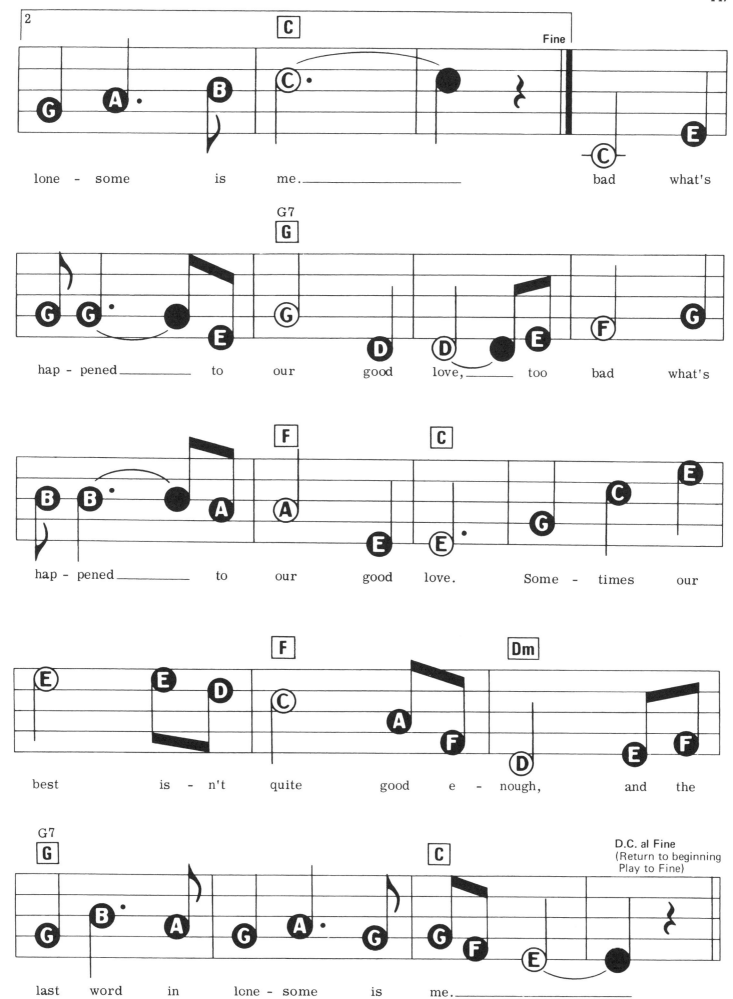

Longneck Bottle

Registration 3
Rhythm: Country Swing or Fox Trot

*Words and Music by Rick Carnes
and Steve Wariner*

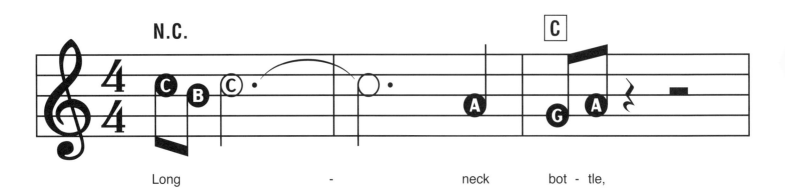

Long - neck bot - tle,

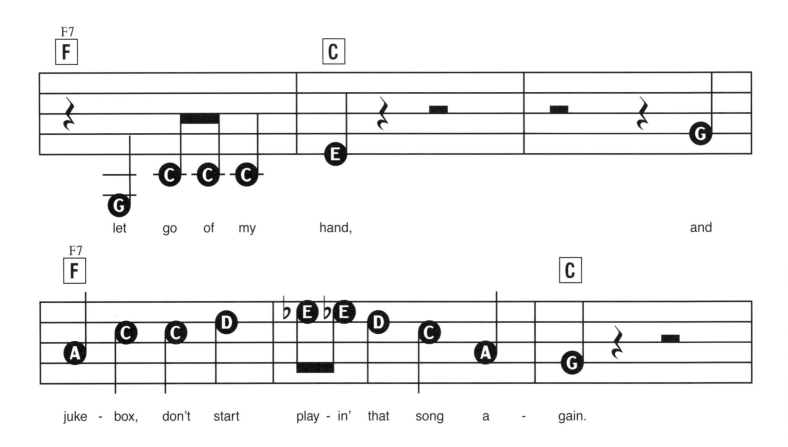

let go of my hand, and

juke - box, don't start play - in' that song a - gain.

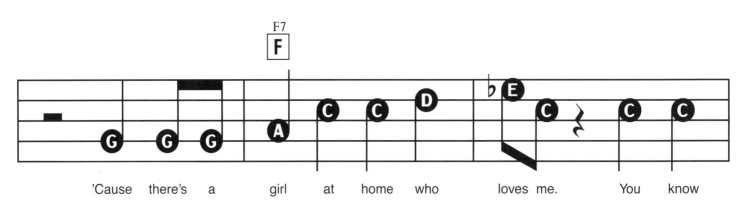

'Cause there's a girl at home who loves me. You know

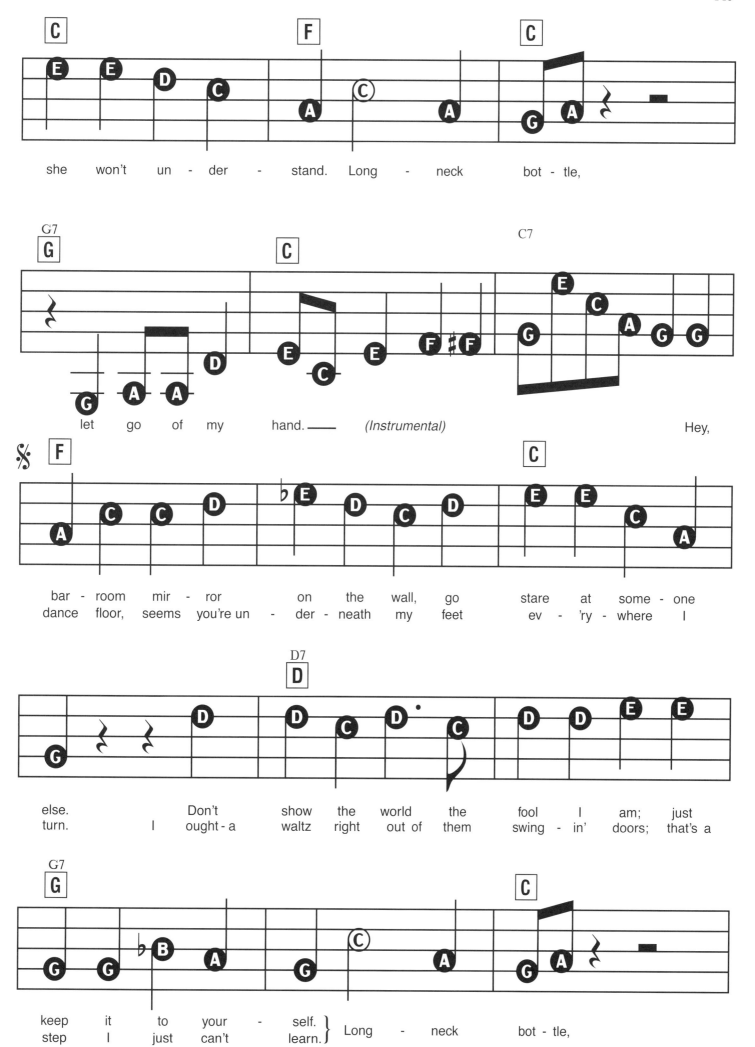

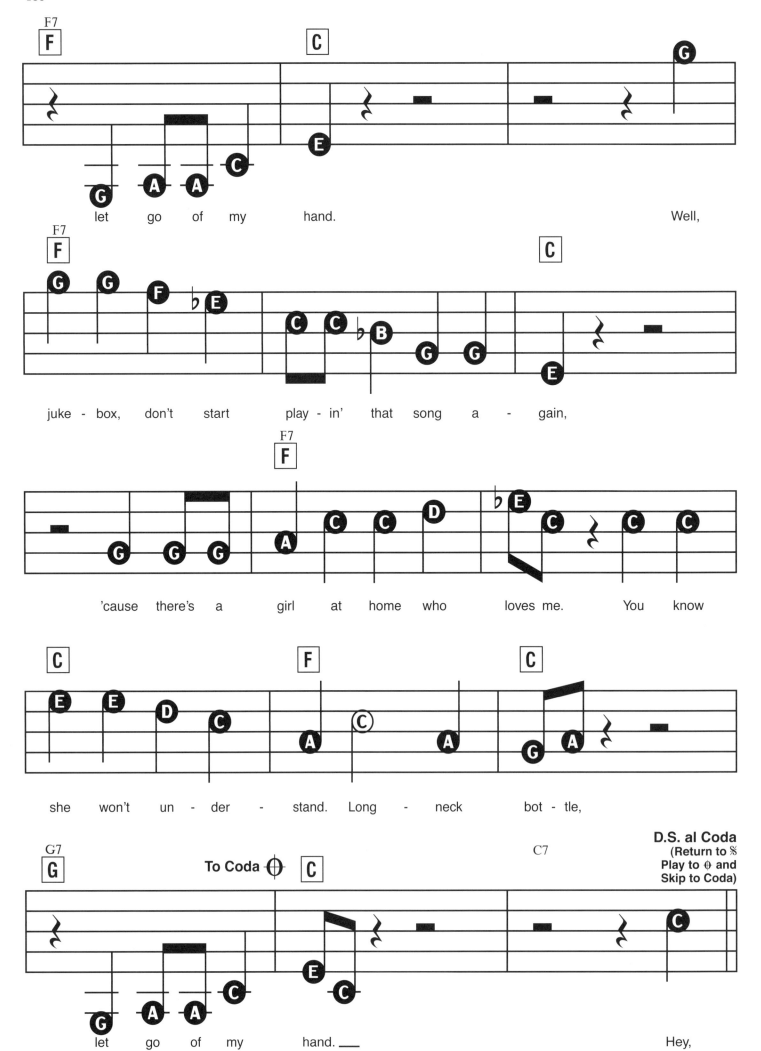

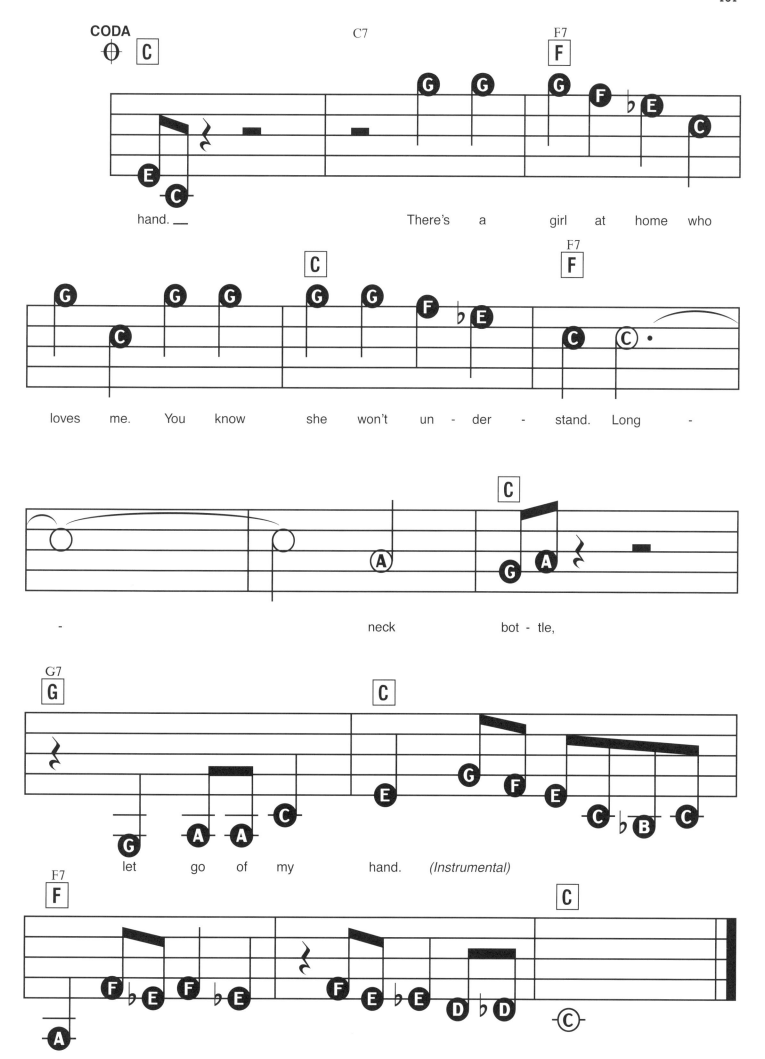

Mammas Don't Let Your Babies Grow Up to Be Cowboys

Registration 2
Rhythm: Waltz

Words and Music by Ed Bruce
and Patsy Bruce

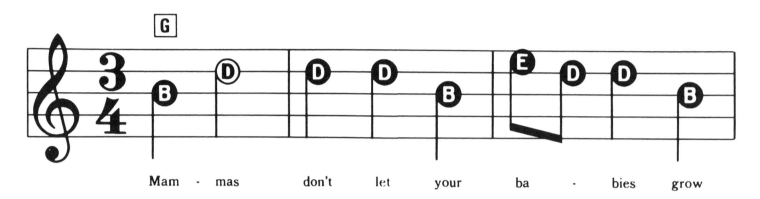

Mam - mas don't let your ba - bies grow

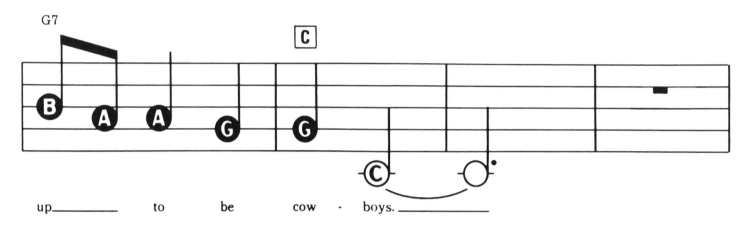

up_____ to be cow - boys. _____

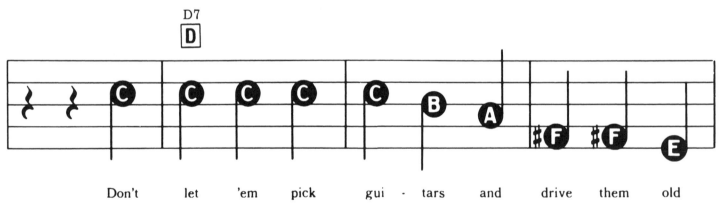

Don't let 'em pick gui - tars and drive them old

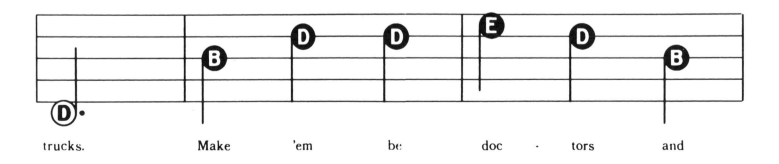

trucks. Make 'em be doc - tors and

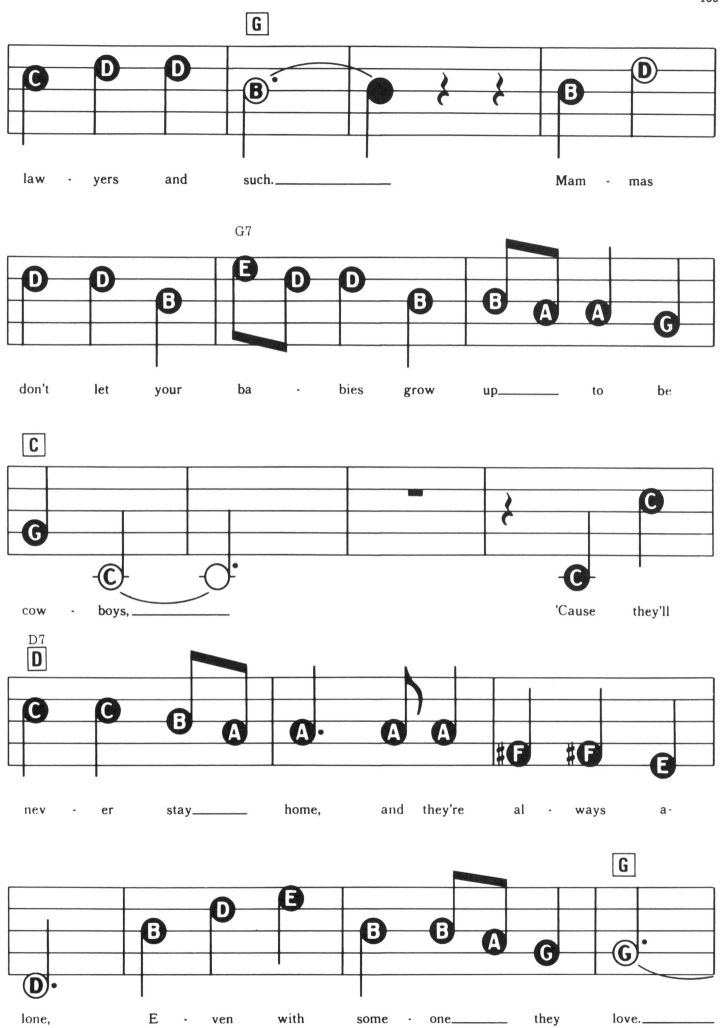

154

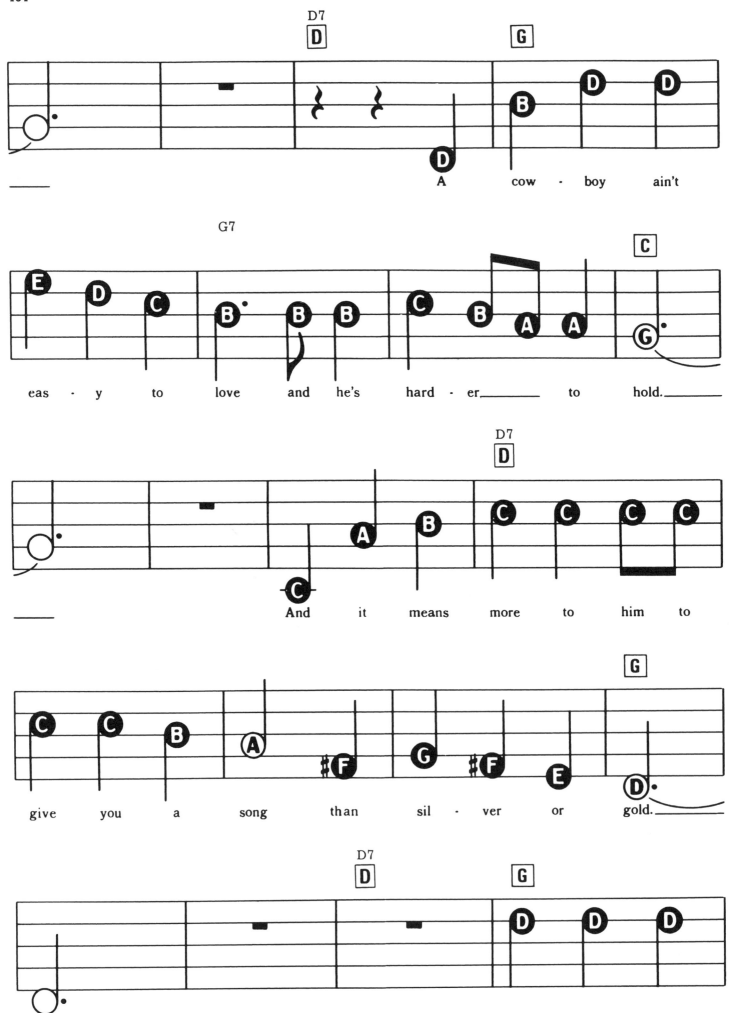

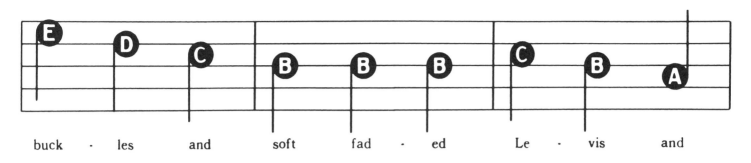

buck - les and soft fad - ed Le - vis and

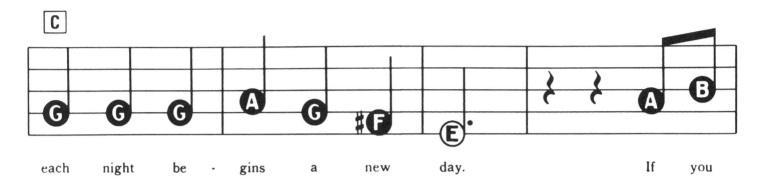

each night be - gins a new day. If you

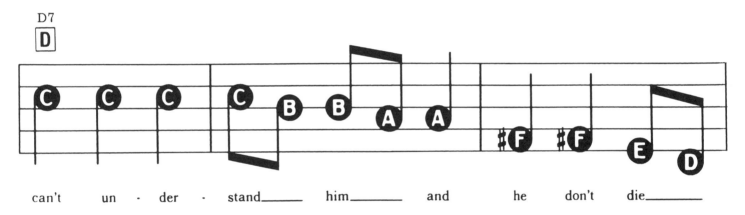

can't un - der - stand___ him___ and he don't die___

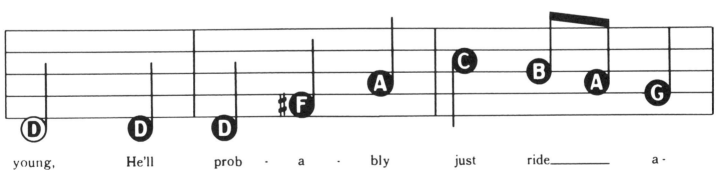

young, He'll prob - a - bly just ride___ a-

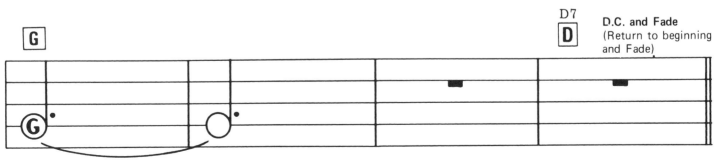

way. ___

Mountain Music

Registration 3
Rhythm: Country or Shuffle

Words and Music by
Randy Owen

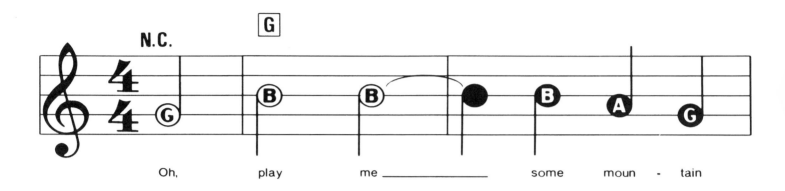

Oh, play me _____ some moun - tain

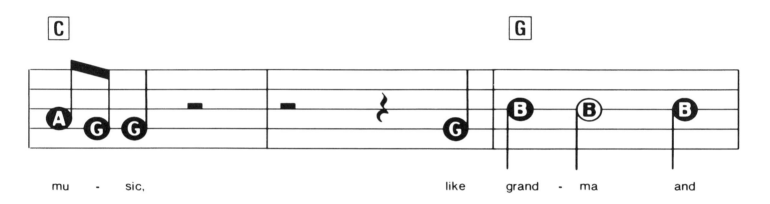

mu - sic, like grand - ma and

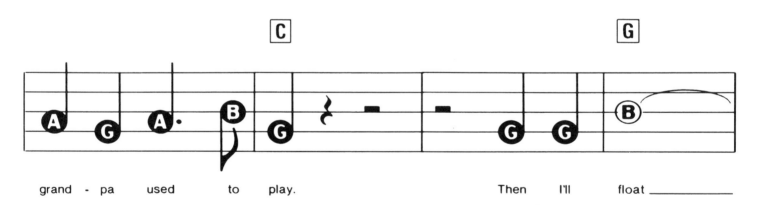

grand - pa used to play. Then I'll float _____

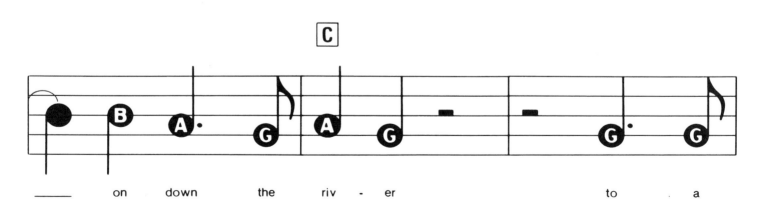

_____ on down the riv - er to a

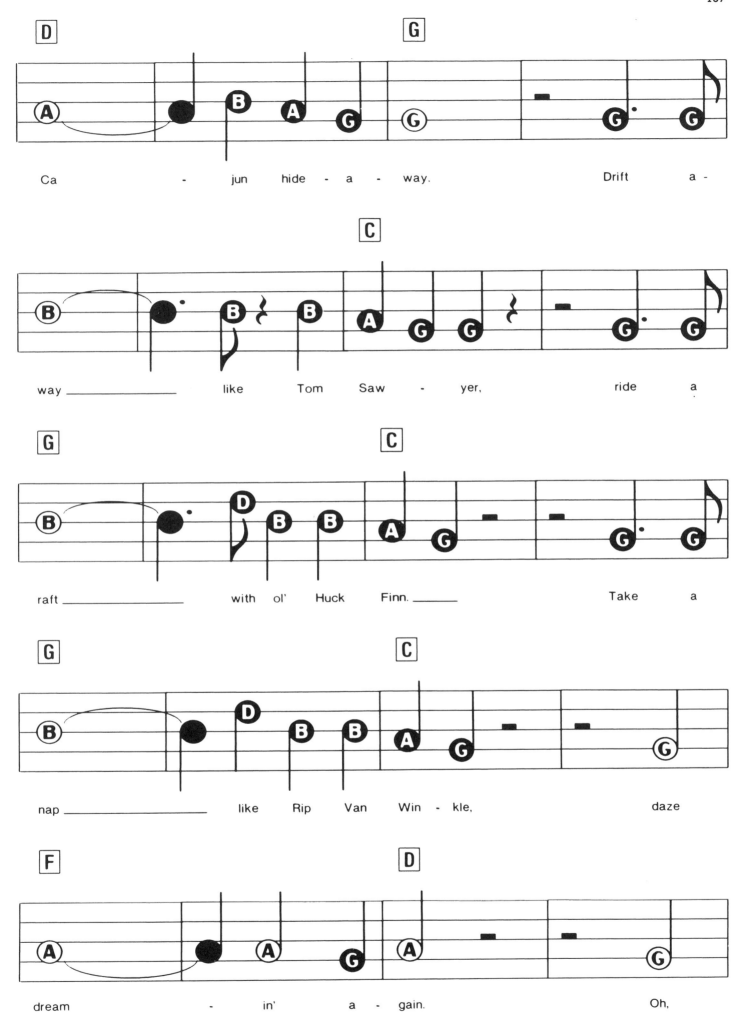

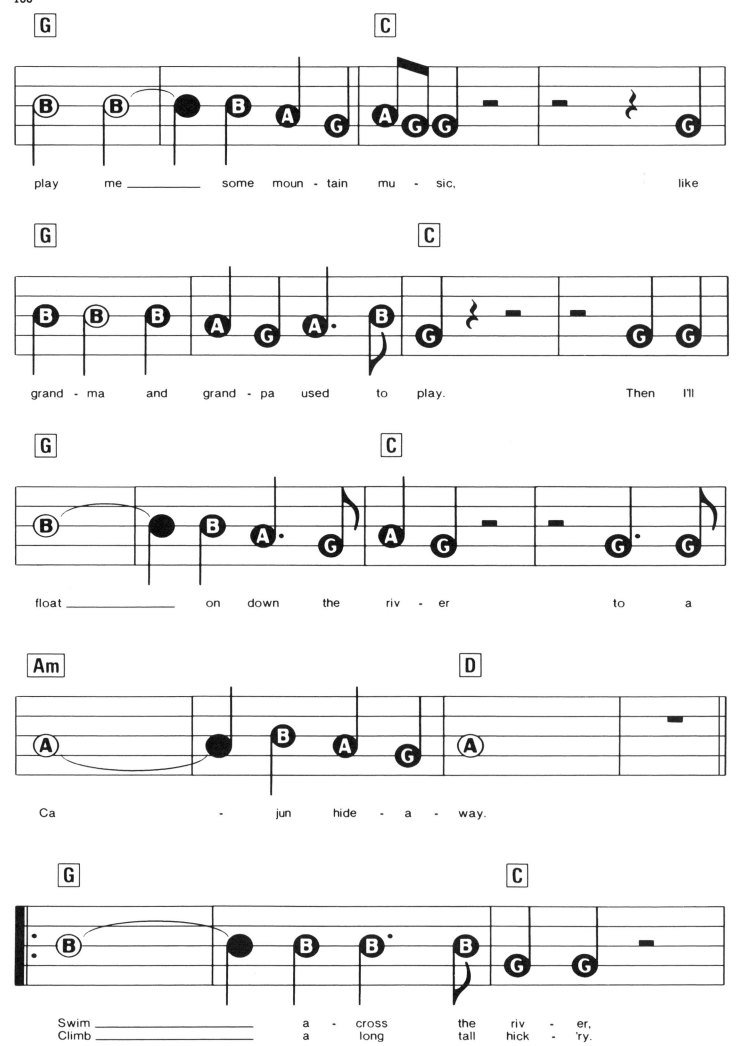

159

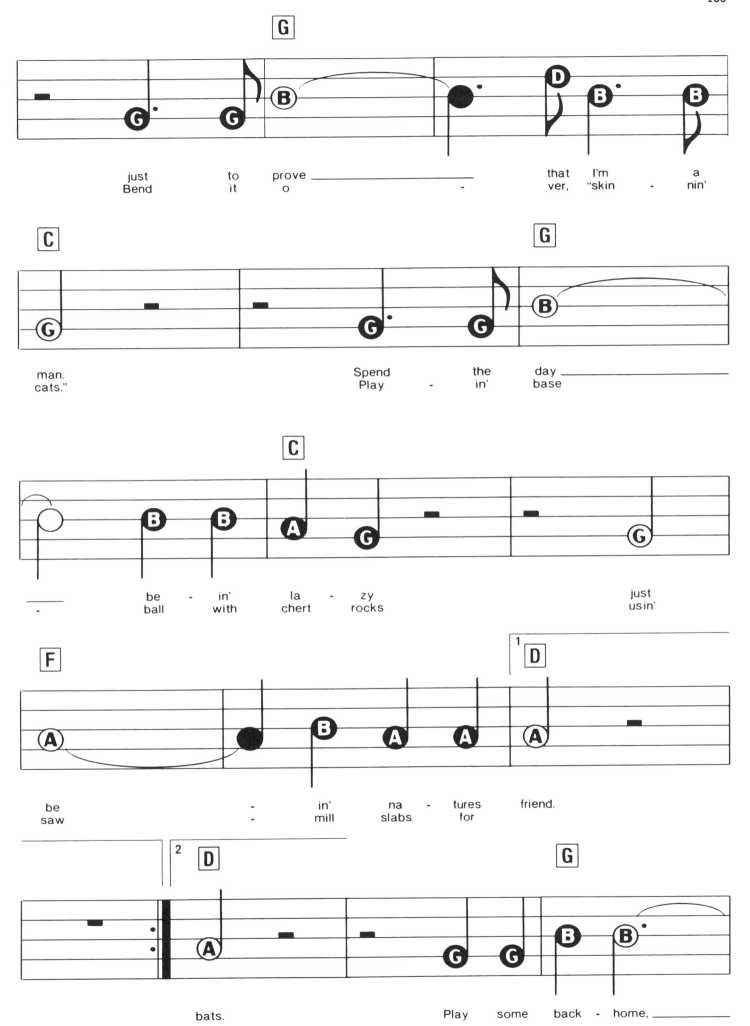

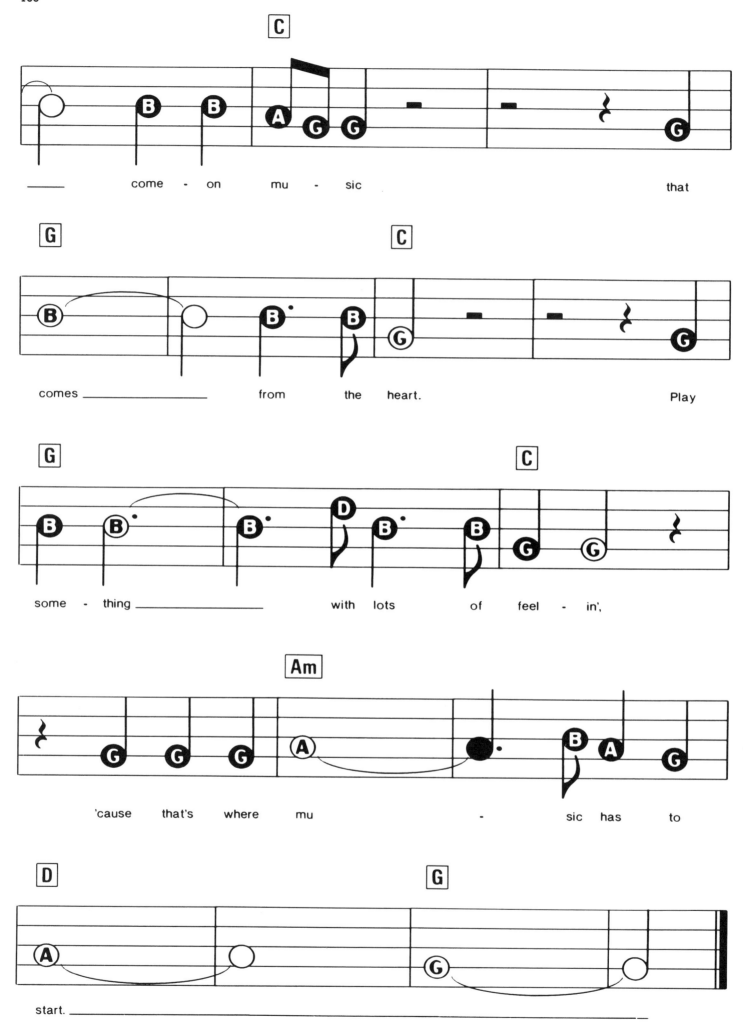

My Heroes Have Always Been Cowboys

Registration 9
Rhythm: Waltz

Words and Music by
Sharon Vaughn

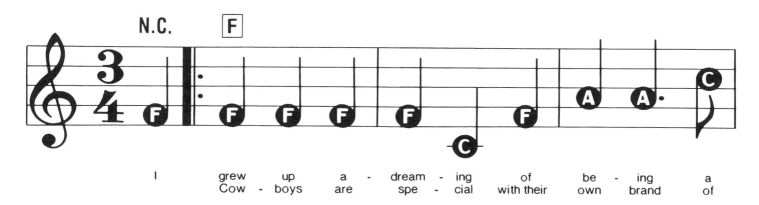

I grew up a - dream - ing of be - ing a
Cow - boys are spe - cial with their own brand of

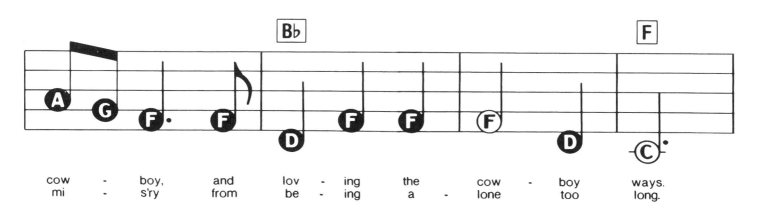

cow - boy, and lov - ing the cow - boy ways.
mi - s'ry and from be - ing a - lone boy too long.

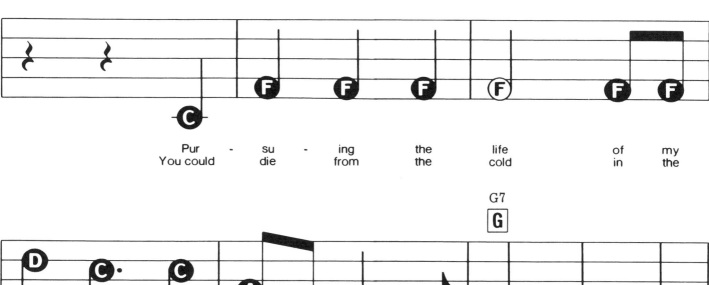

Pur - su - ing the life of my
You could die from the cold in the

high - rid - in' he - roes, _____ I burned up my
arms of a night - mare, _____ knowing well that your

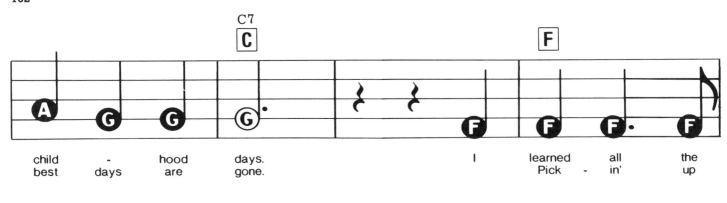

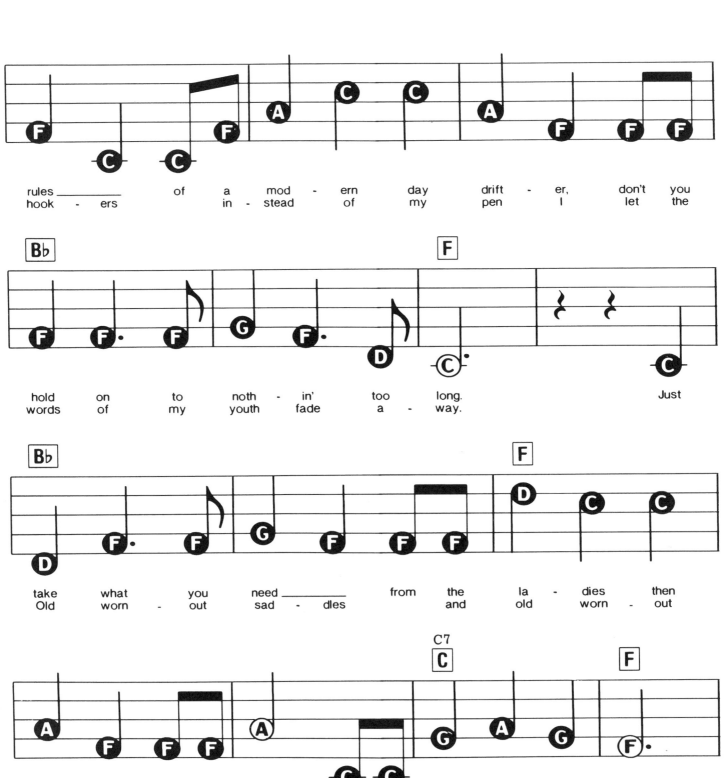

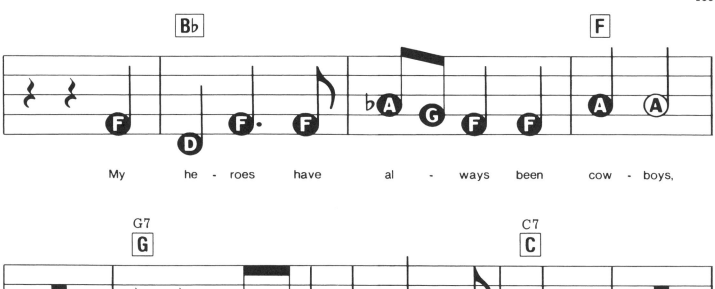

My he - roes have al - ways been cow - boys,

and they still are, it seems.

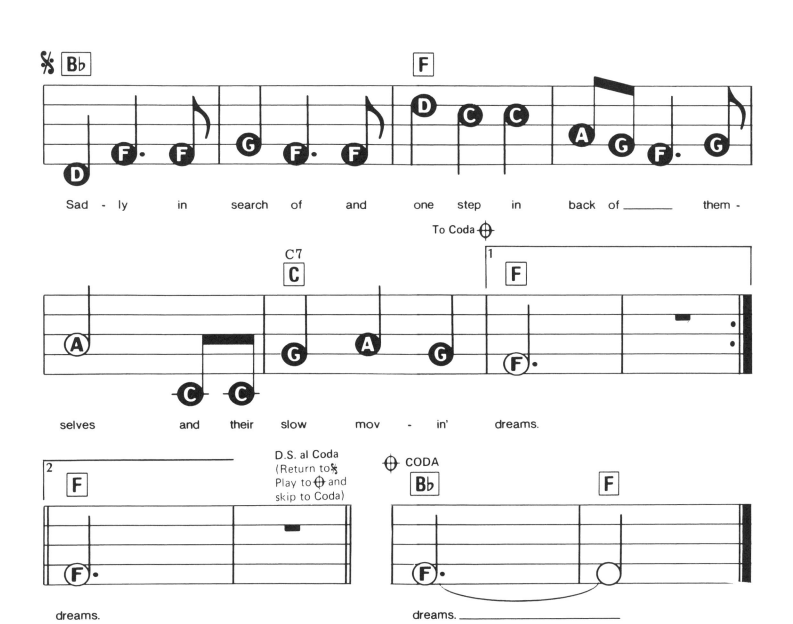

Sad - ly in search of and one step in back of _____ them -

To Coda ⊕

selves and their slow mov - in' dreams.

D.S. al Coda
(Return to 𝄋
Play to ⊕ and
skip to Coda)

⊕ CODA

dreams.

dreams. _____

My Woman My Woman My Wife

Registration 7
Rhythm: 8-Beat or Ballad

Words and Music by
Marty Robbins

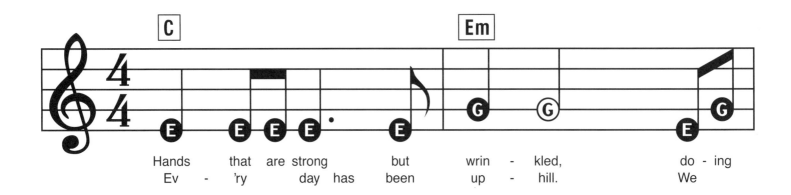

Hands that are strong but wrin - kled, do - ing
Ev - 'ry day has been up - hill. We

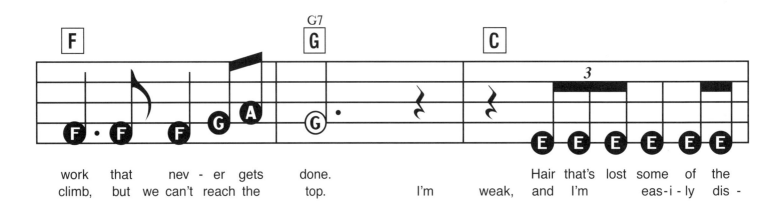

work that nev - er gets done. I'm weak, Hair that's lost some of the
climb, but we can't reach the top. and I'm eas-i - ly dis -

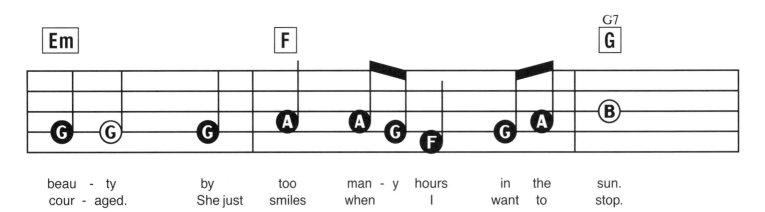

beau - ty by too man - y hours in the sun.
cour - aged. She just smiles when I want to stop.

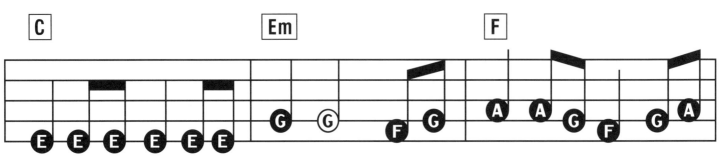

Eyes that show some dis - ap - point - ment, and there's been quite a lot in her
Lips that are wea - ry, but ten - der with love that strength - ens my

165

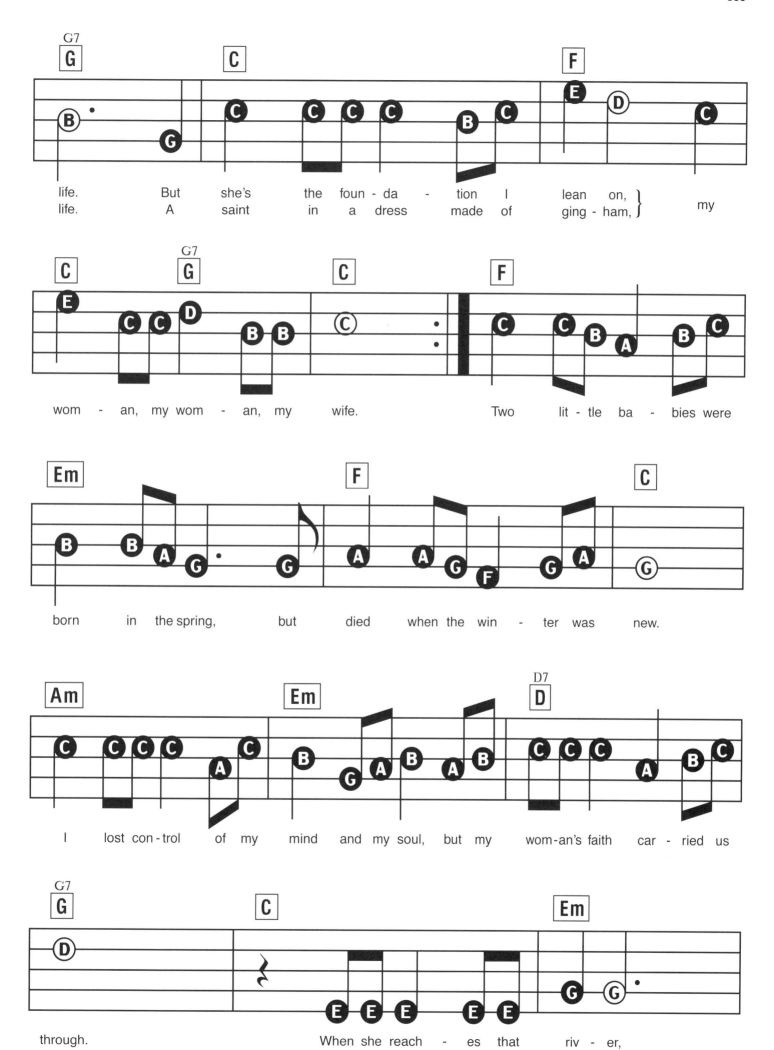

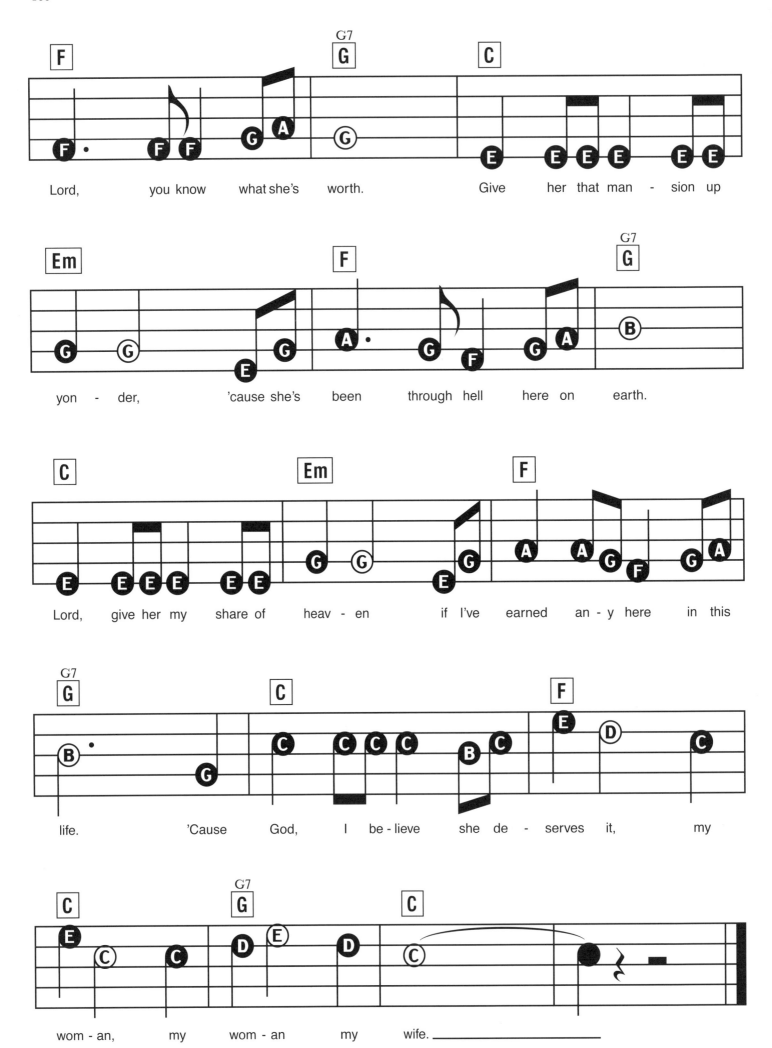

Nine to Five
from NINE TO FIVE

Registration 5
Rhythm: Rock

Words and Music by
Dolly Parton

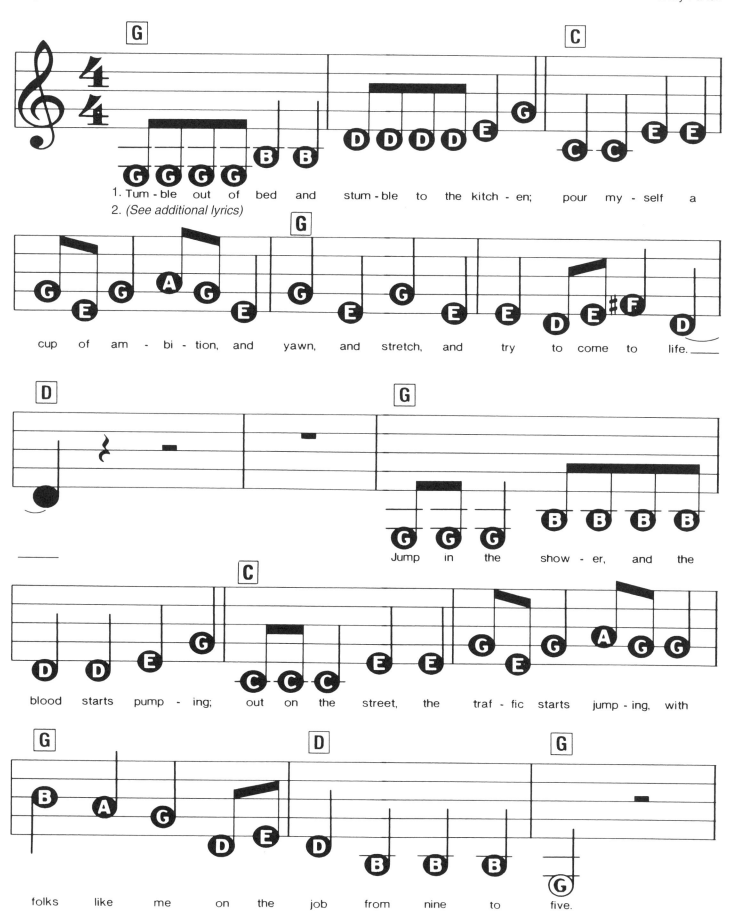

Chorus

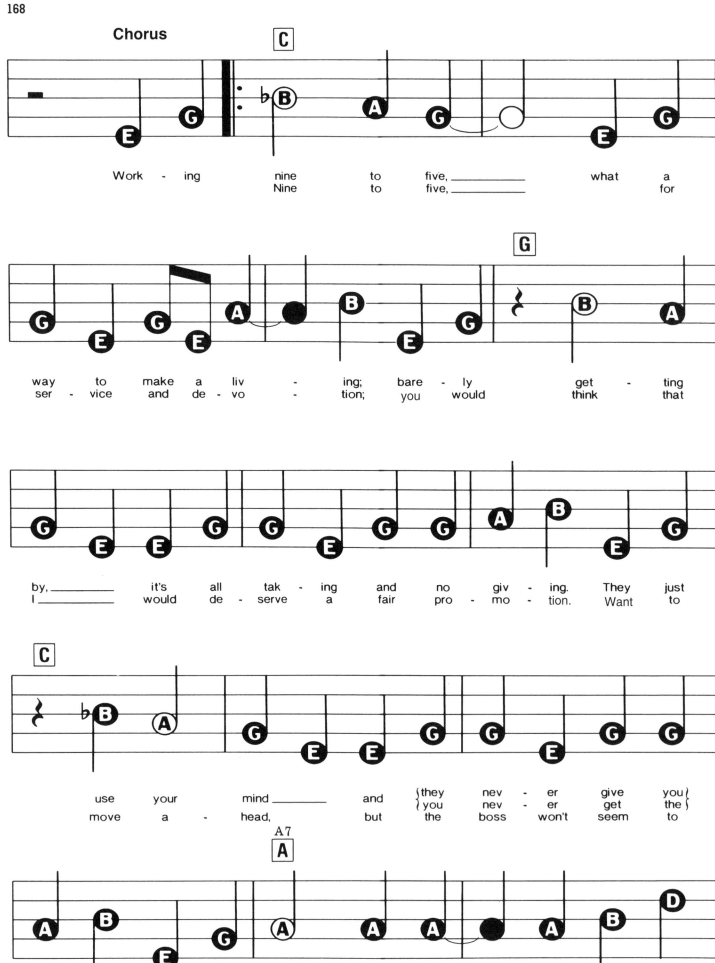

Work - ing nine to five, _____ what a
Nine to five, _____ for

way to make a liv - ing; bare - ly
ser - vice and de - vo - tion; you would

get - ting
think that

by, _____ it's all tak - ing and no giv - ing. They just
I _____ would de - serve a fair pro - mo - tion. Want to

use your mind _____ and {they nev - er give you}
move a - head, but the {you nev - er get the}
boss won't seem to

cred - it; it's e - nough to drive _____ you _____
let me. I swear some - times _____ that man is

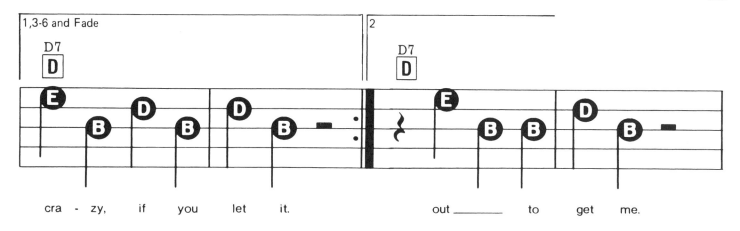

cra - zy, if you let it. out _____ to get me.

D.C. (Fade on Chorus)

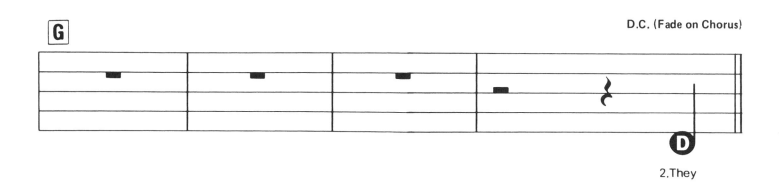

2. They

Additional Lyrics

Verse 2:

They let you dream just to watch them shatter;
You're just a step on the boss man's ladder,
But you've got dreams he'll never take away.
In the same boat with a lot of your friends;
Waitin' for the day your ship'll come in,
And the tide's gonna turn, and it's all gonna roll your way.
Chorus

Chorus 4,6:

Nine to five, they've got you where they want you;
There's a better life, and you dream about it, don't you?
It's a rich man's game, no matter what they call it;
And you spend your life putting money in his pocket.

Ocean Front Property

Registration 3
Rhythm: Country or Swing

Words and Music by Hank Cochran,
Royce Porter and Dean Dillon

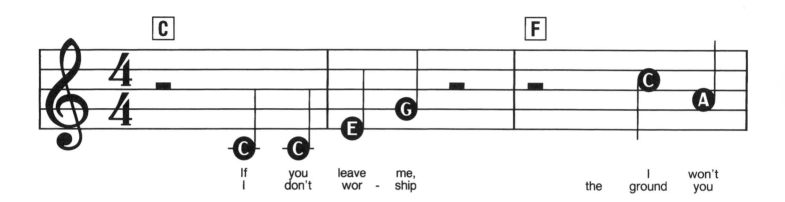

If you leave me,
I don't wor - ship

the I won't
the ground you

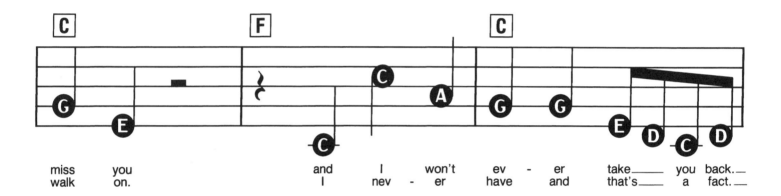

miss you
walk on.

and I won't ev - er take____ you back.____
I nev - er have and that's____ a fact.____

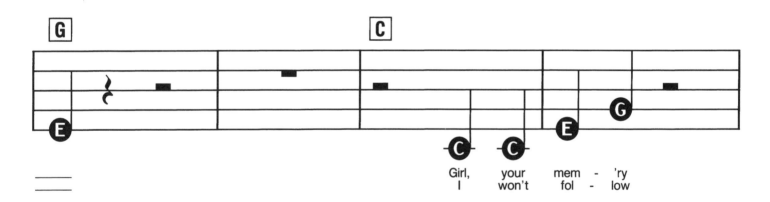

Girl, your mem - 'ry
I won't fol - low

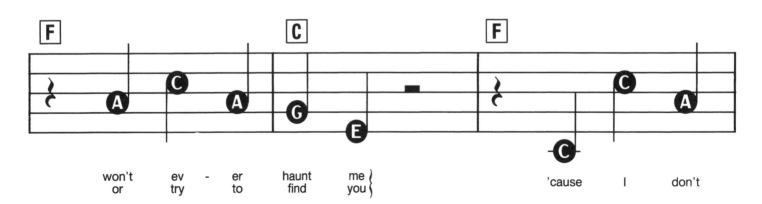

won't ev - er haunt me
or try to find you

'cause I don't

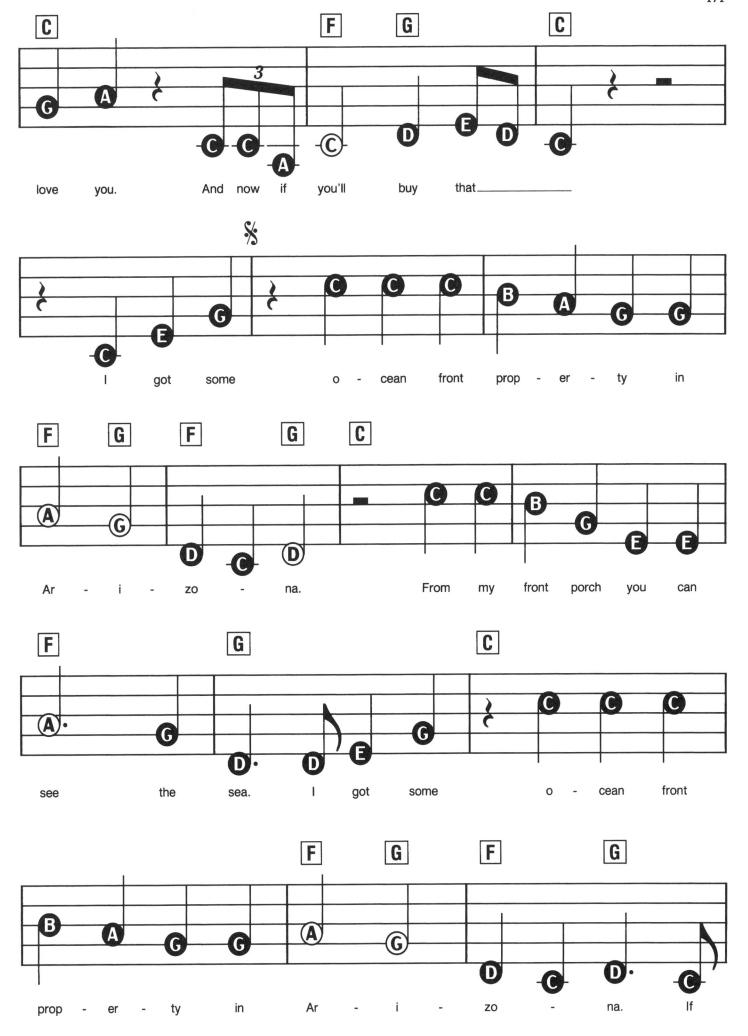

On the Other Hand

Registration 4
Rhythm: Country

Words and Music by Don Schlitz
and Paul Overstreet

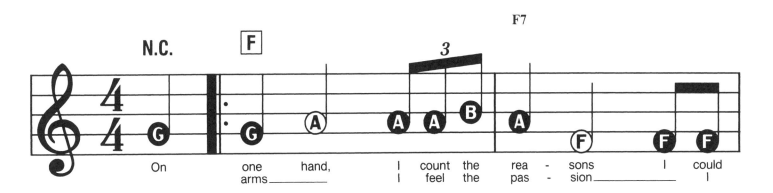

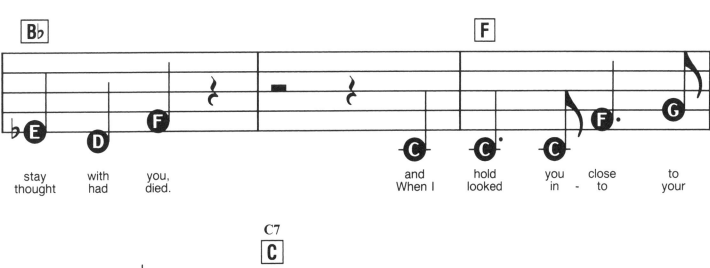

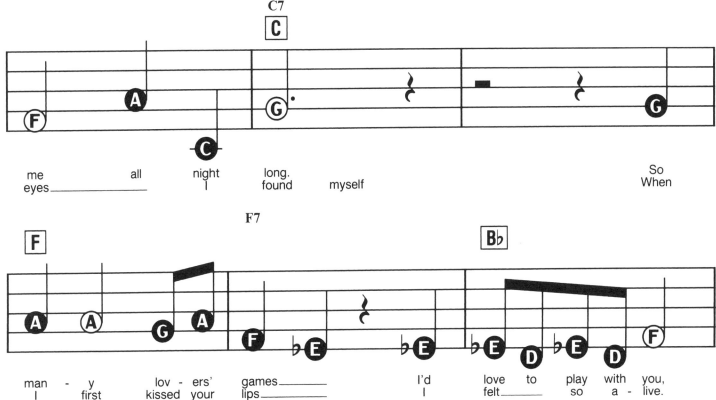

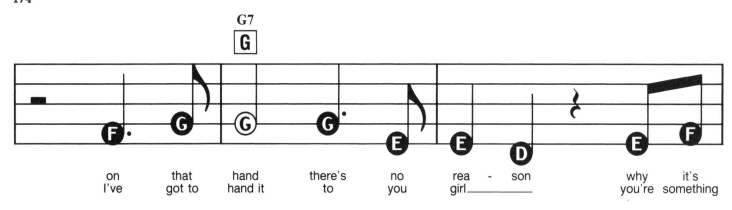

on that hand there's no reason why it's
I've got to hand it to you girl_____ you're something

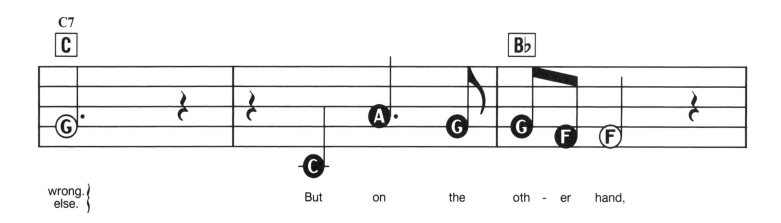

wrong.
else. But on the oth - er hand,

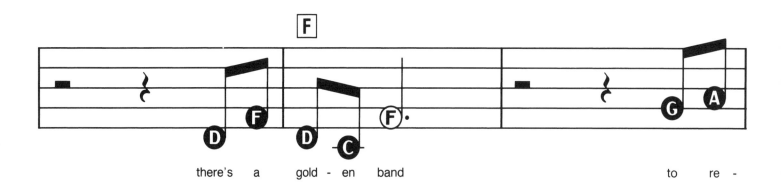

there's a gold - en band to re -

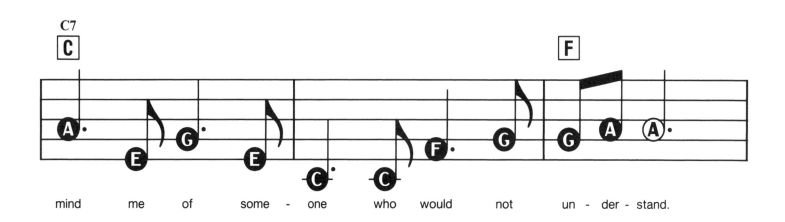

mind me of some - one who would not un - der - stand.

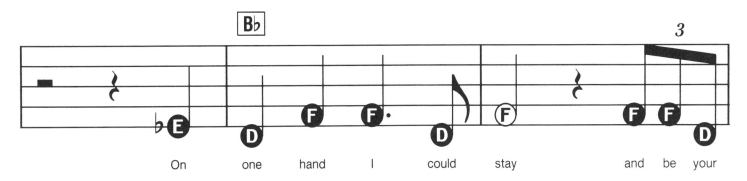

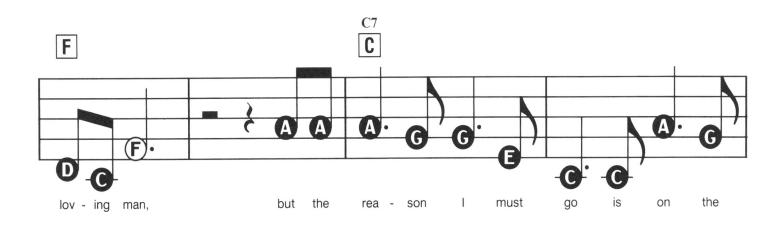

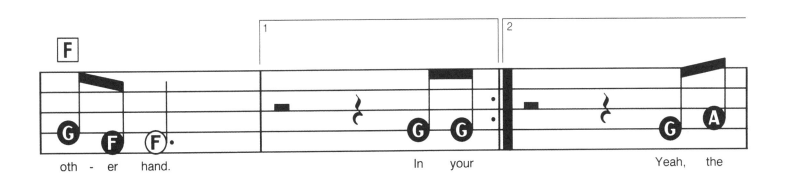

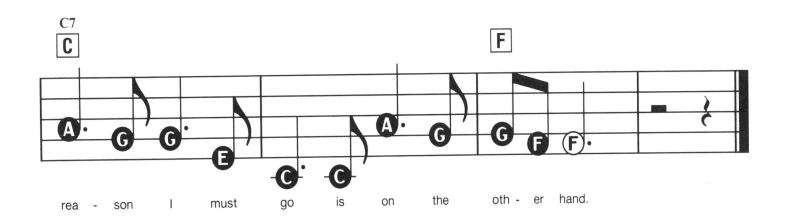

Old Dogs, Children and Watermelon Wine

Registration 5
Rhythm: Country Western

Words and Music by
Tom T. Hall

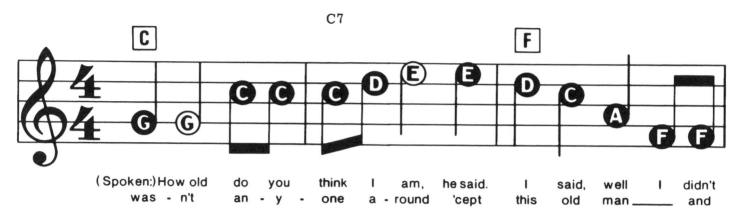

(Spoken:) How old do you think I am, he said. I said, well I didn't
was - n't an - y - one a - round 'cept this old man _____ and

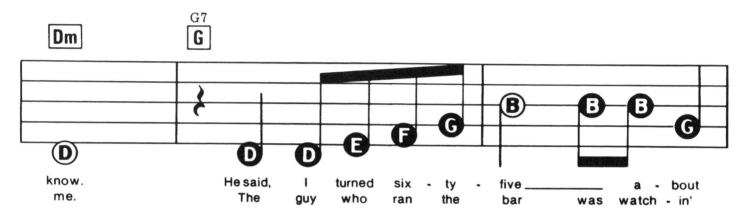

know. He said, I turned six - ty - five _____ a - bout
me. The guy who ran the bar was watch - in'

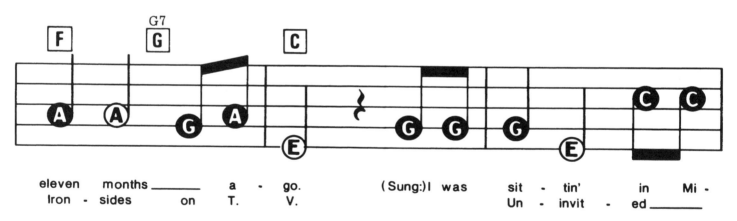

eleven months _____ a - go. (Sung:) I was sit - tin' in Mi -
Iron - sides on T. V. Un - invit - ed _____

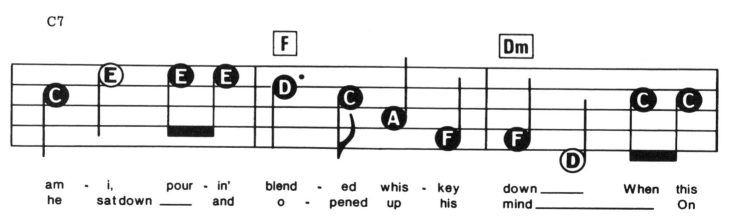

am - i, pour - in' blend - ed whis - key down _____ When this
he sat down _____ and o - pened up his mind _____ On

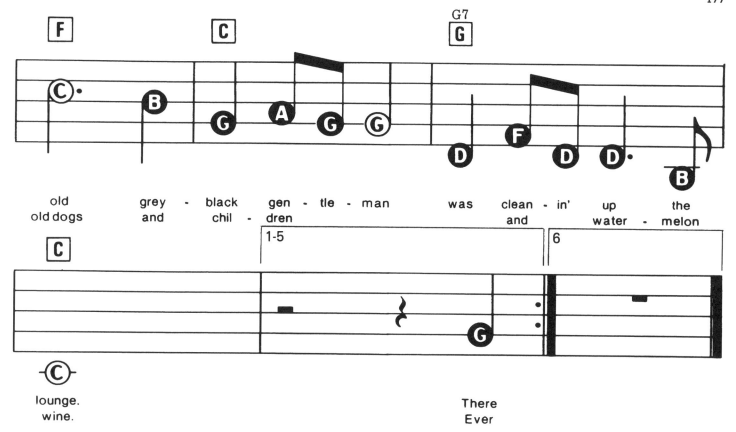

old   grey - black   gen - tle - man   was   clean - in'   up   the
old dogs   and   chil - dren   and   water - melon

lounge.
wine.

There
Ever

3. Ever had a drink of watermelon wine? He asked
   He told me all about it though I didn't answer back.
   Ain't but three things in this world that's worth a solitary dime,
   But old dogs-children and watermelon wine.

4. He said women think about theyselves when menfolk ain't around,
   And friends are hard to find when they discover that you down.
   He said I tried it all when I was young and in my natural prime;
   Now it's old dogs-children and watermelon wine.

5. Old dogs care about you even when you make mistakes.
   God bless little children while they're still too young to hate.
   When he moved away, I found my pen and copied down that line
   'Bout old dogs and children and watermelon wine.

6. I had to catch a plane up to Atlanta that next day,
   As I left for my room I saw him pickin' up my change.
   That night I dreamed in peaceful sleep of shady summertime
   Of old dogs and children and watermelon wine.

On the Road Again

Registration 7
Rhythm: Swing

Words and Music by
Willie Nelson

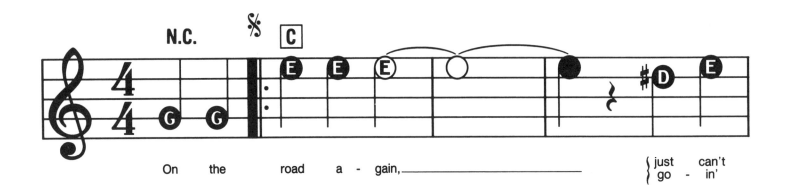

On the road a - gain,_____ { just can't
                                    go - in'

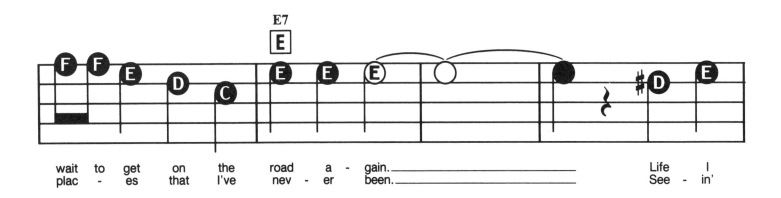

wait to get on the road a - gain._____ Life I
plac - es on that I've nev - er been._____ See - in'

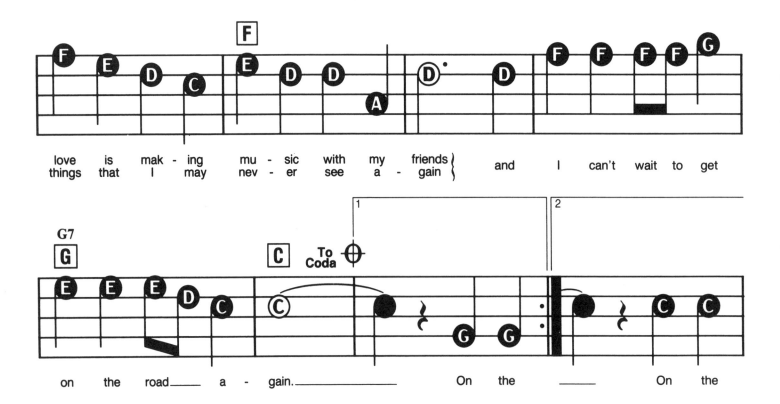

love is mak - ing mu - sic with my friends } and I can't wait to get
things that I may nev - er see a - gain

on the road___ a - gain.___ On the ___ On the

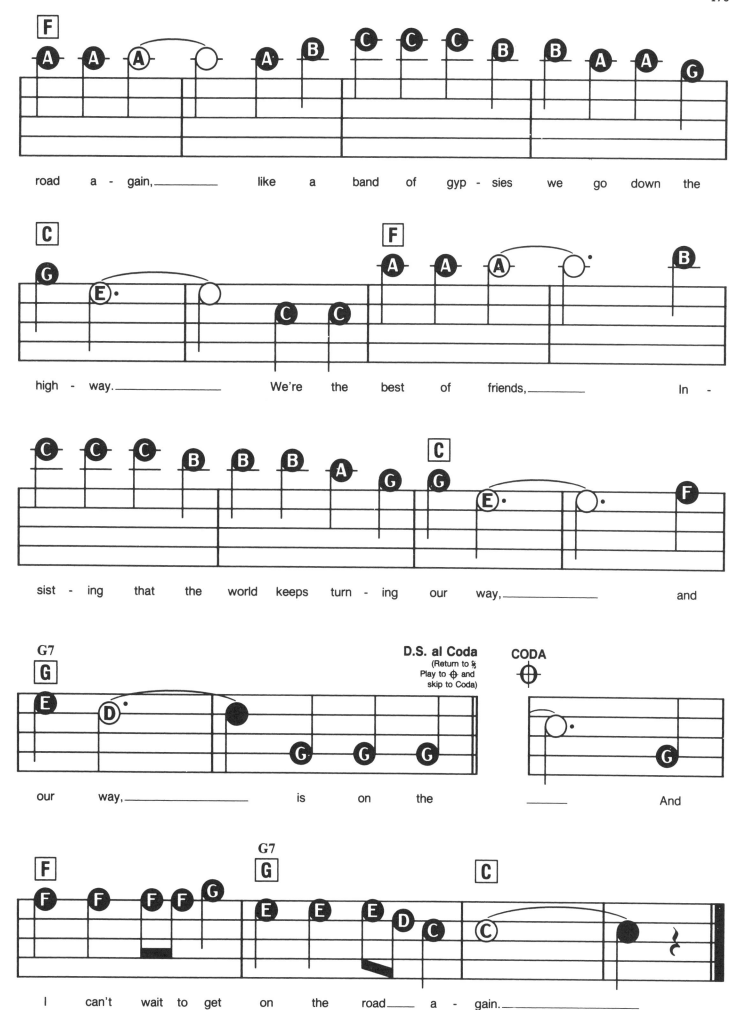

Pickin' Wildflowers

Registration 8
Rhythm: Country Rock or Country Pop

Words and Music by Keith Anderson,
Kim Williams and John Rich

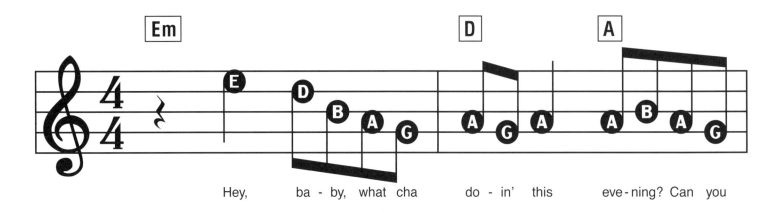

Hey, ba - by, what cha do - in' this eve - ning? Can you

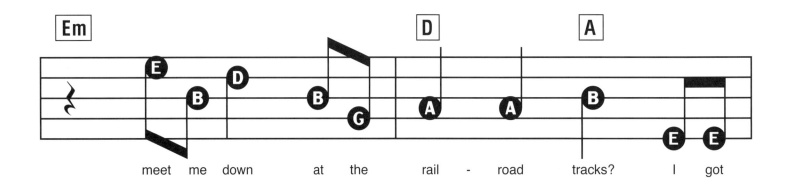

meet me down at the rail - road tracks? I got

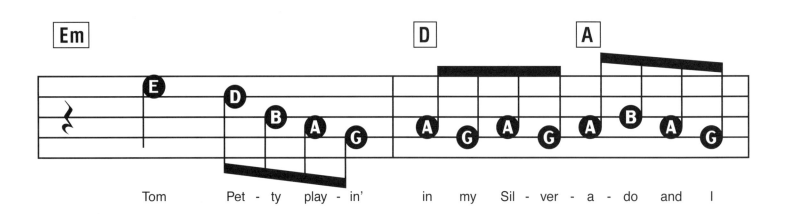

Tom Pet - ty play - in' in my Sil - ver - a - do and I

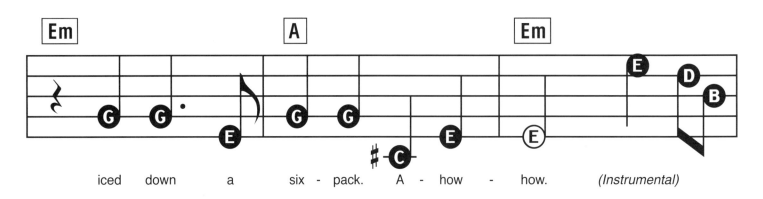

iced down a six - pack. A - how - how. *(Instrumental)*

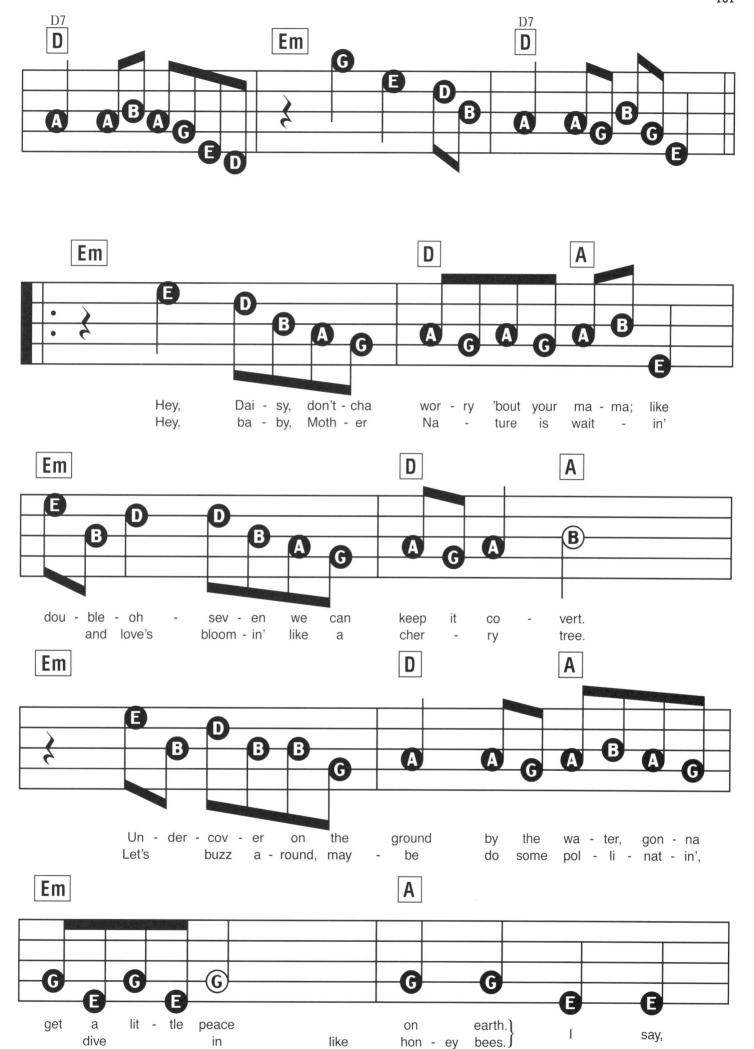

182

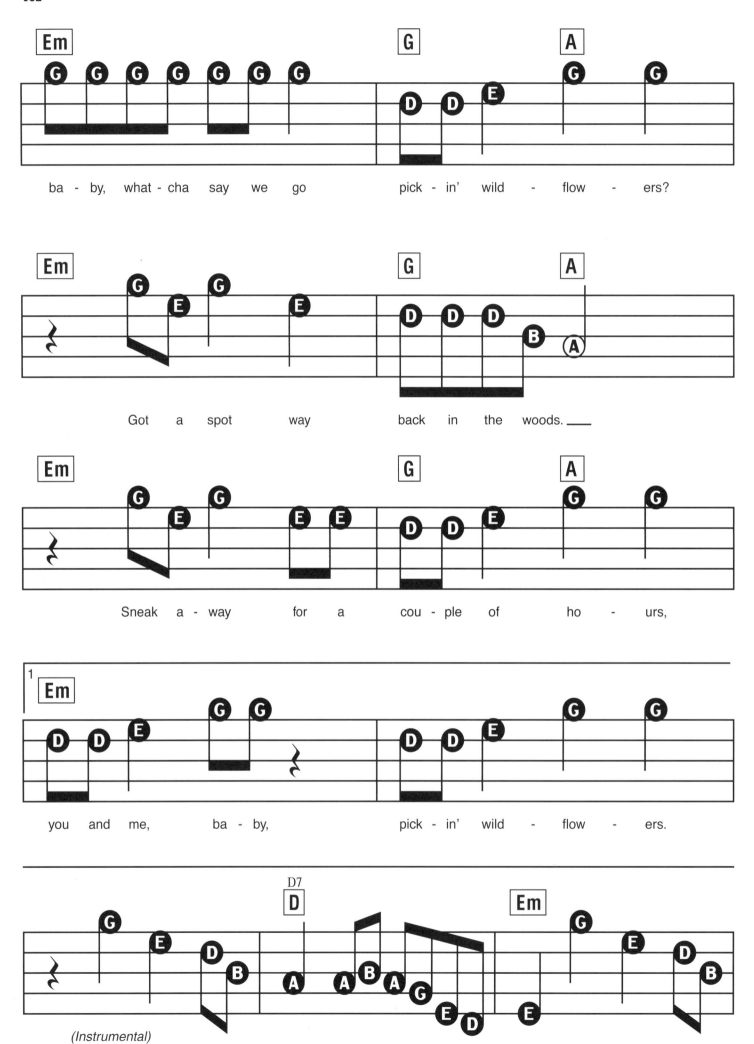

ba - by, what - cha say we go pick - in' wild - flow - ers?

Got a spot way back in the woods. ___

Sneak a - way for a cou - ple of ho - urs,

you and me, ba - by, pick - in' wild - flow - ers.

(Instrumental)

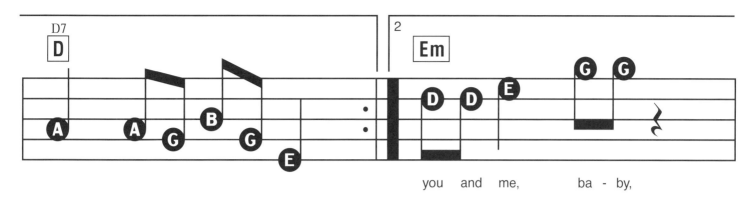

you and me, ba - by,

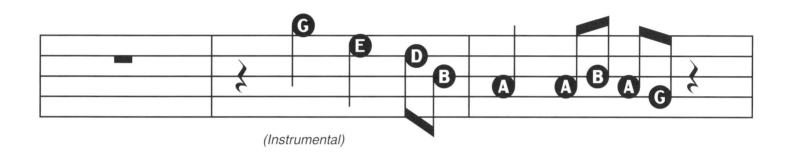

(Instrumental)

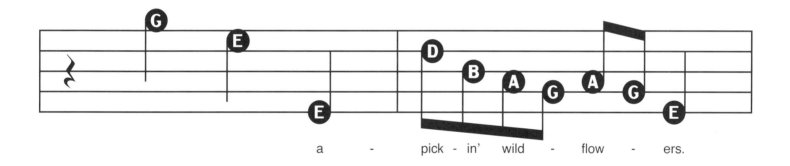

a - pick - in' wild - flow - ers.

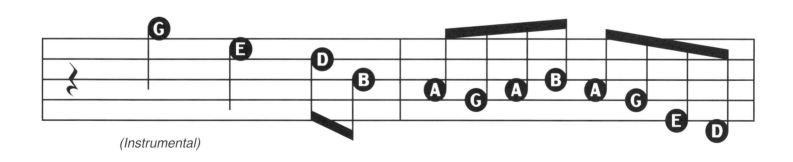

(Instrumental)

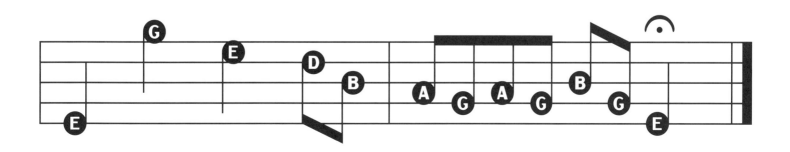

A Rainy Night in Georgia

Registration 5
Rhythm: Ballad or Fox Trot

Words and Music by
Tony Joe White

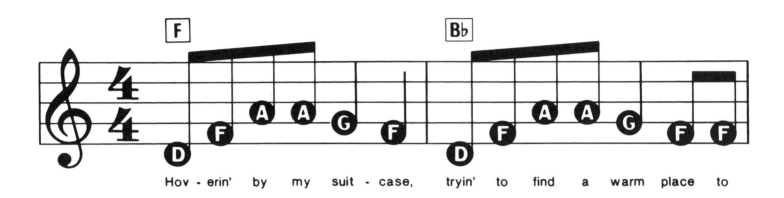

Hov - erin' by my suit - case, tryin' to find a warm place to

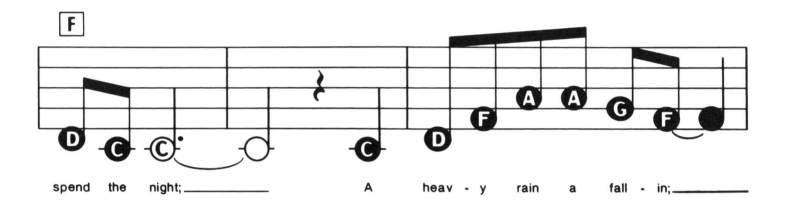

spend the night;_____ A heav - y rain a fall - in;_____

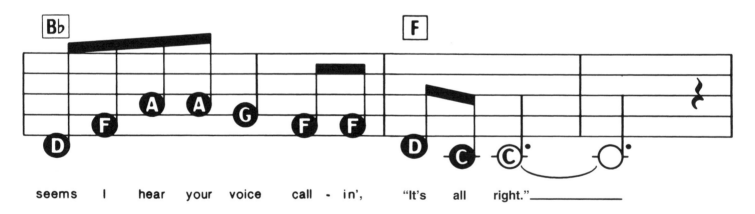

seems I hear your voice call - in', "It's all right."_____

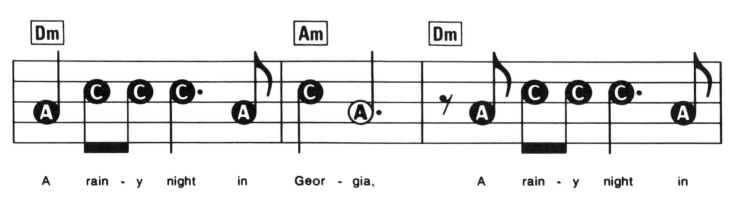

A rain - y night in Geor - gia, A rain - y night in

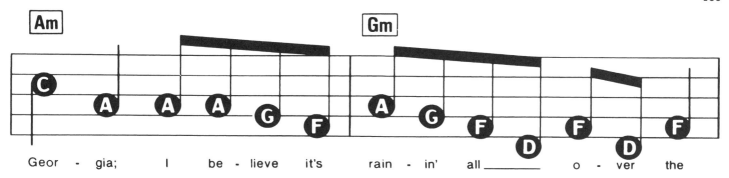

Geor - gia; I be - lieve it's rain - in' all _____ o - ver the

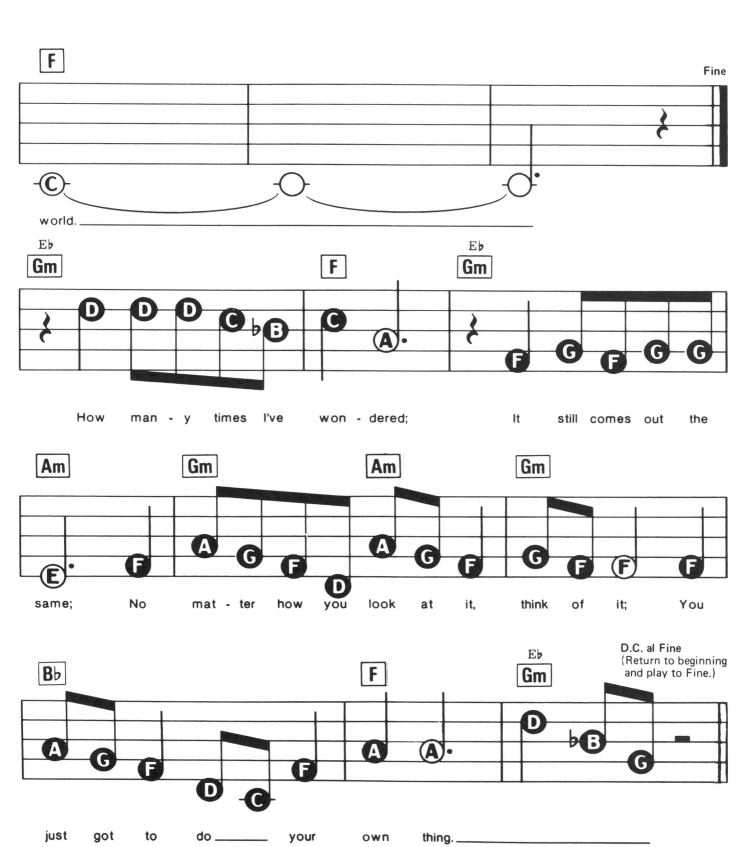

world. _____

How man - y times I've won - dered; It still comes out the

same; No mat - ter how you look at it, think of it; You

D.C. al Fine
(Return to beginning
and play to Fine.)

just got to do _____ your own thing. _____

Ring of Fire

Registration 3
Rhythm: Rock

Words and Music by Merle Kilgore
and June Carter

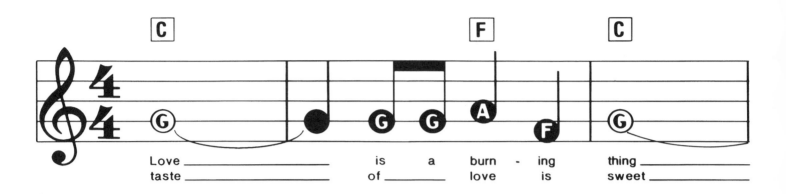

Love _____ is a burn - ing thing _____
taste _____ of _____ love is sweet _____

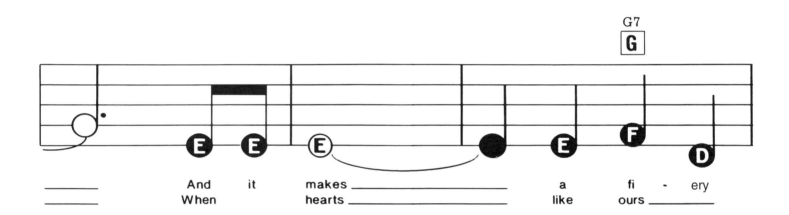

_____ And it makes _____ a fi - ery
_____ When hearts _____ like ours _____

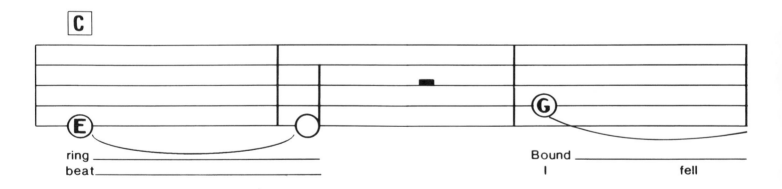

ring _____
beat _____   Bound _____
                                   I   fell

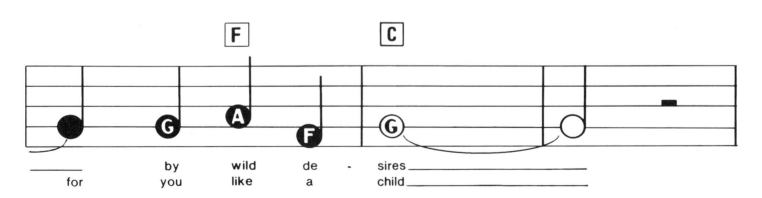

_____ by wild de - sires _____
for   you like a child _____

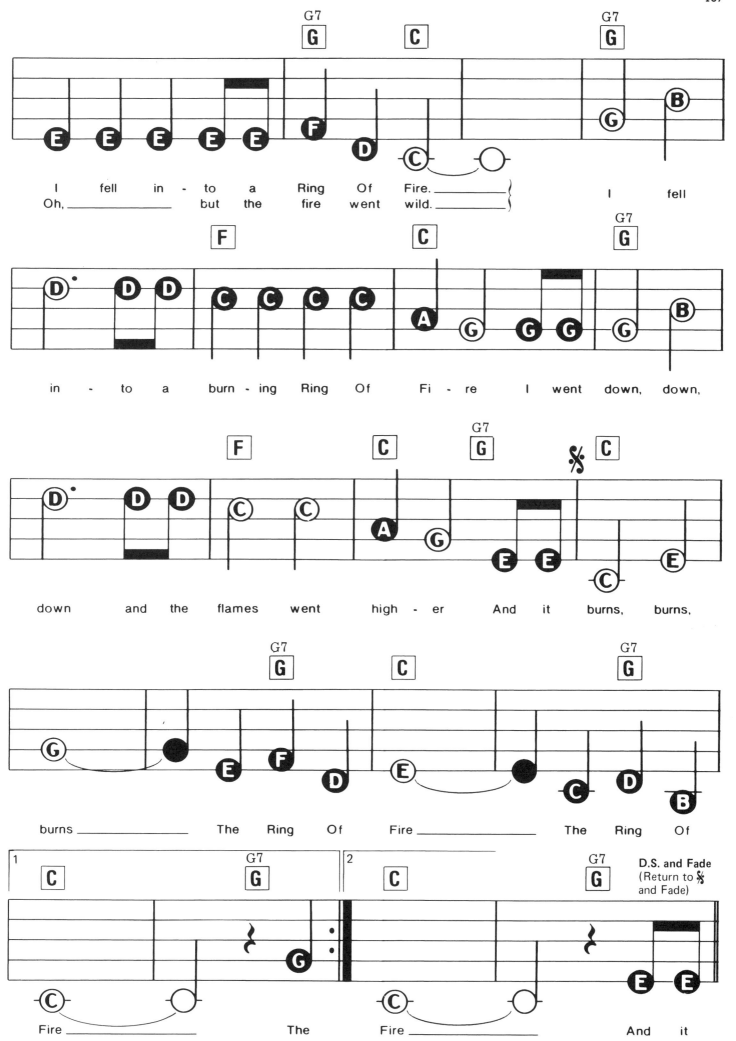

Rocky Top

Registration 8
Rhythm: Western

Words and Music by Boudleaux Bryant
and Felice Bryant

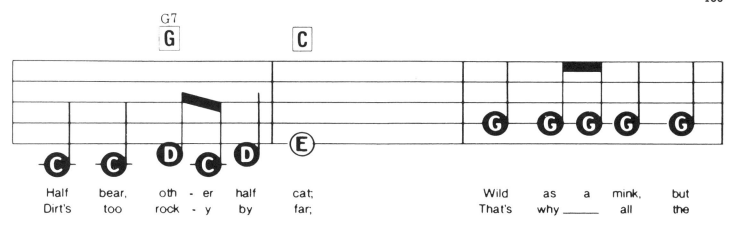

Half bear, oth - er half cat;
Dirt's too rock - y by far;

Wild as a mink, but
That's why _____ all the

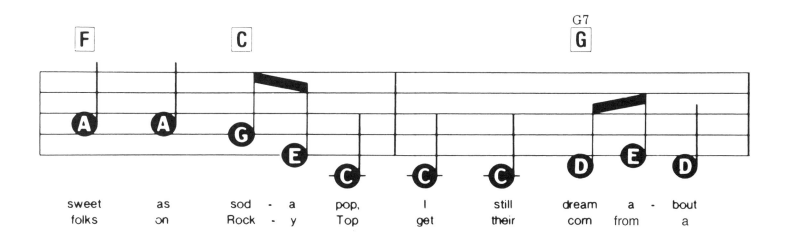

sweet as sod - a pop, I still dream a - bout
folks on Rock - y Top get their corn from a

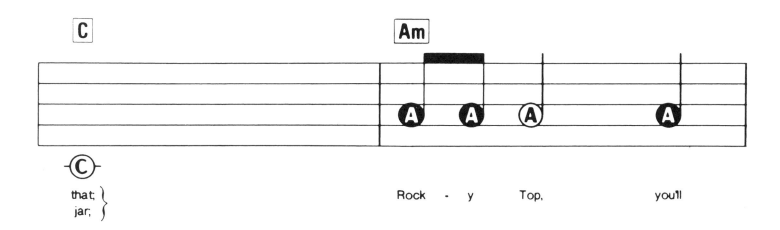

that; }
jar; }

Rock - y Top, you'll

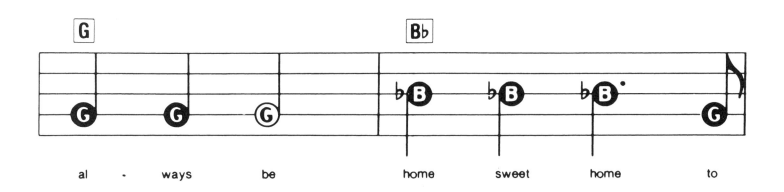

al - ways be home sweet home to

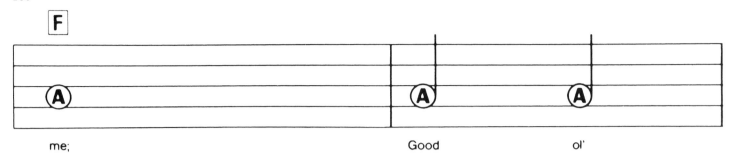

me;　　　　　　　　　Good　　　　ol'

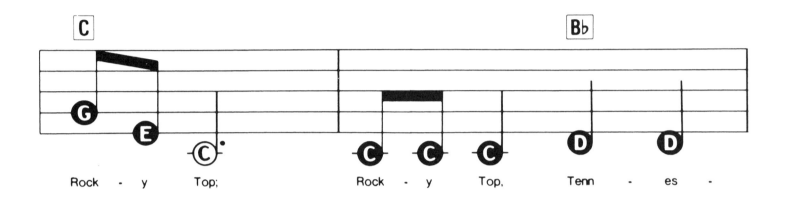

Rock - y　Top;　　　Rock - y　Top,　Tenn - es -

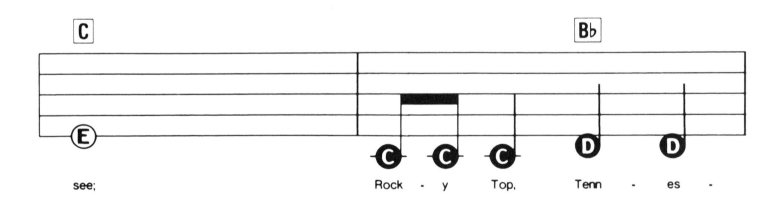

see;　　　　　　　　Rock - y　Top,　Tenn - es -

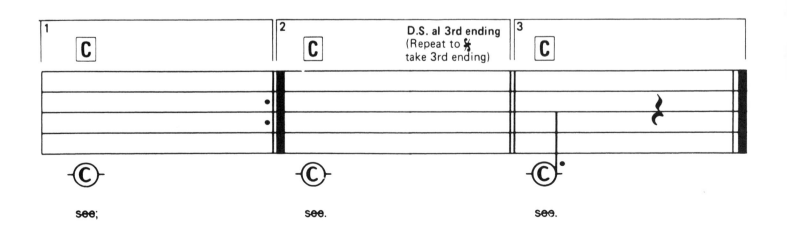

see;　　　　　　　see.　　　　　　see.

Saginaw, Michigan

Registration 8
Rhythm: Country

Words and Music by Don Wayne
and Bill Anderson

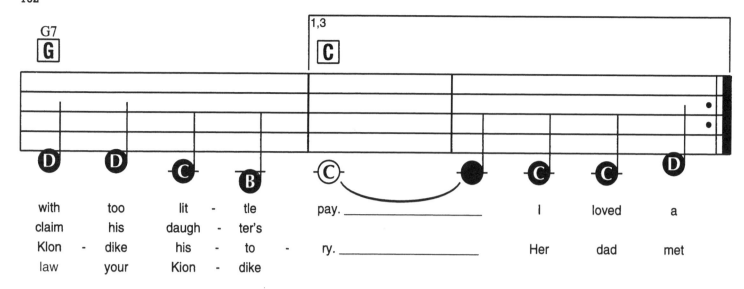

with too lit - tle pay. _____ I loved a
claim his daugh - ter's Klon - dike his - to - ry. _____ Her dad met
law your Kion - dike

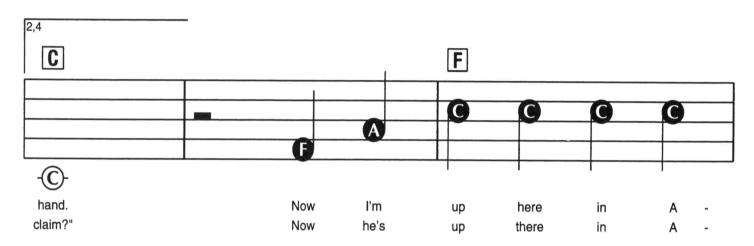

hand. Now I'm up here in A -
claim?" Now he's up there in A -

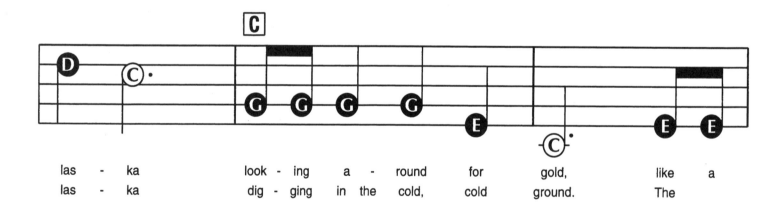

las - ka look - ing a - round for gold, like a
las - ka dig - ging in the cold, cold ground. The

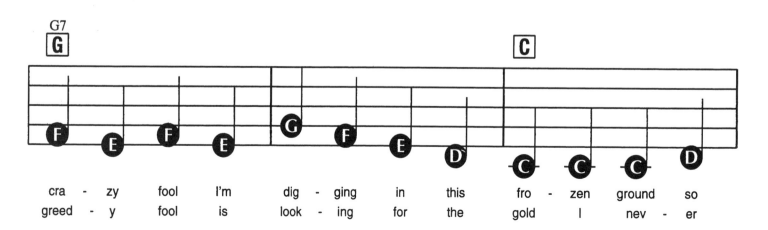

cra - zy fool I'm dig - ging in this fro - zen ground so
greed - y fool is look - ing for the gold I nev - er

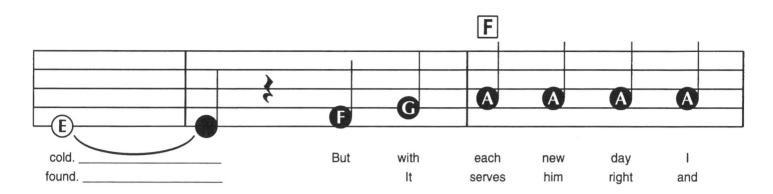

cold. _____ But with each new day I
found. _____ It serves him right and

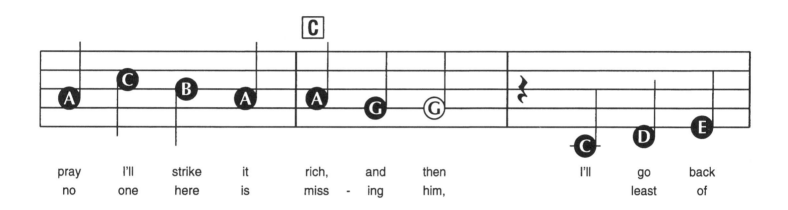

pray I'll strike it rich, and then I'll go back
no one here is miss - ing him, least of

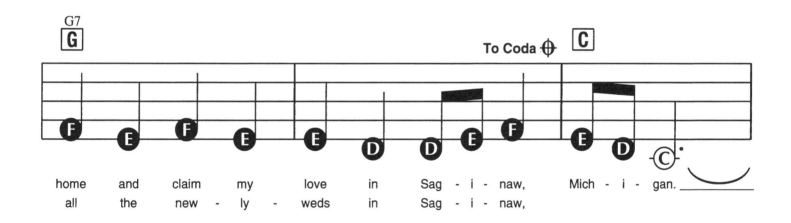

home and claim my love in Sag - i - naw, Mich - i - gan. _____
all the new - ly - weds in Sag - i - naw,

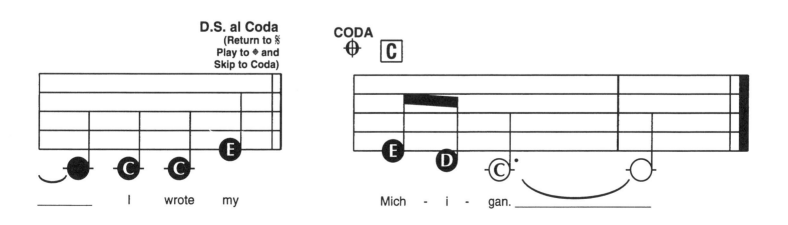

D.S. al Coda
(Return to %
Play to ⊕ and
Skip to Coda)

_____ I wrote my

CODA
⊕

Mich - i - gan. _____

Shameless

Registration 8
Rhythm: Rock

Words and Music by
Billy Joel

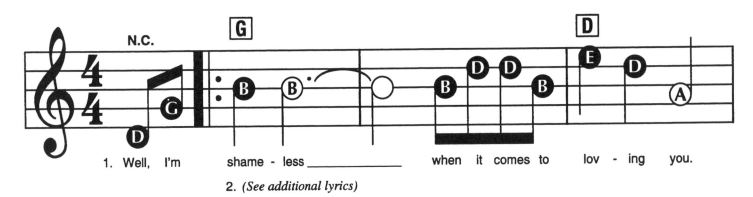

1. Well, I'm shame - less _____ when it comes to lov - ing you.

2. *(See additional lyrics)*

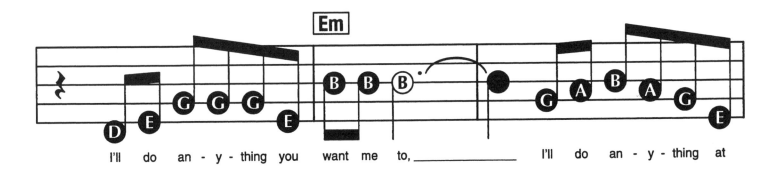

I'll do an - y - thing you want me to, _____ I'll do an - y - thing at

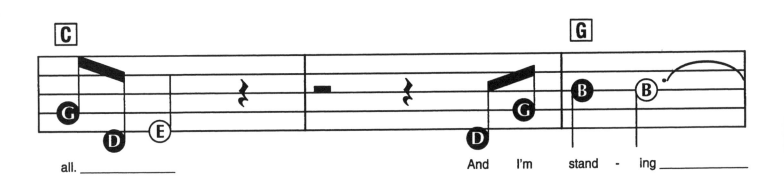

all. _____ And I'm stand - ing _____

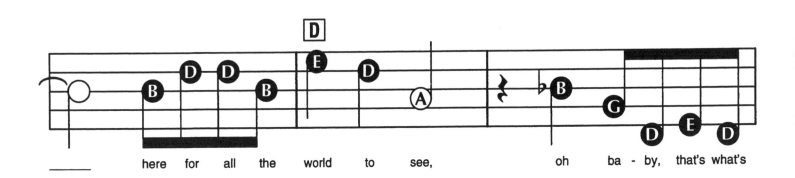

_____ here for all the world to see, oh ba - by, that's what's

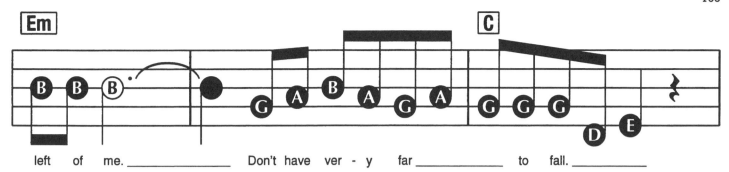

left of me. _____ Don't have ver - y far _____ to fall. _____

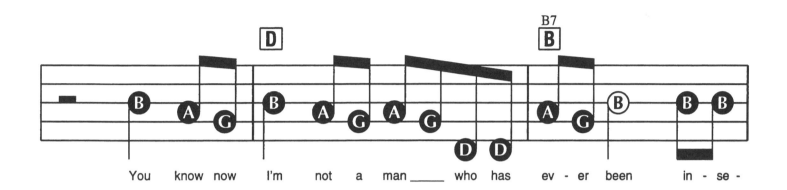

You know now I'm not a man _____ who has ev - er been in - se -

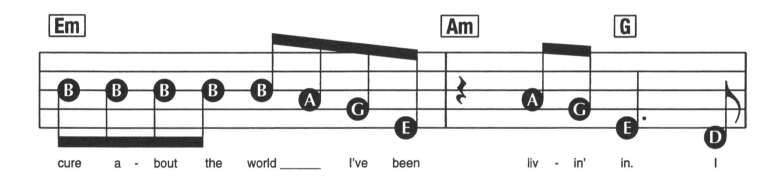

cure a - bout the world _____ I've been liv - in' in. I

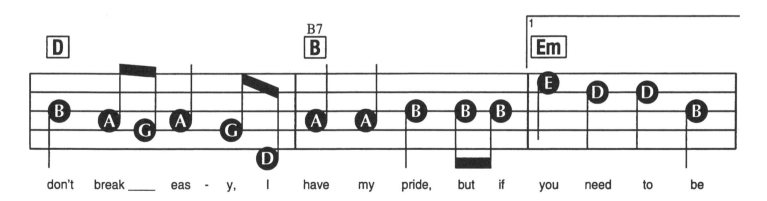

don't break ____ eas - y, I have my pride, but if you need to be

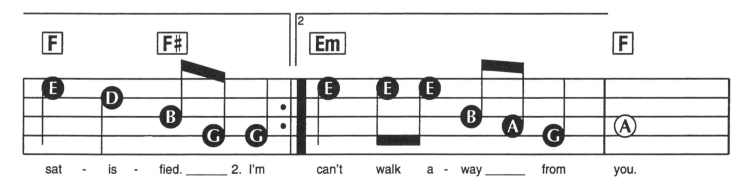

sat - is - fied. _____ 2. I'm can't walk a - way _____ from you.

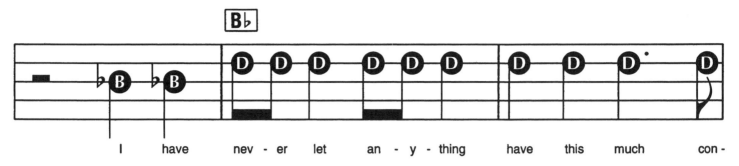

I have nev - er let an - y - thing have this much con -

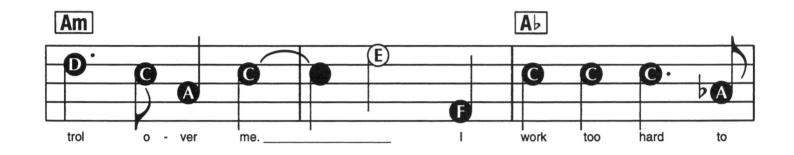

trol o - ver me. _____ I work too hard to

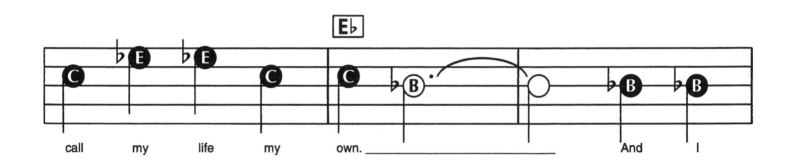

call my life my own. _____ And I

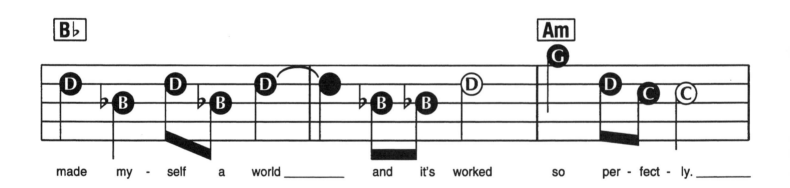

made my - self a world _____ and it's worked so per - fect - ly. _____

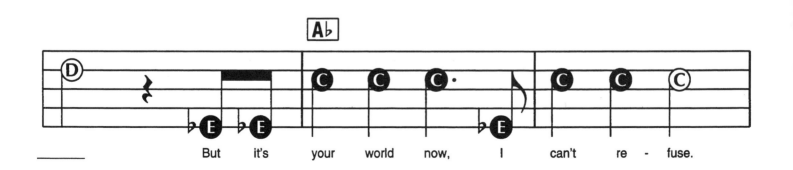

_____ But it's your world now, I can't re - fuse.

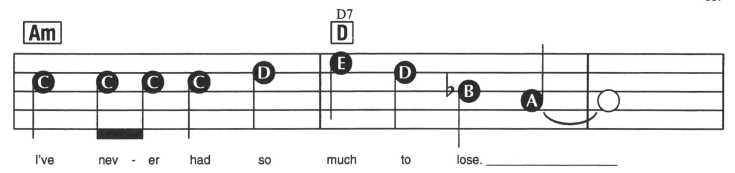

I've nev - er had so much to lose. _____

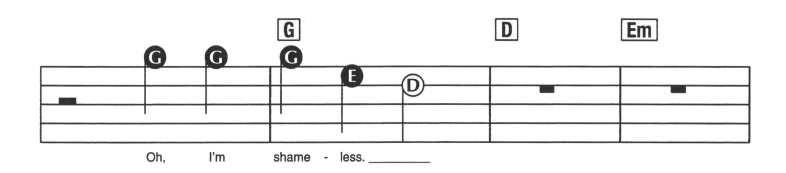

Oh, I'm shame - less. _____

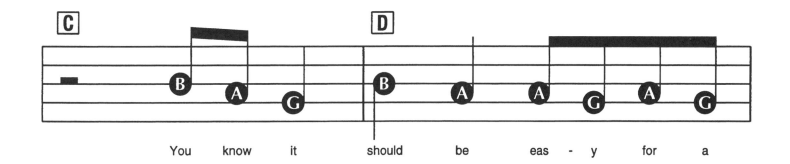

You know it should be eas - y for a

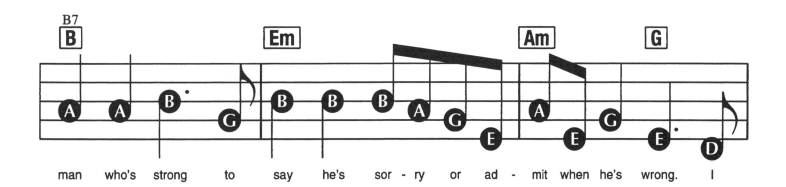

man who's strong to say he's sor - ry or ad - mit when he's wrong. I

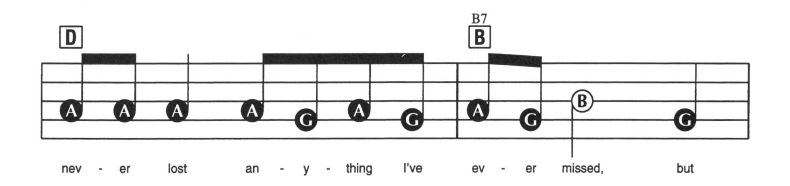

nev - er lost an - y - thing I've ev - er missed, but

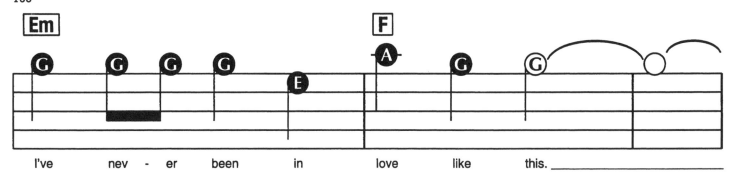

I've nev - er been in love like this. _____

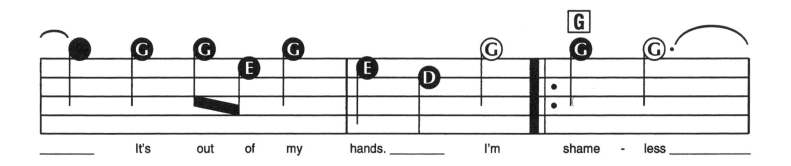

_____ It's out of my hands. _____ I'm shame - less _____

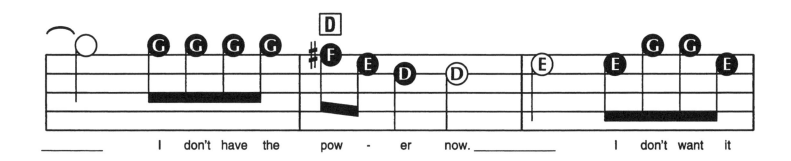

_____ I don't have the pow - er now. _____ I don't want it

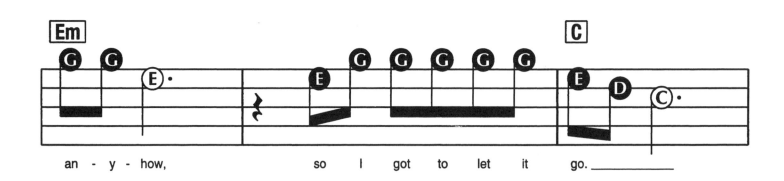

an - y - how, so I got to let it go. _____

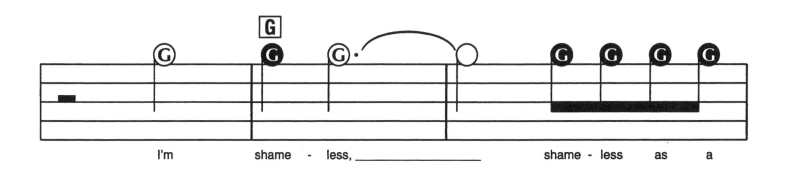

I'm shame - less, _____ shame - less as a

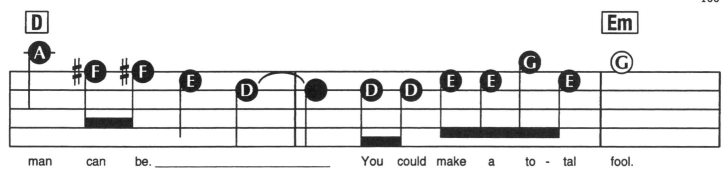

man   can   be. _____   You   could   make   a   to - tal   fool.

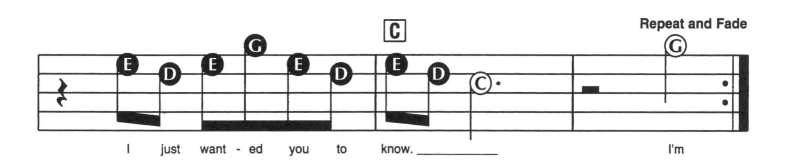

I   just   want - ed   you   to   know. _____   I'm

Additional Lyrics

2. I'm shameless, oh honey, I don't have a prayer.
    Every time I see you standing there,
    I go down upon my knees.
    And I'm changing, swore I'd never compromise.
    Oh, but you convinced me otherwise.
    I'll do anything you please.
    You see, in all my life I've never found
    What I couldn't resist, what I couldn't turn down.
    I could walk away from anyone I ever knew,
    But I can't walk away from you.

She Believes in Me

Registration 5
Rhythm: Ballad

Words and Music by
Steve Gibb

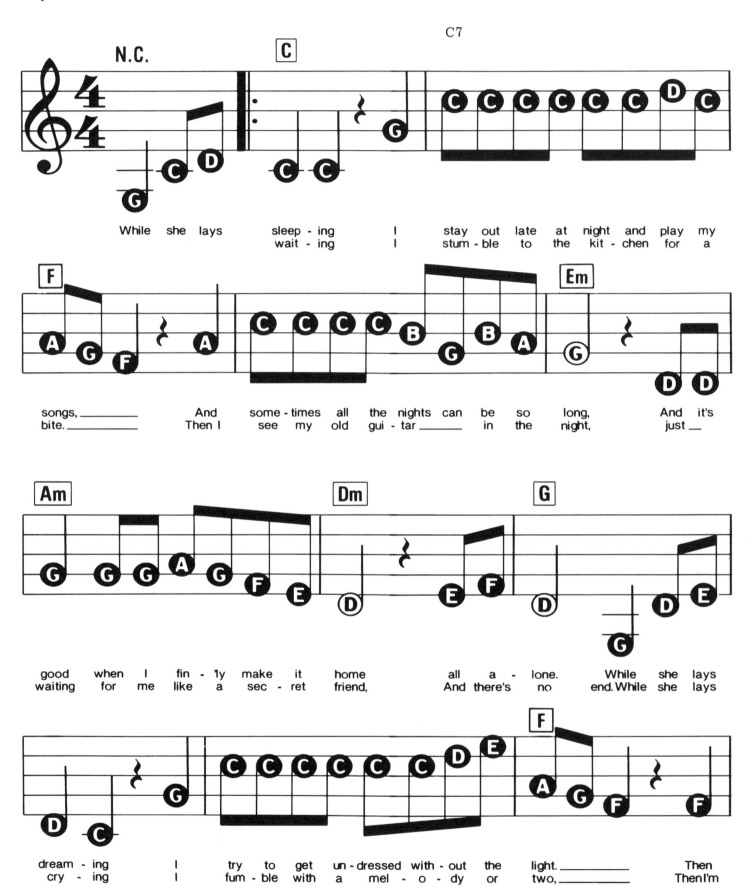

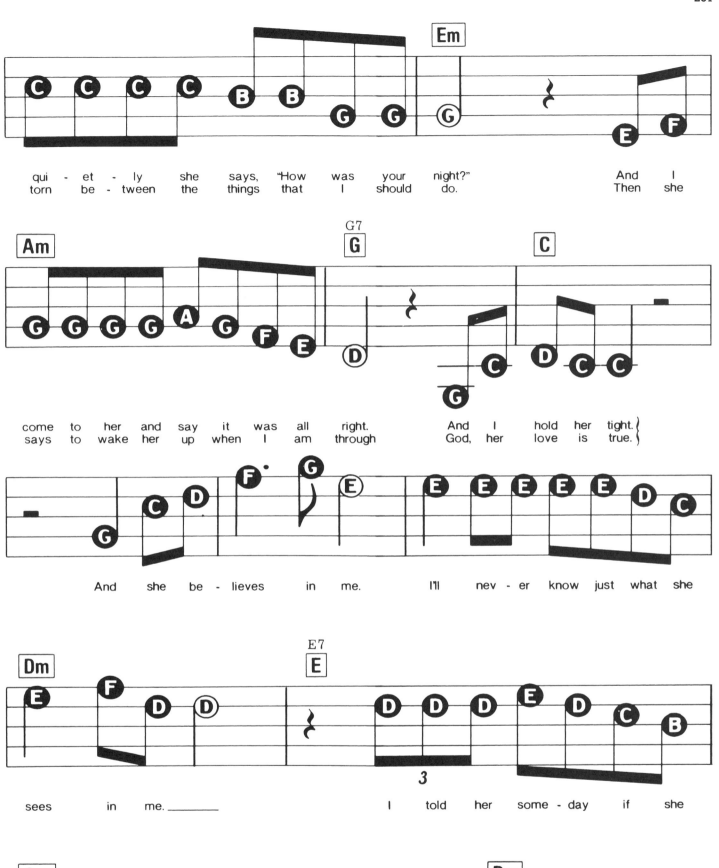

quiet - ly she says, "How was your night?"
torn be - tween the things that I should do.

And I
Then she

come to her and say it was all right.
says to wake her up when I am through

And I hold her tight.
God, her love is true.

And she be - lieves in me. I'll nev - er know just what she

sees in me. _____ I told her some - day if she

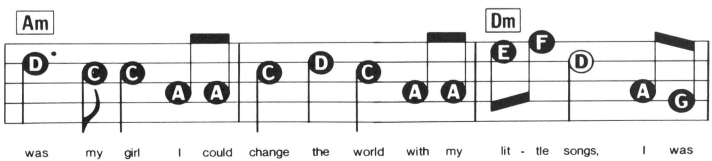

was my girl I could change the world with my lit - tle songs, I was

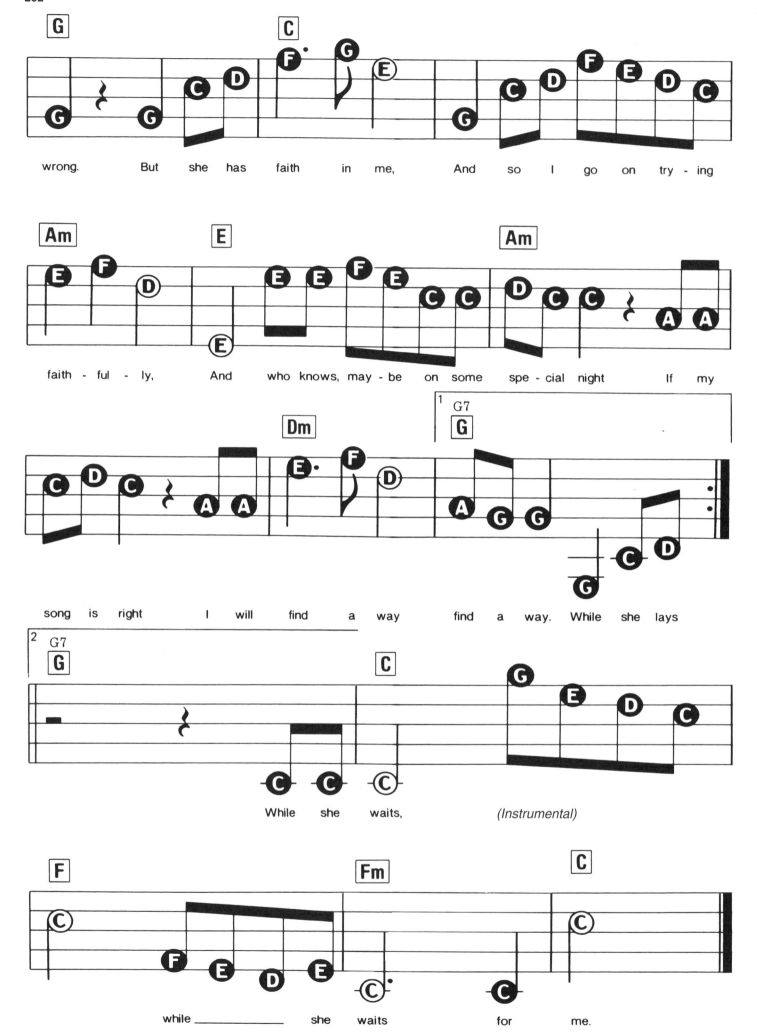

Singing the Blues

Registration 9
Rhythm: Shuffle

Words and Music by
Melvin Endsley

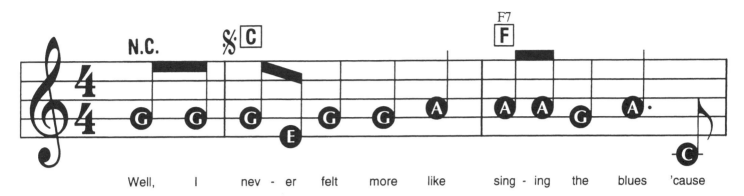

Well, I nev - er felt more like sing - ing the blues 'cause

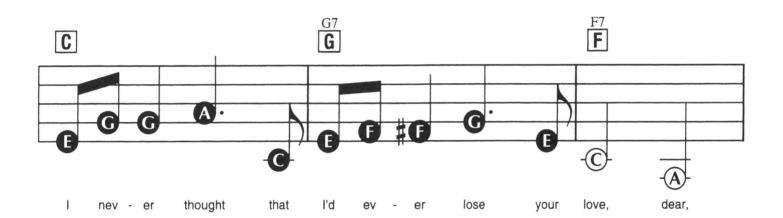

I nev - er thought that I'd ev - er lose your love, dear,

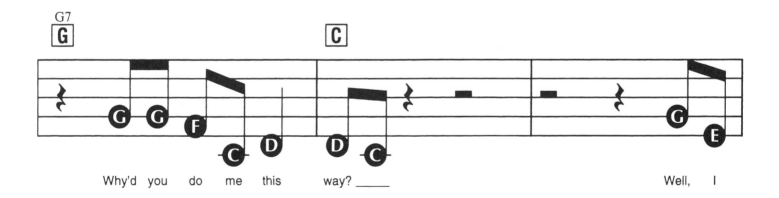

Why'd you do me this way? _____ Well, I

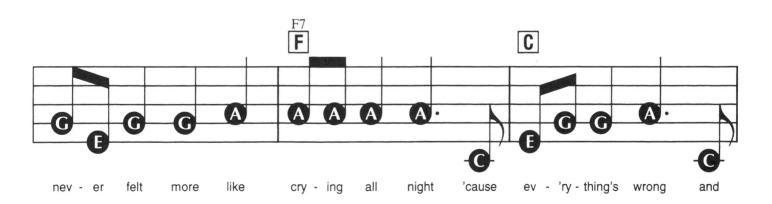

nev - er felt more like cry - ing all night 'cause ev - 'ry - thing's wrong and

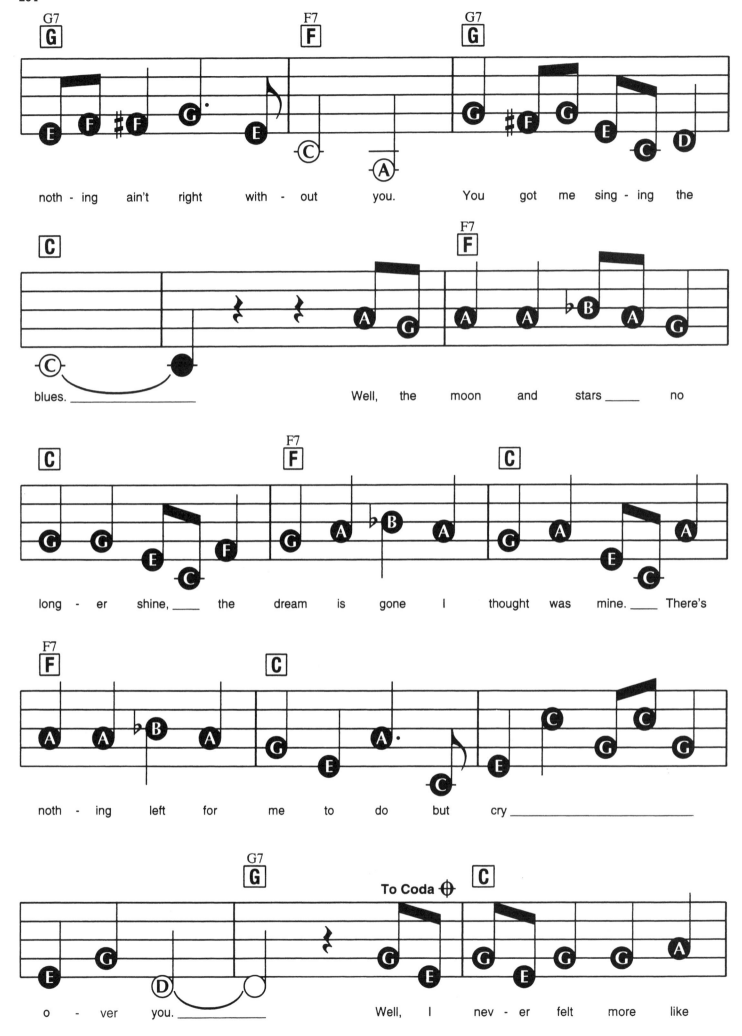

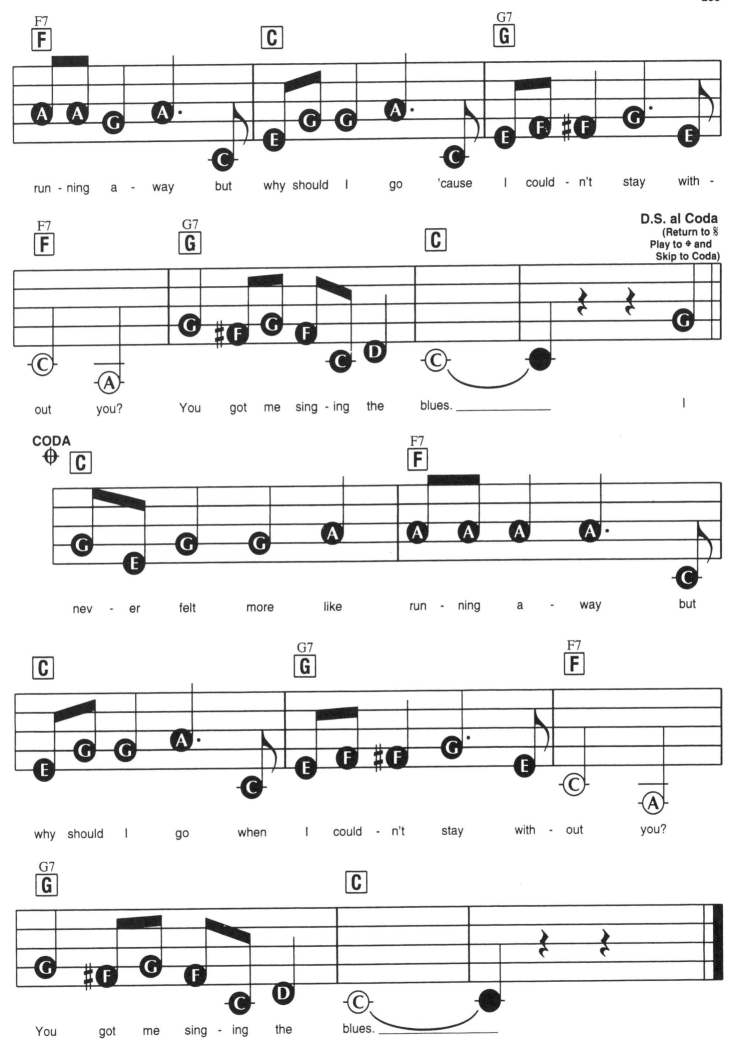

run - ning a - way but why should I go 'cause I could - n't stay with -

D.S. al Coda
(Return to %
Play to ⊕ and
Skip to Coda)

out you? You got me sing - ing the blues. _____ I

CODA

nev - er felt more like run - ning a - way but

why should I go when I could - n't stay with - out you?

You got me sing - ing the blues. _____

She's Got You

Registration 10
Rhythm: Country or Pops

Words and Music by
Hank Cochran

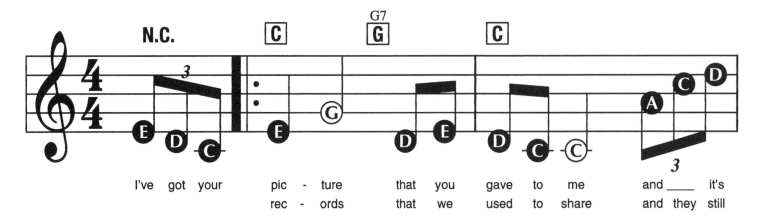

I've got your pic - ture that you gave to me and ____ it's
rec - ords that we used to share and they still

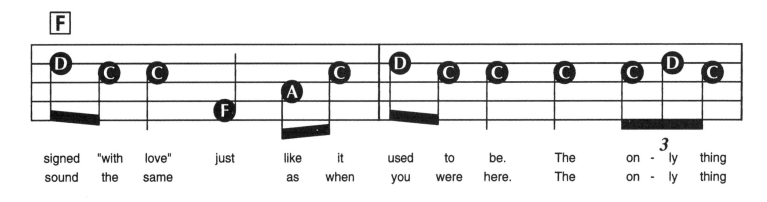

signed "with love" just like it used to be. The on - ly thing
sound the same as when you were here. The on - ly thing

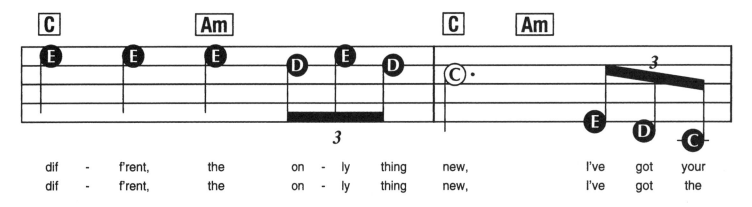

dif - f'rent, the on - ly thing new, I've got your
dif - f'rent, the on - ly thing new, I've got the

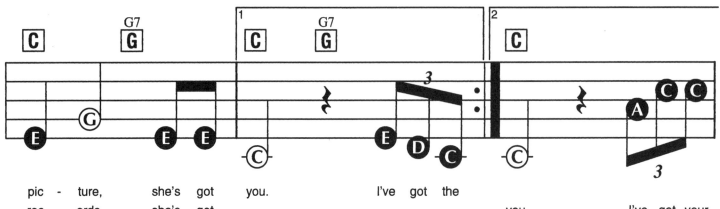

pic - ture, she's got you. I've got the
rec - ords, she's got you. I've got your

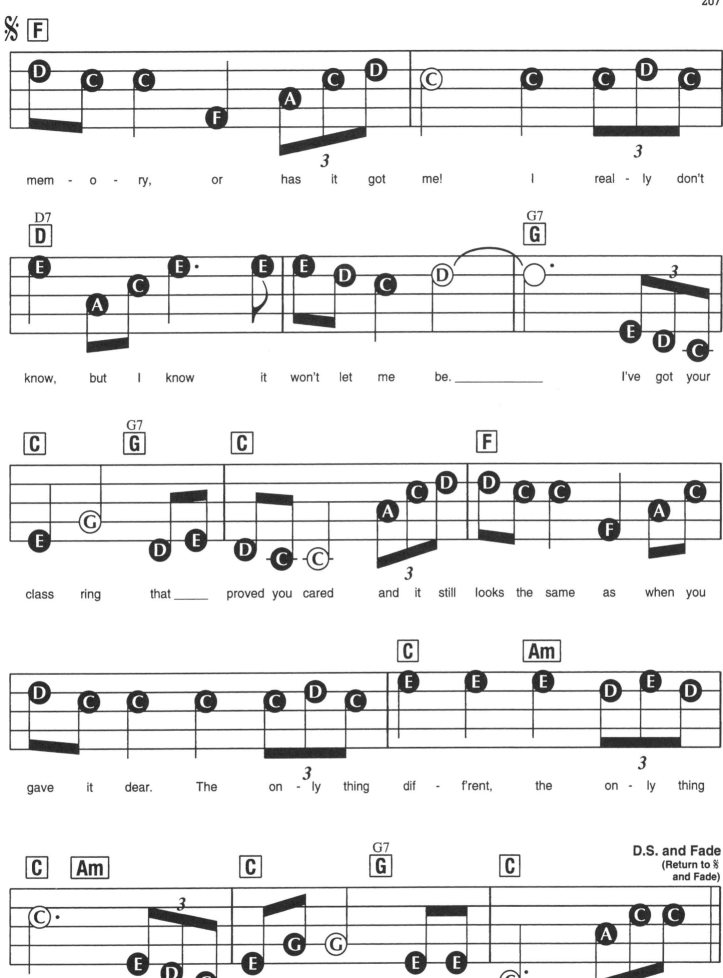

Skip a Rope

Registration 5
Rhythm: Swing

Words and Music by Jack Moran
and Glenn D. Tubb

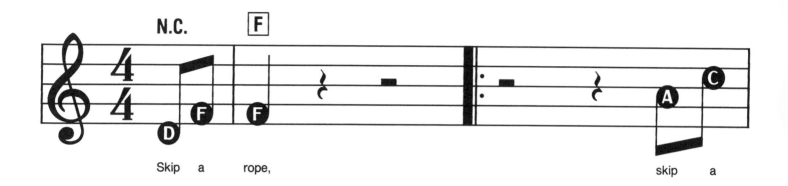

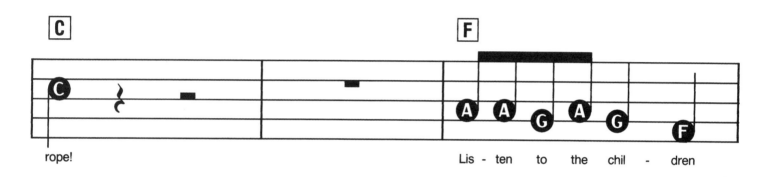

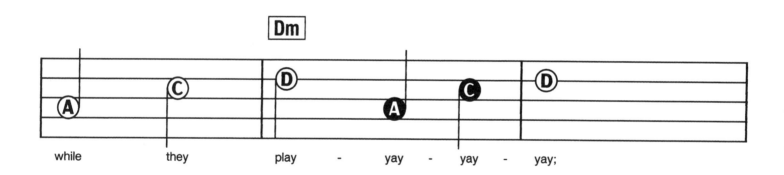

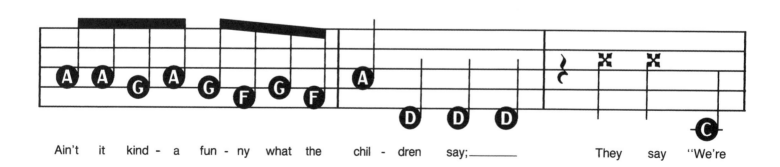

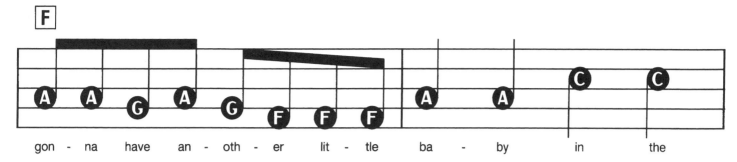

gon - na   have   an - oth - er   lit - tle   ba - by   in   the

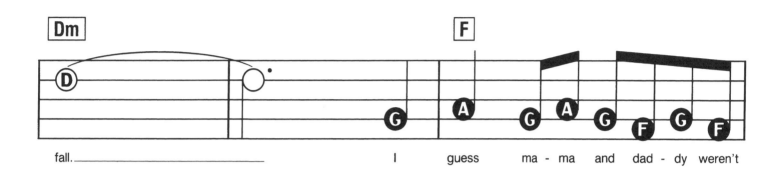

fall._____   I   guess   ma - ma   and   dad - dy   weren't

Repeat as many times as necessary

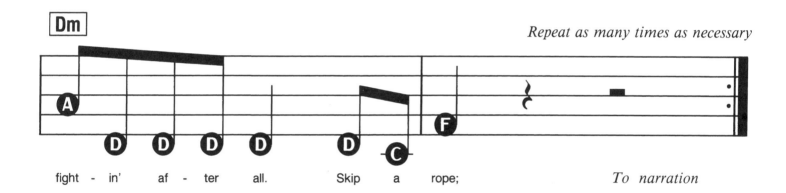

fight - in'   af - ter   all.   Skip   a   rope;   *To narration*

NARRATION

(Lady) You shouldn't say that! (Man) Say what?
Skip A Rope? That's the name of the song, lady.
OK, I'll do the one about the income tax man.

2. (Sing)

The man came to see us about our income tax,
Said we're gonna get some money back,
Daddy's sorta grinning, somethin's on his mind,
He sent the income tax man a valentine.
Skip A Rope, Skip A Rope,
Oh, listen to the children while they play-yay-yay-yay,
Uh-I forgot what I'm suppose to say.

NARRATION

(Other Person) Skip A Rope! Got a joke?
Skip A Rope you dope! Tell a joke about a rope? O.K.
You hear the one about the near sighted rope that fell in
love with a snake?
Oh, you messed up the punch line! Where's the punch line,
I ain't even seen a punch bowl. You know I skip a lot.
You see the doctor gave me these pills and he said take one
a day for three days running and then skip a day,
And this is my day to skip.
I used to skip a well rope. I used to skip a sick rope;
Heck, I even tried to smoke one of those one time.

(Sing)

Skip the jokes, thanks a lot, skip the jokes.
Oh, listen to the children while they play. (Fade out)

Sleeping Single in a Double Bed

Registration 1
Rhythm: Country

Words and Music by Dennis Morgan
and Kye Fleming

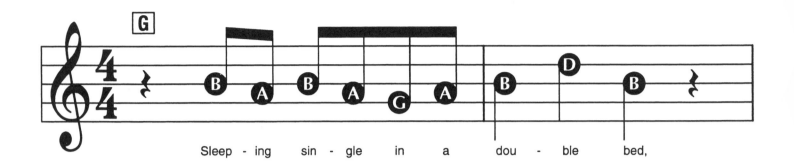

Sleep - ing sin - gle in a dou - ble bed,

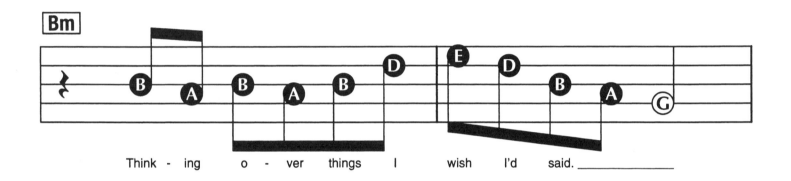

Think - ing o - ver things I wish I'd said. _____

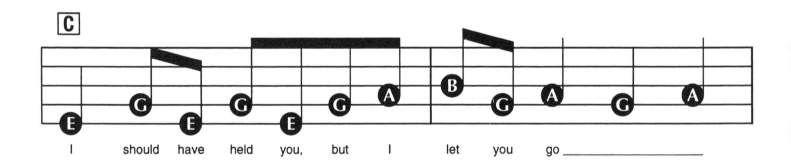

I should have held you, but I let you go _____

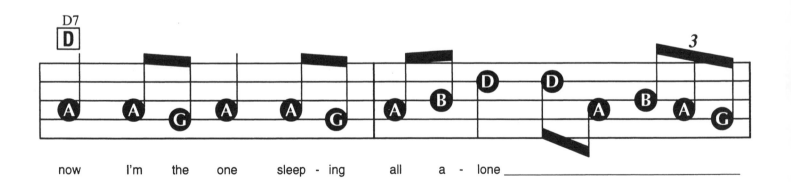

now I'm the one sleep - ing all a - lone _____

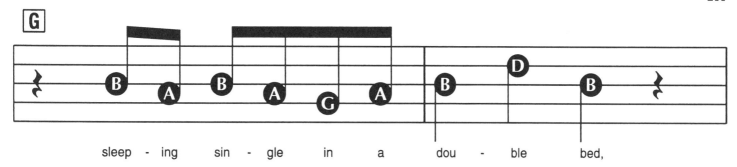

G

sleep - ing sin - gle in a dou - ble bed,

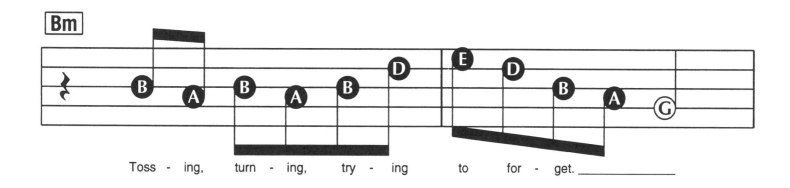

Bm

Toss - ing, turn - ing, try - ing to for - get. _____

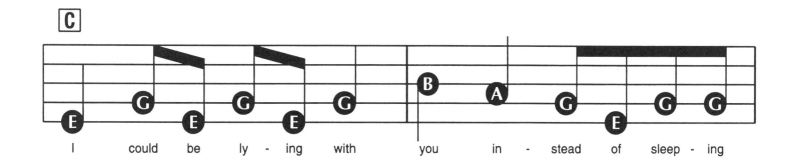

C

I could be ly - ing with you in - stead of sleep - ing

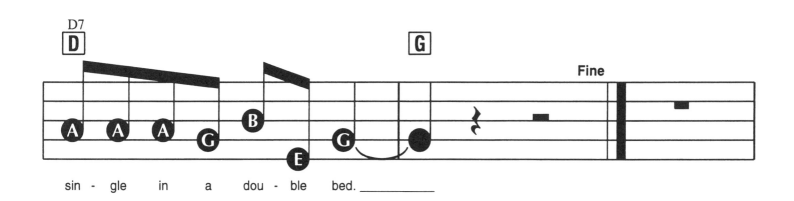

D7
D   G   Fine

sin - gle in a dou - ble bed. _____

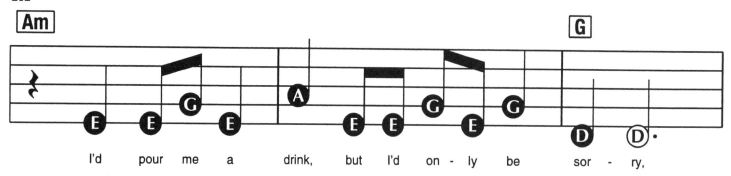

I'd pour me a drink, but I'd on - ly be sor - ry,

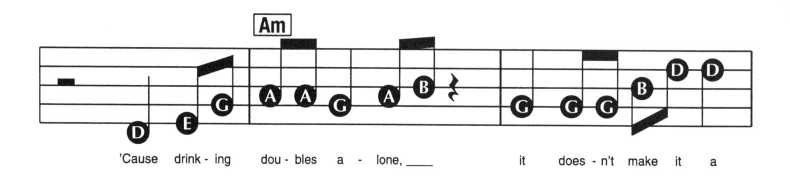

'Cause drink - ing dou - bles a - lone, _____ it does - n't make it a

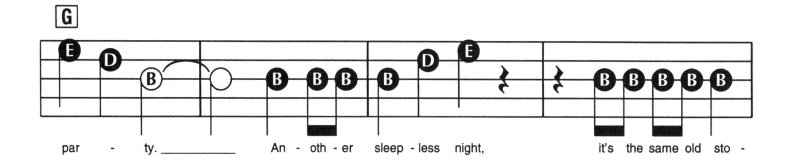

par - ty. _____ An - oth - er sleep - less night, it's the same old sto -

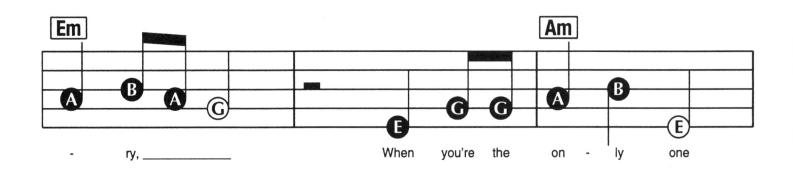

- ry, _____ When you're the on - ly one

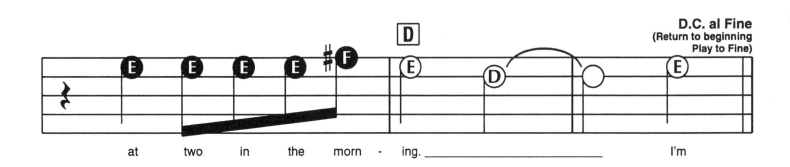

D.C. al Fine
(Return to beginning
Play to Fine)

at two in the morn - ing. _____ I'm

Smoky Mountain Rain

Registration 10
Rhythm: Rock

Words and Music by Kye Fleming
and Dennis Morgan

I thumbed my way from L. A. back to Knox - ville;

I found out those bright lights ain't where ___ I be - long. ___

From a phone booth, in the rain, I called to tell her

I've had a change of dreams, I'm com - ing home; ___

but tears filled my eyes when I found that she was gone. ___

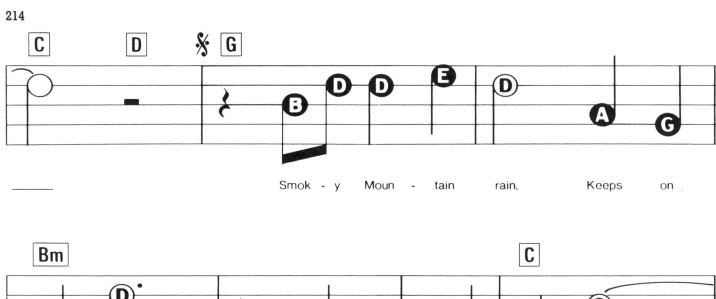

Smok - y Moun - tain rain, Keeps on

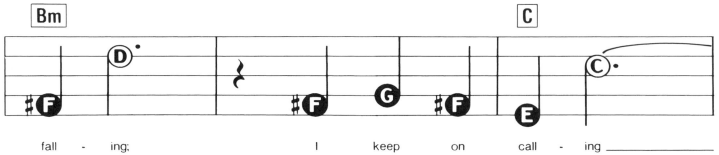

fall - ing; I keep on call - ing ____ her name. ____

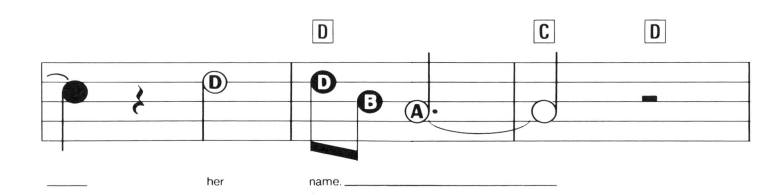

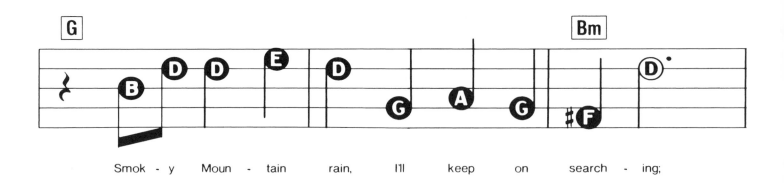

Smok - y Moun - tain rain, I'll keep on search - ing;

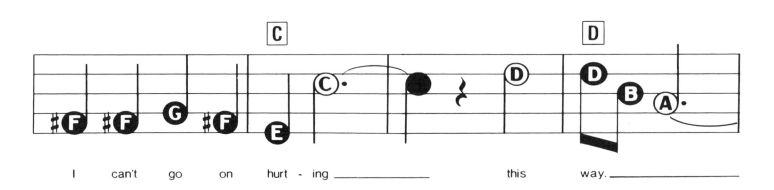

I can't go on hurt - ing ____ this way.

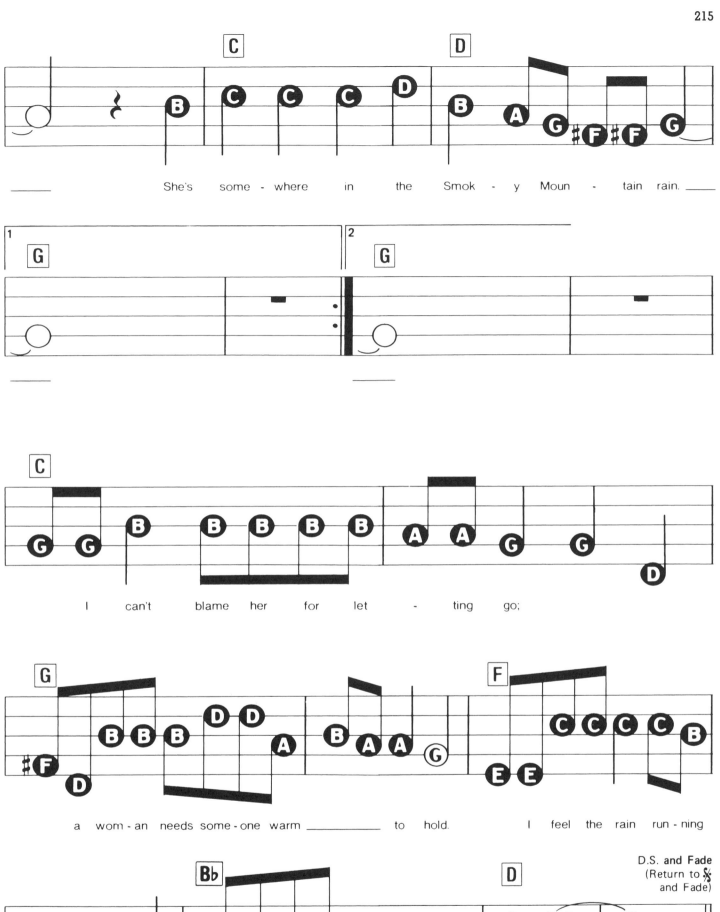

She's some - where in the Smok - y Moun - tain rain.

I can't blame her for let - ting go;

a wom - an needs some - one warm _____ to hold. I feel the rain run - ning

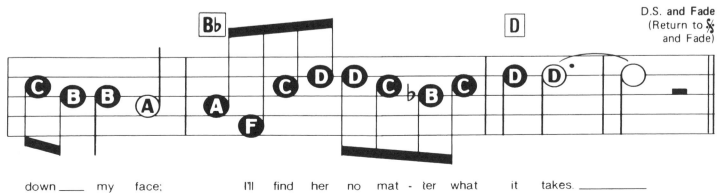

D.S. **and Fade**
(Return to 𝄋
and Fade)

down ___ my face; I'll find her no mat - ter what it takes. _____

Snowbird

Registration 5
Rhythm: Fox Trot or Ballad

Words and Music by
Gene MacLellan

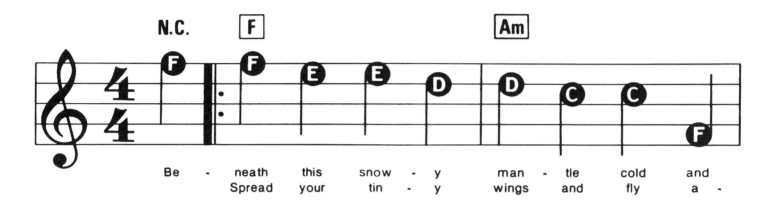

Be - neath this snow - y man - tle cold and
Spread your tin - y wings and fly a -

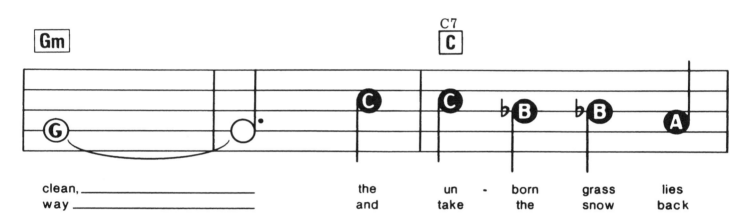

clean, the un - born grass lies
way and take the snow back

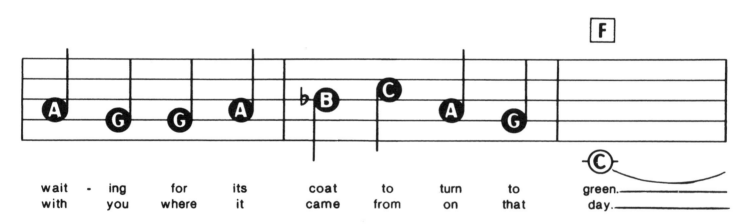

wait - ing for its coat to turn to green.
with you where it came from on to that day.

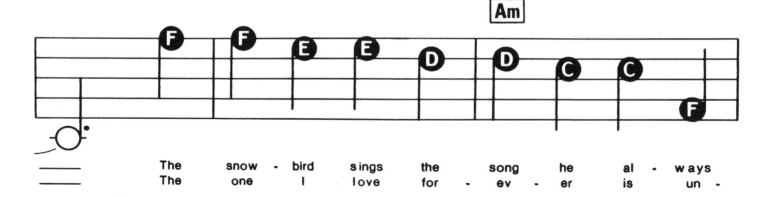

The snow - bird sings the song he al - ways
The one I love for - ev - er is un -

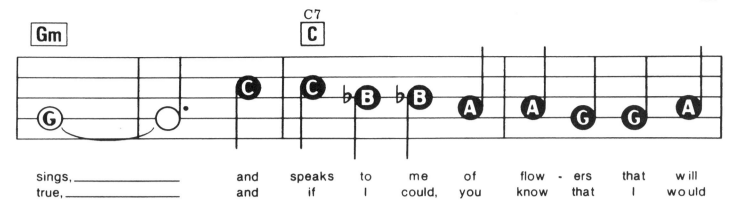

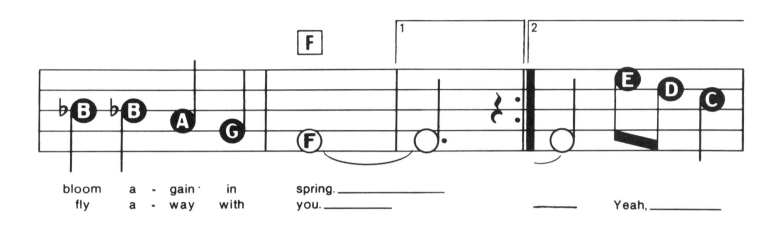

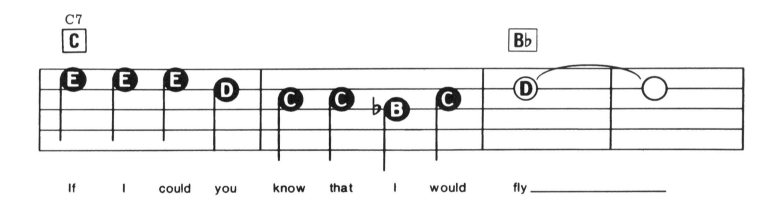

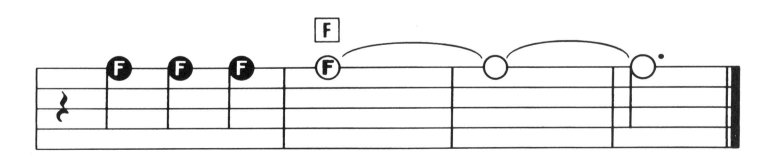

Sunday Mornin' Comin' Down

Registration 4
Rhythm: Ballad

Words and Music by
Kris Kristofferson

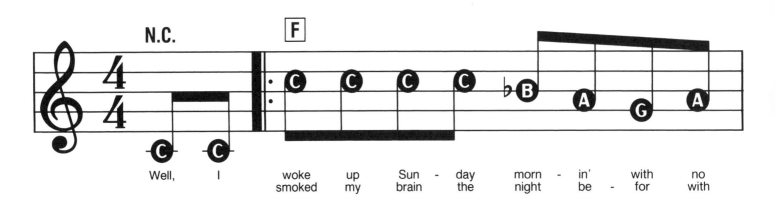

Well, I woke up Sun - day morn - in' with no
smoked up my brain the night be - for with

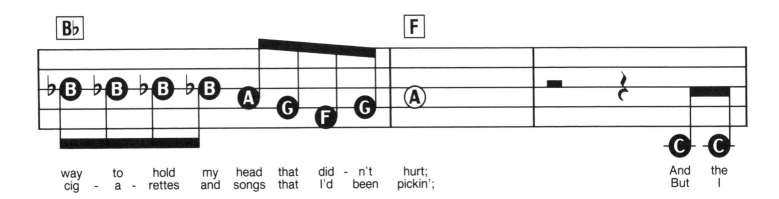

way to hold my head that did - n't hurt; And the
cig - a - rettes and songs that I'd been pickin'; But I

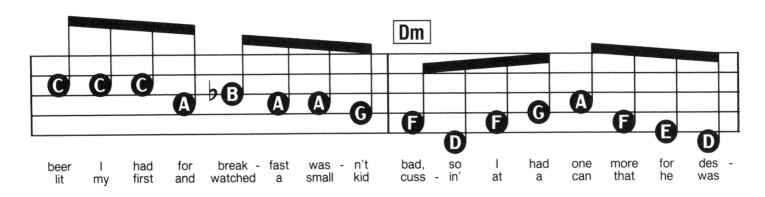

beer I had for break - fast was - n't bad, so I had one more for des
lit my first and watched a small kid cuss - in' at a can that he was

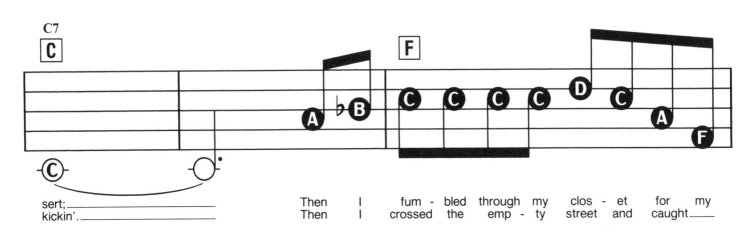

sert;_____
kickin'._____

Then I fum - bled through my clos - et for my
Then I crossed the emp - ty street and caught_____

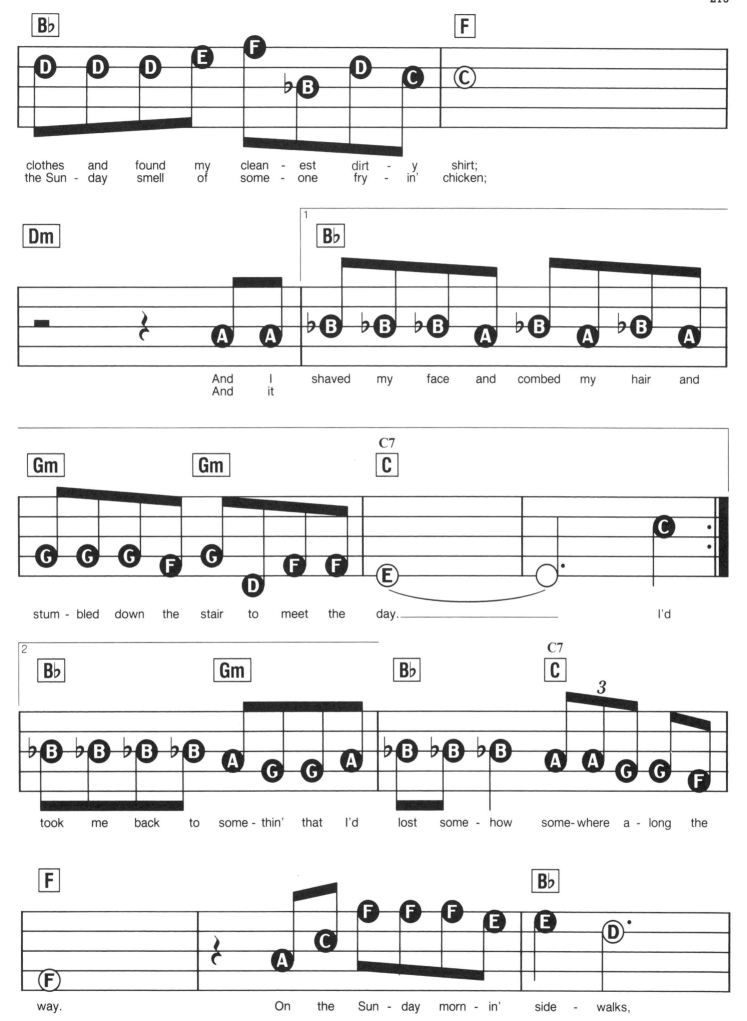

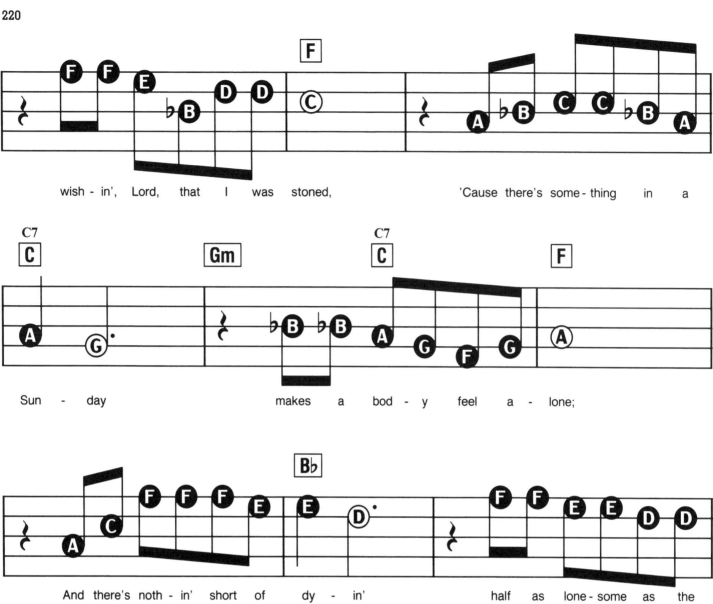

wish - in', Lord, that I was stoned, 'Cause there's some - thing in a

Sun - day makes a bod - y feel a - lone;

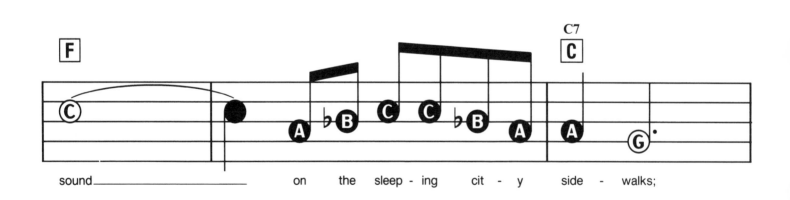

And there's noth - in' short of dy - in' half as lone - some as the

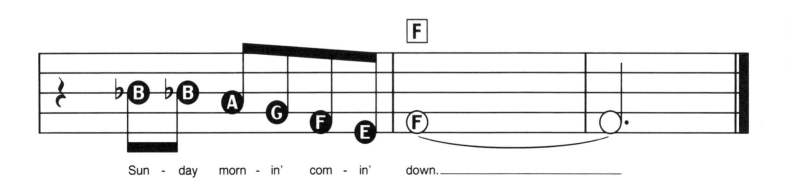

sound_____ on the sleep - ing cit - y side - walks;

Sun - day morn - in' com - in' down._____

Thank God I'm a Country Boy

Registration 4
Rhythm: Country

Words and Music by
John Martin Sommers

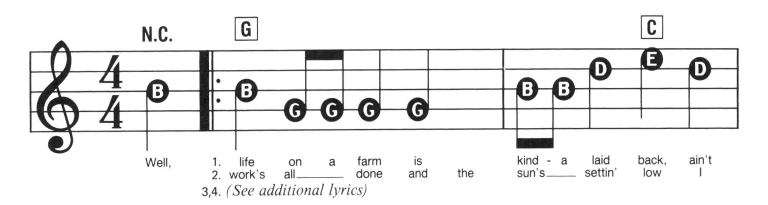

Well, 1. life on a farm is the kind - a laid back, ain't
2. work's all____ done and the sun's____ settin' low I
3,4. *(See additional lyrics)*

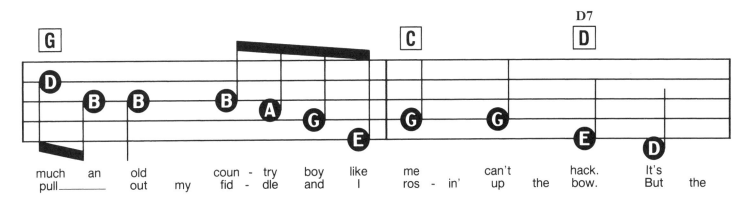

much an old my coun - try boy like me can't hack. It's
pull____ out my fid - dle and I ros - in' up the bow. But the

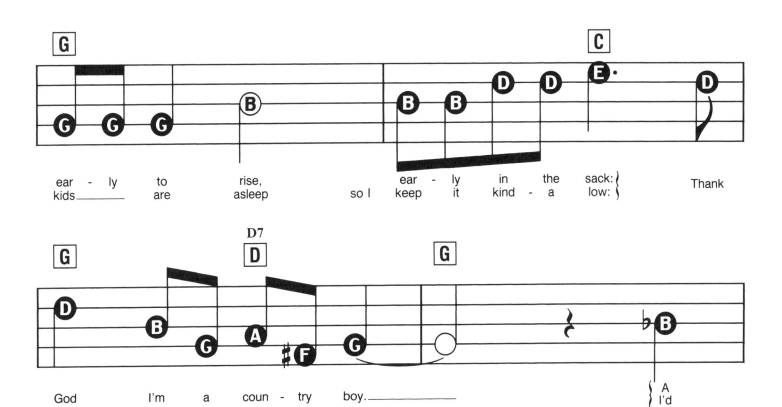

ear - ly to rise, so I keep it ear - ly in the sack: Thank
kids____ are asleep it kind - a low:

God I'm a coun - try boy.____ A I'd

222

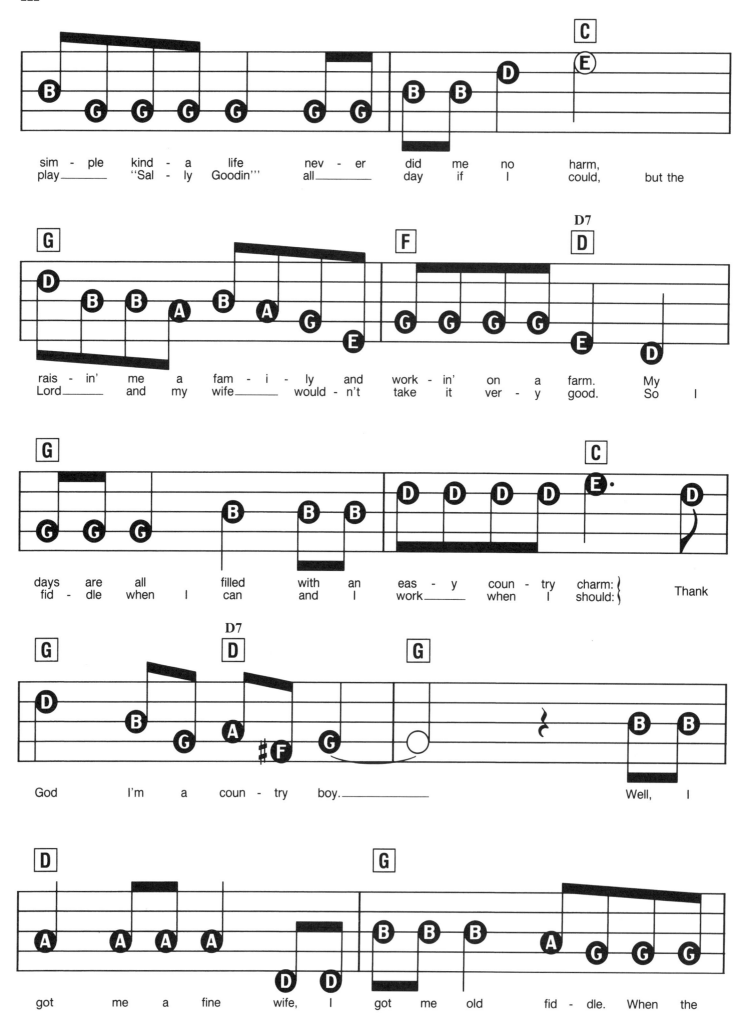

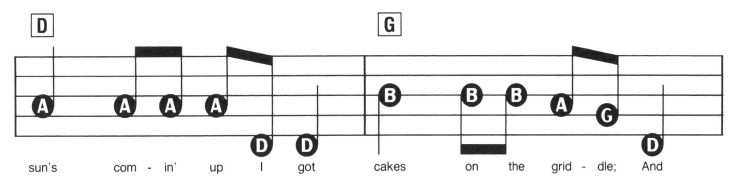

sun's com - in' up I got cakes on the grid - dle; And

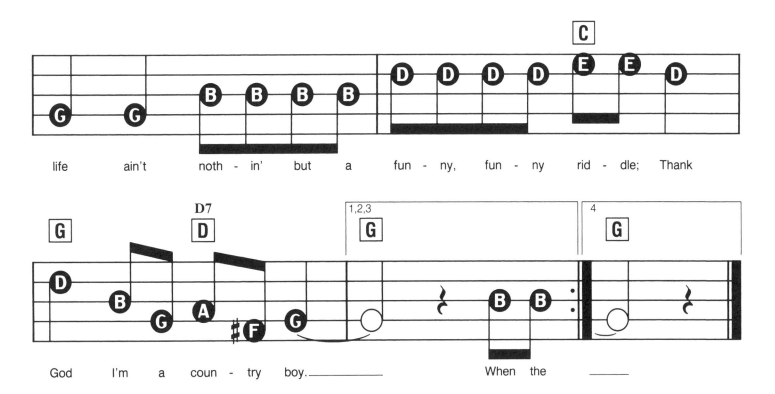

life ain't noth - in' but a fun - ny, fun - ny rid - dle; Thank

God I'm a coun - try boy. When the

Additional Lyrics

Verse 3
I wouldn't trade my life for diamonds or jewels,
I never was one of them money hungry fools.
I'd rather have my fiddle and my farmin' tools:
Thank God I'm a country boy.
Yeah, city folk drivin' in a black limousine,
A lotta sad people thinkin' that's mighty keen.
Well, folks let me tell you now exactly what I mean:
I thank God I'm a country boy.

Verse 4
Well, my fiddle was my daddy's till the day he died,
And he took me by the hand and held me close to his side.
He said, "Live a good life and play my fiddle with pride,
And thank God you're a country boy."
My daddy taught me young how to hunt and how to whittle,
He taught me how to work and play a tune on the fiddle.
He taught me how to love and how to give just a little:
Thank God I'm a country boy.

Take Me Home, Country Roads

Registration 10
Rhythm: Country

Words and Music by John Denver,
Bill Danoff and Taffy Nivert

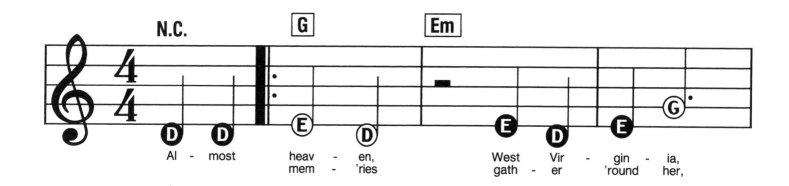

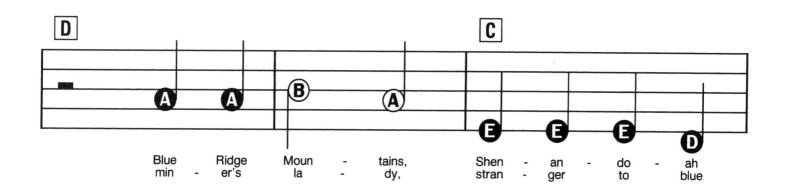

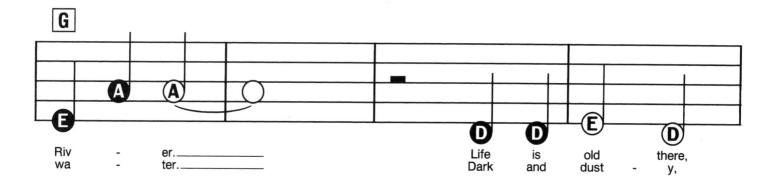

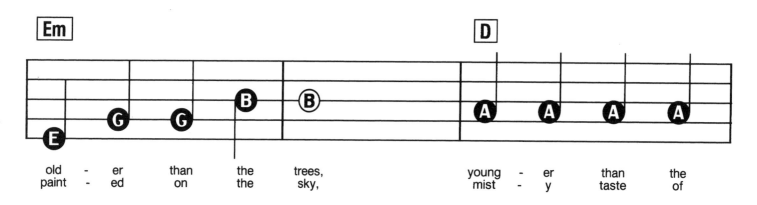

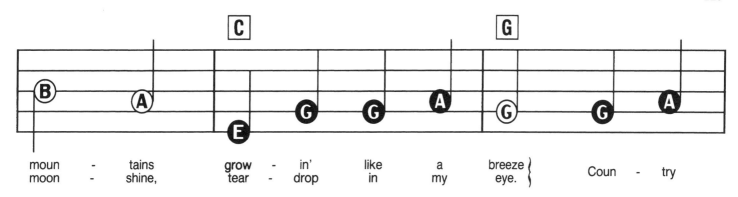

moun - tains grow - in' like a breeze Coun - try
moon - shine, tear - drop in my eye.

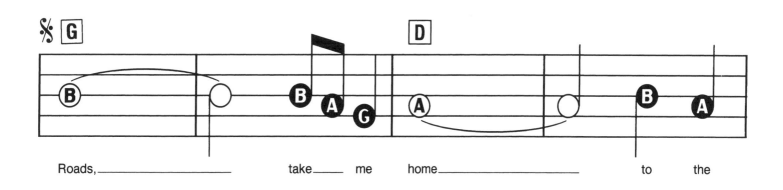

Roads, take me home to the

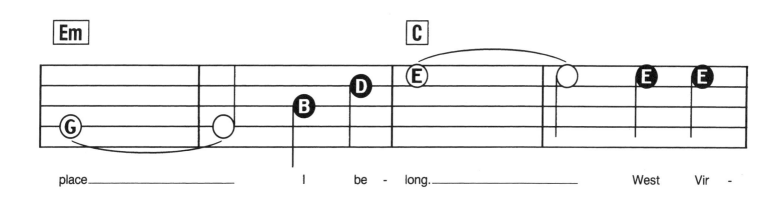

place I be - long. West Vir -

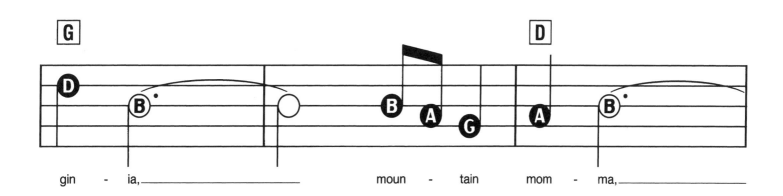

gin - ia, moun - tain mom - ma,

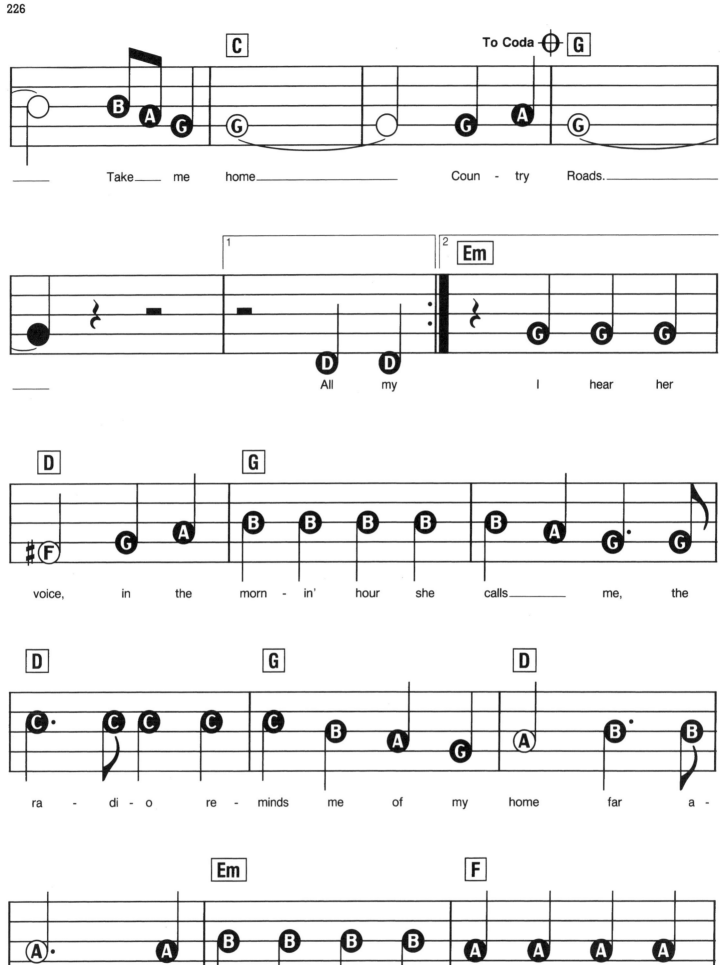

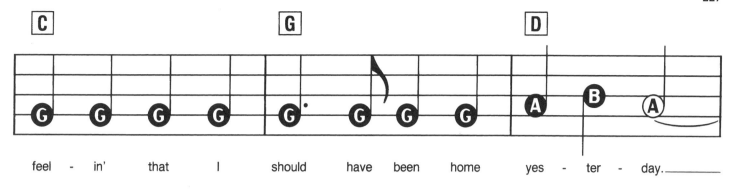

feel - in' that I should have been home yes - ter - day.

D7

D.S. al Coda
(Return to %
play to ⊕ then
skip to Coda)

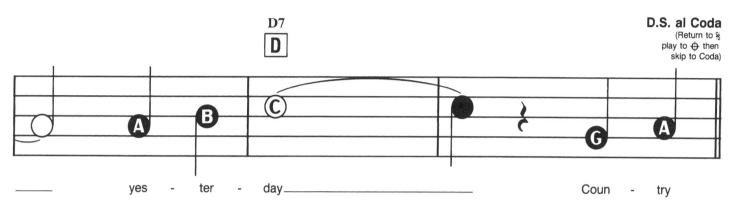

yes - ter - day Coun - try

CODA

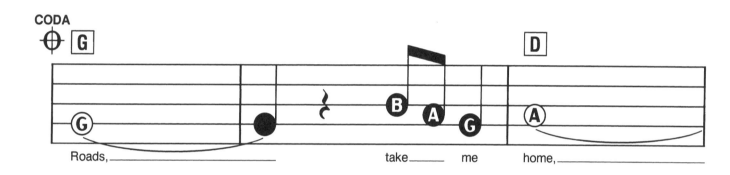

Roads, take me home,

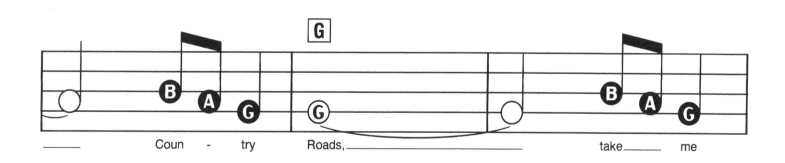

Coun - try Roads, take me

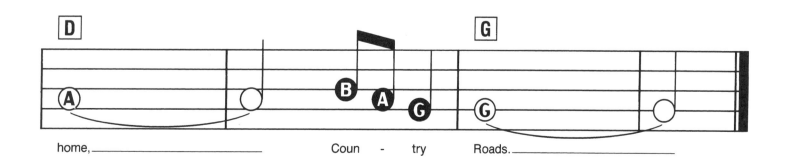

home, Coun - try Roads.

Take These Chains from My Heart

Registration 8
Rhythm: Country Swing or Fox Trot

Words and Music by Fred Rose
and Hy Heath

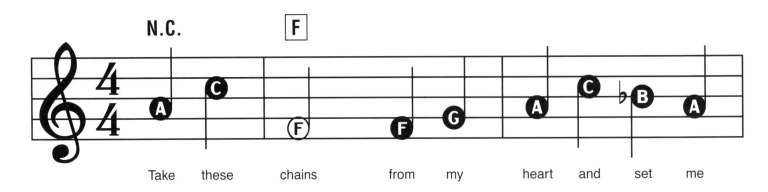

Take these chains from my heart and set me

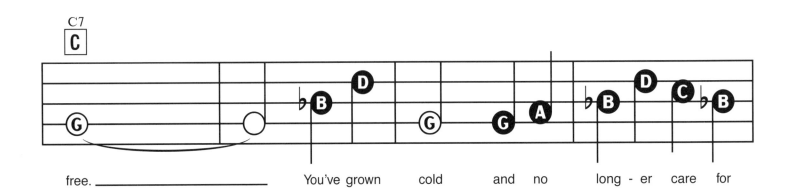

free. _____ You've grown cold and no long-er care for

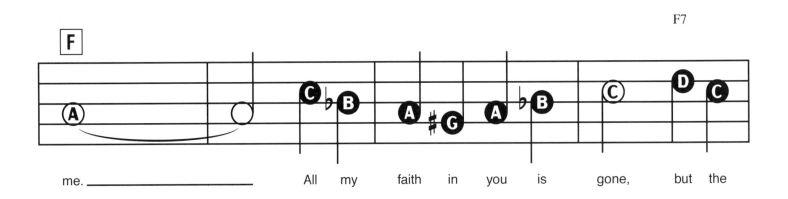

me. _____ All my faith in you is gone, but the

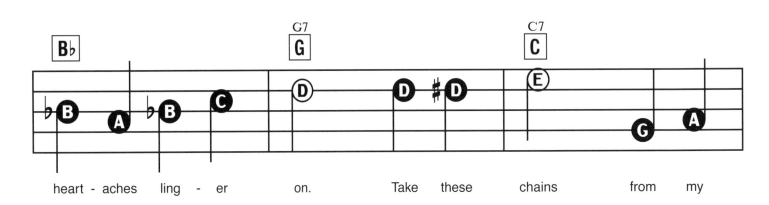

heart-aches ling-er on. Take these chains from my

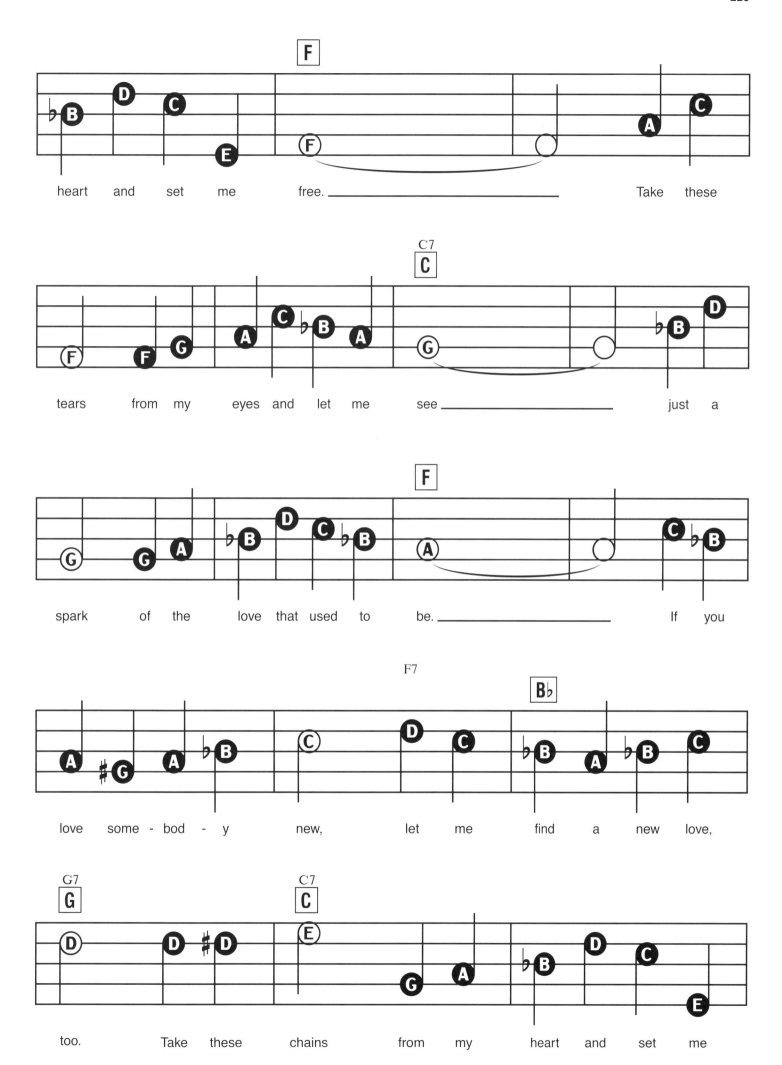

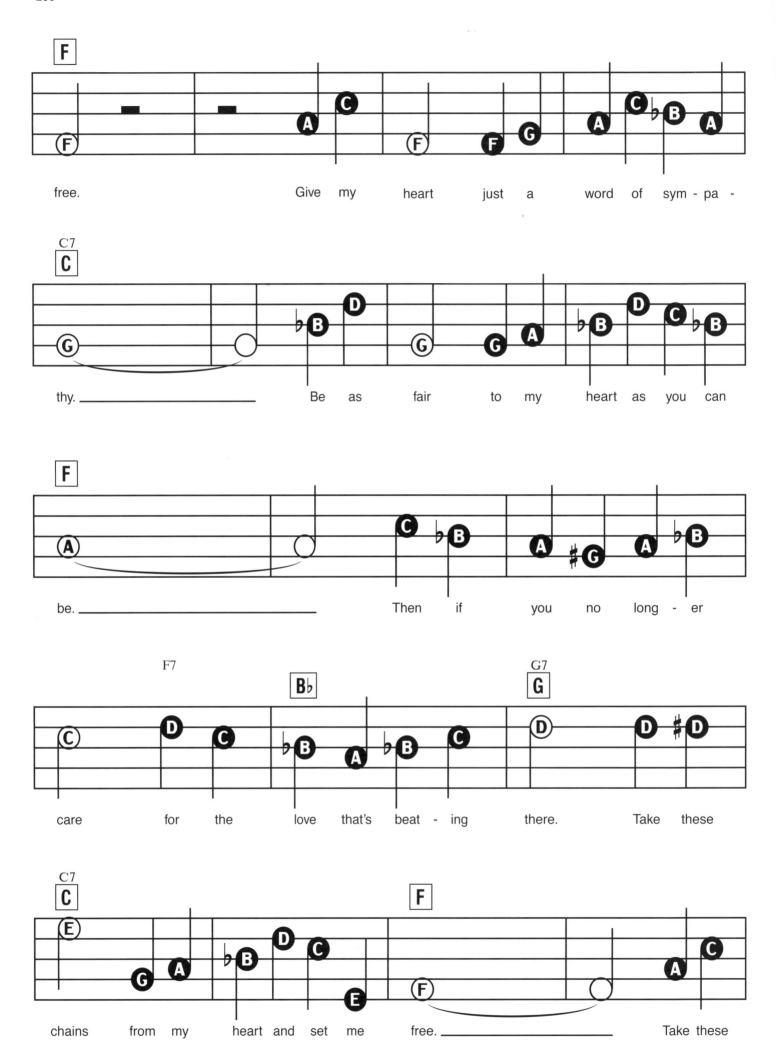

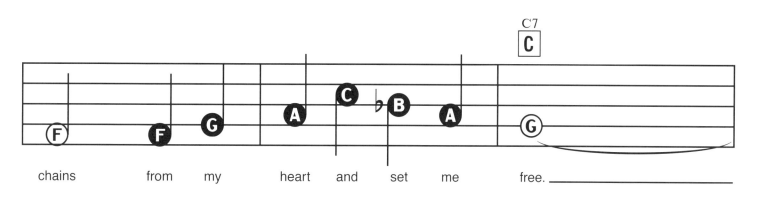

chains　from　my　heart　and　set　me　free.

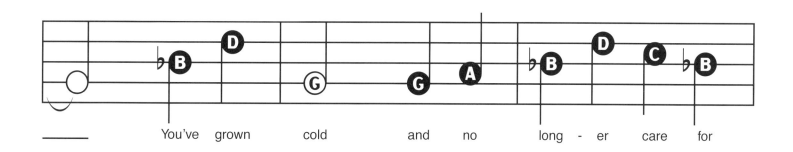

You've　grown　cold　and　no　long - er　care　for

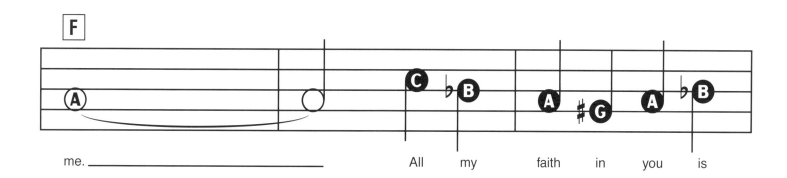

me.　All　my　faith　in　you　is

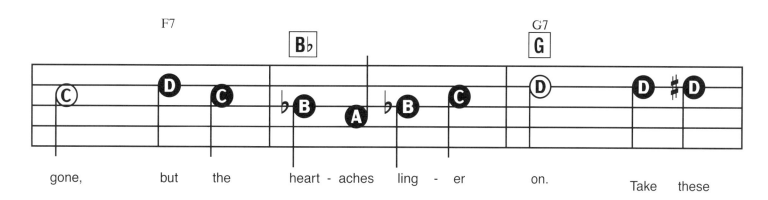

gone,　but　the　heart - aches　ling - er　on.　Take　these

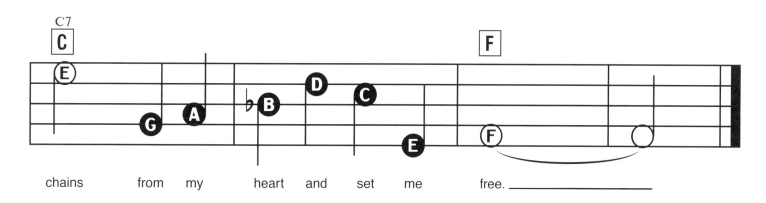

chains　from　my　heart　and　set　me　free.

Talkin' in Your Sleep

Registration 4
Rhythm: Ballad or 8-Beat

Words and Music by Roger Cook
and Bobby Woods

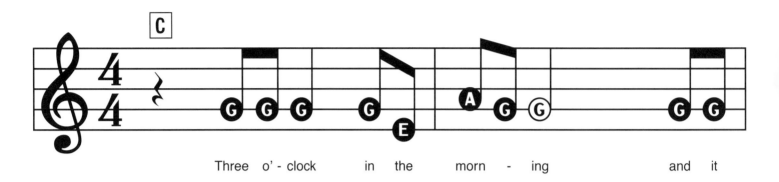

Three o'-clock in the morn - ing and it

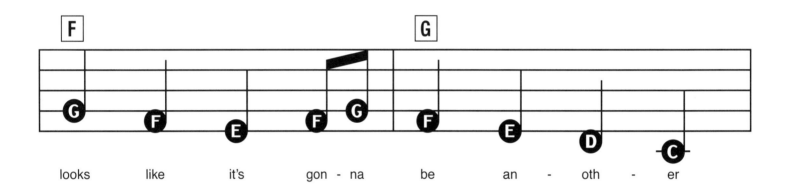

looks like it's gon - na be an - oth - er

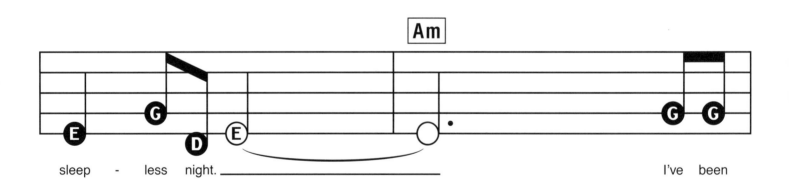

sleep - less night. _____ I've been

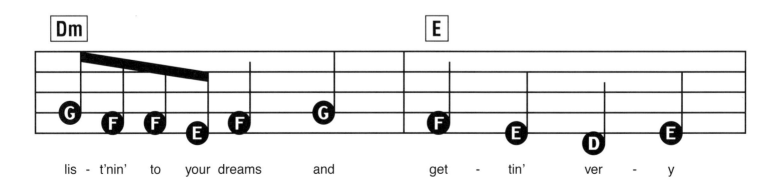

lis - t'nin' to your dreams and get - tin' ver - y

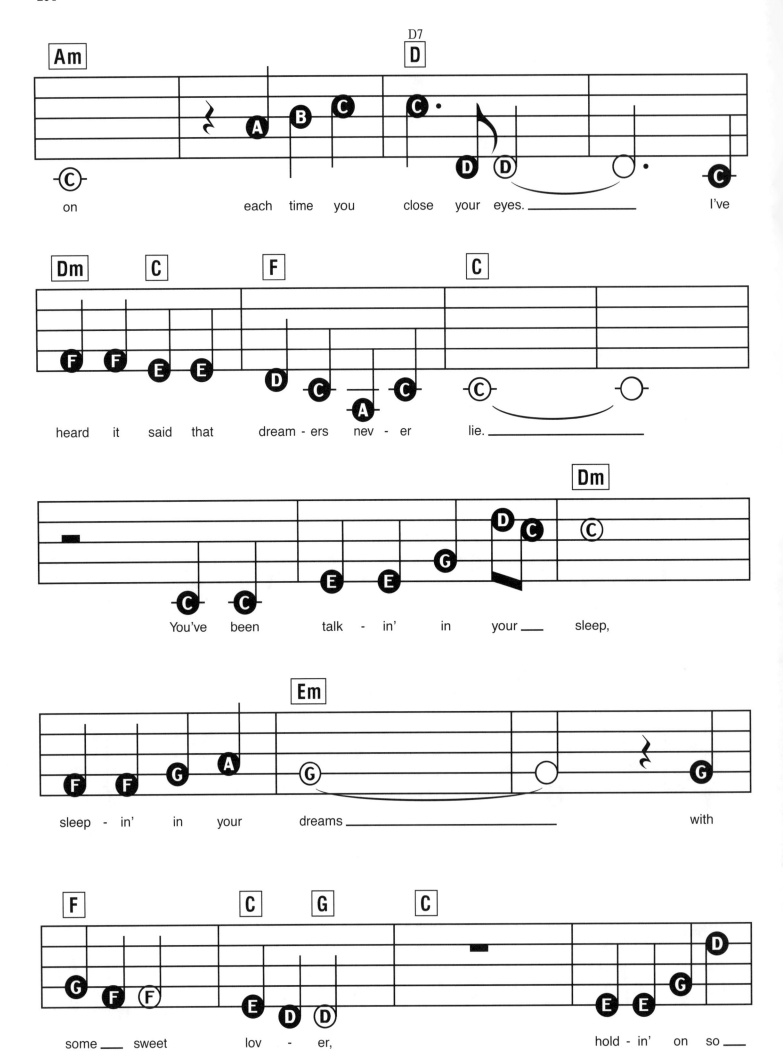

235

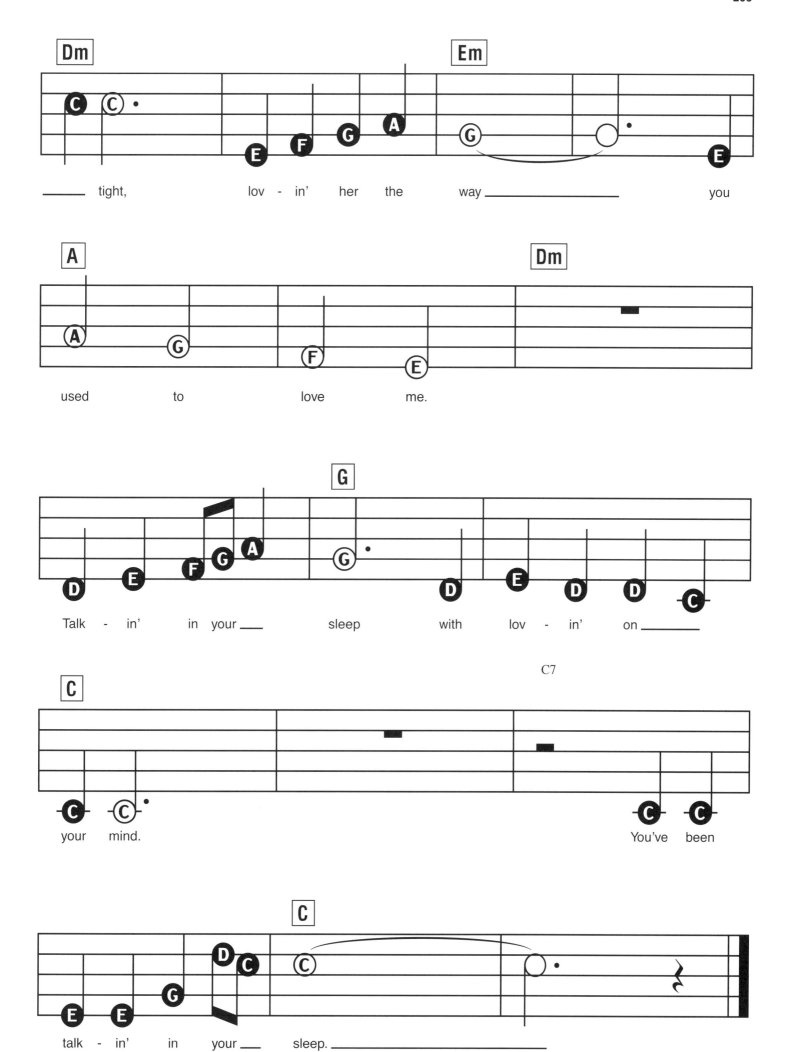

There Goes My Everything

Registration 3
Rhythm: Waltz

Words and Music by
Dallas Frazier

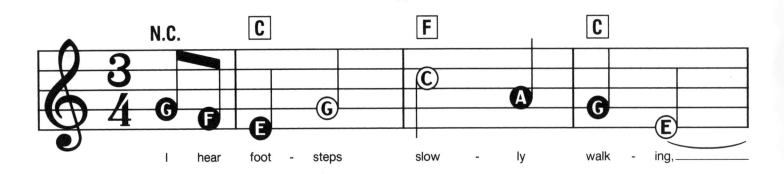

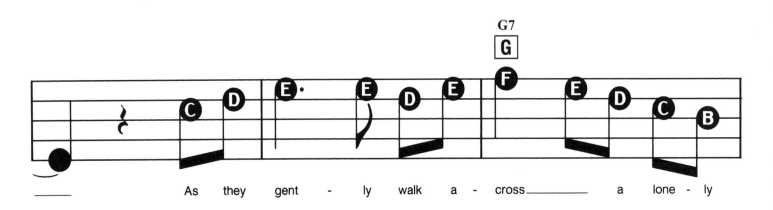

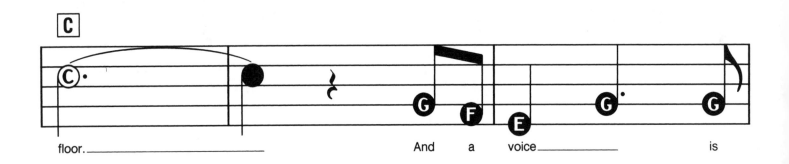

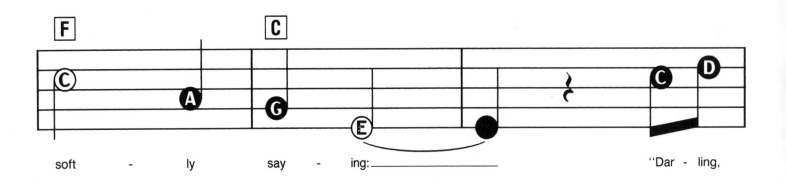

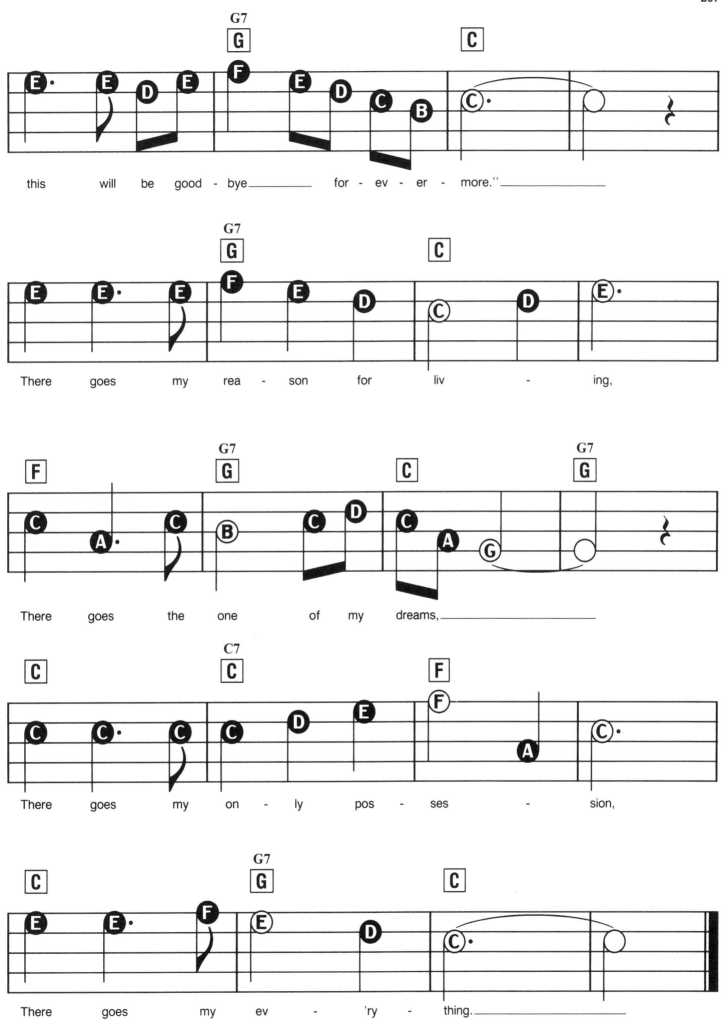

This Kiss

Registration 3
Rhythm: Country Rock or 8-Beat

Words and Music by Annie Roboff,
Beth Nielsen Chapman and Robin Lerner

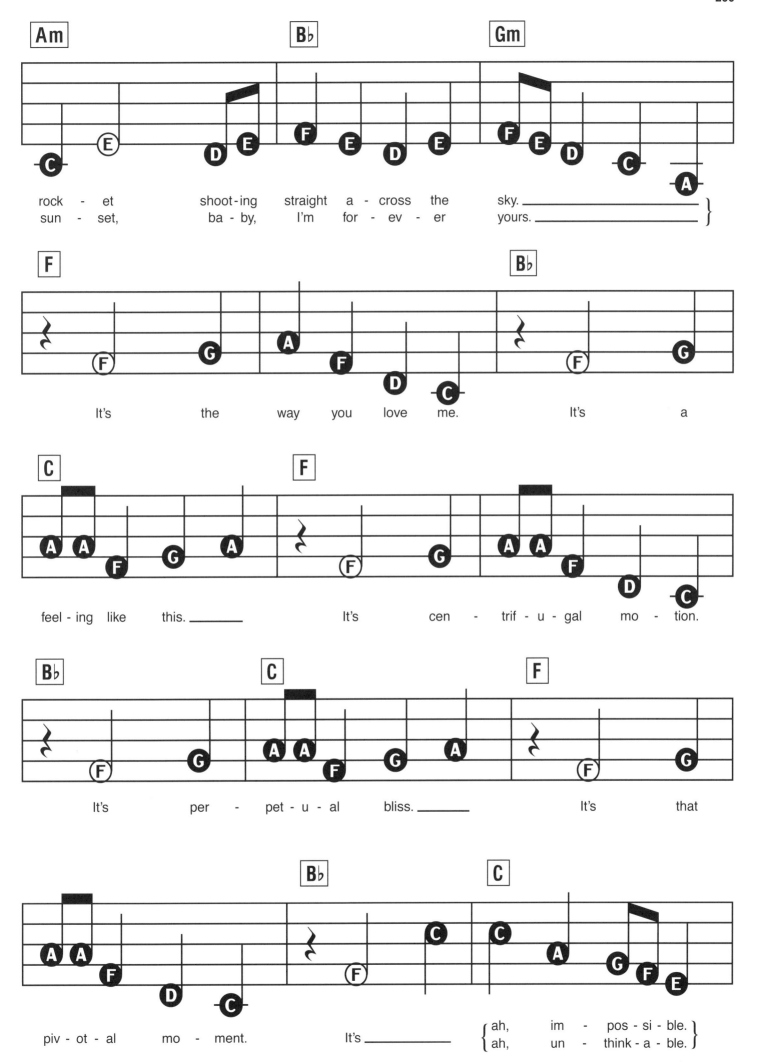

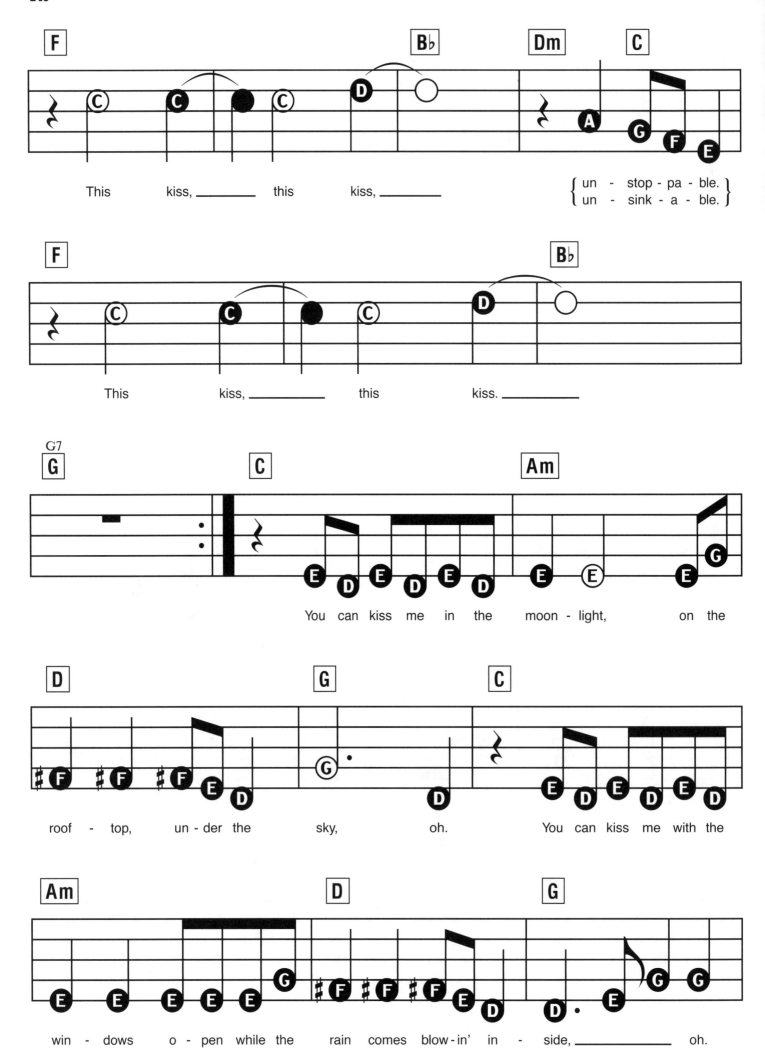

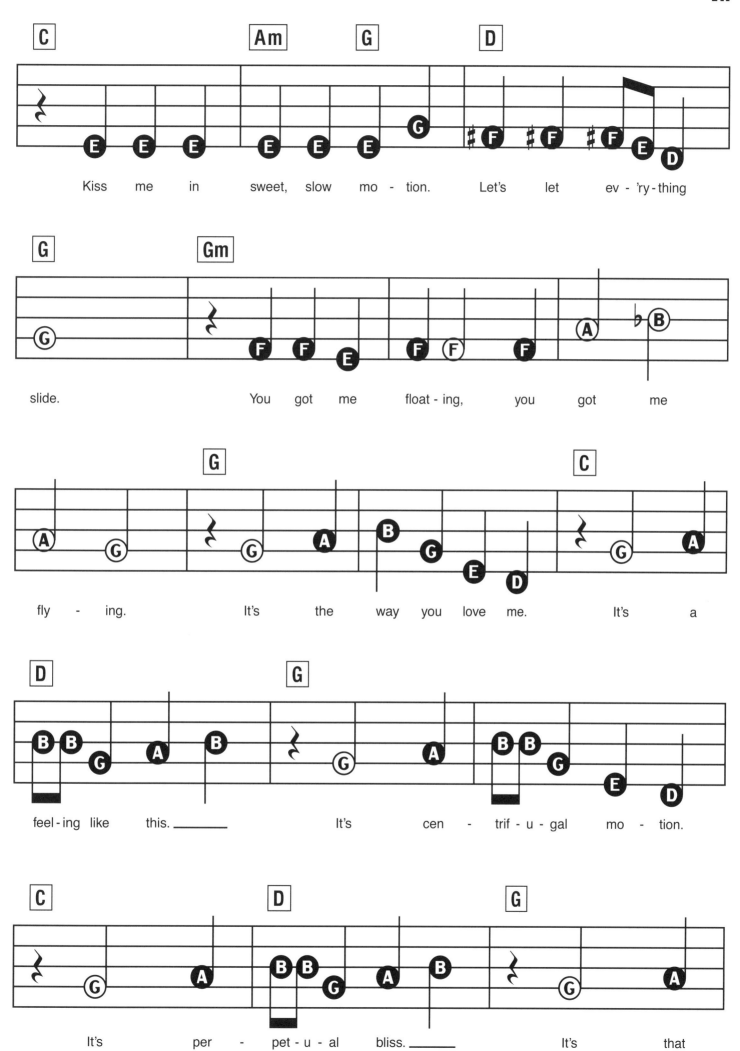

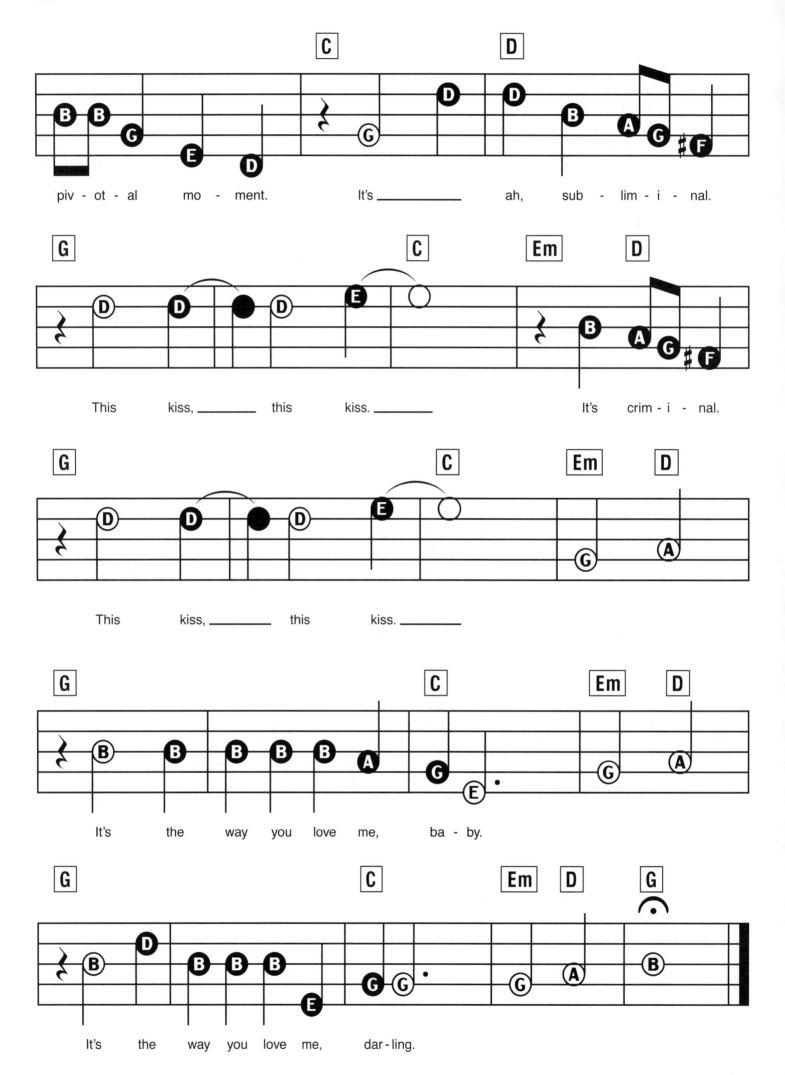

Troubadour

Registration 3
Rhythm: Country Pop or Ballad

Words and Music by Leslie Satcher
and Monty Holmes

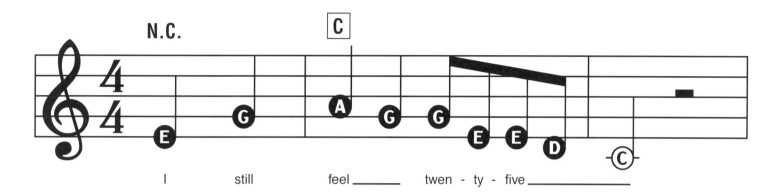

I still feel _____ twen - ty - five _____

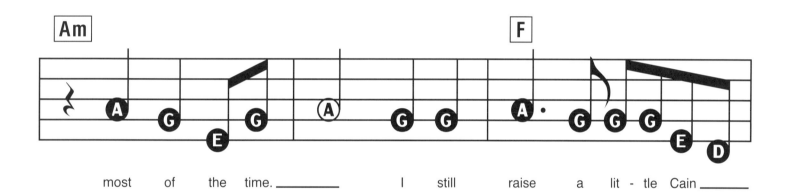

most of the time. _____ I still raise a lit - tle Cain _____

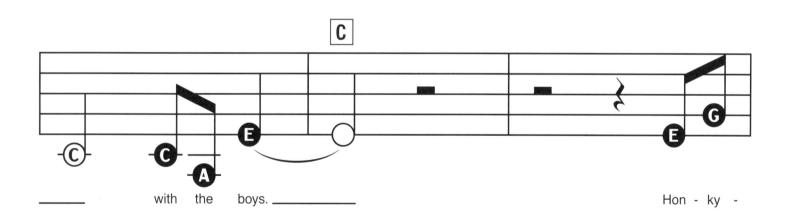

_____ with the boys. _____ Hon - ky -

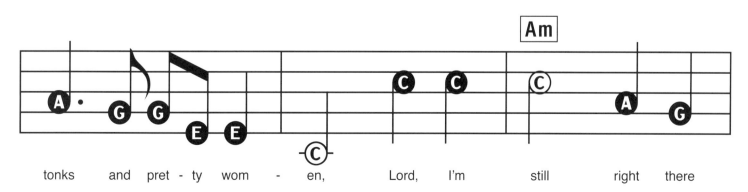

tonks and pret - ty wom - en, Lord, I'm still right there

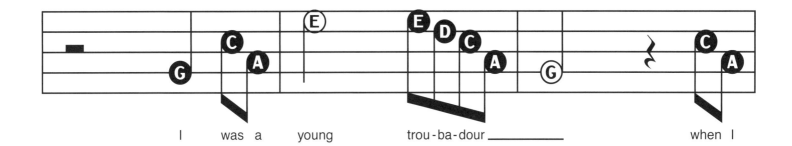

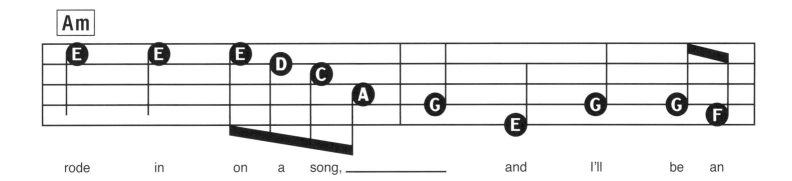

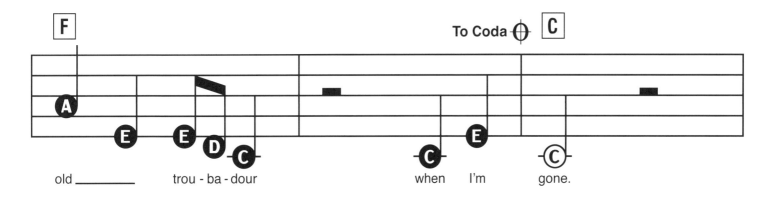

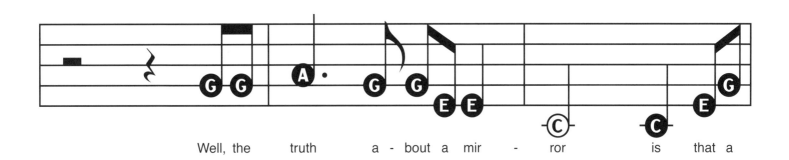

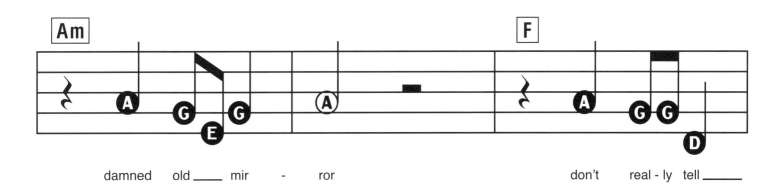

246

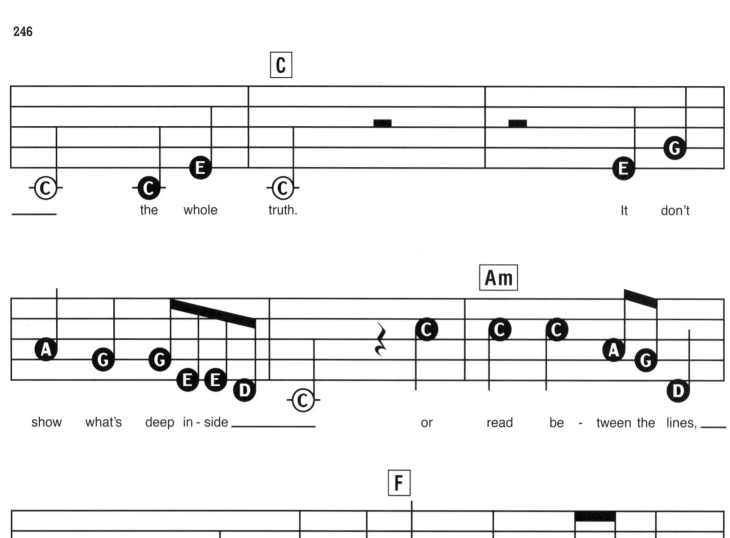

the whole truth. It don't

show what's deep in-side ___ or read be - tween the lines, ___

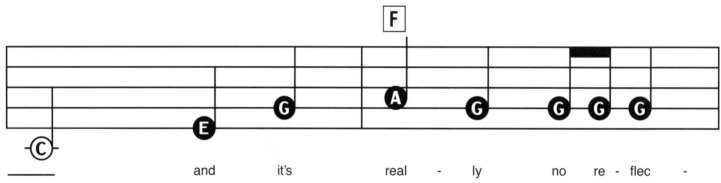

___ and it's real - ly no re - flec -

D.S. al Coda
(Return to 𝄋
Play to ⊕ and
Skip to Coda)

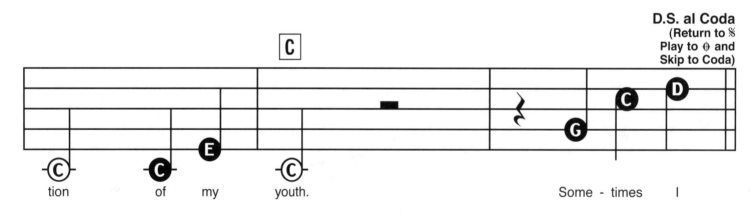

tion of my youth. Some - times I

CODA

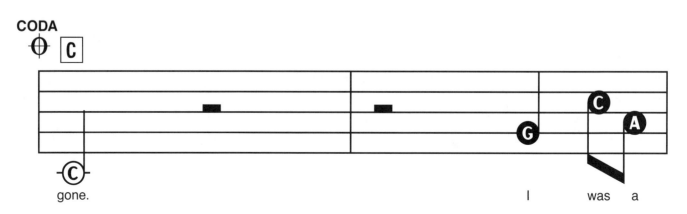

gone. I was a

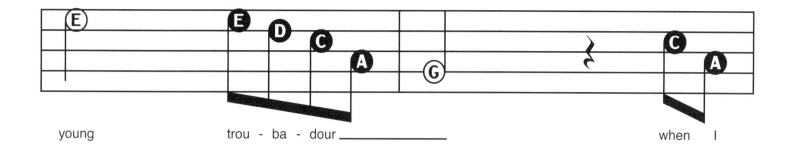

young trou - ba - dour _____ when I

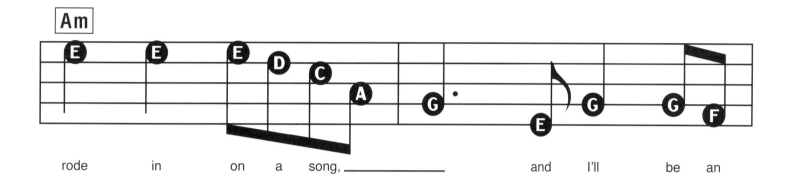

Am

rode in on a song, _____ and I'll be an

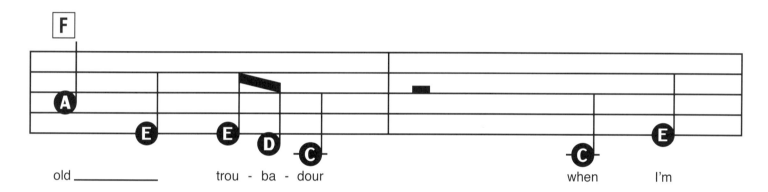

F

old _____ trou - ba - dour when I'm

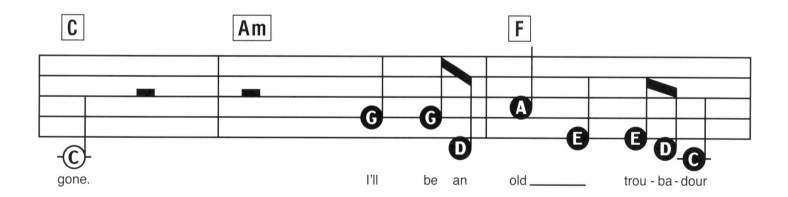

C **Am** **F**

gone. I'll be an old _____ trou - ba - dour

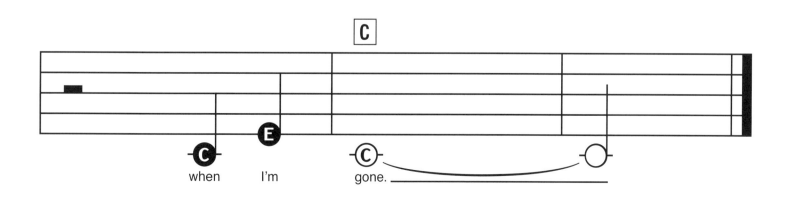

C

when I'm gone. _____

Through the Years

Registration 4
Rhythm: Rock or Slow Rock

Words and Music by Steve Dorff
and Marty Panzer

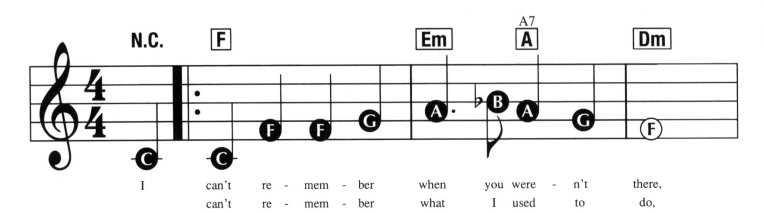

I can't re-mem-ber when you were-n't there,
can't re-mem-ber what I used to do,

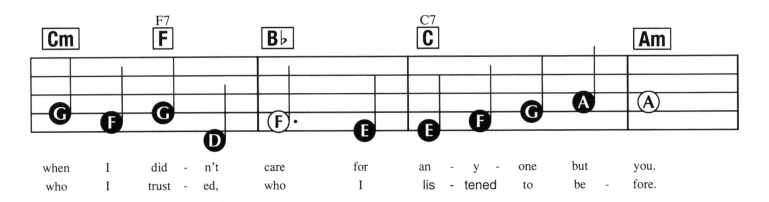

when I did-n't care for an-y-one but you.
who I trust-ed, who I lis-tened to be-fore.

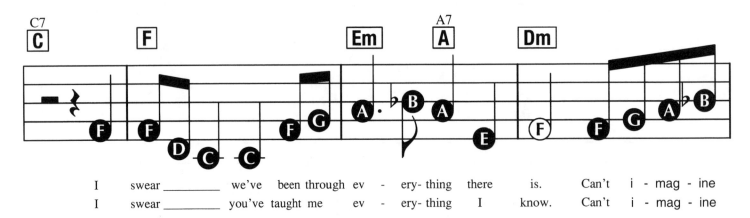

I swear _____ we've been through ev-ery-thing there is. Can't i-mag-ine
I swear _____ you've taught me ev-ery-thing I know. Can't i-mag-ine

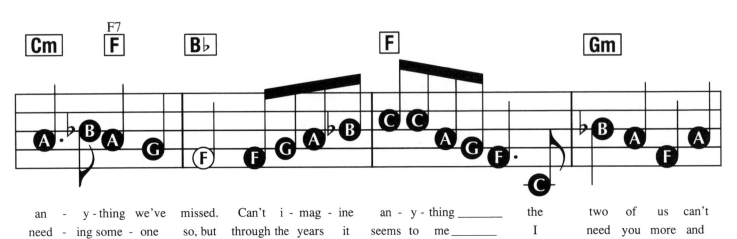

an-y-thing we've missed. Can't i-mag-ine an-y-thing _____ the two of us can't
need-ing some-one so, but through the years it seems to me _____ I need you more and

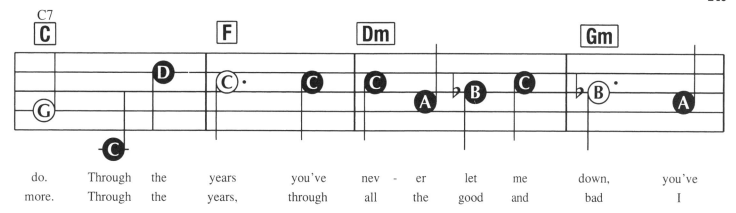

do. Through the years you've nev - er let me down, you've
more. Through the years, through all the good and bad I

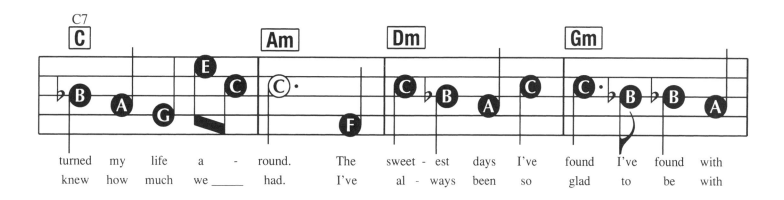

turned my life a - round. The sweet - est days I've found I've found with
knew how much we ___ had. I've al - ways been so glad to be with

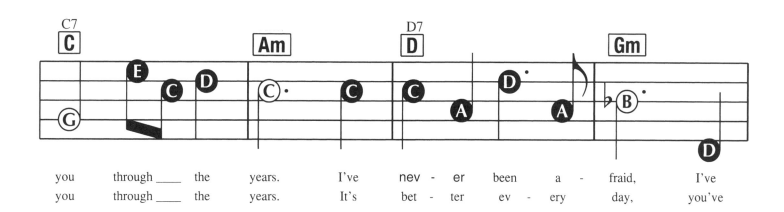

you through ___ the years. I've nev - er been a - fraid, I've
you through ___ the years. It's bet - ter ev - ery day, you've

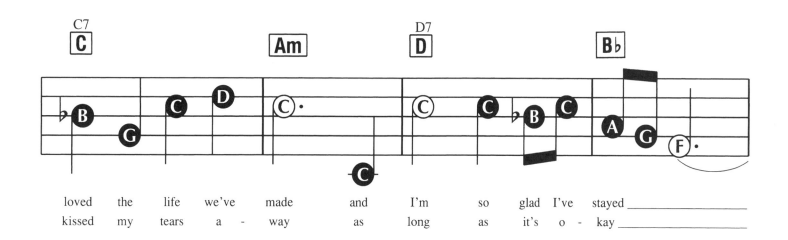

loved the life we've made and I'm so glad I've stayed _____
kissed my tears a - way as long as it's o - kay _____

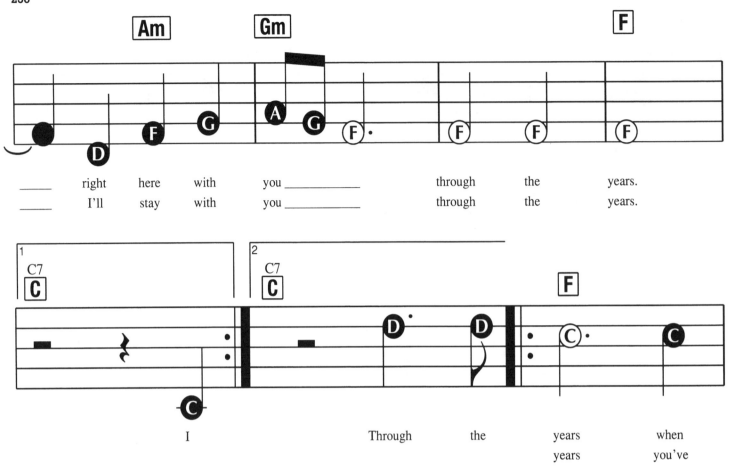

_____ right here with you _____ through the years.
_____ I'll stay with you _____ through the years.

I   Through the years when
                              years you've

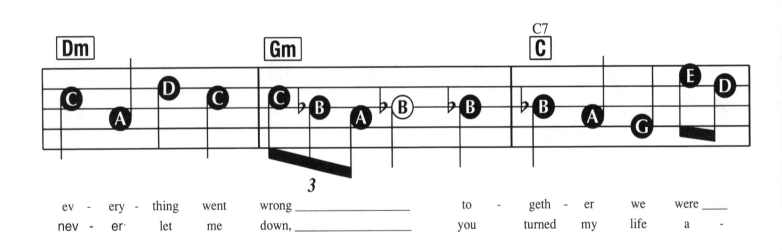

ev - ery - thing went wrong _____ to - geth - er we were _____
nev - er let me down, _____ you turned my life a -

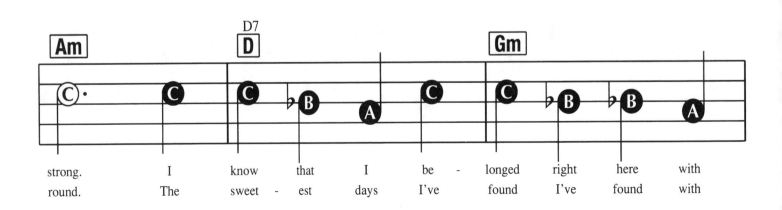

strong.   I know that I be - longed right here with
round.   The sweet - est days I've found I've found with

251

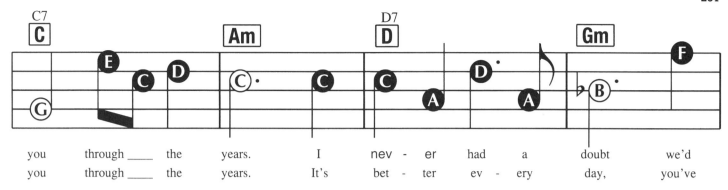

you through ____ the years.   I   nev - er   had   a   doubt   we'd
you through ____ the years.   It's   bet - ter   ev - ery   day,   you've

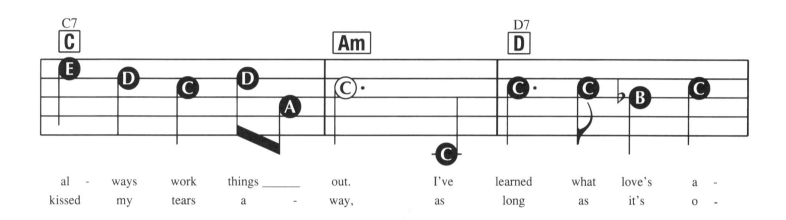

al - ways   work   things _____ out.   I've   learned   what   love's   a -
kissed my   tears   a - way,   as   long   as   it's   o -

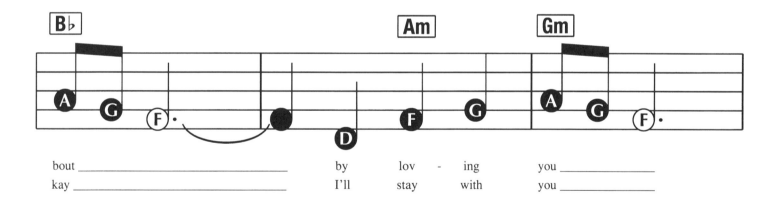

bout _____   by   lov - ing   you _____
kay _____   I'll   stay   with   you _____

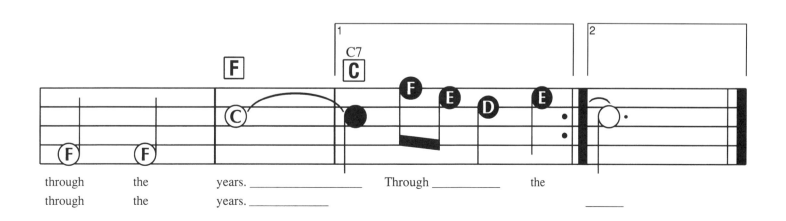

through   the   years. _____   Through _____ the
through   the   years. _____   _____

The Tip of My Fingers

Registration 3
Rhythm: Waltz

Words and Music by
Bill Anderson

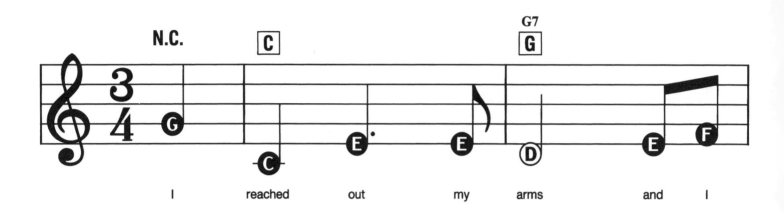

I reached out my arms and I

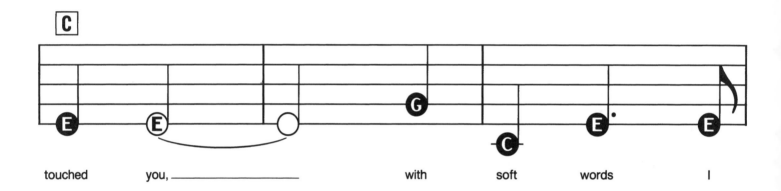

touched you, with soft words I

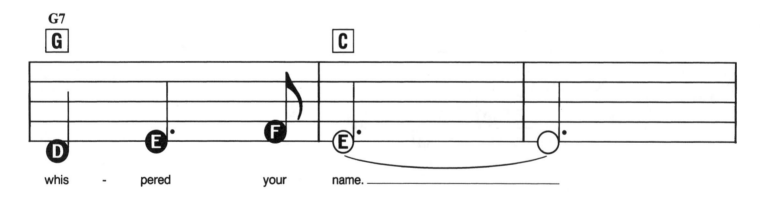

whis - pered your name.

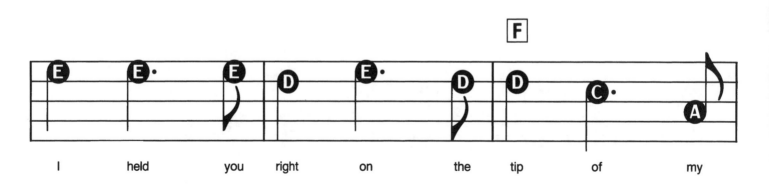

I held you right on the tip of my

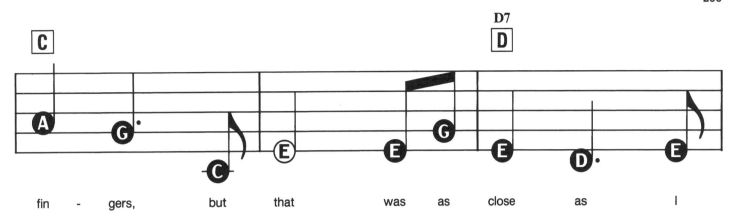

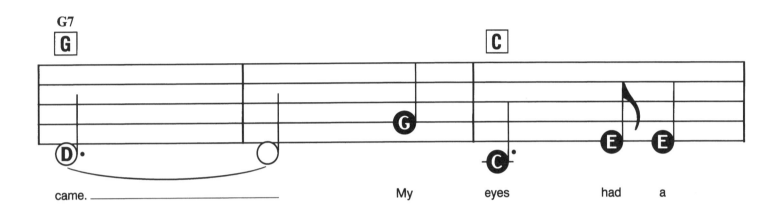

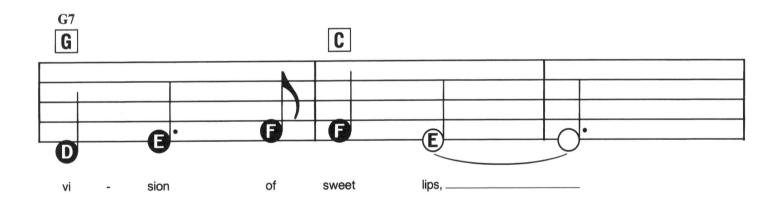

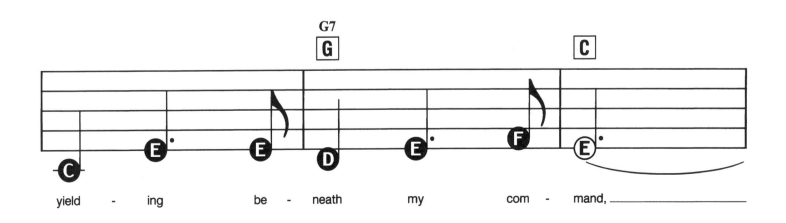

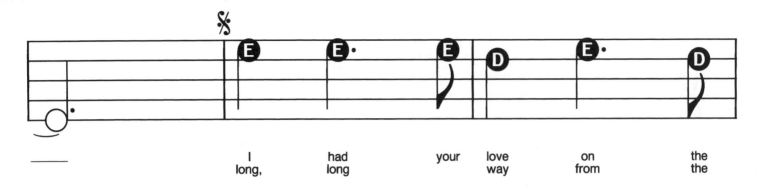

I   had   your   love   on   the
long,   long   way   from   the

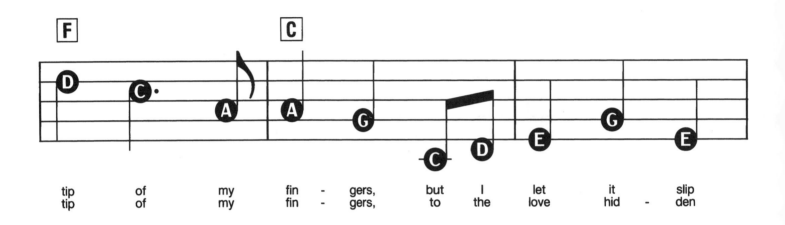

tip   of   my   fin - gers,   but   I   let   it   slip
tip   of   my   fin - gers,   to   the   love   hid - den

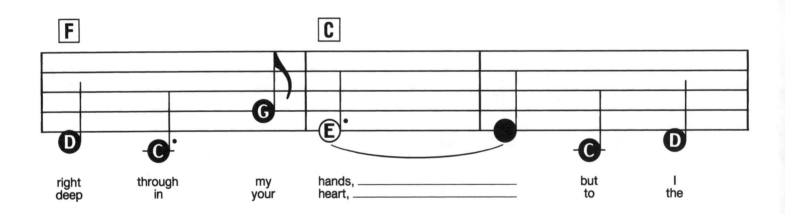

right   through   my   hands, _____   but   I
deep   in   your   heart, _____   to   the

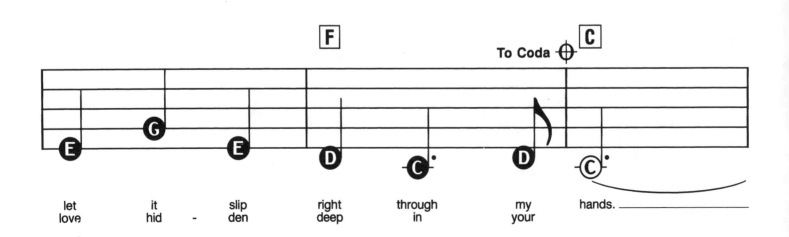

let   it   slip   right   through   my   hands. _____
love   it   hid - den   deep   in   your

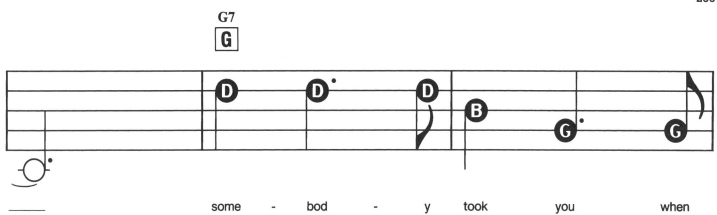

some - bod - y took you when

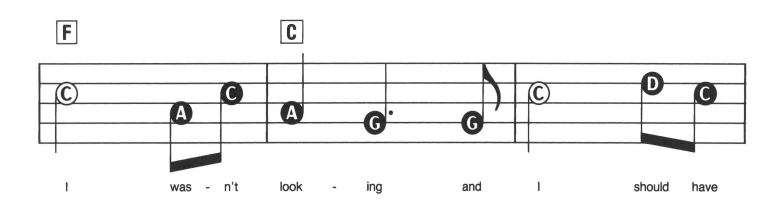

I was - n't look - ing and I should have

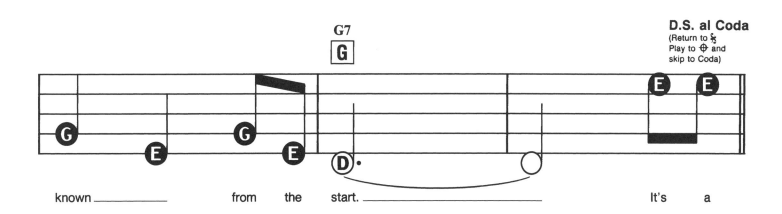

known _____ from the start. _____ It's a

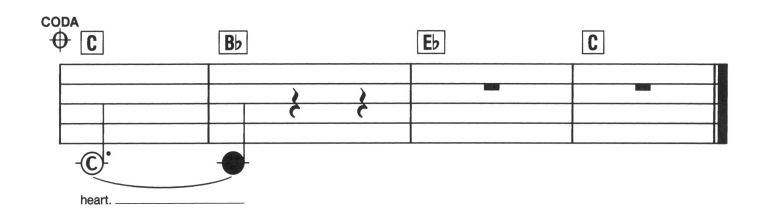

heart. _____

T-R-O-U-B-L-E

Registration 4
Rhythm: Fox Trot or Country Pop

Words and Music by
Jerry Chesnut

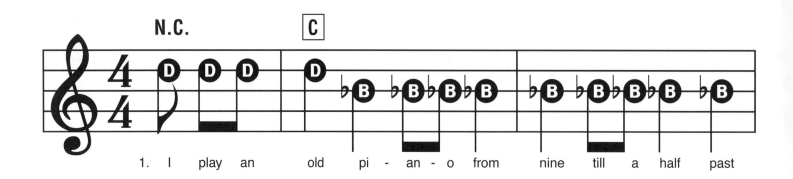

1. I play an old pi - an - o from nine till a half past

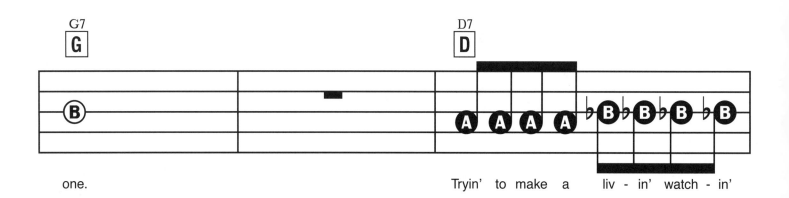

one. Tryin' to make a liv - in' watch - in'

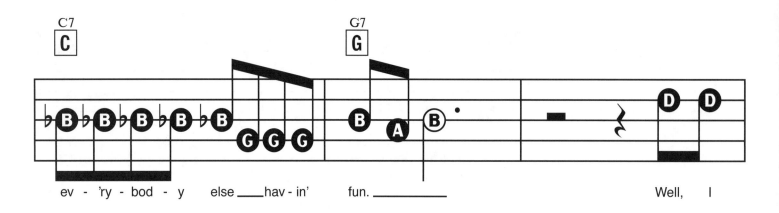

ev - 'ry - bod - y else ___ hav - in' fun. ___ Well, I

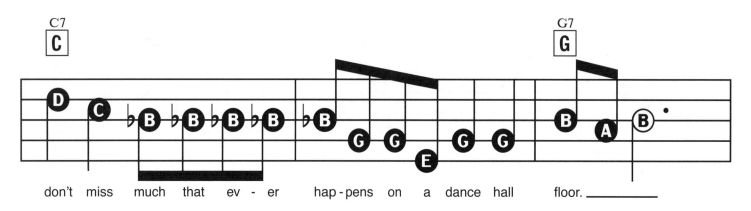

don't miss much that ev - er hap - pens on a dance hall floor. ___

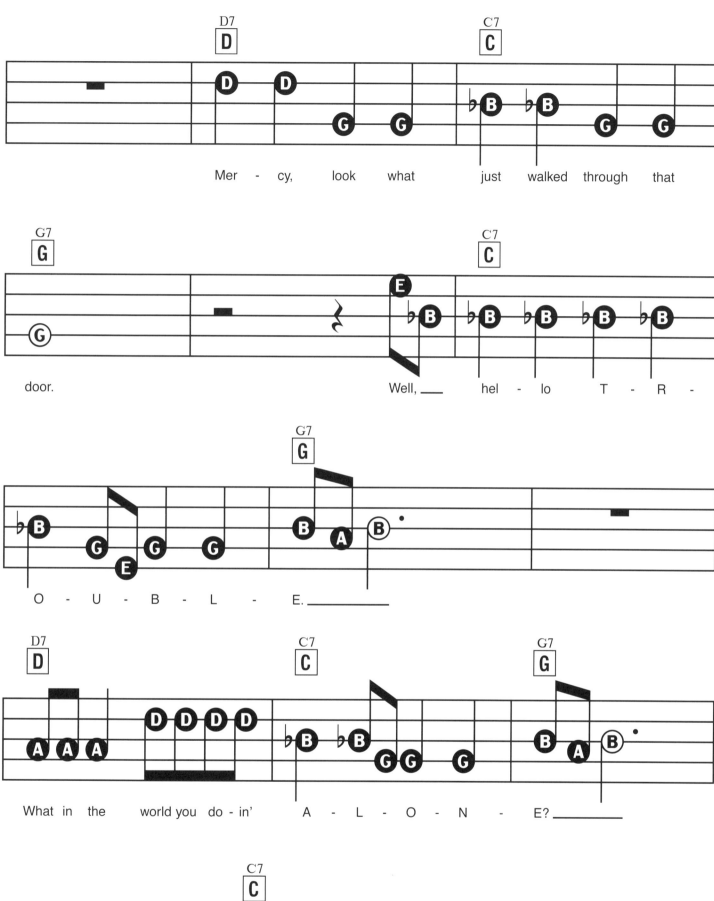

Mer - cy, look what just walked through that

door. Well, ___ hel - lo T - R -

O - U - B - L - E. _____

What in the world you do - in' A - L - O - N - E? _____

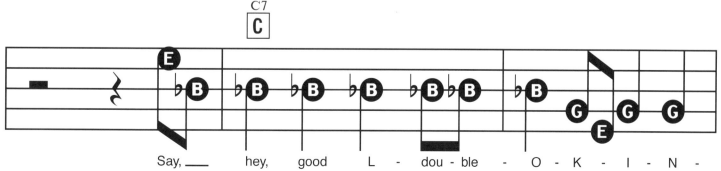

Say, ___ hey, good L - dou - ble - O - K - I - N -

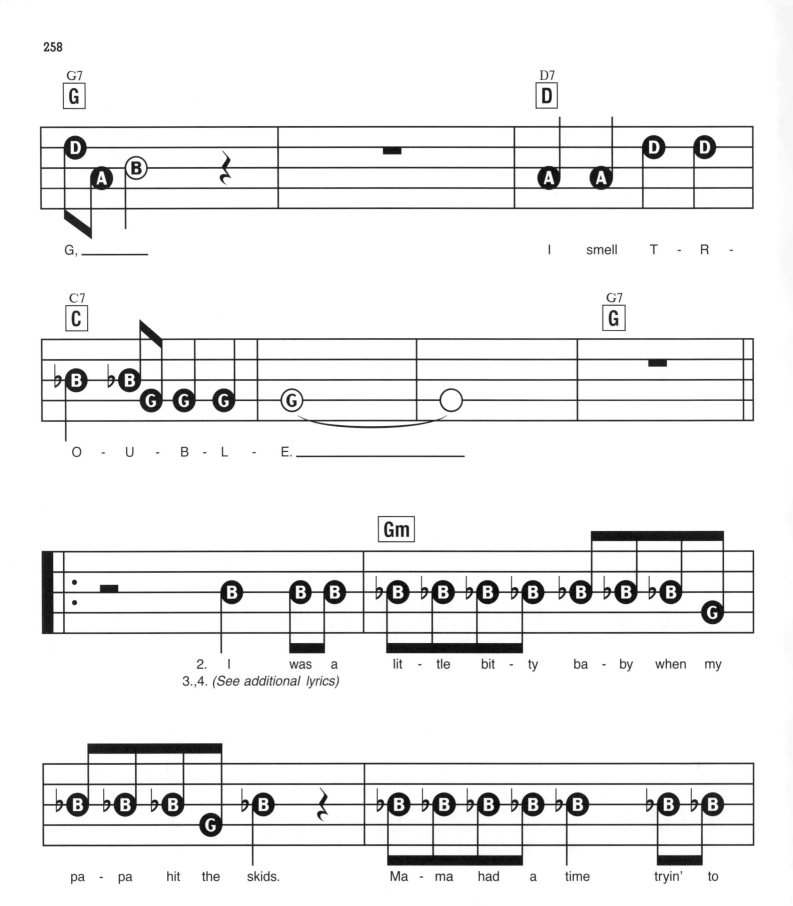

G, _____ I smell T - R -

O - U - B - L - E. _____

2. I was a lit - tle bit - ty ba - by when my
3.,4. *(See additional lyrics)*

pa - pa hit the skids. Ma - ma had a time tryin' to

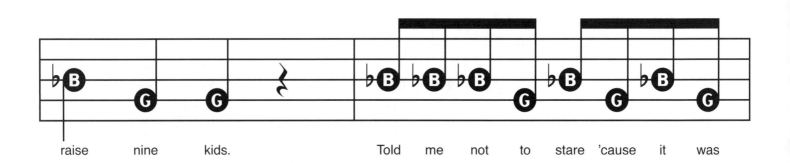

raise nine kids. Told me not to stare 'cause it was

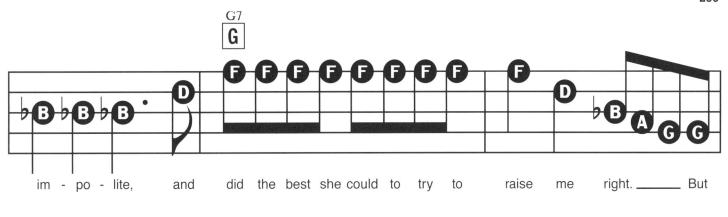

im - po - lite, and did the best she could to try to raise me right. _____ But

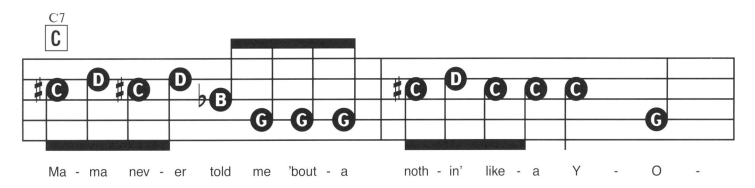

Ma - ma nev - er told me 'bout - a noth - in' like - a Y - O -

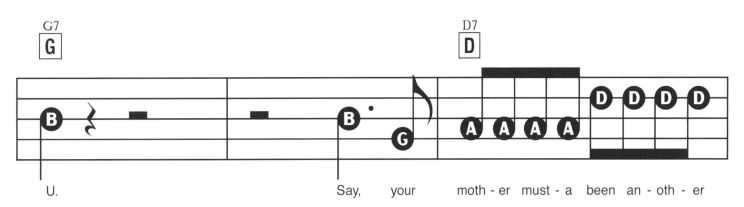

U. Say, your moth - er must - a been an - oth - er

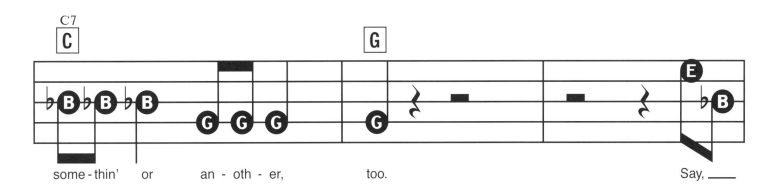

some - thin' or an - oth - er, too. Say, _____

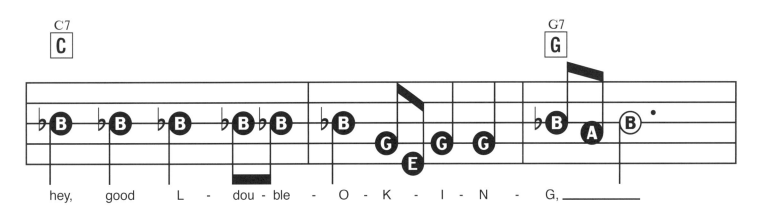

hey, good L - dou - ble - O - K - I - N - G, _____

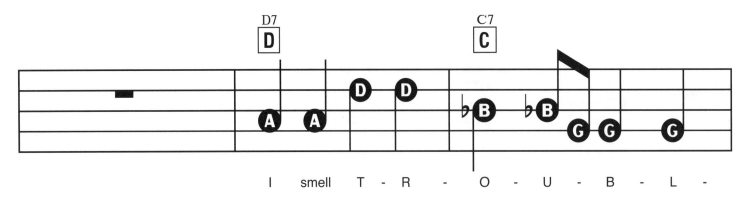

I smell T - R - O - U - B - L -

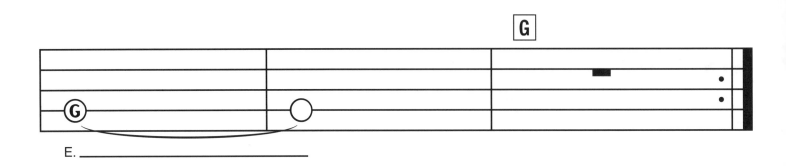

E.

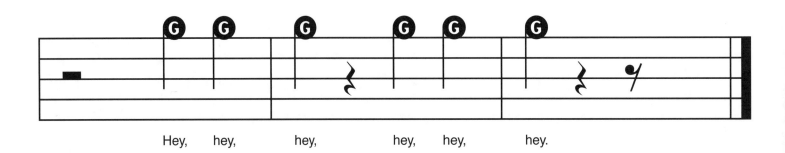

Hey, hey, hey, hey, hey, hey.

Additional Lyrics

3. Well, you talk about a woman, I've seen a lotta others
   With too much somethin' and not enough of another,
   Lookin' like glory and walkin' like a dream.
   Mother Nature's sure been good to Y-O-U.
   Well, your mother musta been another good lookin' mother, too.
   Say, hey, good L-double-O-K-I-N-G, I smell T-R-O-U-B-L-E.

4. Well, you talk about a trouble makin' hunka' pokey bait
   The men are gonna love and all the women gonna hate.
   Remindin' them of everything they're never gonna be,
   Maybe the beginnin' of a World War Three.
   'Cause the world ain't ready for nothing like a Y-O-U.
   I bet your mother musta been another somethin' or the other, too.
   Say, hey, good L-double-O-K-I-N-G, I smell T-R-O-U-B-L-E.

Walk a Mile in My Shoes

Registration 4
Rhythm: Country Rock or 8-Beat

Words and Music by
Joe South

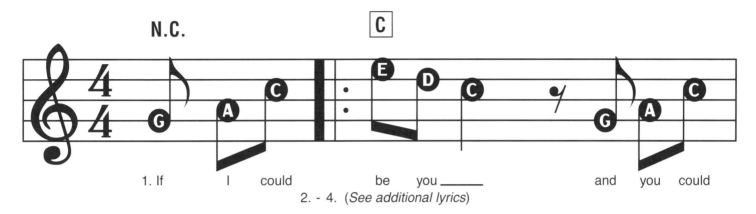

1. If I could be you _____ and you could
2. - 4. (*See additional lyrics*)

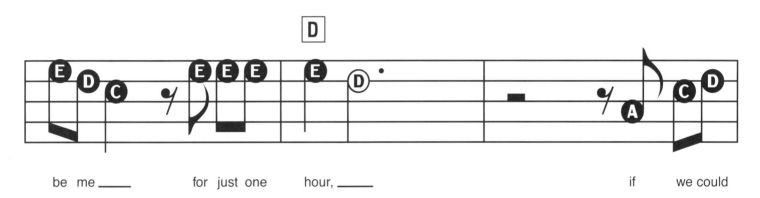

be me _____ for just one hour, _____ if we could

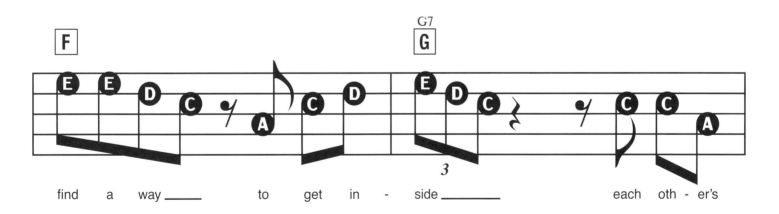

find a way _____ to get in - side _____ each oth - er's

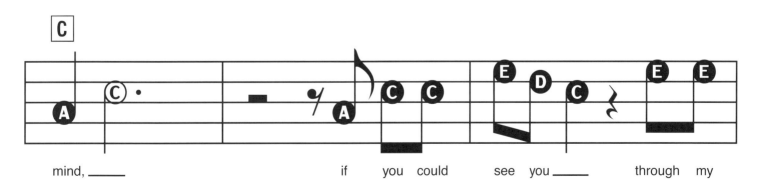

mind, _____ if you could see you _____ through my

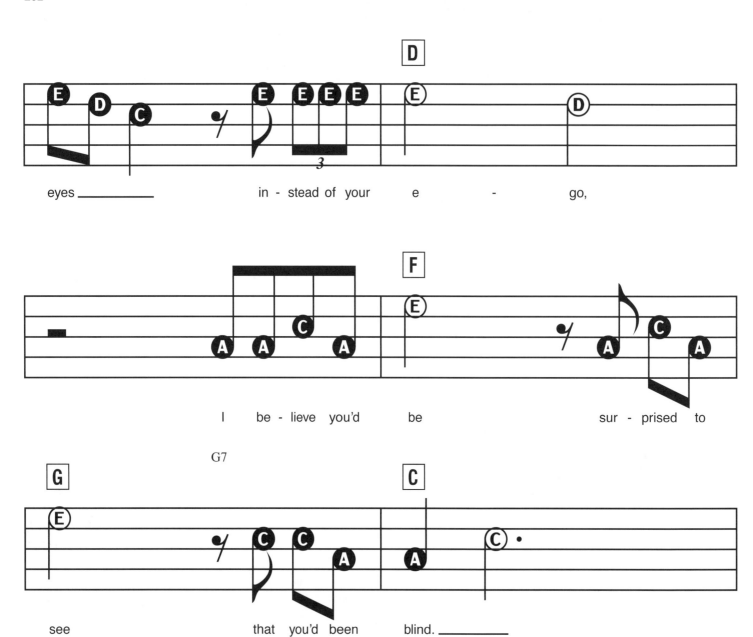

eyes _____ in - stead of your e - go,

I be - lieve you'd be sur - prised to

see that you'd been blind. _____

Chorus

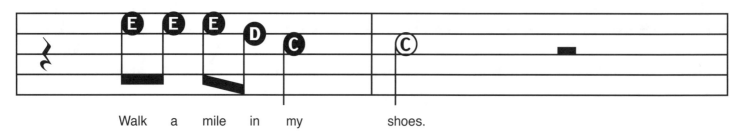

Walk a mile in my shoes.

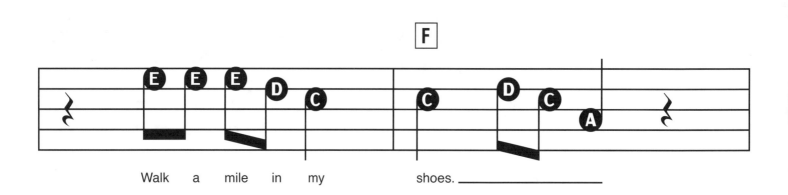

Walk a mile in my shoes. _____

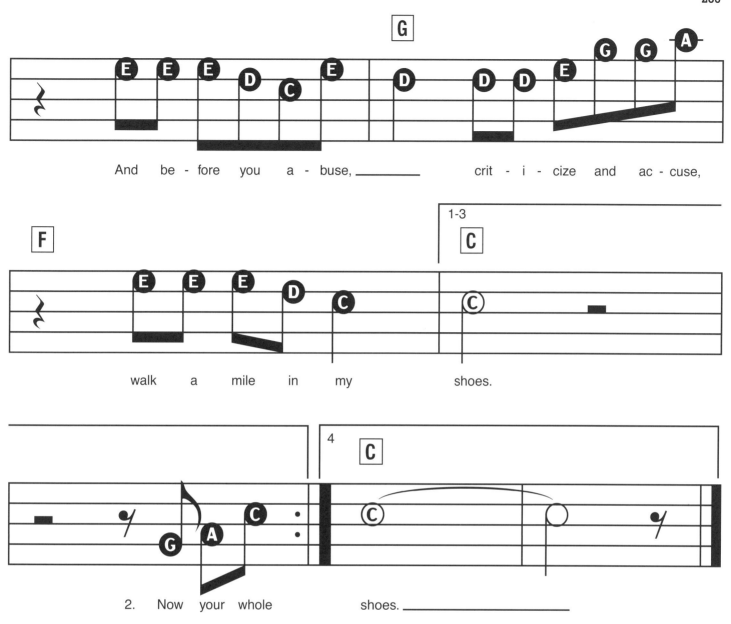

And be - fore you a - buse, _____ crit - i - cize and ac - cuse,

walk a mile in my shoes.

2. Now your whole shoes. _____

Additional Lyrics

2. Now, your whole world you see around you is just a reflection,
And the law of karma says you reap just what you sow.
So, unless you've lived a life of total perfection,
You'd better be careful of every stone that you should throw.
Chorus

3. And yet, we spend the day throwing stones at one another
'Cause I don't think or wear my hair the same way you do.
Well, I may be common people, but I'm your brother,
And when you strike out and try to hurt me it's a-hurtin' you.
Chorus

4. There are people on reservations and out in the ghettos,
And, brother, there but for the grace of God go you and I.
If I only had the wings of a little angel,
Don't you know I'd fly to the top of the mountain and then I'd cry.
Chorus

Two Doors Down

Registration 4
Rhythm: Country Pop or 8 Beat

Words and Music by
Dolly Parton

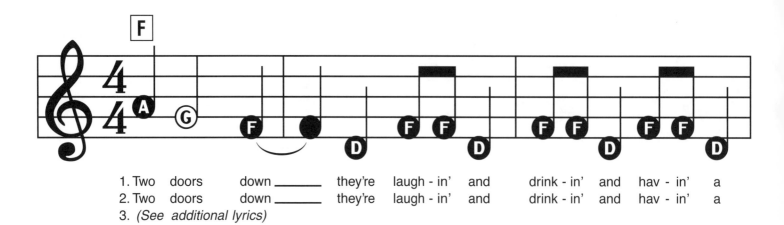

1. Two doors down _____ they're laugh - in' and drink - in' and hav - in' a
2. Two doors down _____ they're laugh - in' and drink - in' and hav - in' a
3. *(See additional lyrics)*

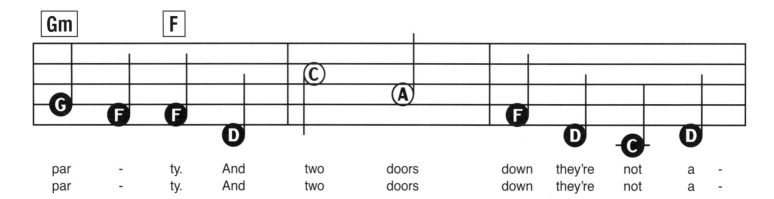

par - ty. And two doors down they're not a -
par - ty. And two doors down they're not a -

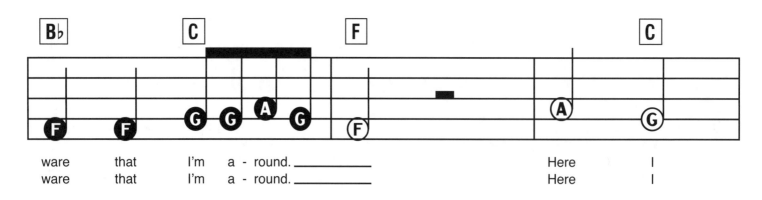

ware that I'm a - round. _____ Here I
ware that I'm a - round. _____ Here I

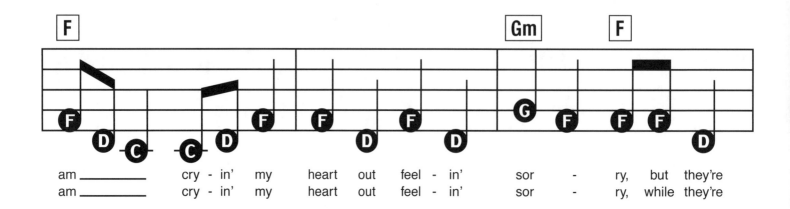

am _____ cry - in' my heart out feel - in' sor - ry, but they're
am _____ cry - in' my heart out feel - in' sor - ry, while they're

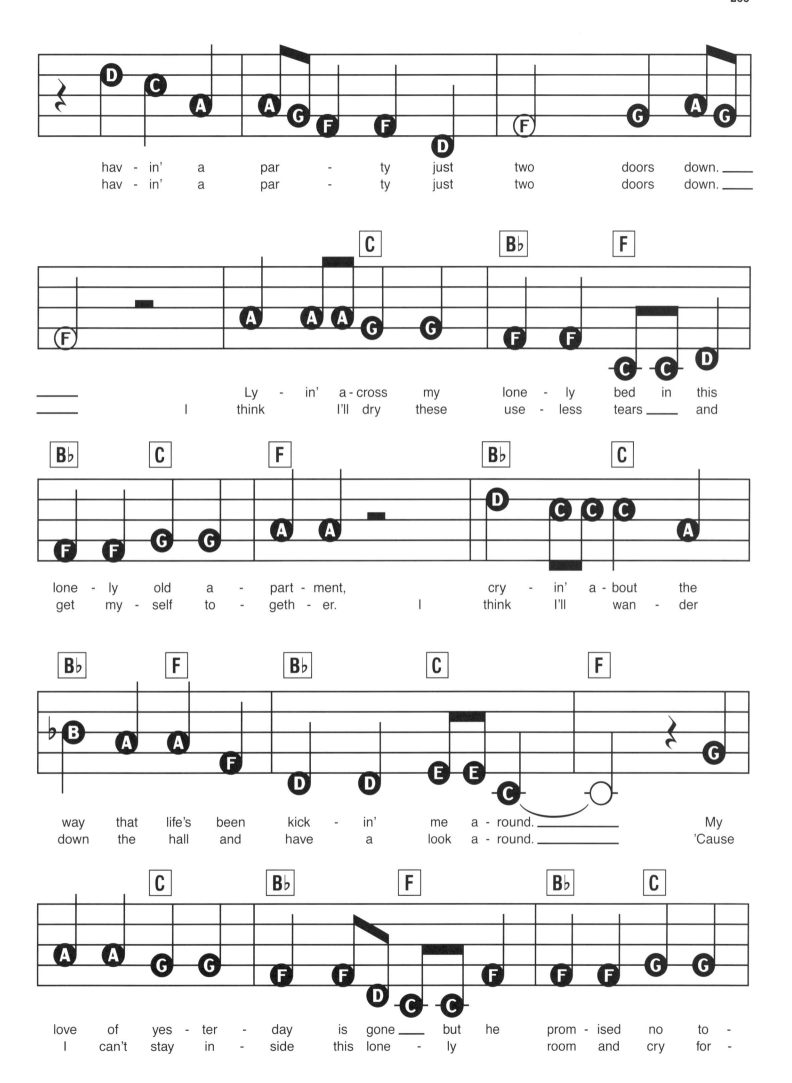

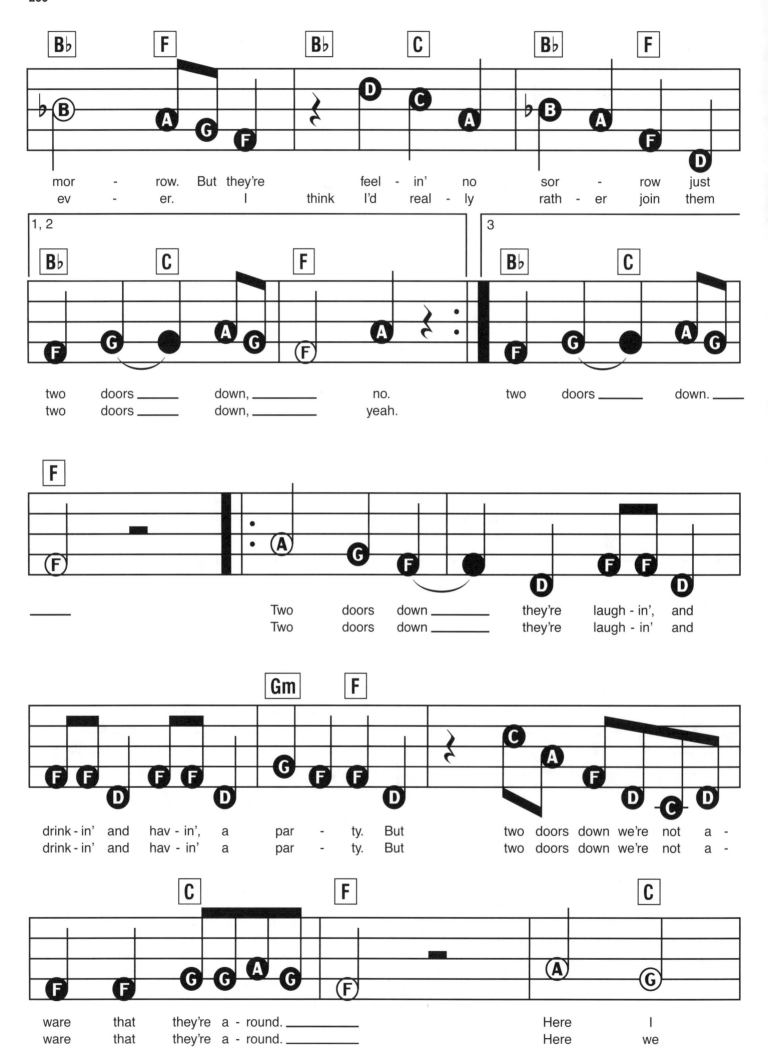

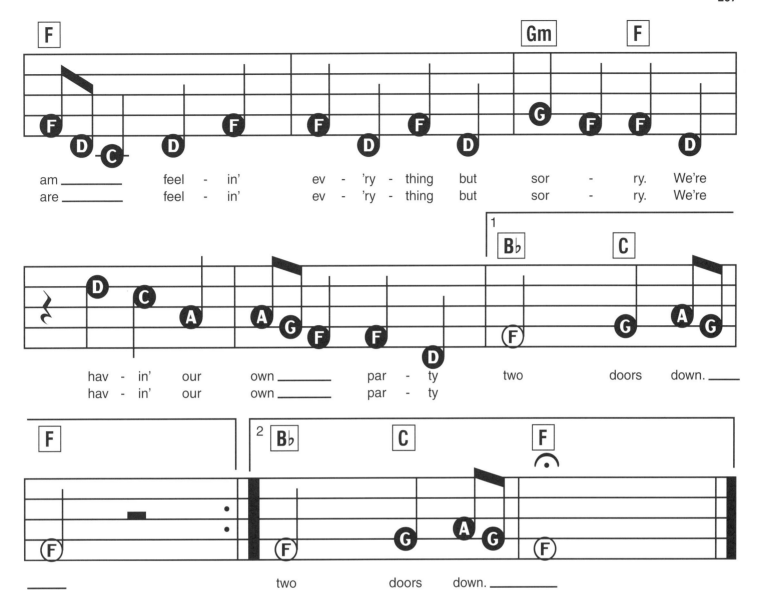

Additional Lyrics

3. Two doors down they're laughin' and drinkin' and havin' a party.
   And two doors down they're all aware that I'm around.
   'Cause here I am no longer cryin', feelin' sorry.
   We're havin' a party just two doors down.

   I can't believe I'm standin' here dry-eyed all smiles and talkin'.
   Makin' conversation with the new love I have found.
   I ask him if he'd like to be alone; so we start walkin'
   Down the hall to my place waitin' two doors down.

Walking in the Sunshine

Registration 5
Rhythm: Country

Words and Music by
Roger Miller

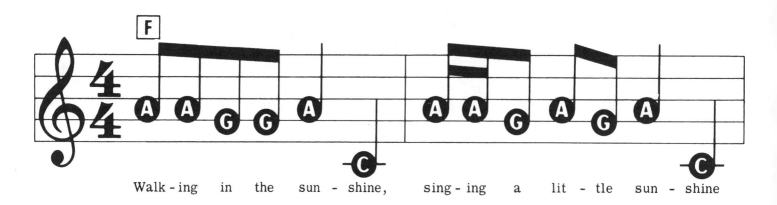

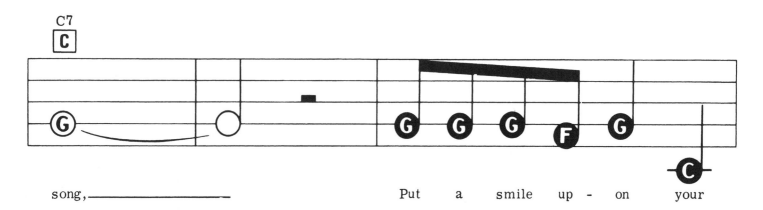

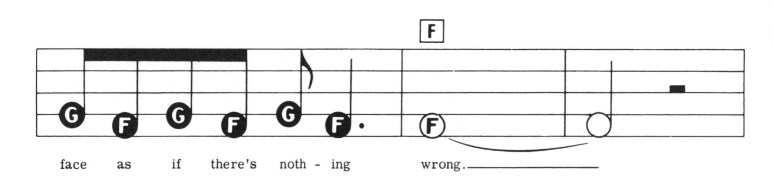

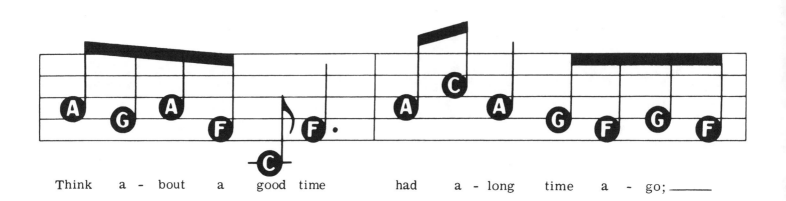

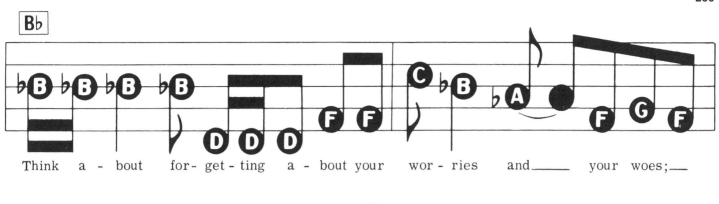

Think a - bout for - get - ting a - bout your wor - ries and____ your woes;____

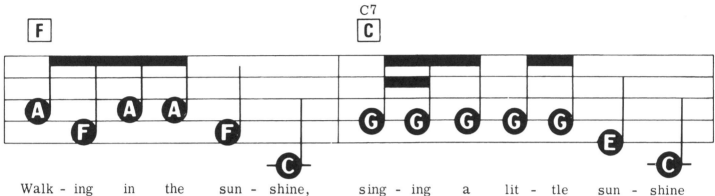

Walk - ing in the sun - shine, sing - ing a lit - tle sun - shine

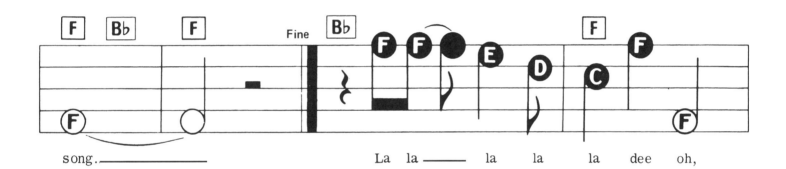

song.____ La la ____ la la la dee oh,

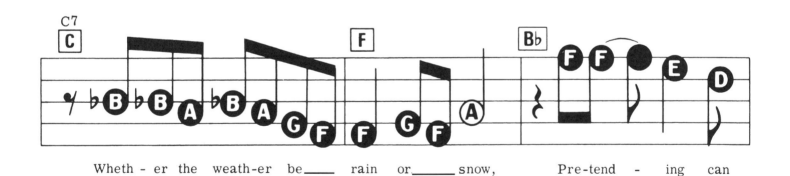

Wheth - er the weath-er be____ rain or____ snow, Pre-tend - ing can

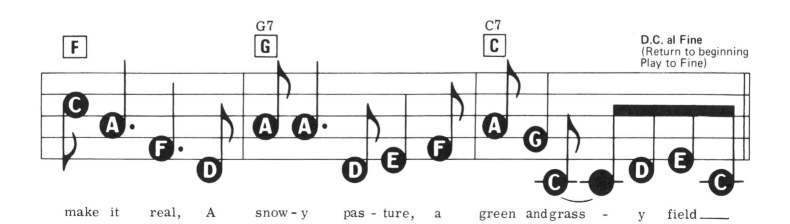

make it real, A snow-y pas - ture, a green and grass - y field____

When My Blue Moon Turns to Gold Again

Registration 1
Rhythm: Country or Fox Trot

Words and Music by Wiley Walker
and Gene Sullivan

N.C. / **B♭**

Mem - o - ries that lin - ger in my
lips that used to in thrill me
cas - tles we built of dreams to -

F7 / **F**

heart, _____ mem - o - ries that make my heart grow
so, _____ your kiss - es were meant for on - ly
geth - er _____ were the sweet - est sto - ries ev - er

B♭

cold; _____ but some day they'll live a - gain, sweet -
me; _____ In my dreams they'll live a - gain, sweet -
told; _____ May - be we will live them all a -

F7 / **F**

heart, _____ and my blue moon a - gain will turn to
heart, _____ but my gol - den moon is just a mem - o -
gain, _____ and my blue moon a - gain will turn to

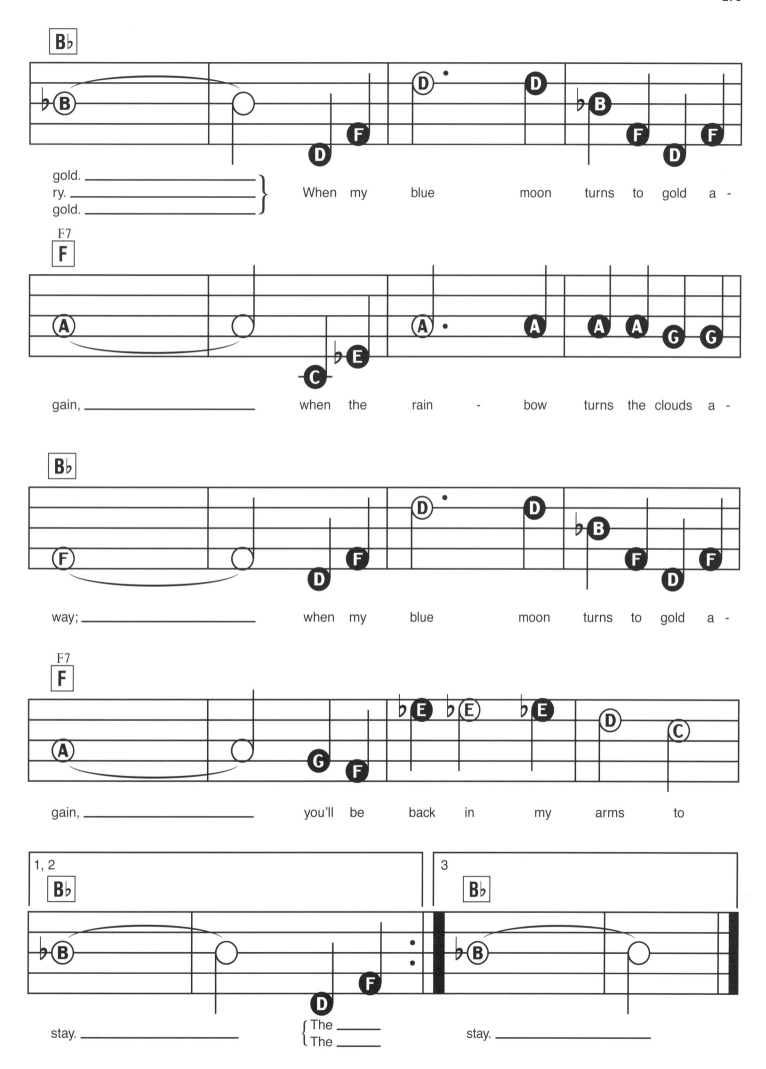

Whiskey River

Registration 2
Rhythm: Country Pop or Fox Trot

Words and Music by
J.B. Shinn III

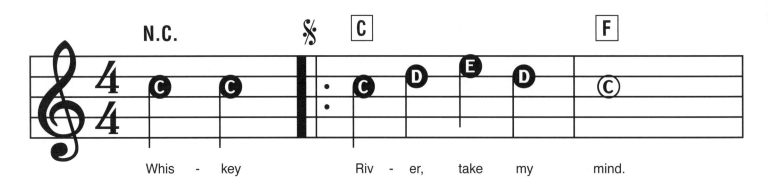

Whis - key   Riv - er, take my mind.

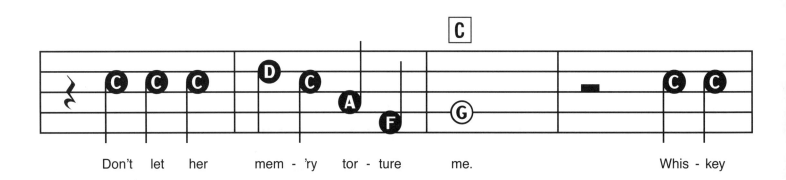

Don't let her mem - 'ry tor - ture me.   Whis - key

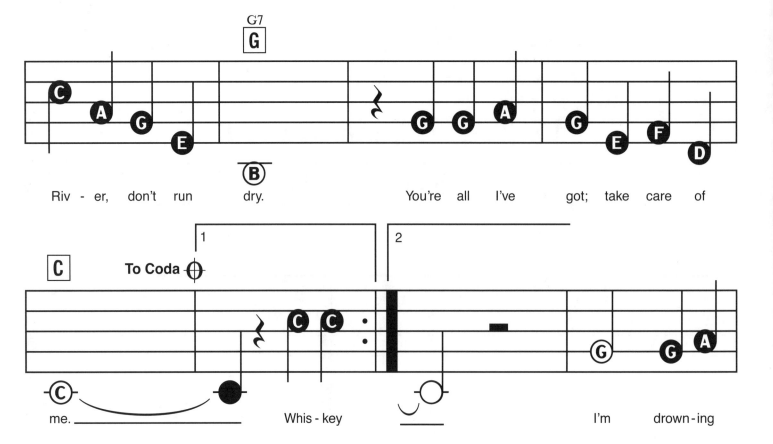

Riv - er, don't run dry.   You're all I've got; take care of

me. _____   Whis - key ___   I'm drown - ing

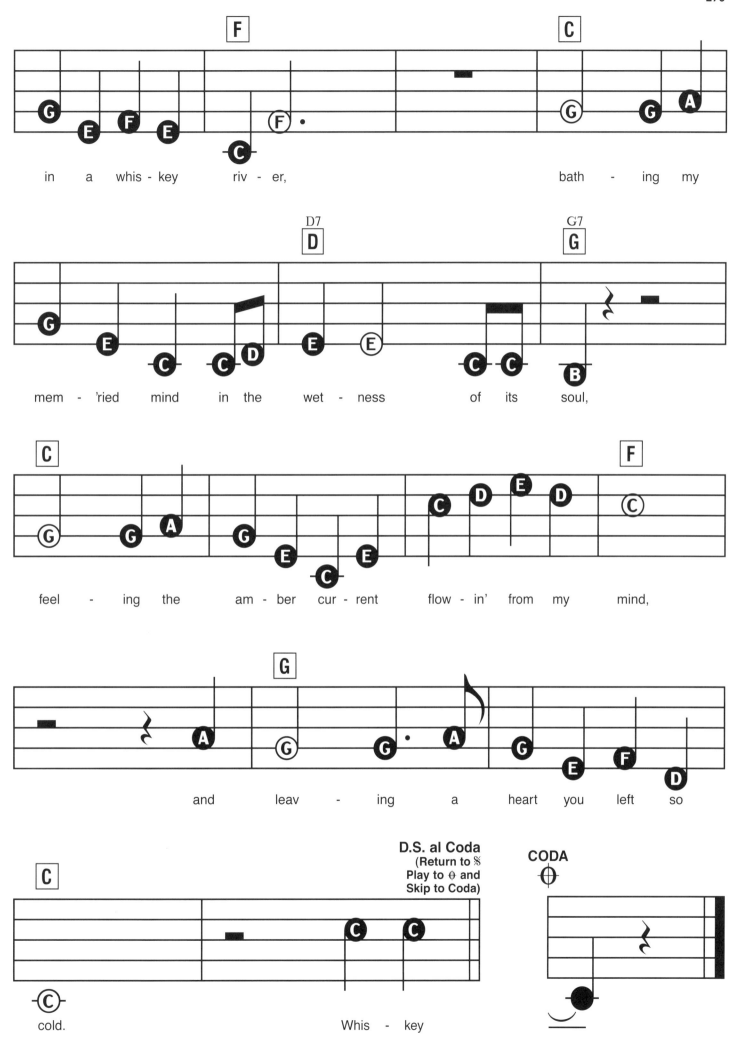

You Are My Sunshine

Registration 4
Rhythm: Fox Trot

Words and Music by Jimmie Davis
and Charles Mitchell

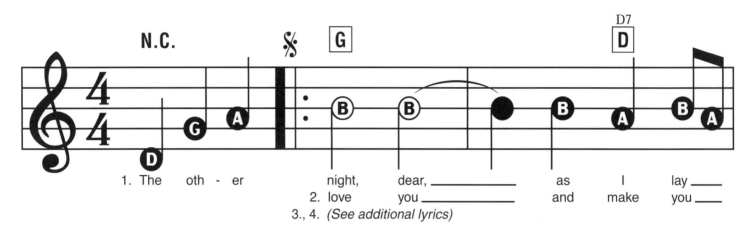

1. The oth - er night, dear, _____ as I lay _____
2. love you _____ and make you _____
3., 4. *(See additional lyrics)*

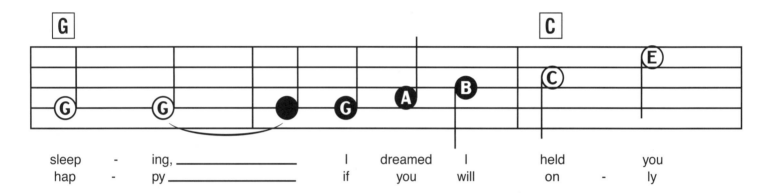

sleep - ing, _____ I dreamed I held you
hap - py _____ if you will on - ly

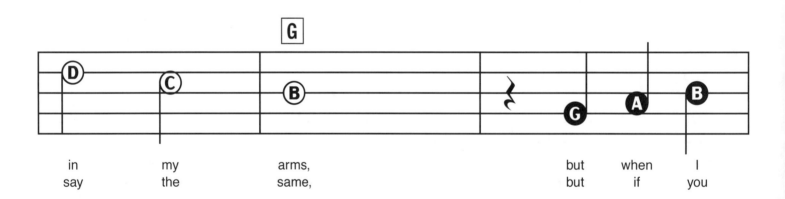

in my arms, but when I
say the same, but if you

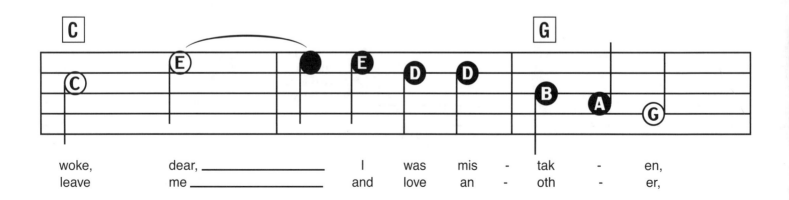

woke, dear, _____ I was mis - tak - en,
leave me _____ and love an - oth - er,

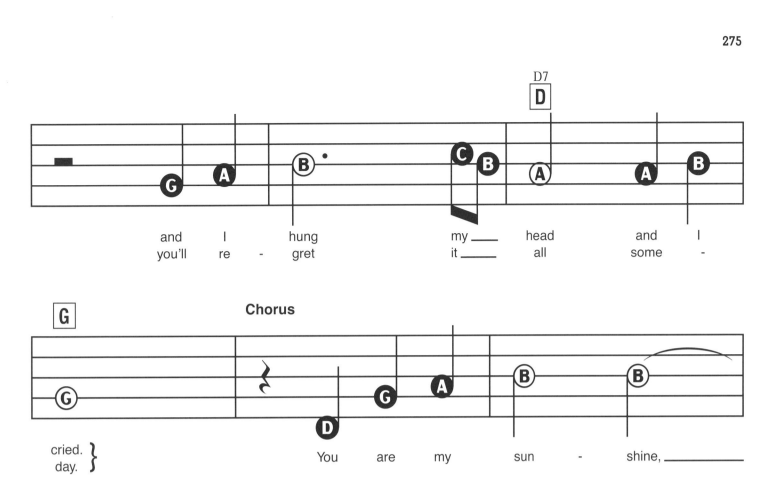

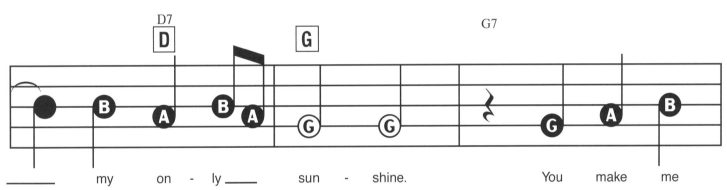

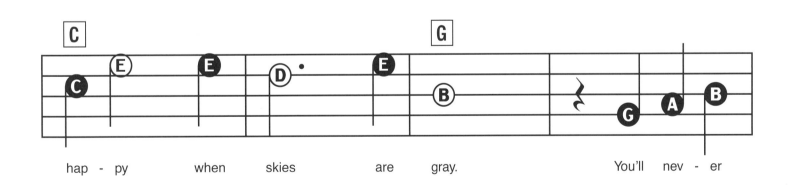

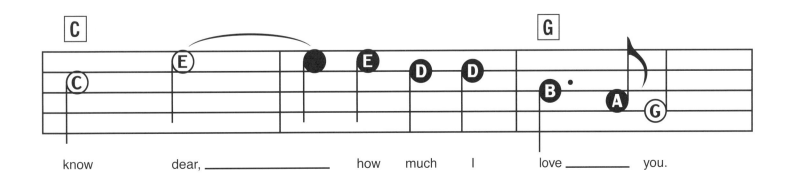

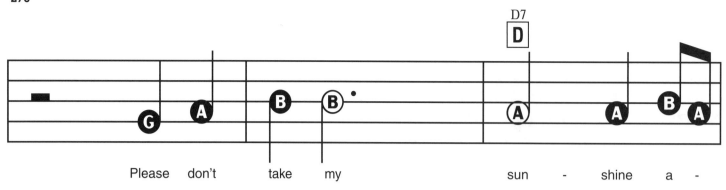

Please don't take my sun - shine a -

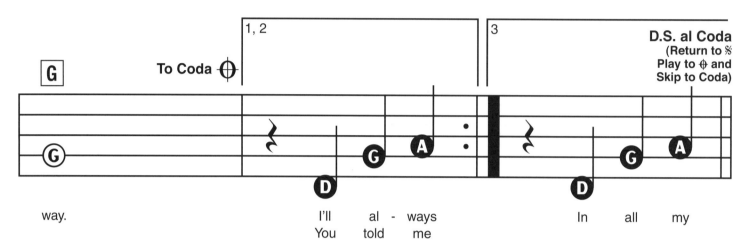

way.   I'll al - ways   In all my
                      You told me

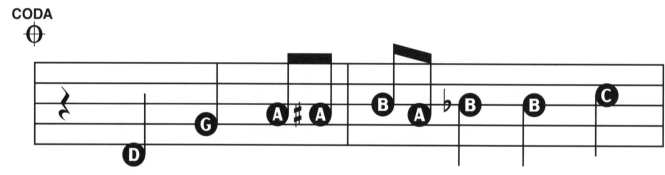

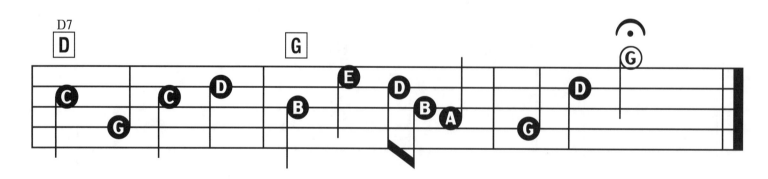

Additional Lyrics

3. You told me once, dear, you really loved me
   And no one could come between,
   But now you've left me to love another.
   You have shattered all of my dreams.
   Chorus

4. In all my dreams, dear, you seem to leave me.
   When I awake my poor heart pains.
   So won't you come back and make me happy?
   I'll forgive dear I'll take all the blame.
   Chorus

You Decorated My Life

Registration 1
Rhythm: Ballad or Fox Trot

Words and Music by Debbie Hupp
and Bob Morrison

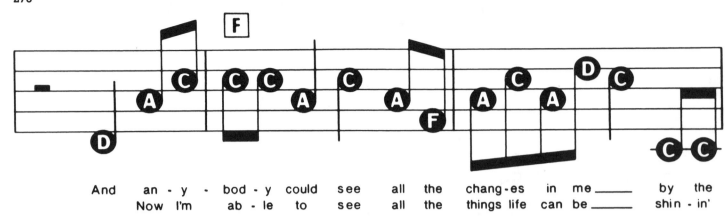

And an-y-bod-y could see all the chang-es in me _____ by the
Now I'm ab-le to see all the things life can be _____ shin-in'

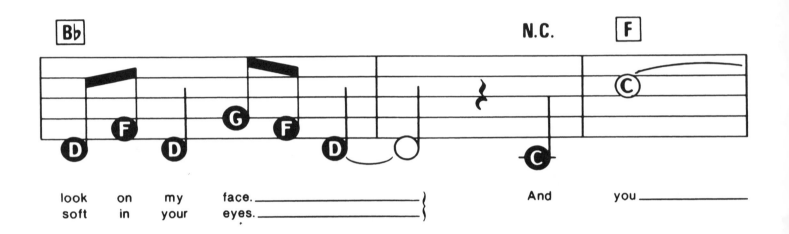

look on my face. _____
soft in your eyes. _____

And you _____

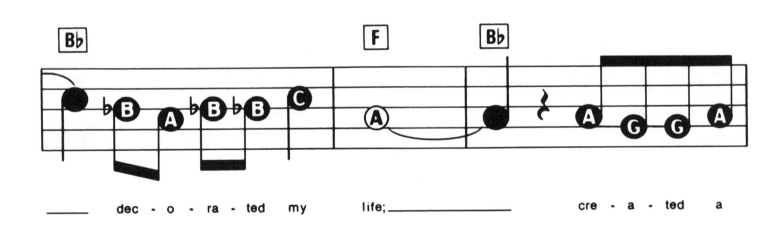

_____ dec-o-ra-ted my life; _____ cre-a-ted a

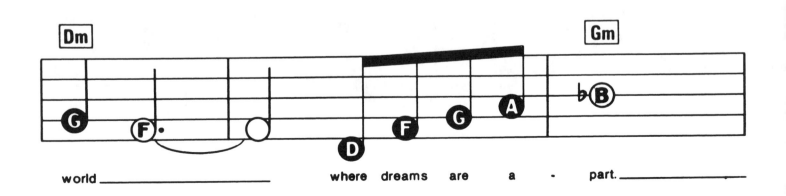

world _____ where dreams are a - part. _____

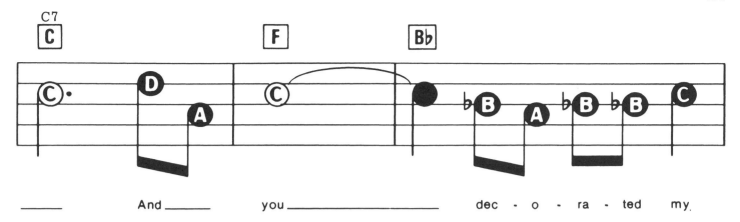

And _____ you _____ dec - o - ra - ted my

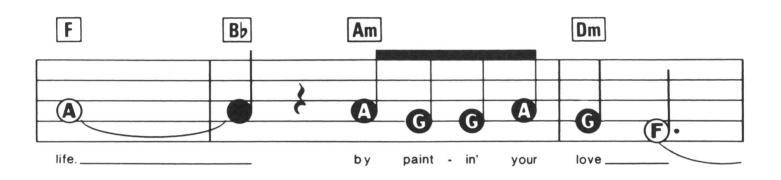

life. _____ by paint - in' your love _____

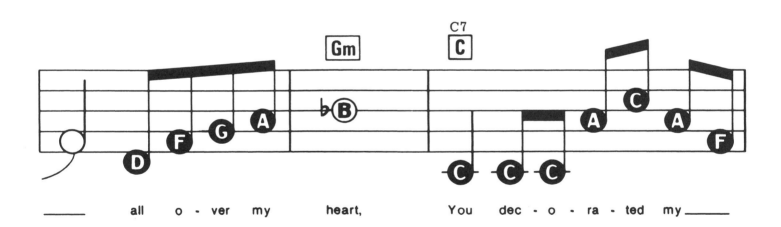

_____ all o - ver my heart, You dec - o - ra - ted my _____

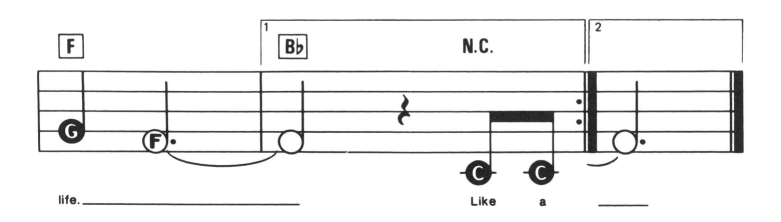

life. _____ Like a _____

You Belong to Me

Registration 4
Rhythm: Ballad

Words and Music by Pee Wee King,
Redd Stewart and Chilton Price

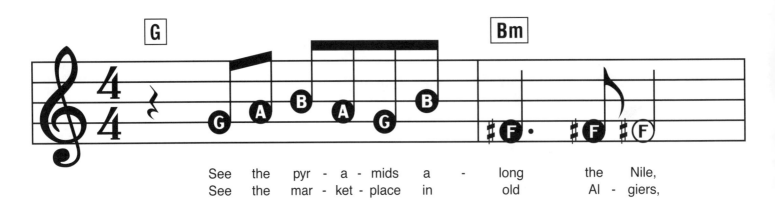

See the pyr - a - mids a - long the Nile,
See the mar - ket - place in old Al - giers,

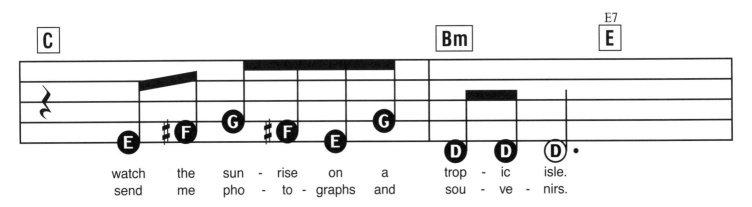

watch the sun - rise on a trop - ic isle.
send me pho - to - graphs and sou - ve - nirs.

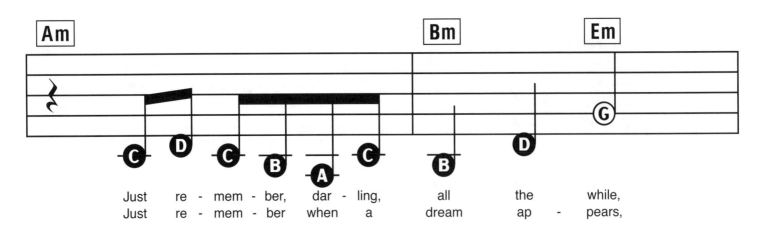

Just re - mem - ber, dar - ling, all the while,
Just re - mem - ber when a dream ap - pears,

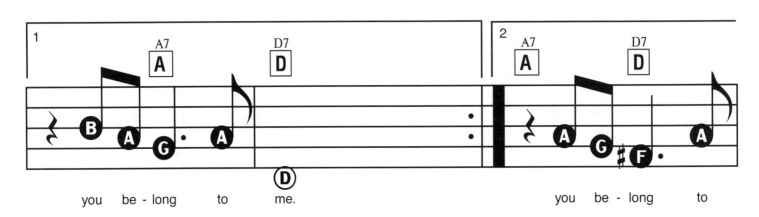

you be - long to me.

you be - long to

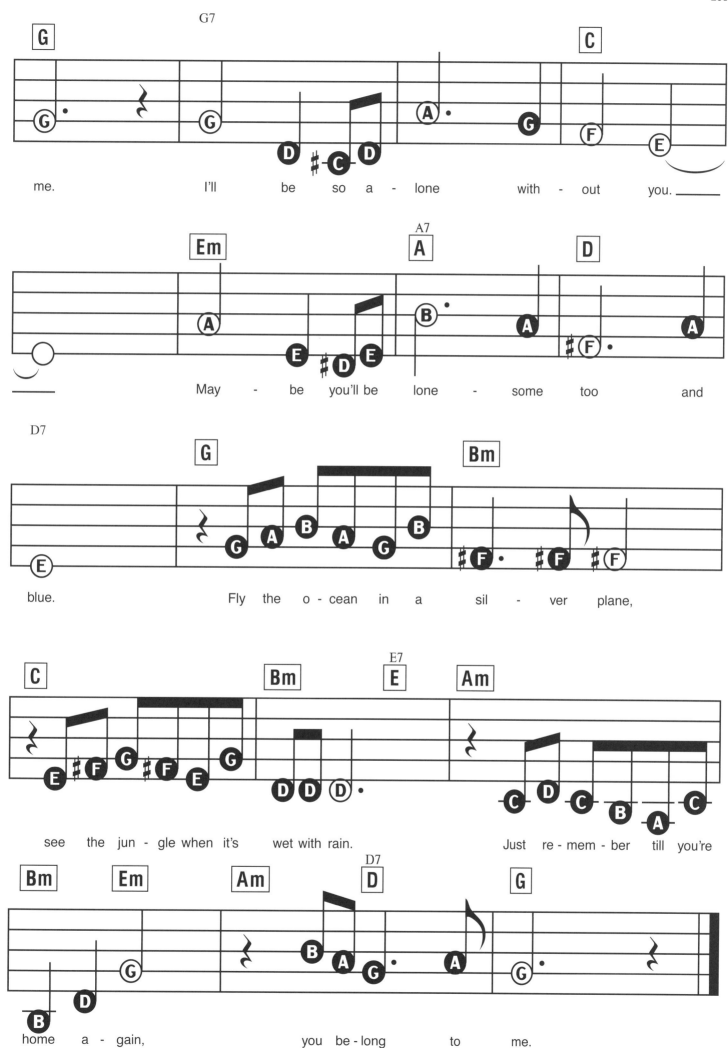

You Belong with Me

Registration 4
Rhythm: Dance or Rock

Words and Music by Taylor Swift
and Liz Rose

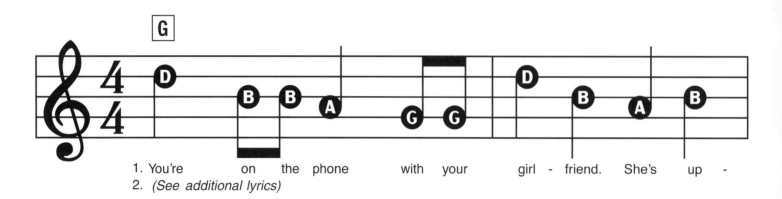

1. You're on the phone with your girl - friend. She's up -
2. *(See additional lyrics)*

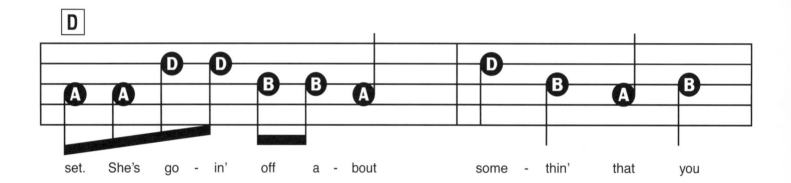

set. She's go - in' off a - bout some - thin' that you

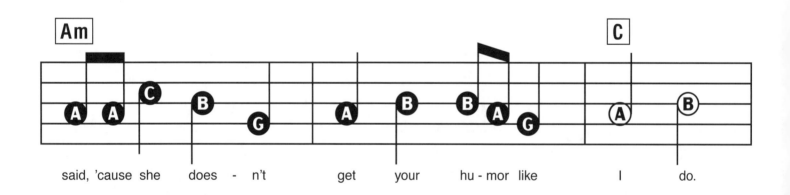

said, 'cause she does - n't get your hu - mor like I do.

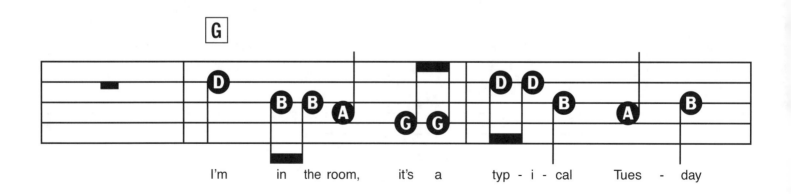

I'm in the room, it's a typ - i - cal Tues - day

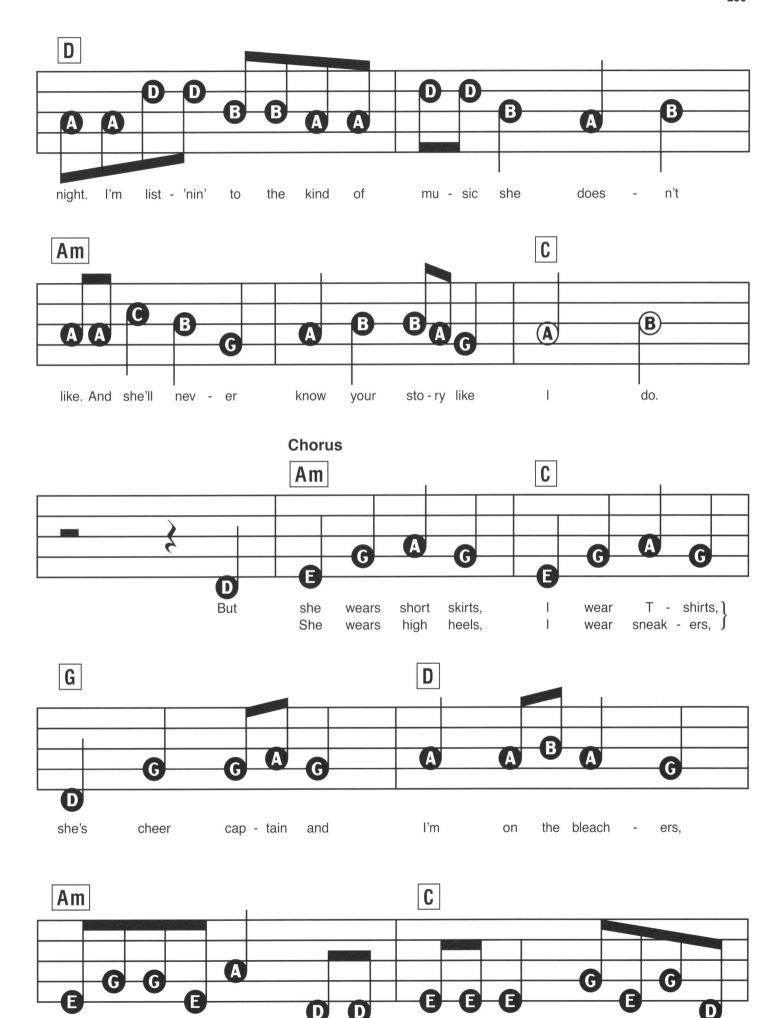

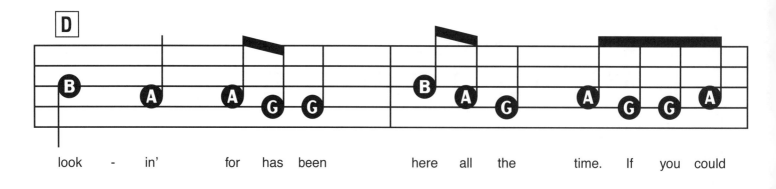

look - in' for has been here all the time. If you could

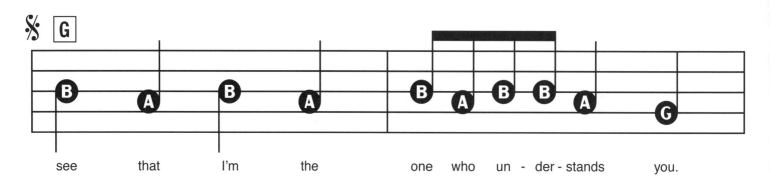

see that I'm the one who un - der - stands you.

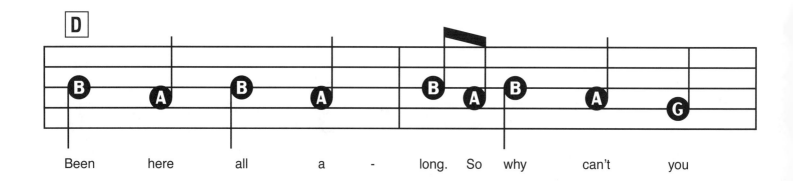

Been here all a - long. So why can't you

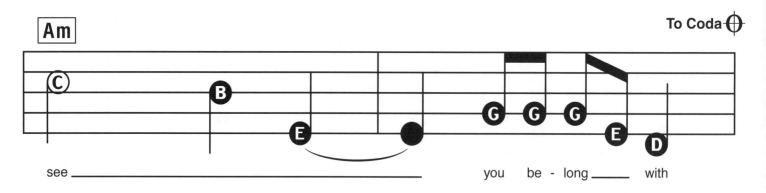

see _____ you be - long _____ with

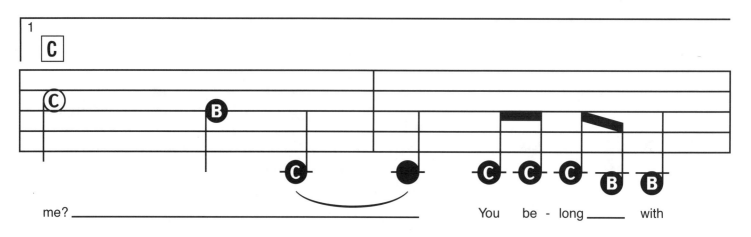

me? _____ You be - long _____ with

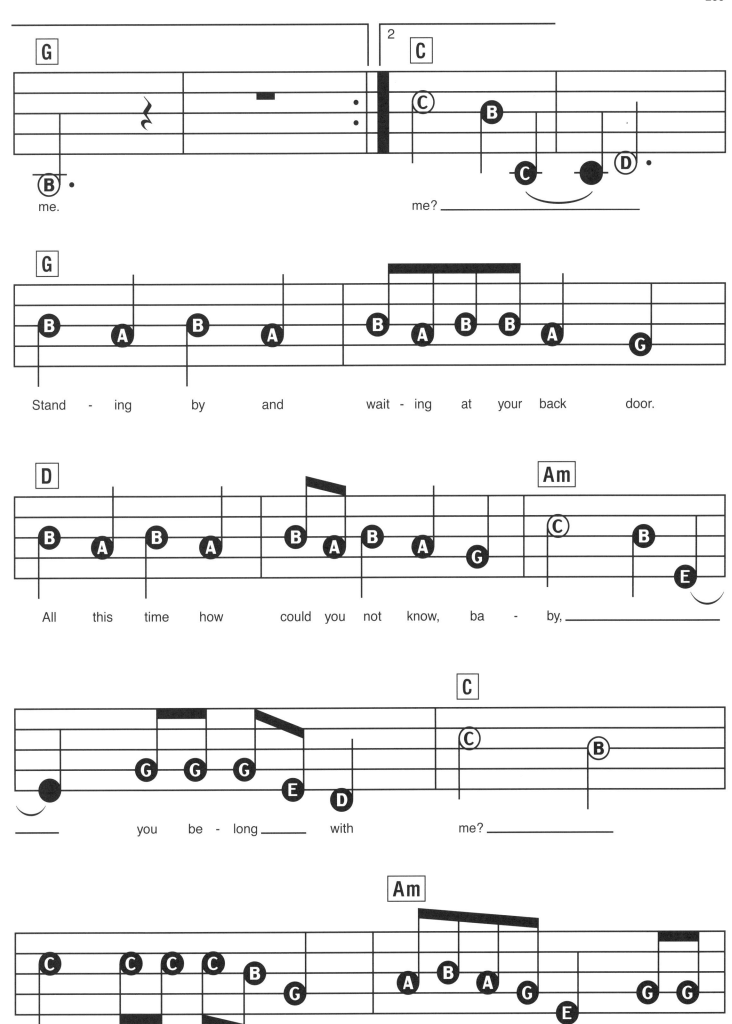

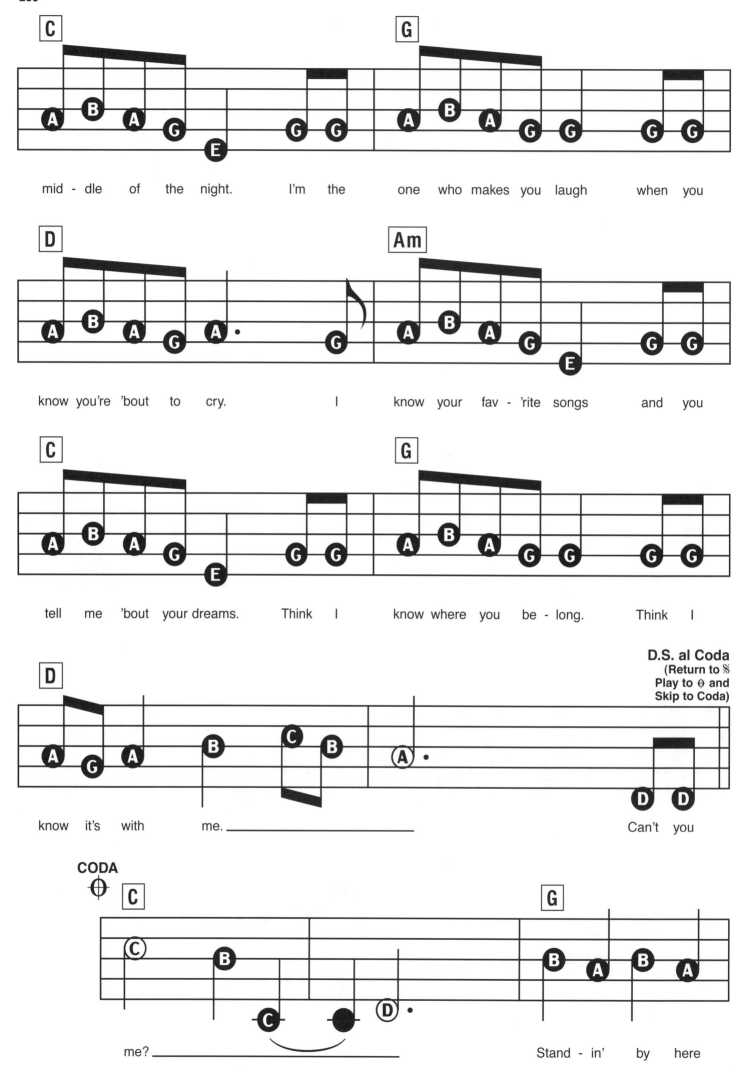

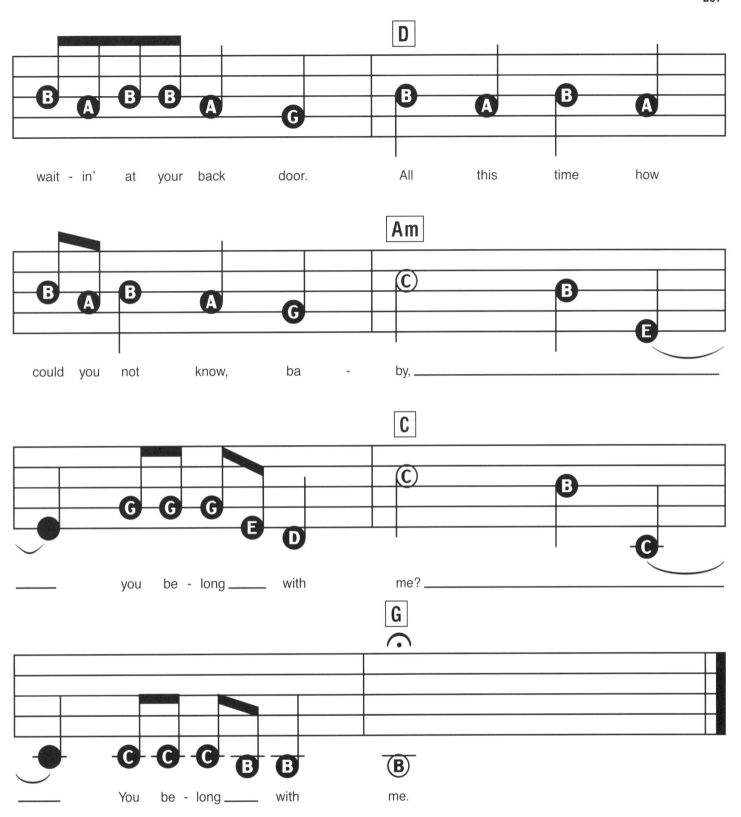

Additional Lyrics

2. Walkin' the streets with you in your worn out jeans,
   I can't help thinkin' this is how it ought to be.
   Laughin' on a park bench, thinkin' to myself,
   "Hey, isn't this easy?"
   And you've got a smile that could light up this whole town.
   I haven't seen it in a while since she brought you down.
   You say you're fine. I know better than that.
   Hey, what you doin' with a girl like that?
   Chorus

You Don't Know Me
from CLAMBAKE

Registration 5
Rhythm: Slow Rock or Rock

Words and Music by Cindy Walker
and Eddy Arnold

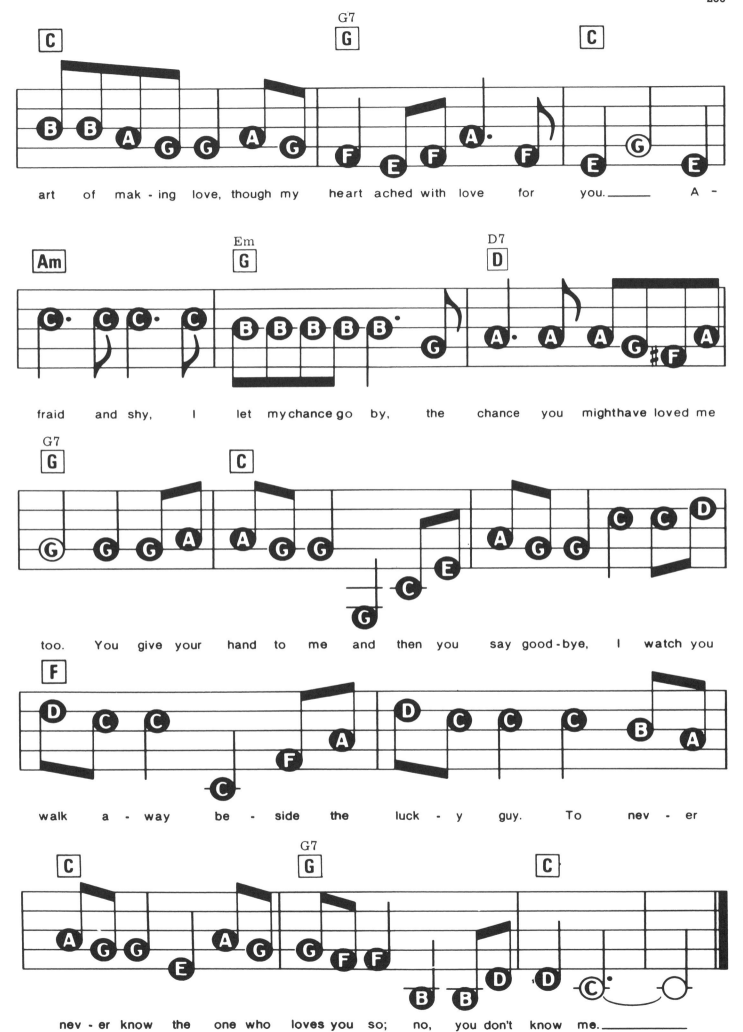

You Win Again

Registration 2
Rhythm: Country Western or Ballad

Words and Music by
Hank Williams

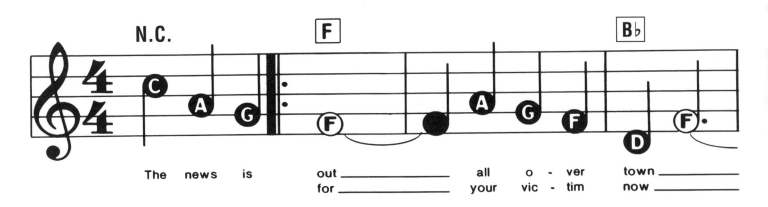

The news is out _____ all o - ver town _____
for _____ your vic - tim now _____

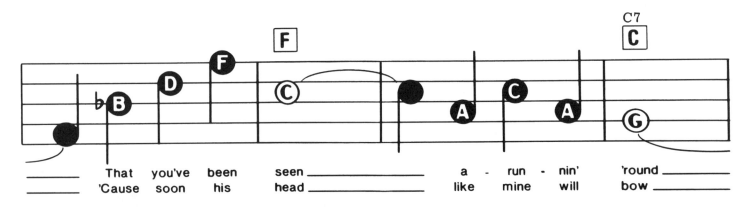

_____ That you've been seen _____ a - run - nin' 'round _____
_____ 'Cause soon his head _____ like mine will bow _____

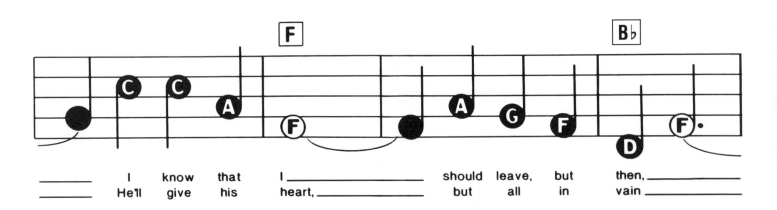

_____ I know that I _____ should leave, but then, _____
_____ He'll give his heart, _____ but all in vain _____

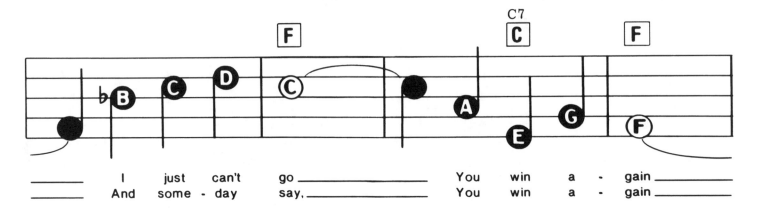

_____ I just can't go _____ You win a - gain _____
_____ And some - day say, _____ You win a - gain _____

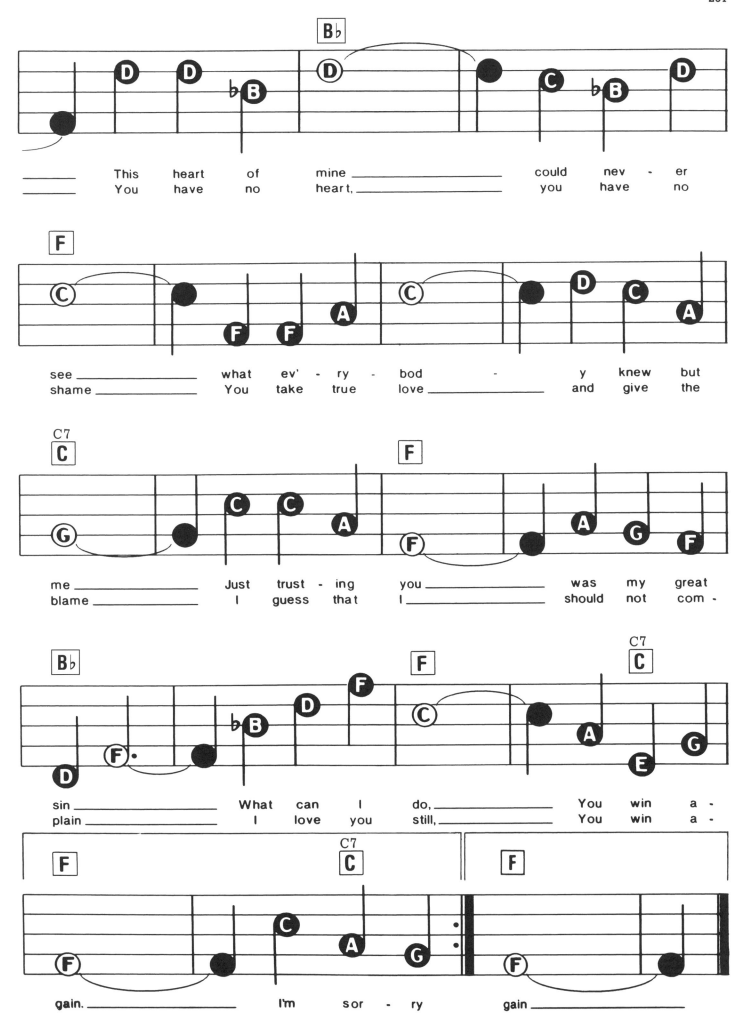

You're the Reason
God Made Oklahoma

Words and Music by Sandy Pinkard,
Larry Collins, Boudleaux Bryant
and Felice Bryant

Registration 10
Rhythm: Blues

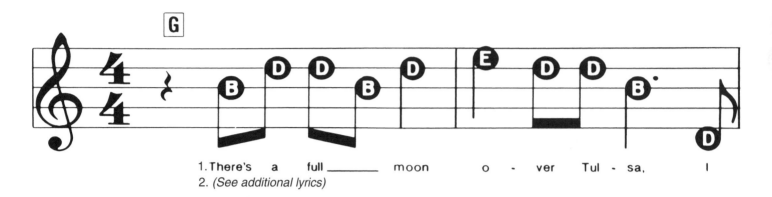

1. There's a full _____ moon o - ver Tul - sa, I
2. (See additional lyrics)

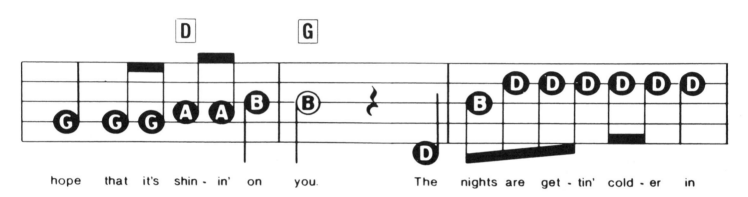

hope that it's shin - in' on you. The nights are get - tin' cold - er in

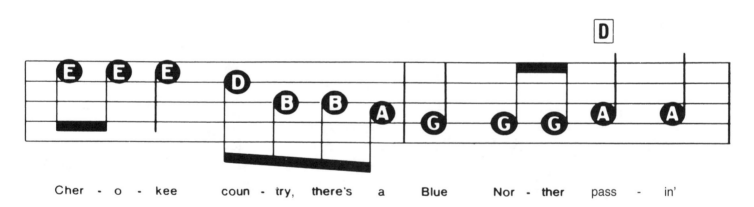

Cher - o - kee coun - try, there's a Blue Nor - ther pass - in'

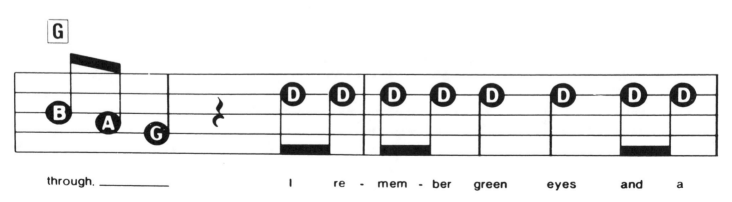

through. _____ I re - mem - ber green eyes and a

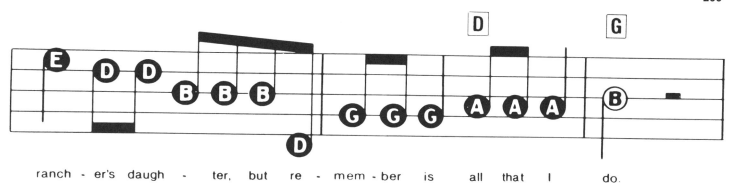

ranch - er's daugh - ter, but re - mem - ber is all that I do.

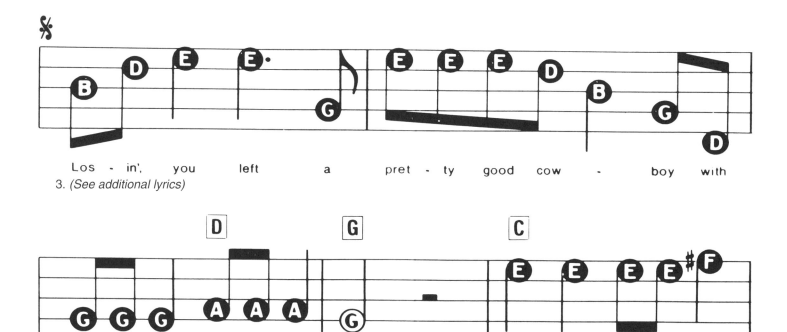

Los - in', you left a pret - ty good cow - boy with

3. *(See additional lyrics)*

noth - in' to hold on to. Sun - down came and I

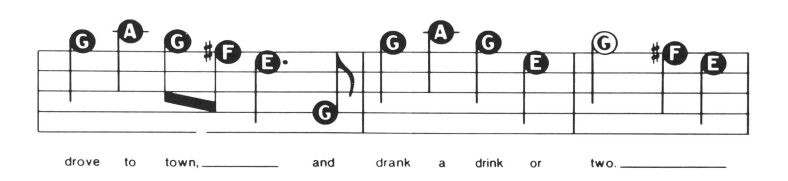

drove to town,_____ and drank a drink or two._____

CHORUS

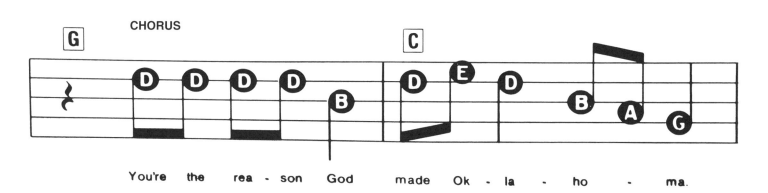

You're the rea - son God made Ok - la - ho - ma.

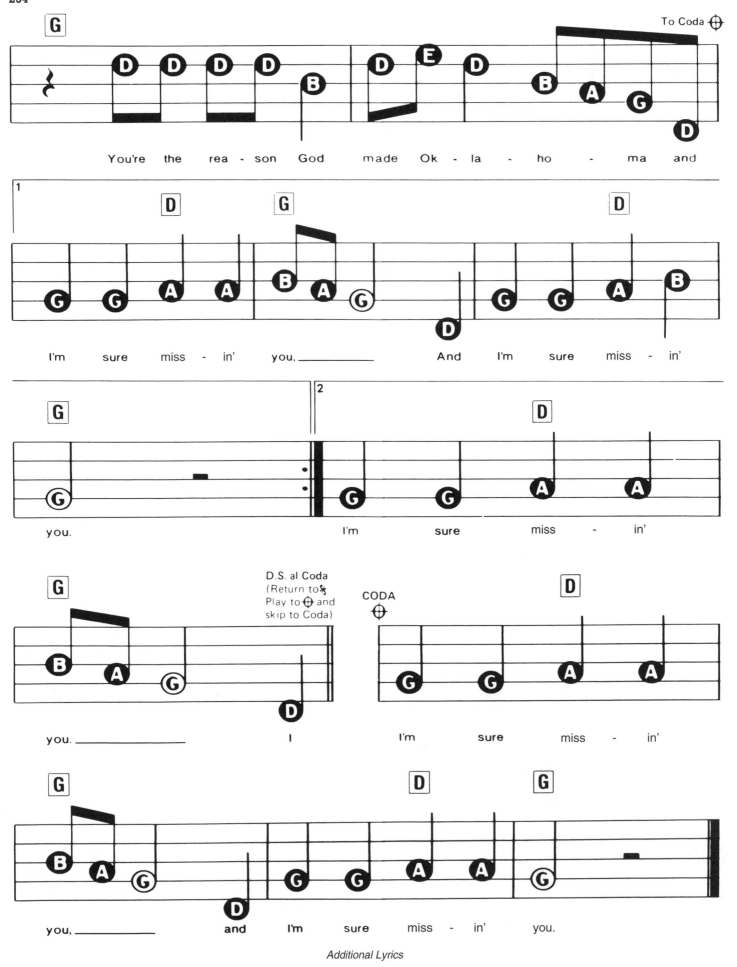

Additional Lyrics

2. Here the city lights outshine the moon
   I was just now thinking of you
   Sometimes when the wind blows
   You can see the mountains
   And all the way to Malibu
   Everyone's a star here in L.A. County

You ought to see the things that they do.
All the cowboys down on the Sunset Strip
Wish they could be like you.
The Santa Monica Freeway
Sometimes makes a country girl blue
Chorus

3. I worked ten hours on a John Deere tractor,
   Just thinkin of you all day . . . .
   I've got a calico cat and a two
   room flat, on a
   street in West L.A.
   Chorus

Registration Guide

• Match the Registration number on the song to the corresponding numbered category below. Select and activate an instrumental sound available on your instrument.

• Choose an automatic rhythm appropriate to the mood and style of the song. (Consult your Owner's Guide for proper operation of automatic rhythm features.)

• Adjust the tempo and volume controls to comfortable settings.

Registration

1	Mellow	Flutes, Clarinet, Oboe, Flugel Horn, Trombone, French Horn, Organ Flutes
2	Ensemble	Brass Section, Sax Section, Wind Ensemble, Full Organ, Theater Organ
3	Strings	Violin, Viola, Cello, Fiddle, String Ensemble, Pizzicato, Organ Strings
4	Guitars	Acoustic/Electric Guitars, Banjo, Mandolin, Dulcimer, Ukulele, Hawaiian Guitar
5	Mallets	Vibraphone, Marimba, Xylophone, Steel Drums, Bells, Celesta, Chimes
6	Liturgical	Pipe Organ, Hand Bells, Vocal Ensemble, Choir, Organ Flutes
7	Bright	Saxophones, Trumpet, Mute Trumpet, Synth Leads, Jazz/Gospel Organs
8	Piano	Piano, Electric Piano, Honky Tonk Piano, Harpsichord, Clavi
9	Novelty	Melodic Percussion, Wah Trumpet, Synth, Whistle, Kazoo, Perc. Organ
10	Bellows	Accordion, French Accordion, Mussette, Harmonica, Pump Organ, Bagpipes

E-Z PLAY® TODAY PUBLICATIONS

The E-Z Play® Today songbook series is the shortest distance between beginning music and playing fun! Check out this list of highlights and visit www.halleonard.com for a complete listing of all volumes and songlists.

00102278 1. Favorite Songs with 3 Chords $7.95	00100127 103. Greatest Songs of the Last Century $16.95	00101933 230. Songs of the '40s..............................$14.95
00100374 2. Country Sound $8.95	00100256 107. The Best Praise & Worship Songs Ever ...$16.99	00101934 231. Songs of the '50s..............................$14.95
00100167 3. Contemporary Disney......................$15.99	00100363 108. Classical Themes (English/Spanish) ...$6.95	00101935 232. Songs of the '60s..............................$14.95
00100382 4. Dance Band Greats........................$7.95	00102232 109. Motown's Greatest Hits.................$12.95	00101936 233. Songs of the '70s..............................$14.95
00100305 5. All-Time Standards........................$7.95	00101566 110. Neil Diamond Collection...............$14.99	00101581 235. Elvis Presley Anthology...................$15.95
00100428 6. Songs of The Beatles $9.99	00100119 111. Season's Greetings.....................$14.95	00100165 236. Irving Berlin's God Bless America®
00100442 7. Hits from Musicals........................$7.95	00101498 112. Best of The Beatles...................$19.95	& Other Songs for a Better Nation......$9.95
00100490 8. Patriotic Songs...........................$7.95	00100134 113. Country Gospel USA...................$10.95	00290059 238. 25 Top Christmas Songs.................$9.95
00100355 9. Christmas Time...........................$7.95	00101612 115. The Greatest Waltzes..................$9.95	00290170 239. Big Book of Children's Songs...........$14.95
00100435 10. Hawaiian Songs..........................$7.95	00100257 116. Amy Grant – Greatest Hits............$9.95	00290120 240. Frank Sinatra........................$14.95
00100386 12. Danceable Favorites......................$7.95	00100136 118. 100 Kids' Songs......................$12.95	00100158 243. Oldies! Oldies! Oldies!................$10.95
00102248 13. Three-Chord Country Songs..............$12.95	00101990 119. 57 Super Hits........................$12.95	00290242 244. Songs of the '80s....................$14.95
00100300 14. All-Time Requests.......................$7.95	00100433 120. Gospel of Bill & Gloria Gaither.......$14.95	00100041 245. Best of Simon & Garfunkel.............$8.95
00100370 15. Country Pickin's.........................$7.95	00100333 121. Boogies, Blues and Rags..............$7.95	00100269 247. Essential Songs – Broadway...........$17.99
00100335 16. Broadway's Best.........................$7.95	00100146 122. Songs for Praise & Worship...........$8.95	00100175 249. Elv1s – 30 #1 Hits...................$9.95
00100362 18. Classical Portraits.......................$7.99	00100001 125. Great Big Book of Children's Songs....$12.95	00102113 251. Phantom of the Opera (Broadway) ..$14.95
00102277 20. Hymns.................................$7.95	00101563 127. John Denver's Greatest Hits...........$8.95	00100065 252. Andy Griffith – I Love to Tell the Story .$7.95
00100570 22. Sacred Sounds.........................$7.95	00100037 129. The Groovy Years....................$12.95	00100064 253. Best Movie Songs Ever $14.95
00100214 23. Essential Songs – The 1920s............$16.95	00102318 131. Doo-Wop Songbook..................$10.95	00100176 254. Bossa Nova.........................$7.95
00100206 24. Essential Songs – The 1930s............$16.95	00100171 135. All Around the U.S.A................$10.95	00100203 256. Very Best of Lionel Richie.............$8.95
00100207 25. Essential Songs – The 1940s............$16.95	00001256 136. Christmas Is for Kids................$7.95	00100178 259. Norah Jones – Come Away with Me...$9.95
00100100 26. Holly Season...........................$8.95	00100144 137. Children's Movie Hits................$7.95	00102306 261. Best of Andrew Lloyd Webber $12.95
00001236 27. 60 of the World's Easiest to	00100038 138. Nostalgia Collection.................$14.95	00100063 266. Latin Hits..........................$7.95
Play Songs with 3 Chords..............$8.95	00101956 140. Best of George Strait...............$12.95	00100062 269. Love That Latin Beat.................$7.95
00101598 28. Fifty Classical Themes...................$9.95	00100290 141. All Time Latin Favorites.............$7.95	00100179 270. Christian Christmas Songbook.........$14.95
00100135 29. Love Songs............................$7.95	00100013 144. All Time TV Favorites...............$17.95	00101425 272. ABBA Gold – Greatest Hits $7.95
00100030 30. Country Connection....................$8.95	00100597 146. Hank Williams – His Best............$7.95	00102248 275. Classical Hits –
00001289 32. Sing-Along Favorites....................$7.95	00100420 147. Folk Songs of England,	Bach, Beethoven & Brahms.........$6.95
00100253 34. Inspirational Ballads...................$10.95	Scotland & Ireland..................$7.99	00100186 277. Stevie Wonder – Greatest Hits $9.95
00102254 35. Frank Sinatra – Romance...............$8.95	00101548 150. Best Big Band Songs Ever............$16.95	00100237 280. Dolly Parton........................$9.99
00100122 36. Good Ol' Songs........................$10.95	00100152 151. Beach Boys – Greatest Hits..........$8.95	00100068 283. Best Jazz Standards Ever $15.95
00100410 37. Favorite Latin Songs....................$7.95	00101592 152. Fiddler on the Roof.................$9.99	00100244 287. Josh Groban........................$10.95
00100032 38. Songs of the '90s......................$12.95	00100004 153. Our God Reigns....................$10.95	00100022 288. Sing-a-Long Christmas...............$10.95
00100425 41. Songs of Gershwin, Porter & Rodgers...$7.95	00101549 155. Best of Billy Joel..................$10.99	00100023 289. Sing-a-Long Christmas Carols.........$9.95
00100123 42. Baby Boomers Songbook...............$9.95	00100033 156. Best of Rodgers & Hart.............$7.95	00100073 290. "My Heart Will Go On" &
00100576 43. Sing-along Requests.....................$8.95	00001264 157. Easy Favorites.....................$7.99	15 Other Top Movie Hits...............$7.95
00102135 44. Best of Willie Nelson...................$8.95	00100049 162. Lounge Music......................$10.95	00102124 293. Movie Classics......................$9.95
00100460 45. Love Ballads..........................$8.99	00101530 164. Best Christmas Songbook............$9.95	00100069 294. Old Fashioned Love Songs............$9.95
00100343 48. Gospel Songs of Johnny Cash...........$7.95	00101895 165. Rodgers & Hammerstein Songbook ...$9.95	00100075 296. Best of Cole Porter..................$7.95
00100043 49. Elvis, Elvis, Elvis.......................$9.95	00100140 167. Christian Children's Songbook........$10.95	00102126 297. Best TV Themes.....................$7.95
00102114 50. Best of Patsy Cline.....................$9.95	00100148 169. A Charlie Brown Christmas™..........$7.95	00102130 298. Beautiful Love Songs.................$7.95
00100208 51. Essential Songs – The 1950s............$17.95	00101900 170. Kenny Rogers – Greatest Hits.........$9.95	00001102 301. Kid's Songfest......................$9.95
00100209 52. Essential Songs – The 1960s............$17.95	00101537 171. Best of Elton John..................$7.95	00100191 303. Best Contemporary Christian
00100210 53. Essential Songs – The 1970s............$19.95	00100149 176. Charlie Brown Collection™...........$7.99	Songs Ever.........................$16.95
00100211 54. Essential Songs – The 1980s............$19.95	00100019 177. I'll Be Seeing You –	00102147 306. Irving Berlin Collection..............$14.95
00100342 55. Johnny Cash..........................$9.95	50 Songs of World War II............$14.95	00102182 308. Greatest American Songbook..........$9.95
00100118 57. More of the Best Songs Ever...........$17.95	00102325 179. Love Songs of The Beatles...........$10.99	00100194 309. 3-Chord Rock 'n' Roll................$8.95
00100353 59. Christmas Songs.......................$8.95	00101610 181. Great American Country Songbook ..$12.95	00001580 311. The Platters Anthology...............$7.95
00102282 60. Best of Eric Clapton...................$10.95	00001246 182. Amazing Grace....................$12.95	00100195 313. Tunes for Tots.....................$6.95
00102314 61. Jazz Standards........................$10.95	00450133 183. West Side Story....................$9.99	00100196 314. Chicago...........................$8.95
00100409 62. Favorite Hymns........................$6.95	00100151 185. Carpenters........................$9.99	00100197 315. VH1's 100 Greatest Songs of
00100360 63. Classical Music (Spanish/English) $6.95	00101606 186. 40 Pop & Rock Song Classics.......$12.95	Rock & Roll........................$19.95
00100223 64. Wicked.............................$7.95	00100155 187. Ultimate Christmas.................$17.95	00100080 322. Dixieland..........................$7.95
00100217 65. Hymns with 3 Chords..................$7.95	00102276 189. Irish Favorites.....................$7.95	00100082 327. Tonight at the Lounge................$7.95
00102312 66. Torch Songs..........................$14.95	00101939 190. 17 Super Christmas Hits.............$8.95	00100092 333. Great Gospel Favorites...............$7.95
00100218 67. Music from the Motion Picture *Ray* ..$8.95	00100053 191. Jazz Love Songs...................$8.95	00100252 335. More of the Best
00100449 69. It's Gospel...........................$7.95	00101998 192. 65 Standard Hits...................$15.95	Broadway Songs Ever $17.95
00100432 70. Gospel Greats.........................$7.95	00101941 194. 67 Standard Hits...................$16.95	00102235 346. Big Book of Christmas Songs $14.95
00100255 71. Worship Classics.......................$7.95	00101609 196. Best of George Gershwin............$9.99	00102140 350. Best of Billboard: 1955-1959..........$19.95
00100117 72. Canciones Románticas..................$6.95	00100057 198. Songs in 3/4 Time..................$9.95	00100088 355. Smoky Mountain
00100121 73. Movie Love Songs......................$7.95	00100453 199. Jumbo Songbook...................$19.95	Gospel Favorites....................$8.95
00100568 75. Sacred Moments.......................$6.95	00101539 200. Best Songs Ever....................$19.95	00100095 359. 100 Years of Song..................$17.95
00100572 76. The Sound of Music...................$8.95	00101540 202. Best Country Songs Ever............$17.95	00100096 360. More 100 Years of Song.............$19.95
00100489 77. My Fair Lady.........................$6.95	00101541 203. Best Broadway Songs Ever...........$17.99	00100103 375. Songs of Bacharach & David..........$7.95
00100424 81. Frankie Yankovic – Polkas & Waltzes ...$7.95	00101542 204. Best Easy Listening Songs Ever........$17.95	00100107 392. Disney Favorites....................$19.95
00100579 86. Songs from Musicals....................$7.95	00101543 205. Best Love Songs Ever...............$17.95	00100108 393. Italian Favorites....................$7.95
00100577 89. Songs for Children.....................$7.95	00101585 206. Favorite Children's Songs............$7.95	00100111 394. Best Gospel Songs Ever.............$17.95
00290104 90. Elton John Anthology..................$16.99	00100058 208. Easy Listening Favorites.............$7.95	00100114 398. Disney's Princess Collections..........$10.99
00100034 91. 30 Songs for a Better World.............$8.95	00100059 210. '60s Pop Rock Hits................$12.95	00100115 400. Classical Masterpieces...............$10.95
00100036 93. Country Hits..........................$10.95	00101546 213. Disney Classics....................$14.95	
00100139 94. Jim Croce – Greatest Hits.............$8.95	00101533 215. Best Christmas Songs Ever...........$19.95	
00100219 95. The Phantom of the Opera (Movie) $10.95	00100156 219. Christmas Songs with 3 Chords.......$7.95	
00100263 96. Mamma Mia – Movie Soundtrack $7.99	00102080 225. Lawrence Welk Songbook...........$9.95	
00102317 97. Elvis Presley – Songs of Inspiration.....$9.95	00101482 226. Award Winning Songs of the	
00100125 99. Children's Christmas Songs............$7.95	Country Music Association............$19.95	
00100602 100. Winter Wonderland...................$8.95	00101931 228. Songs of the '20s...................$13.95	
00001309 102. Carols of Christmas..................$7.99	00101932 229. Songs of the '30s...................$13.95	

FOR MORE INFORMATION, SEE YOUR LOCAL MUSIC DEALER,
OR WRITE TO:

HAL•LEONARD®
CORPORATION
7777 W. BLUEMOUND RD. P.O. BOX 13819 MILWAUKEE, WI 53213

Prices, contents, and availability subject to change without notice.

0410